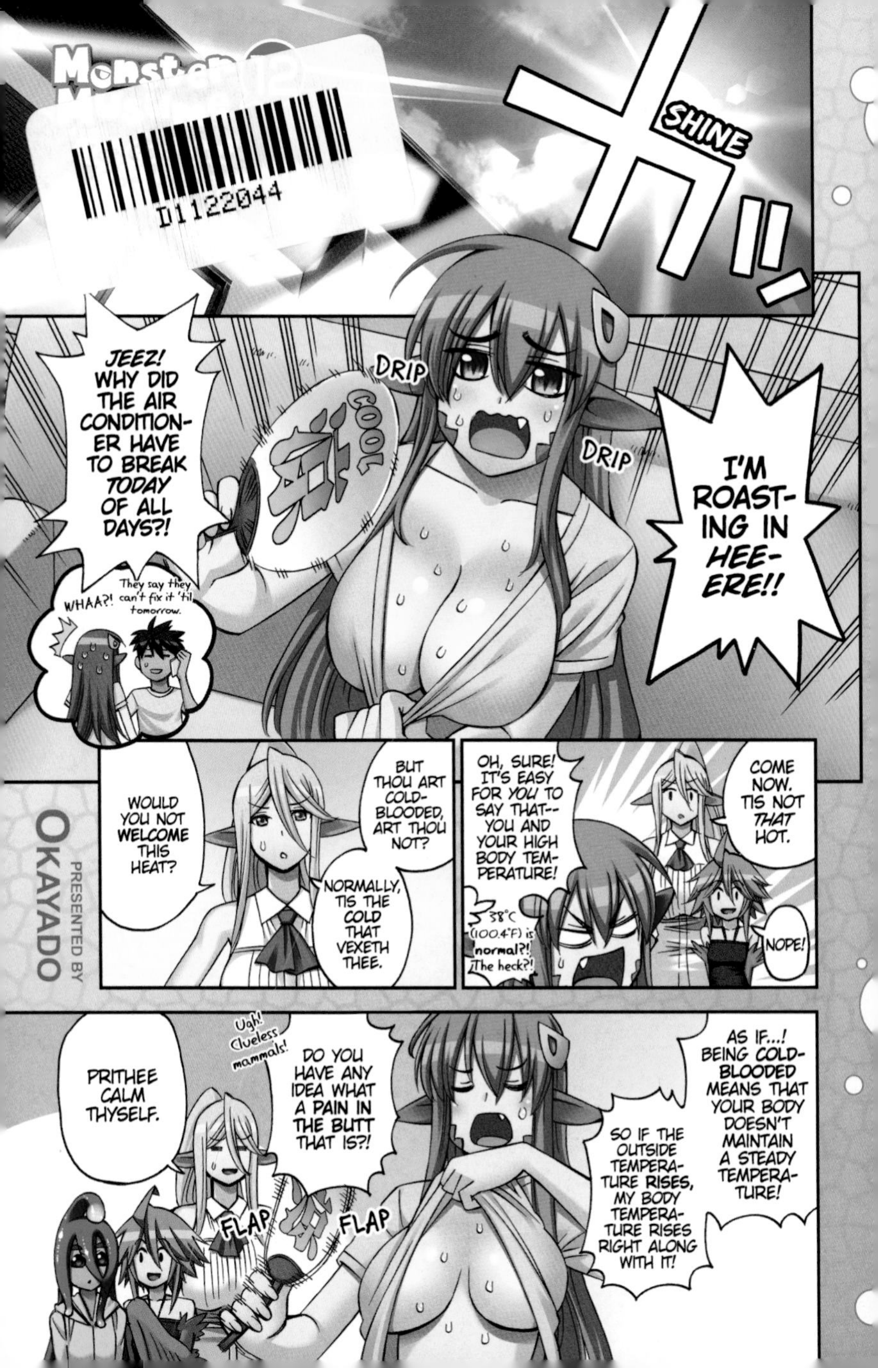

SHINE
I'M ROASTING IN HEE-ERE!!
DRIP
DRIP
COOL
JEEZ! WHY DID THE AIR CONDITIONER HAVE TO BREAK TODAY OF ALL DAYS?!
They say they can't fix it 'til tomorrow.
WHAA?!
COME NOW. TIS NOT THAT HOT.
NOPE!
OH, SURE! IT'S EASY FOR YOU TO SAY THAT-- YOU AND YOUR HIGH BODY TEMPERATURE!
38°C (100.4°F) is normal?! The heck?!
BUT THOU ART COLD-BLOODED, ART THOU NOT?
NORMALLY, TIS THE COLD THAT VEXETH THEE.
WOULD YOU NOT WELCOME THIS HEAT?
PRESENTED BY OKAYADO
AS IF...! BEING COLD-BLOODED MEANS THAT YOUR BODY DOESN'T MAINTAIN A STEADY TEMPERATURE!
SO IF THE OUTSIDE TEMPERATURE RISES, MY BODY TEMPERATURE RISES RIGHT ALONG WITH IT!
DO YOU HAVE ANY IDEA WHAT A PAIN IN THE BUTT THAT IS?!
Ugh! Clueless mammals!
FLAP
FLAP
PRITHEE CALM THYSELF.

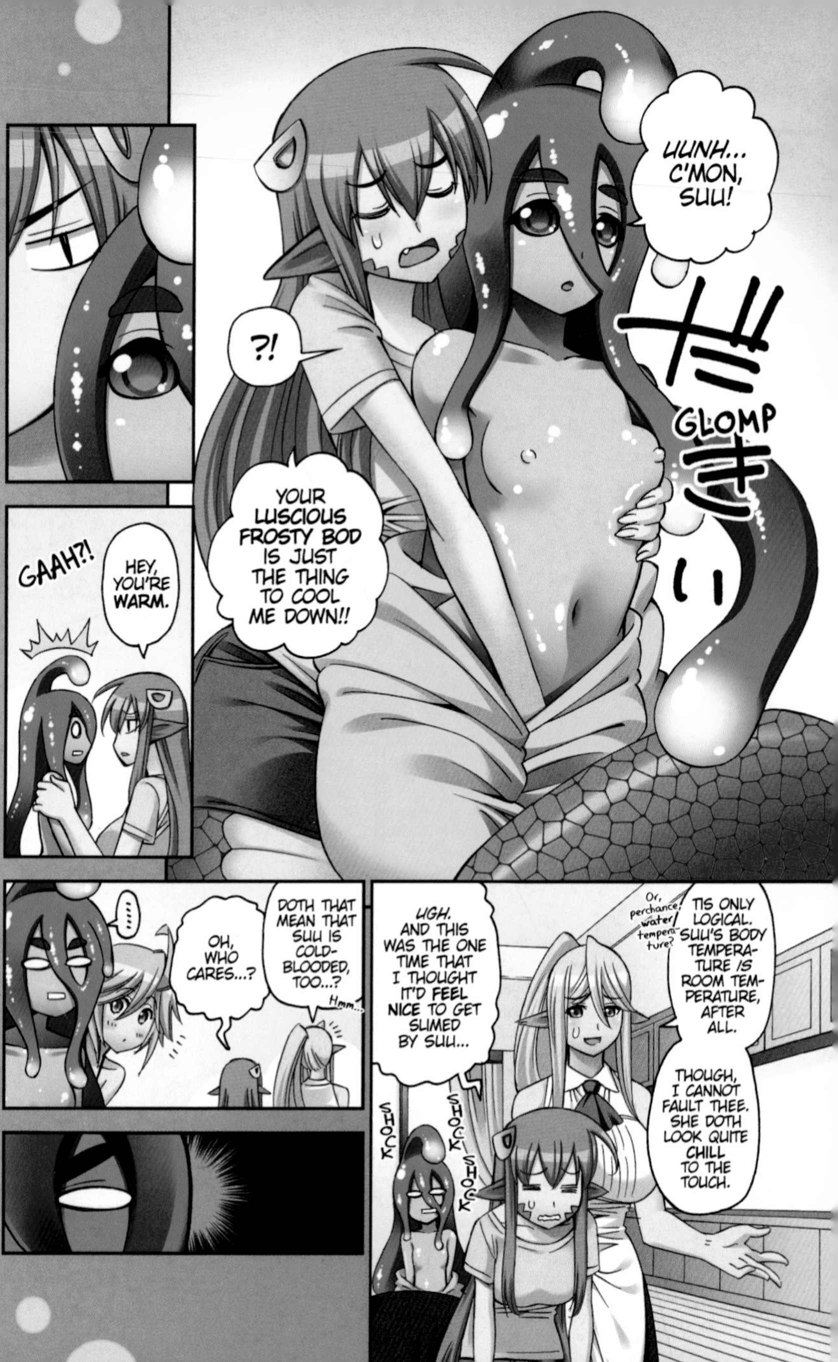
UUNH... C'MON, SUU!
だき
GLOMP
い
?!
YOUR LUSCIOUS FROSTY BOD IS JUST THE THING TO COOL ME DOWN!!
HEY, YOU'RE WARM.
GAAH?!
TIS ONLY LOGICAL. SUU'S BODY TEMPERATURE IS ROOM TEMPERATURE, AFTER ALL.
Or, perchance, water temperature?
UGH. AND THIS WAS THE ONE TIME THAT I THOUGHT IT'D FEEL NICE TO GET SLIMED BY SUU...
THOUGH, I CANNOT FAULT THEE. SHE DOTH LOOK QUITE CHILL TO THE TOUCH.
SHOCK SHOCK SHOCK
DOTH THAT MEAN THAT SUU IS COLD-BLOODED, TOO...?
Hmm...
OH, WHO CARES...?
......

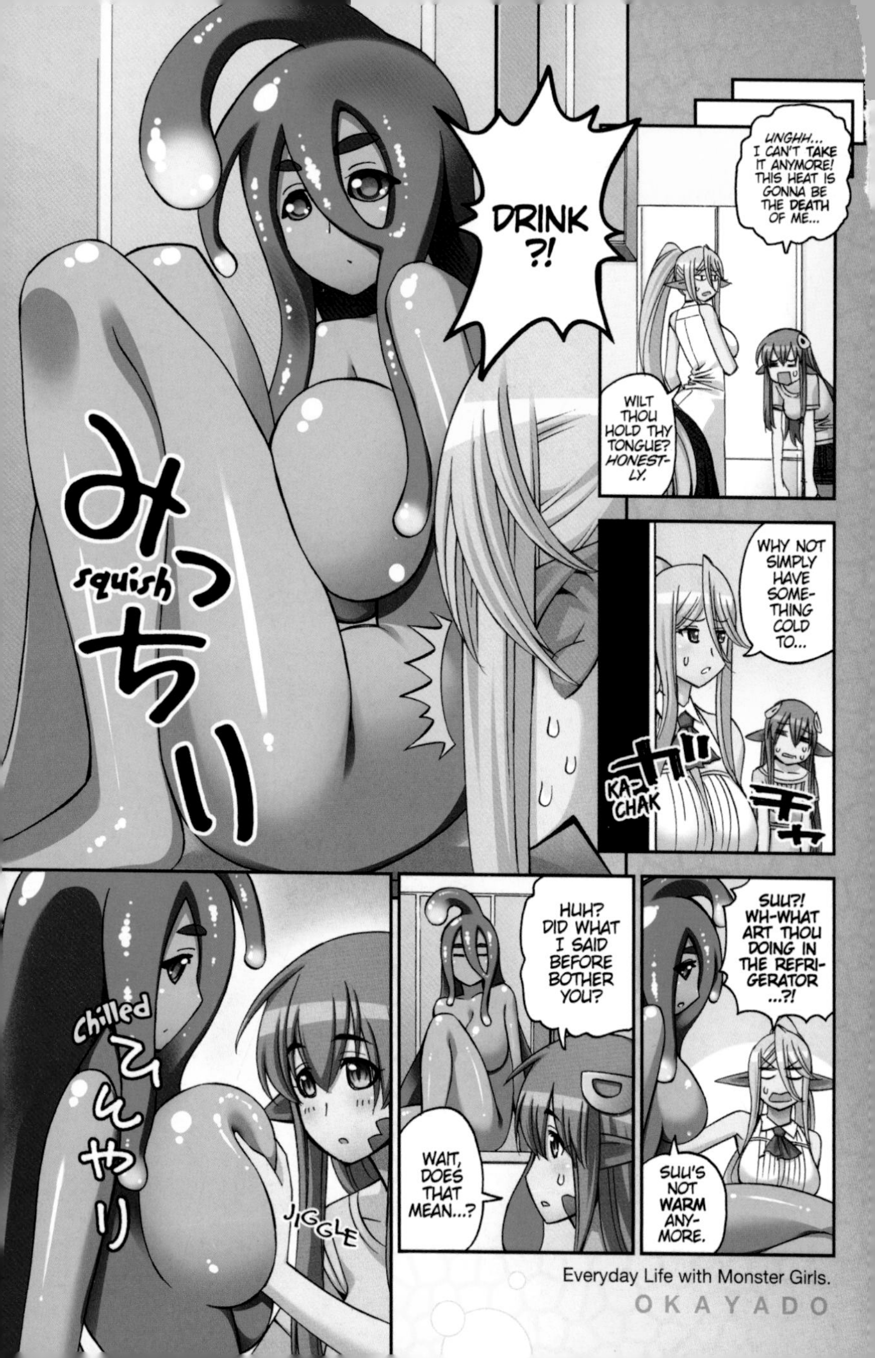
UNGHH... I CAN'T TAKE IT ANYMORE! THIS HEAT IS GONNA BE THE DEATH OF ME...
WILT THOU HOLD THY TONGUE? HONESTLY.
WHY NOT SIMPLY HAVE SOMETHING COLD TO...
ガチャ
KA-CHAK
DRINK ?!
みっちり
squish
SUU?! WH-WHAT ART THOU DOING IN THE REFRIGERATOR ...?!
SUU'S NOT WARM ANYMORE.
HUH? DID WHAT I SAID BEFORE BOTHER YOU?
WAIT, DOES THAT MEAN...?
ひんやり
Chilled
JIGGLE

Everyday Life with Monster Girls.

OKAYADO

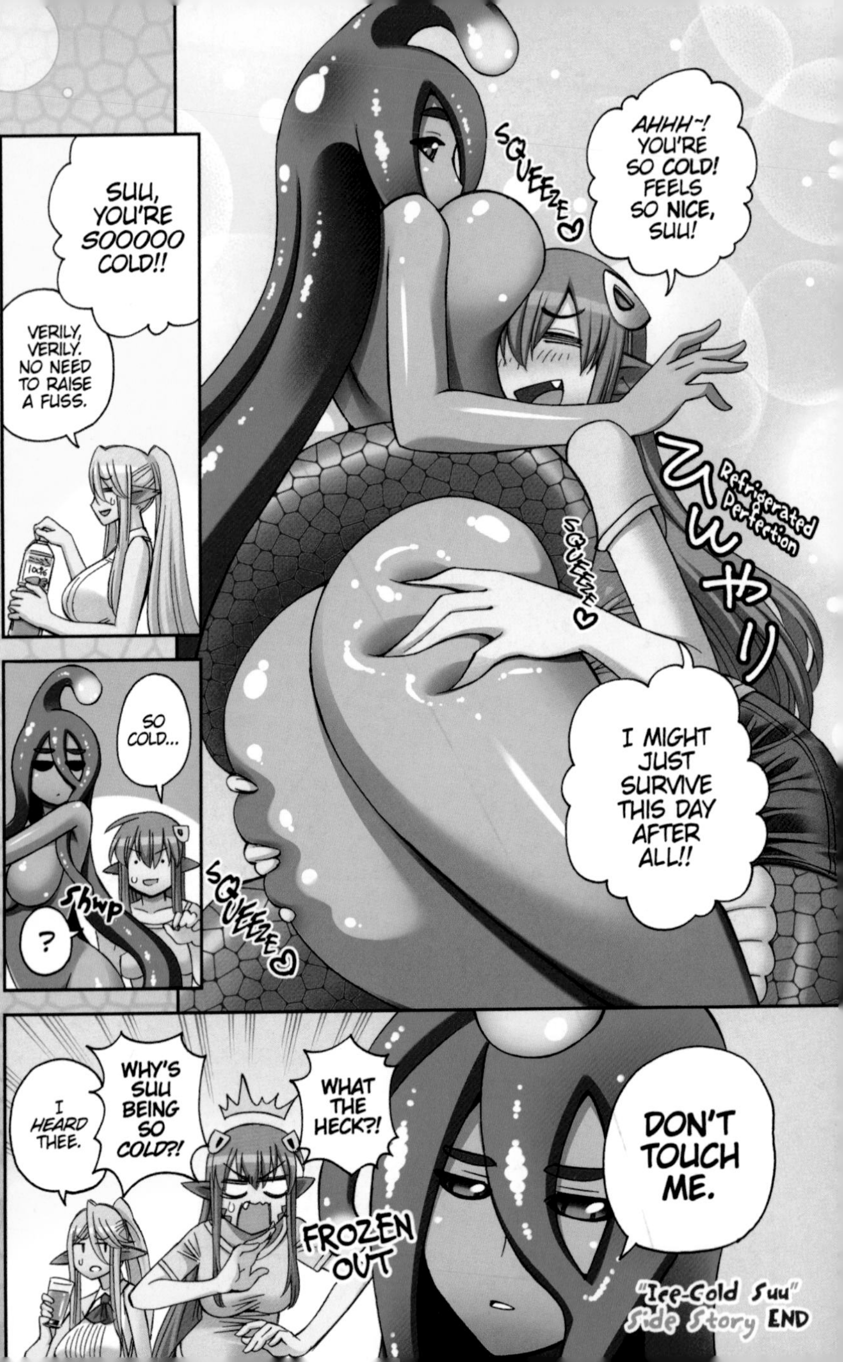
SQUEEZE♥
AHHH~! YOU'RE SO COLD! FEELS SO NICE, SUU!
ひんやり
Refrigerated Perfection
SQUEEZE♥
I MIGHT JUST SURVIVE THIS DAY AFTER ALL!!
SQUEEZE♥
SUU, YOU'RE SOOOOO COLD!!
VERILY, VERILY. NO NEED TO RAISE A FUSS.
SO COLD...
Shwp
?
DON'T TOUCH ME.
WHAT THE HECK?!
WHY'S SUU BEING SO COLD?!
I HEARD THEE.
FROZEN OUT
"Ice-Cold Suu" Side Story END

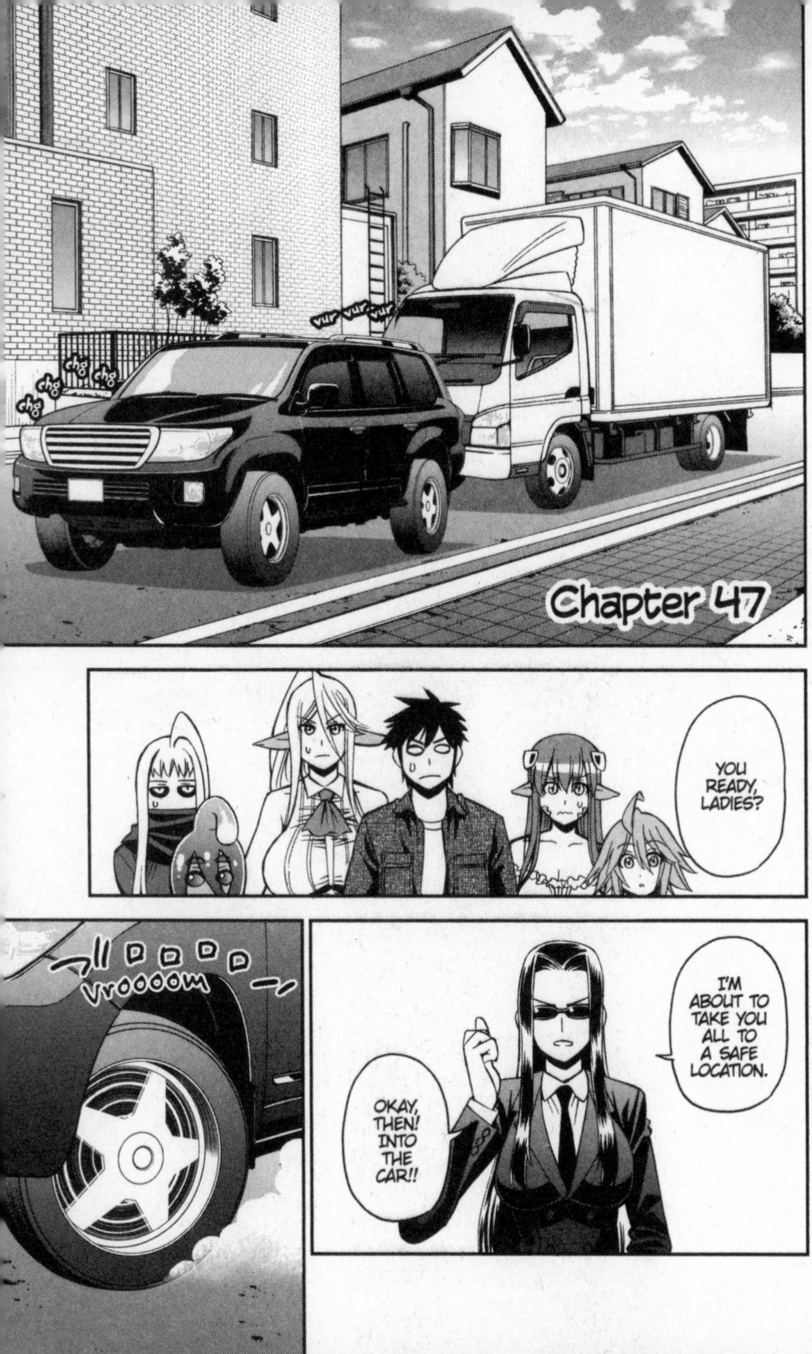
vur vur vur
chg chg chg chg
Chapter 47
YOU READY, LADIES?
I'M ABOUT TO TAKE YOU ALL TO A SAFE LOCATION.
OKAY, THEN! INTO THE CAR!!
vroooom

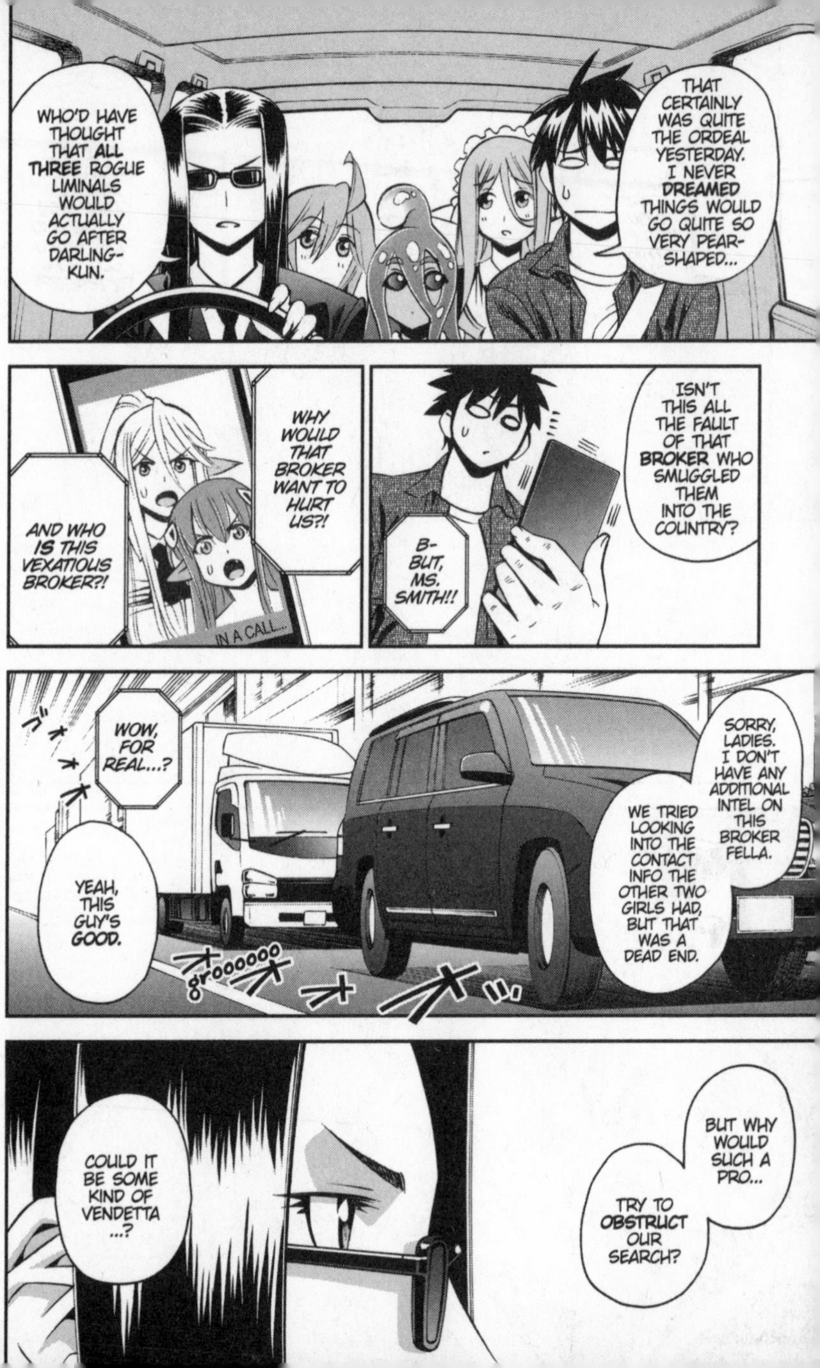

THAT CERTAINLY WAS QUITE THE ORDEAL YESTERDAY. I NEVER **DREAMED** THINGS WOULD GO QUITE SO VERY PEAR-SHAPED...
WHO'D HAVE THOUGHT THAT **ALL THREE** ROGUE LIMINALS WOULD ACTUALLY GO AFTER DARLING-KUN.
ISN'T THIS ALL THE FAULT OF THAT **BROKER** WHO SMUGGLED THEM INTO THE COUNTRY?
B-BUT, MS. SMITH!!
WHY WOULD THAT BROKER WANT TO HURT US?!
*AND WHO **IS** THIS VEXATIOUS BROKER?!*
IN A CALL...
SORRY, LADIES. I DON'T HAVE ANY ADDITIONAL INTEL ON THIS BROKER FELLA.
WE TRIED LOOKING INTO THE CONTACT INFO THE OTHER TWO GIRLS HAD, BUT THAT WAS A DEAD END.
WOW, FOR REAL...?
YEAH, THIS GUY'S **GOOD.**
grooooo
BUT WHY WOULD SUCH A PRO...
TRY TO **OBSTRUCT** OUR SEARCH?
COULD IT BE SOME KIND OF VENDETTA ...?

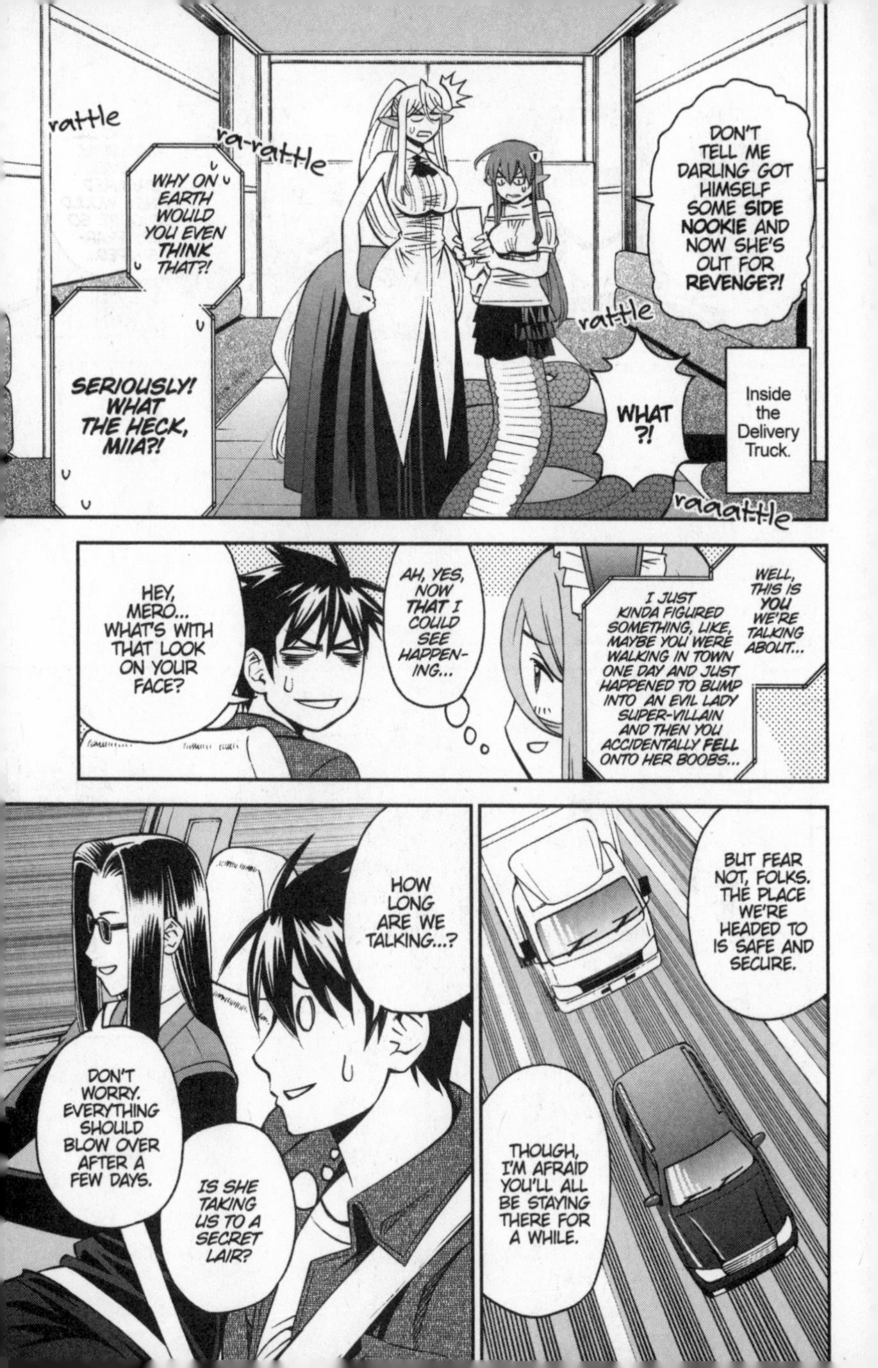
DON'T TELL ME DARLING GOT HIMSELF SOME SIDE NOOKIE AND NOW SHE'S OUT FOR REVENGE?!
Inside the Delivery Truck.
rattle
ra-rattle
WHY ON EARTH WOULD YOU EVEN THINK THAT?!
rattle
WHAT?!
SERIOUSLY! WHAT THE HECK, MIIA?!
raaattle
WELL, THIS IS YOU WE'RE TALKING ABOUT...
I JUST KINDA FIGURED SOMETHING, LIKE, MAYBE YOU WERE WALKING IN TOWN ONE DAY AND JUST HAPPENED TO BUMP INTO AN EVIL LADY SUPER-VILLAIN AND THEN YOU ACCIDENTALLY FELL ONTO HER BOOBS...
AH, YES, NOW THAT I COULD SEE HAPPENING...
HEY, MERO... WHAT'S WITH THAT LOOK ON YOUR FACE?
BUT FEAR NOT, FOLKS. THE PLACE WE'RE HEADED TO IS SAFE AND SECURE.
THOUGH, I'M AFRAID YOU'LL ALL BE STAYING THERE FOR A WHILE.
HOW LONG ARE WE TALKING...?
DON'T WORRY. EVERYTHING SHOULD BLOW OVER AFTER A FEW DAYS.
IS SHE TAKING US TO A SECRET LAIR?

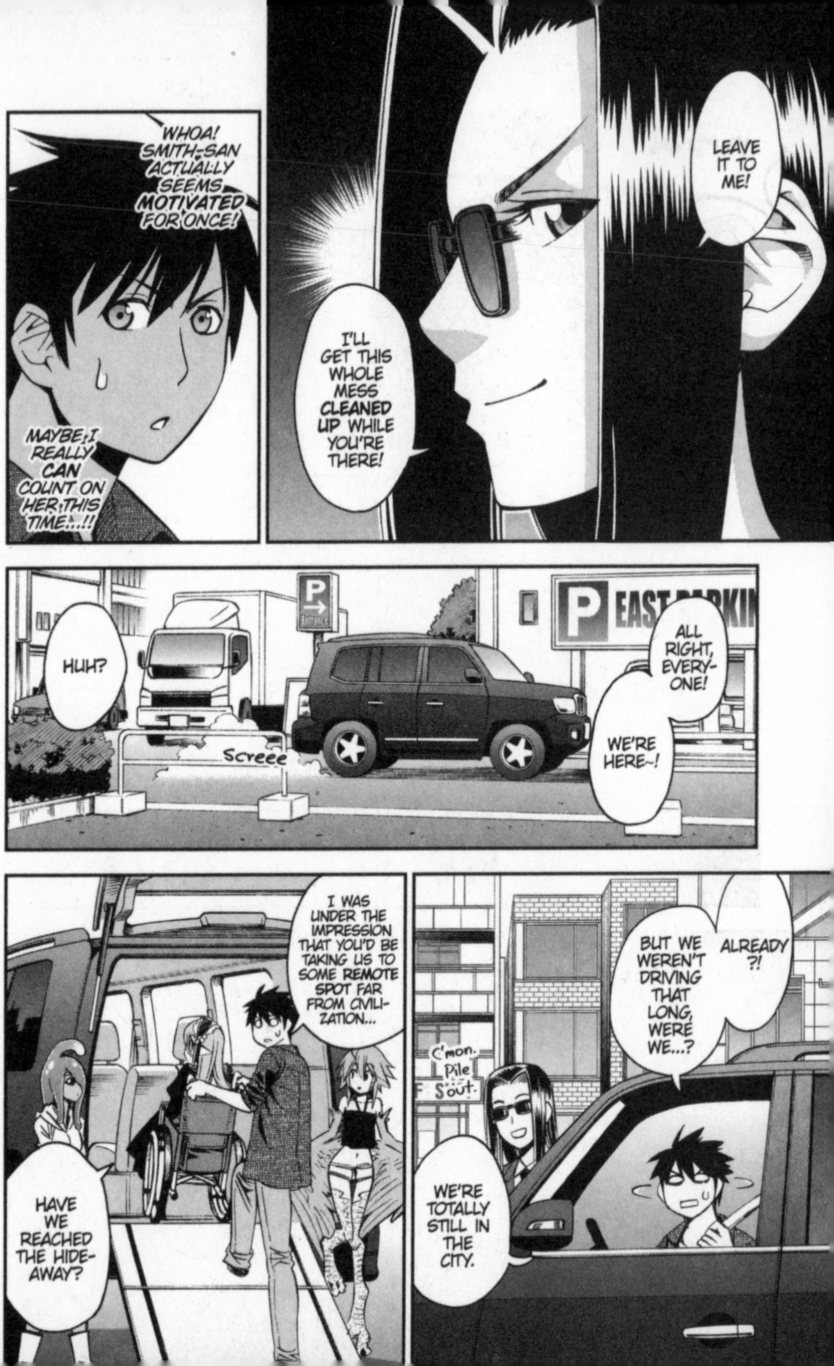
LEAVE IT TO ME!
I'LL GET THIS WHOLE MESS CLEANED UP WHILE YOU'RE THERE!
WHOA! SMITH-SAN ACTUALLY SEEMS MOTIVATED FOR ONCE!
MAYBE I REALLY CAN COUNT ON HER THIS TIME...!!
P EAST PARKIN
ALL RIGHT, EVERYONE!
WE'RE HERE~!
P Entrance
Screee
HUH?
ALREADY ?!
BUT WE WEREN'T DRIVING THAT LONG, WERE WE...?
C'mon. Pile out.
WE'RE TOTALLY STILL IN THE CITY.
I WAS UNDER THE IMPRESSION THAT YOU'D BE TAKING US TO SOME REMOTE SPOT FAR FROM CIVILI-ZATION...
HAVE WE REACHED THE HIDE-AWAY?

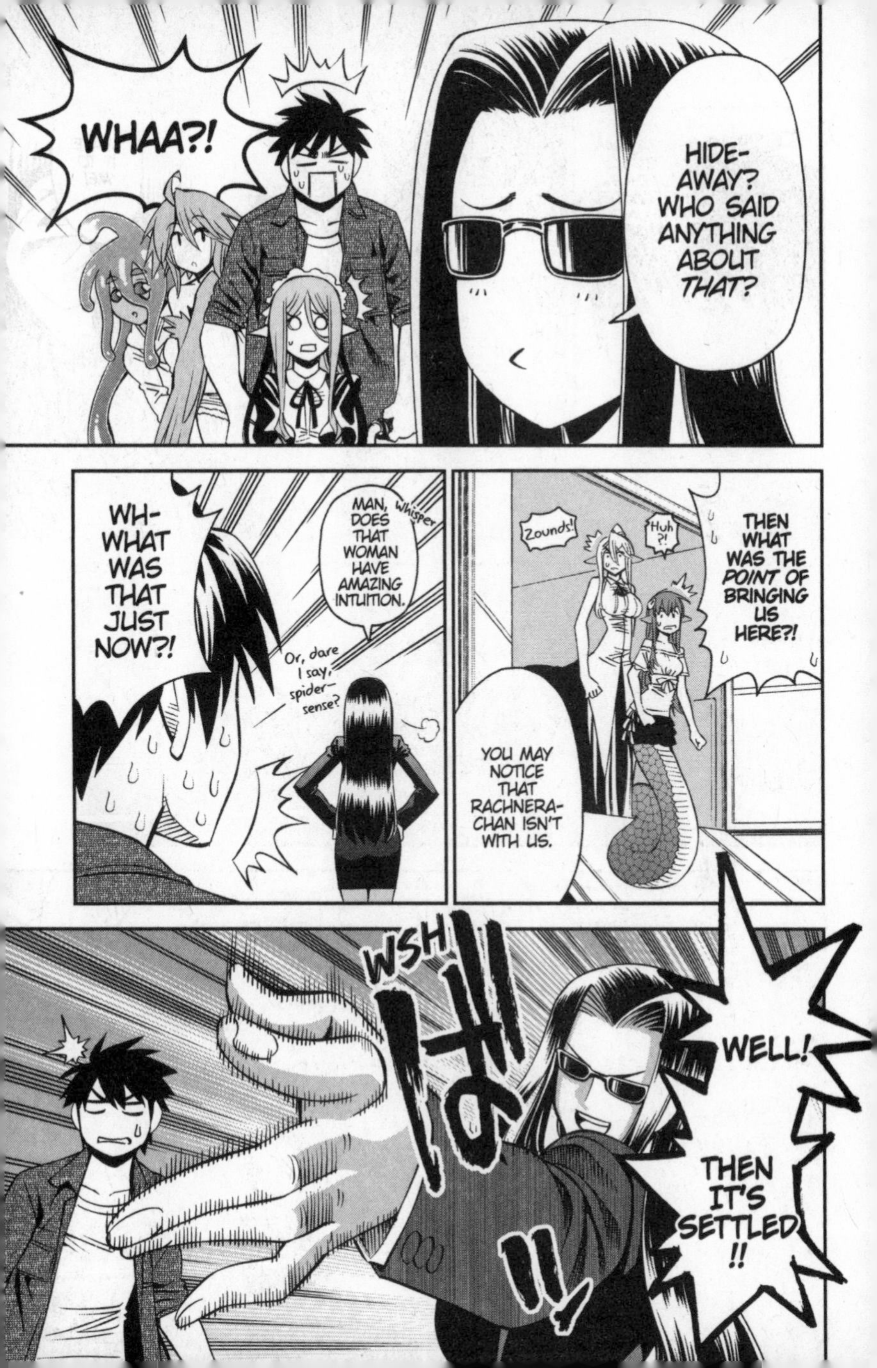
HIDE-AWAY? WHO SAID ANYTHING ABOUT *THAT?*
WHAA?!
THEN WHAT WAS THE *POINT* OF BRINGING US HERE?!
Huh?!
Zounds!
YOU MAY NOTICE THAT RACHNERA-CHAN ISN'T WITH US.
WH-WHAT WAS THAT JUST NOW?!
Whisper
MAN, DOES THAT WOMAN HAVE AMAZING INTUITION.
Or, dare I say, spider-sense?
WELL!
WSH
THEN IT'S SETTLED!!

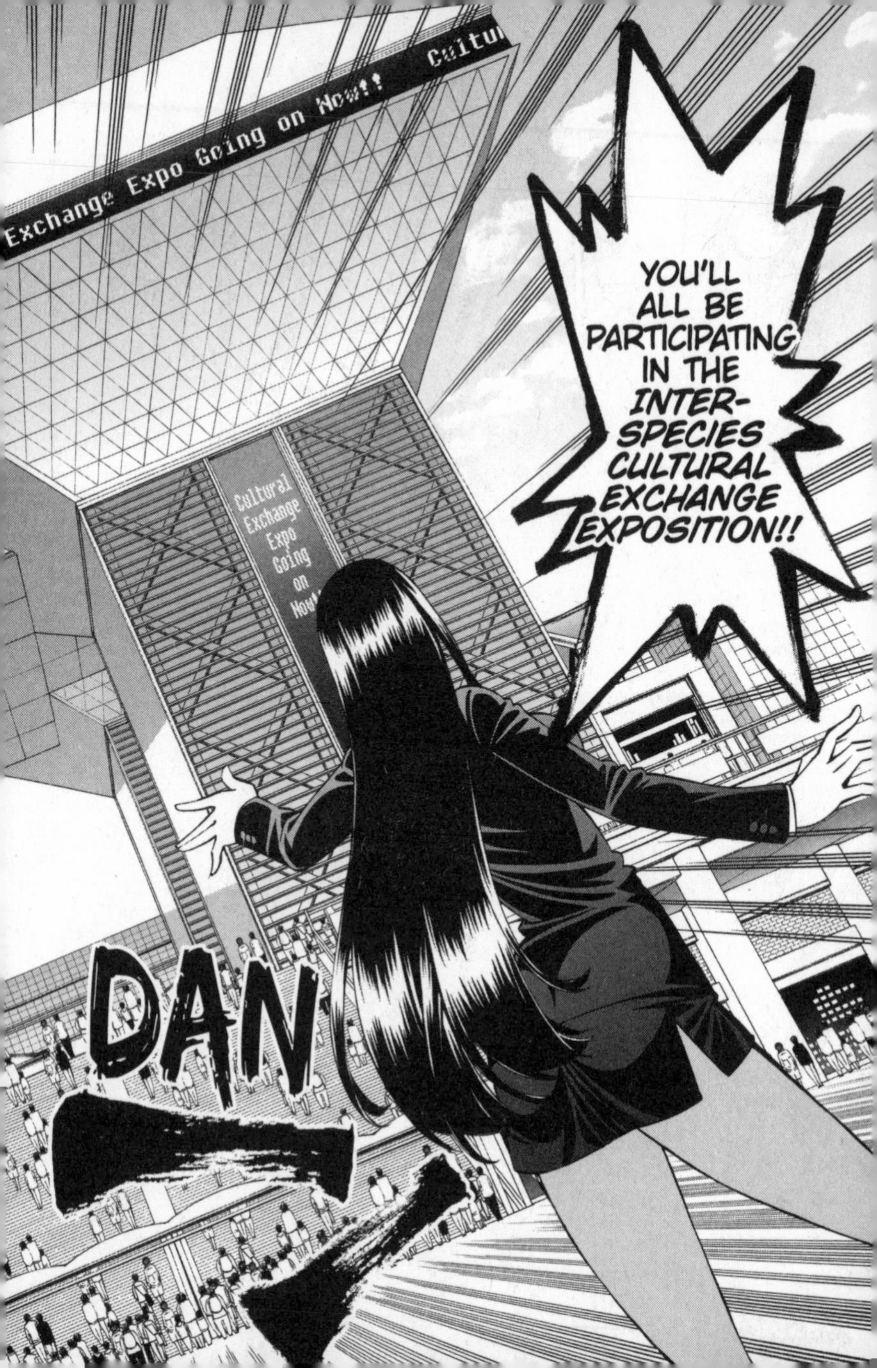
YOU'LL ALL BE PARTICIPATING IN THE INTER-SPECIES CULTURAL EXCHANGE EXPOSITION!!
Exchange Expo Going on Now!! Cultu
Cultural Exchange Expo Going on Now!
DAN

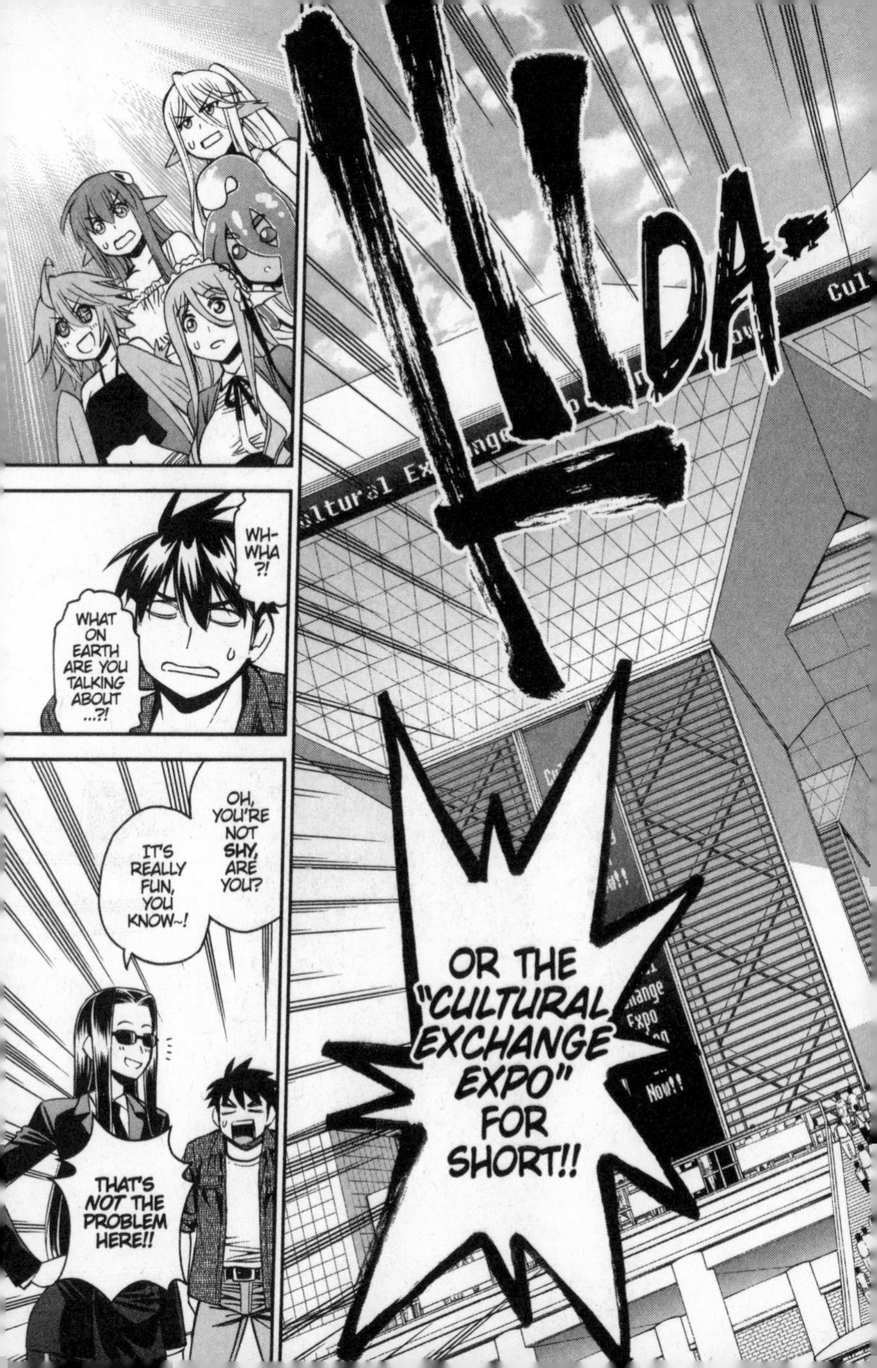
OR THE "CULTURAL EXCHANGE EXPO" FOR SHORT!!
WH-WHA?!
WHAT ON EARTH ARE YOU TALKING ABOUT ...?!
OH, YOU'RE NOT SHY, ARE YOU?
IT'S REALLY FUN, YOU KNOW~!
THAT'S *NOT* THE PROBLEM HERE!!

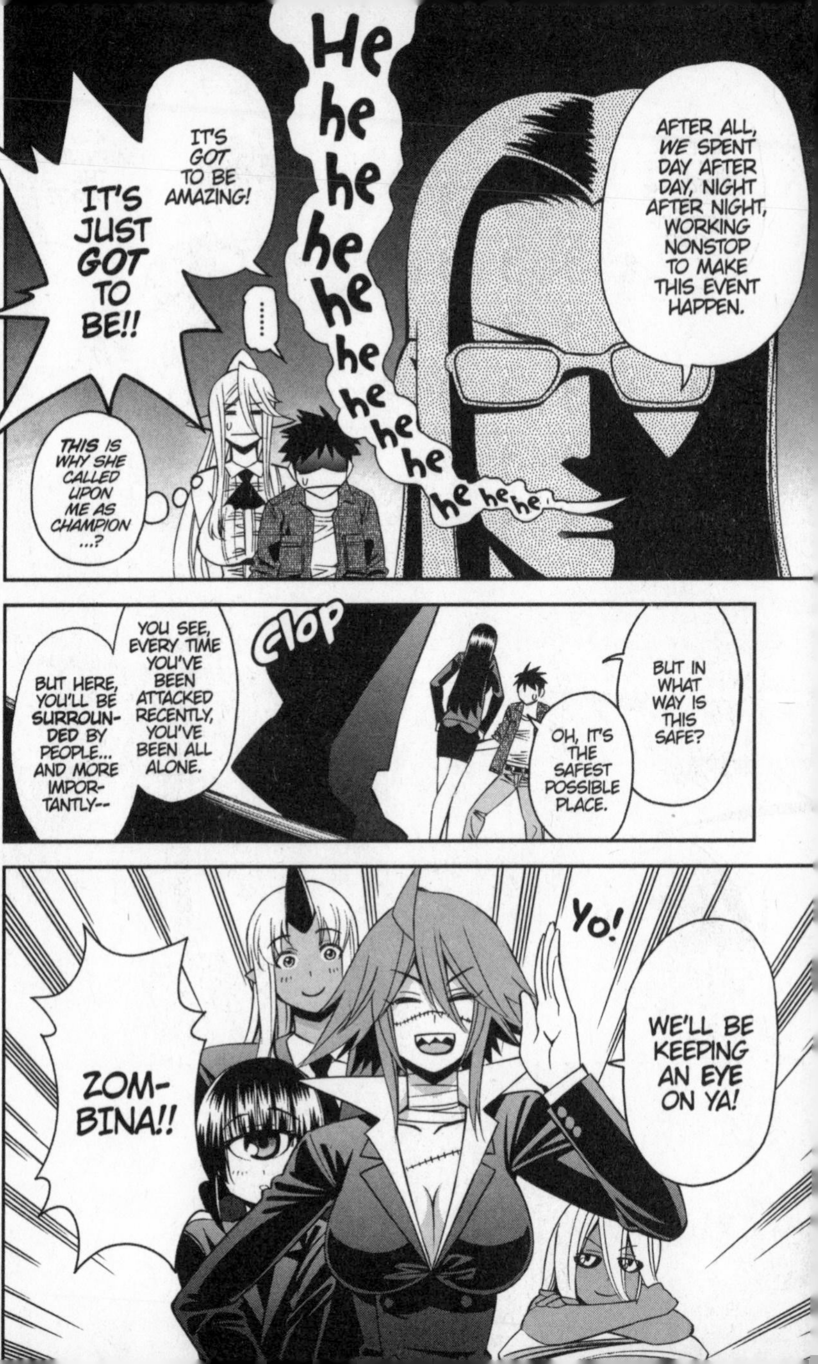
AFTER ALL, WE SPENT DAY AFTER DAY, NIGHT AFTER NIGHT, WORKING NONSTOP TO MAKE THIS EVENT HAPPEN.
He he he he he he he he he he he he he he
IT'S GOT TO BE AMAZING!
IT'S JUST GOT TO BE!!
......
THIS IS WHY SHE CALLED UPON ME AS CHAMPION ...?
BUT IN WHAT WAY IS THIS SAFE?
OH, IT'S THE SAFEST POSSIBLE PLACE.
Clop
YOU SEE, EVERY TIME YOU'VE BEEN ATTACKED RECENTLY, YOU'VE BEEN ALL ALONE.
BUT HERE, YOU'LL BE SURROUNDED BY PEOPLE... AND MORE IMPORTANTLY--
YO!
WE'LL BE KEEPING AN EYE ON YA!
ZOM-BINA!!

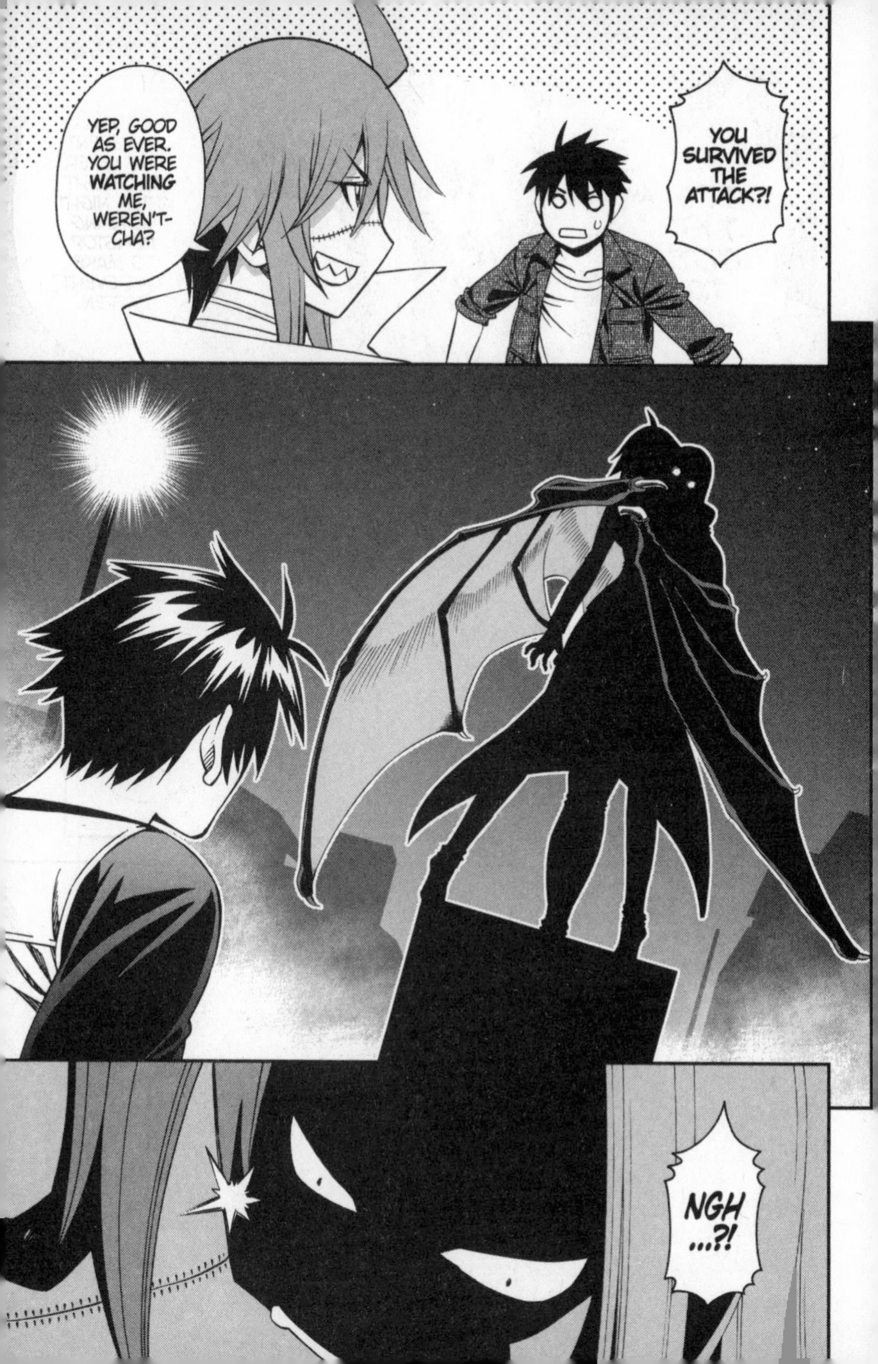
YOU SURVIVED THE ATTACK?!
YEP, GOOD AS EVER. YOU WERE WATCHING ME, WEREN'T-CHA?
NGH ...?!

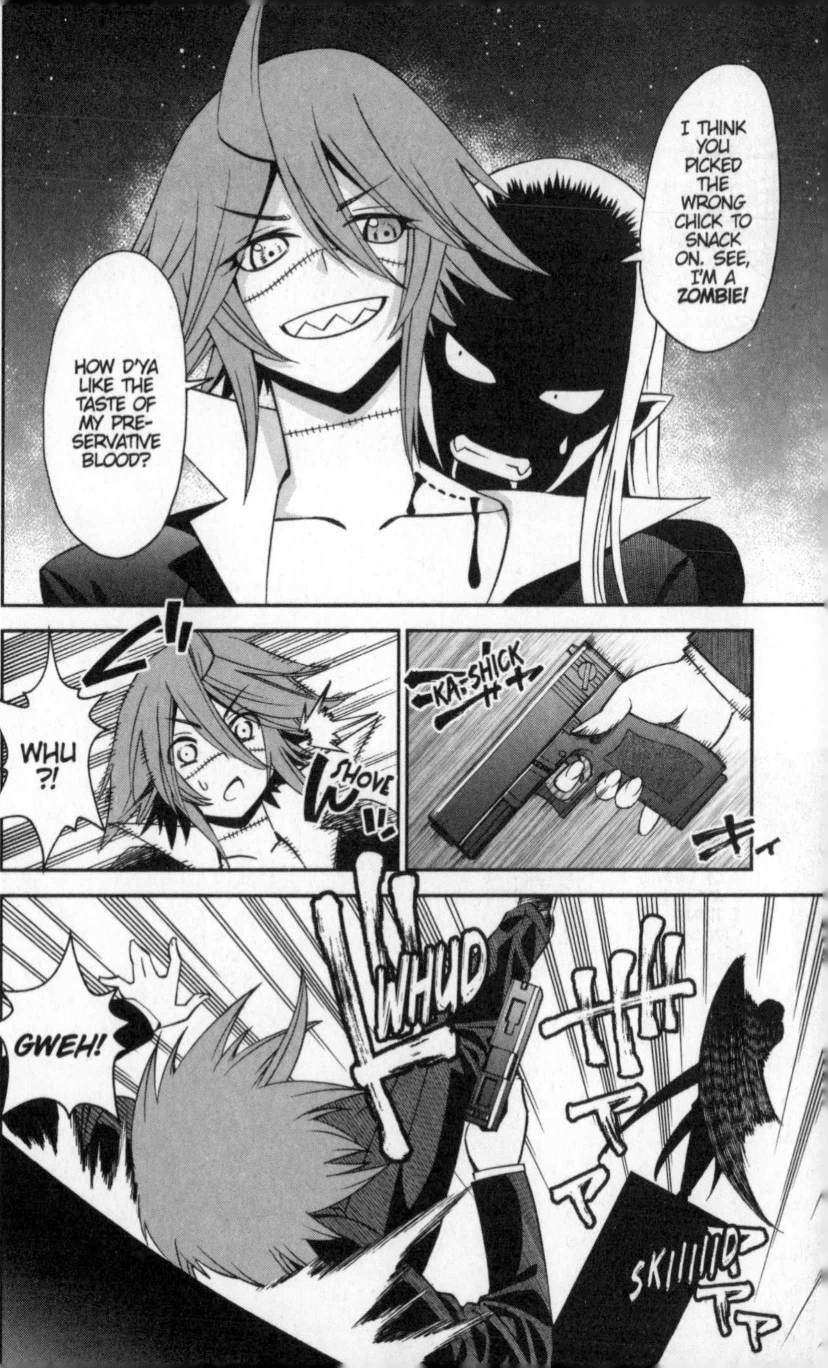
I THINK YOU PICKED THE WRONG CHICK TO SNACK ON. SEE, I'M A ZOMBIE!
HOW D'YA LIKE THE TASTE OF MY PRE-SERVATIVE BLOOD?
KA-SHICK
WHU ?!
SHOVE
WHUD
GWEH!
SKIIIID

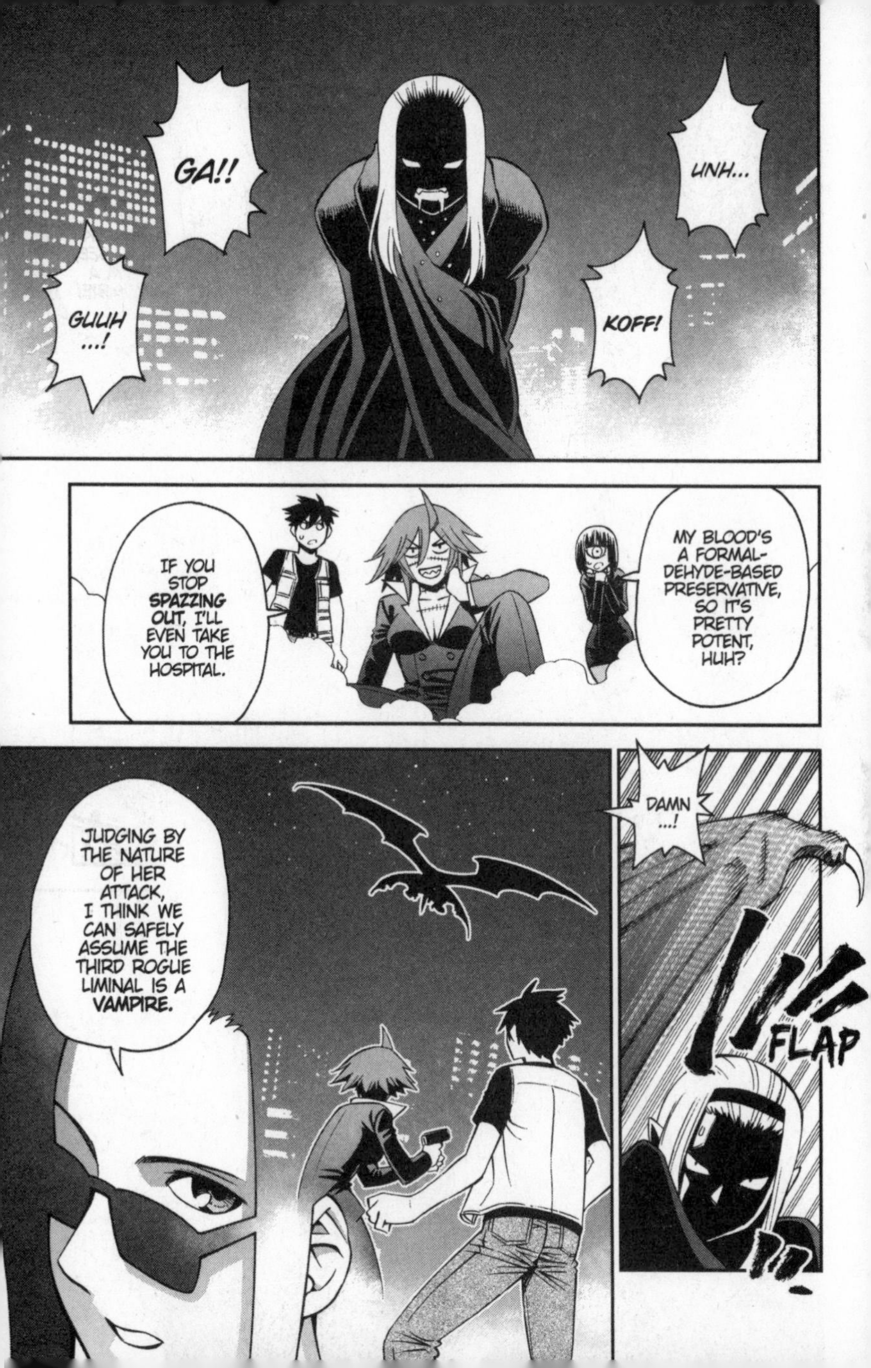
UNH...
GA!!
KOFF!
GUUH ...!
MY BLOOD'S A FORMAL-DEHYDE-BASED PRESERVATIVE, SO IT'S PRETTY POTENT, HUH?
IF YOU STOP SPAZZING OUT, I'LL EVEN TAKE YOU TO THE HOSPITAL.
DAMN ...!
FLAP
JUDGING BY THE NATURE OF HER ATTACK, I THINK WE CAN SAFELY ASSUME THE THIRD ROGUE LIMINAL IS A VAMPIRE.

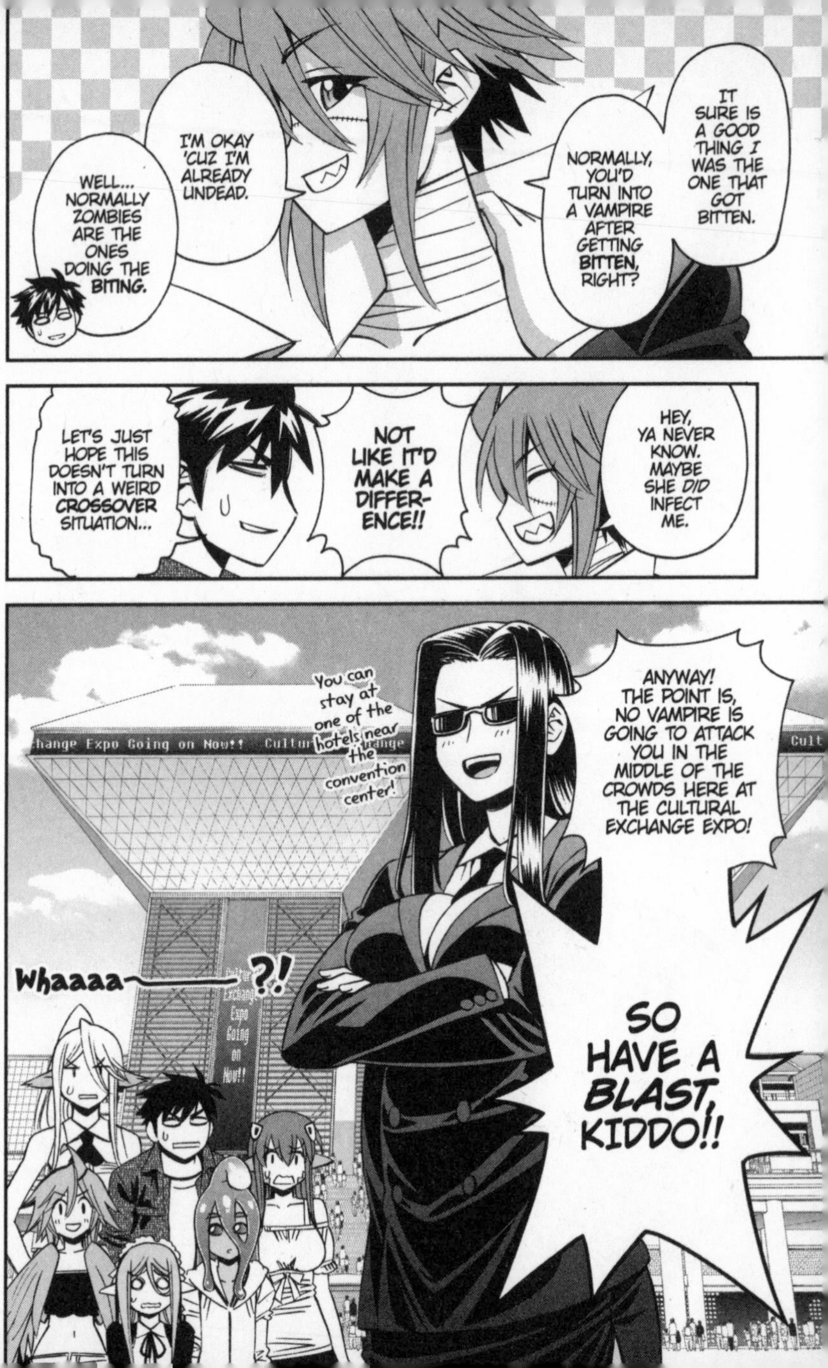
IT SURE IS A GOOD THING *I* WAS THE ONE THAT GOT BITTEN.
NORMALLY, YOU'D TURN INTO A VAMPIRE AFTER GETTING BITTEN, RIGHT?
I'M OKAY 'CUZ I'M ALREADY UNDEAD.
WELL... NORMALLY ZOMBIES ARE THE ONES DOING THE BITING.
HEY, YA NEVER KNOW. MAYBE SHE *DID* INFECT ME.
NOT LIKE IT'D MAKE A DIFFERENCE!!
LET'S JUST HOPE THIS DOESN'T TURN INTO A WEIRD CROSSOVER SITUATION...
ANYWAY! THE POINT IS, NO VAMPIRE IS GOING TO ATTACK YOU IN THE MIDDLE OF THE CROWDS HERE AT THE CULTURAL EXCHANGE EXPO!
You can stay at one of the hotels near the convention center!
SO HAVE A *BLAST,* KIDDO!!
Whaaaa——?!

Monster Musume

Everyday Life with Monster Girls

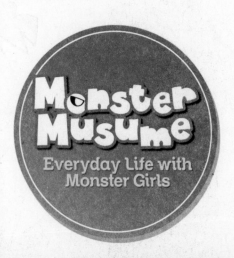

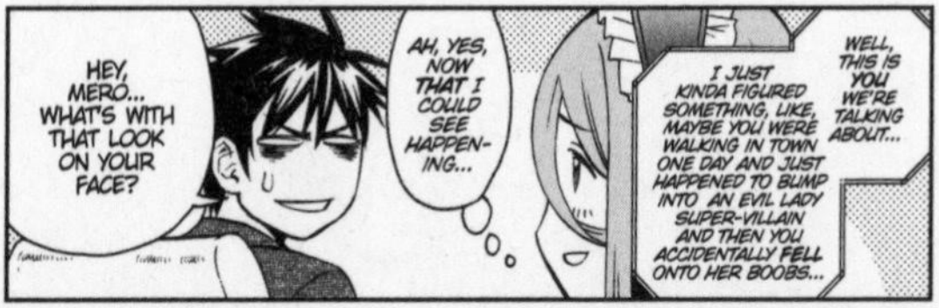
WELL, THIS IS YOU WE'RE TALKING ABOUT...
I JUST KINDA FIGURED SOMETHING, LIKE, MAYBE YOU WERE WALKING IN TOWN ONE DAY AND JUST HAPPENED TO BUMP INTO AN EVIL LADY SUPER-VILLAIN AND THEN YOU ACCIDENTALLY FELL ONTO HER BOOBS...
AH, YES, NOW THAT I COULD SEE HAPPENING...
HEY, MERO... WHAT'S WITH THAT LOOK ON YOUR FACE?

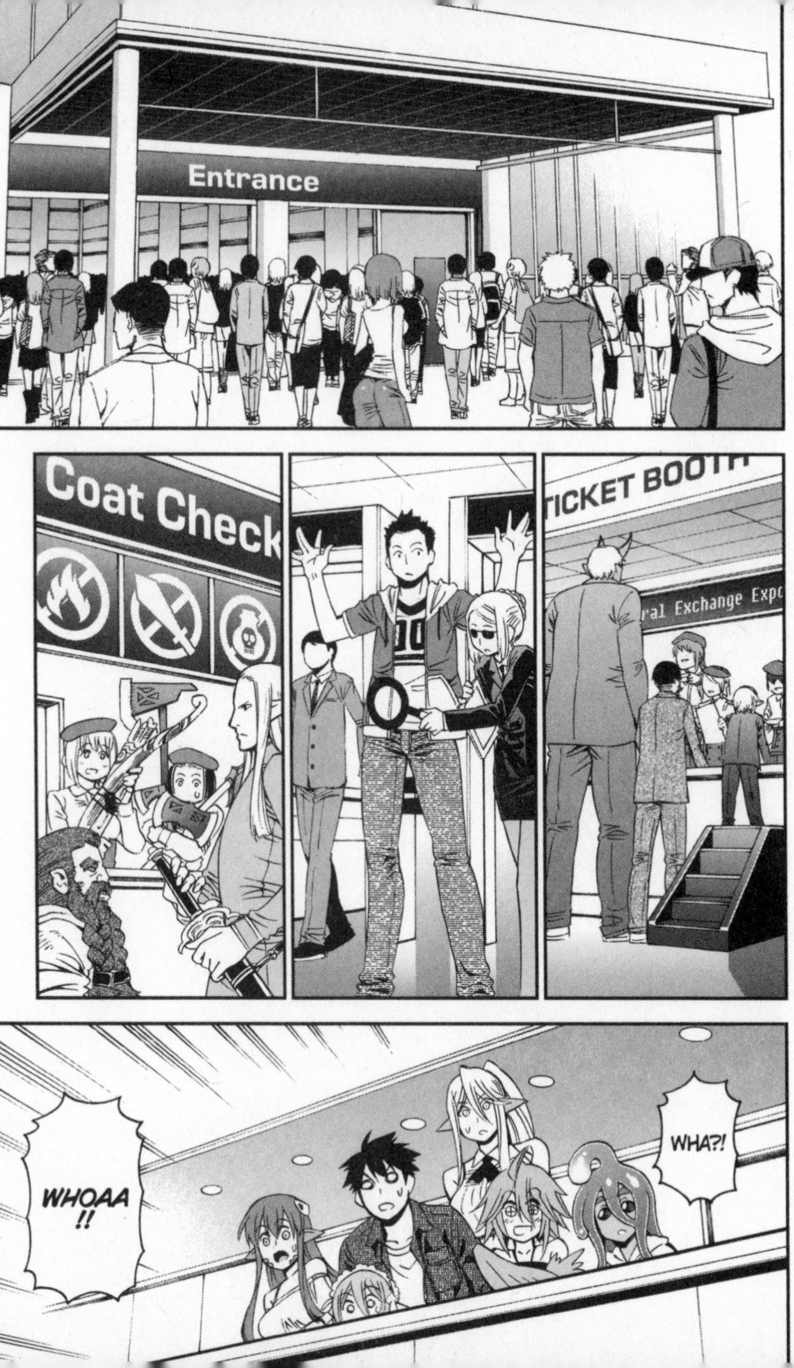
Entrance
TICKET BOOTH
ral Exchange Expo
Coat Check
WHA?!
WHOAA !!

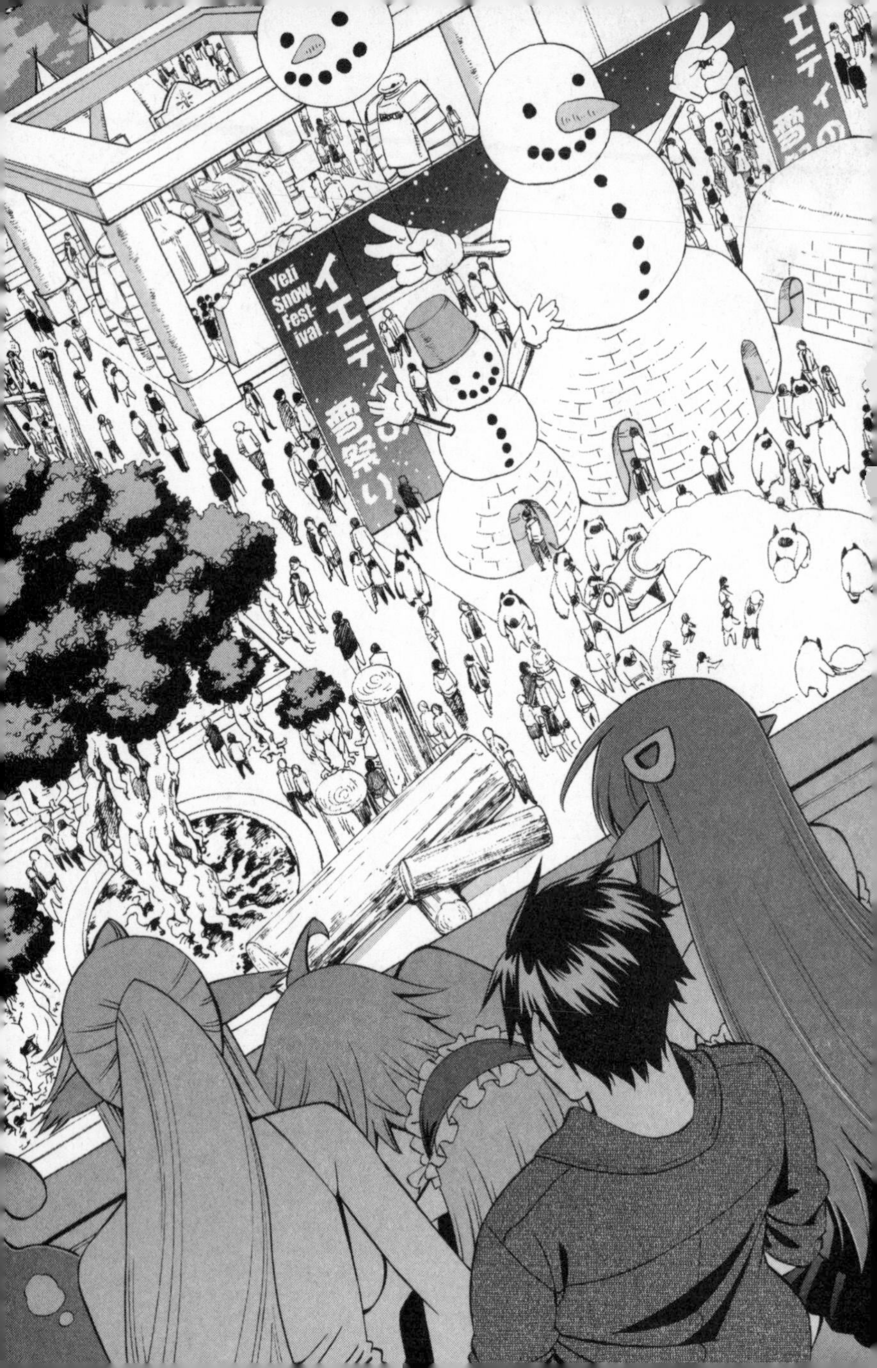
Yeti Snow Fest-ival

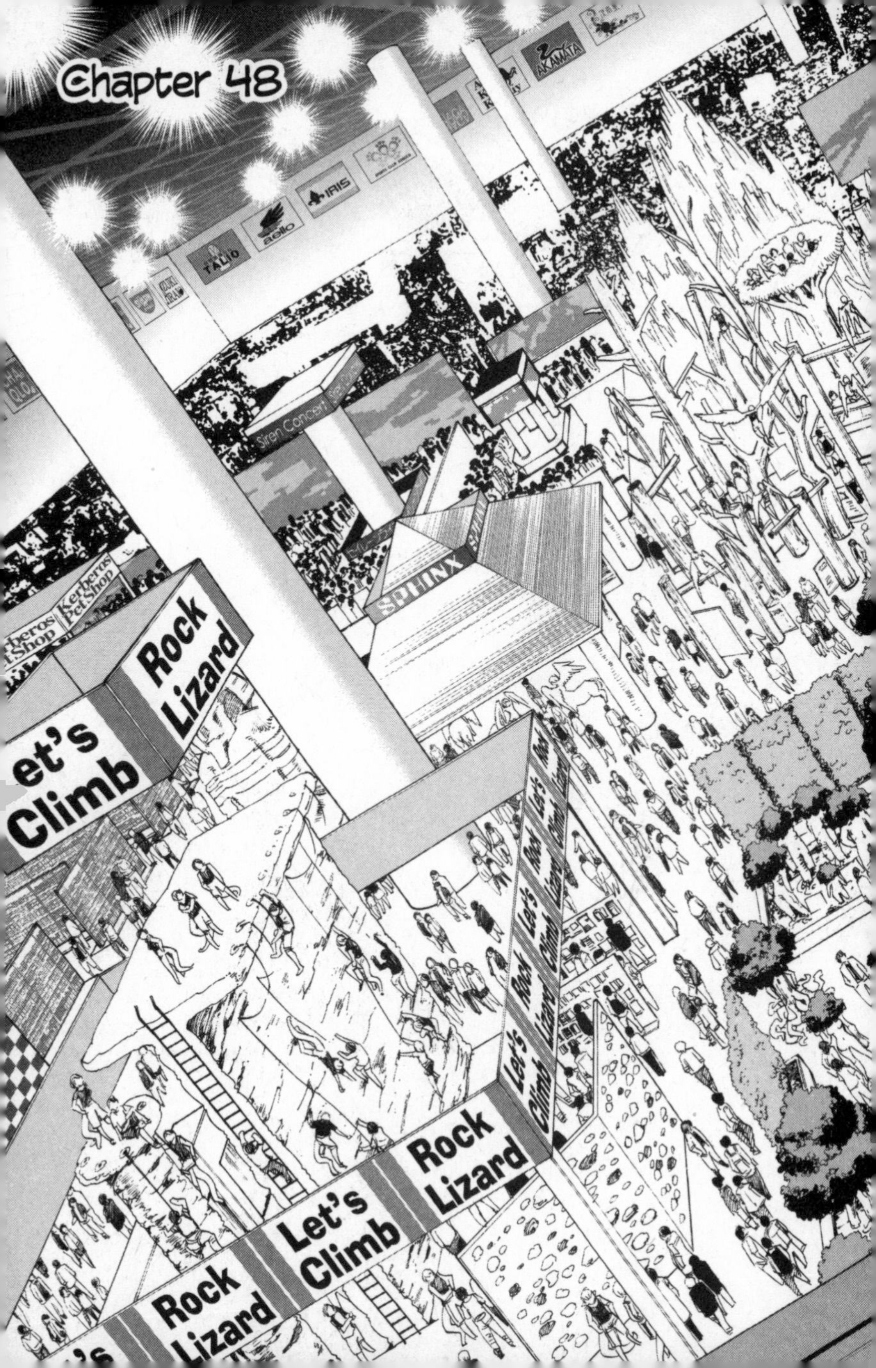
Chapter 48
AKAMATA
IRIS
aello
TALIO
Siren Concert
SPHINX
Kerberos Pet Shop
Rock Lizard
Let's Climb
Let's Climb
Rock Lizard
Rock Lizard
Let's Climb
Rock Lizard
Let's Climb
Rock Lizard

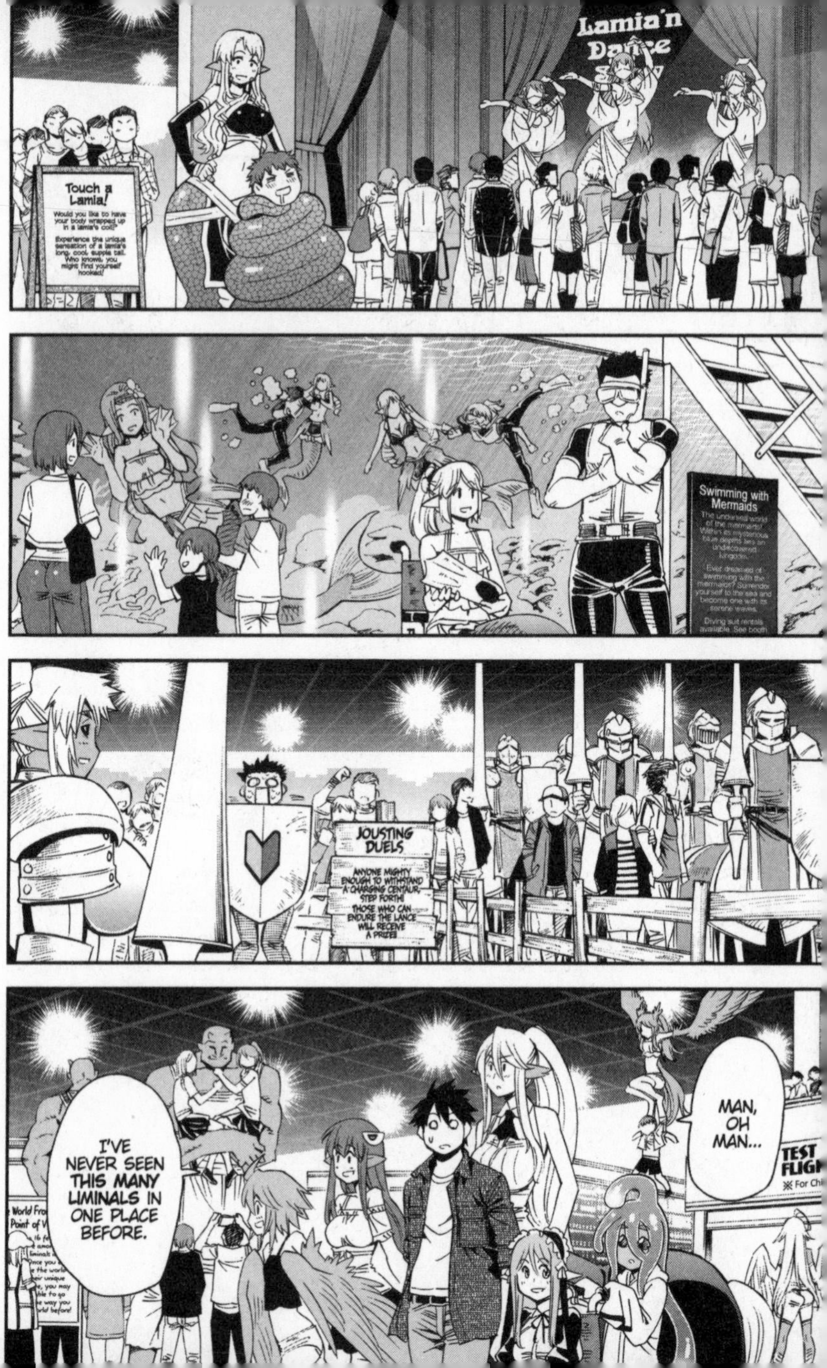
Lamia'n Dance
Touch a Lamia!
Would you like to have your body wrapped up in a lamia's coil?
Experience the unique sensation of a lamia's long, cool, supple tail. Who knows, you might find yourself hooked!
Swimming with Mermaids
The undersea world of the mermaids! Within its mysterious blue depths lies an undiscovered kingdom.
Ever dreamed of swimming with the mermaids? Surrender yourself to the sea and become one with its serene waves.
Diving suit rentals available. See booth
JOUSTING DUELS
ANYONE MIGHTY ENOUGH TO WITHSTAND A CHARGING CENTAUR, STEP FORTH!
THOSE WHO CAN ENDURE THE LANCE WILL RECEIVE A PRIZE!!
MAN, OH MAN...
TEST
I'VE NEVER SEEN THIS MANY LIMINALS IN ONE PLACE BEFORE.

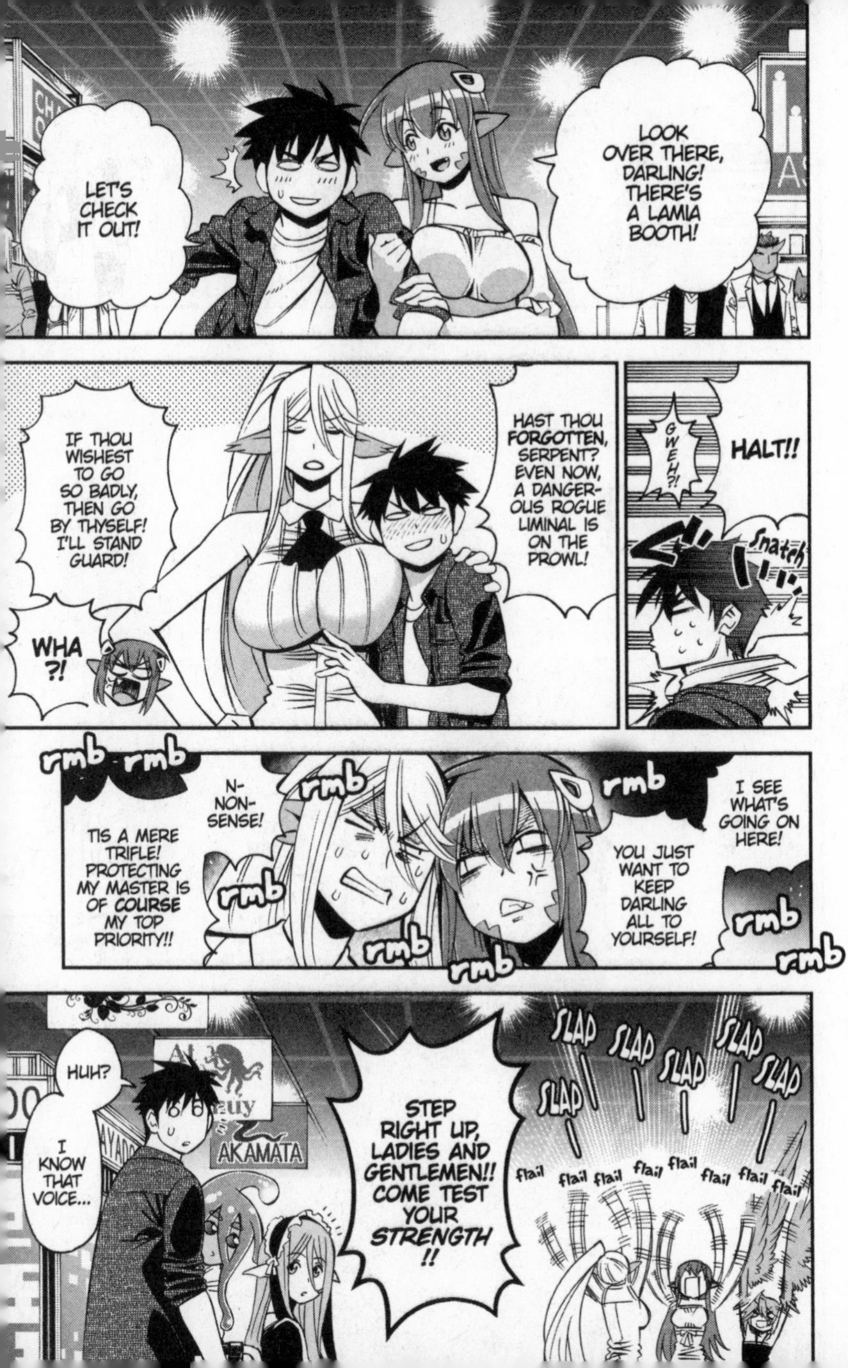
LOOK OVER THERE, DARLING! THERE'S A LAMIA BOOTH!
LET'S CHECK IT OUT!
HALT!!
GWEH?!
Snatch
HAST THOU FORGOTTEN, SERPENT? EVEN NOW, A DANGEROUS ROGUE LIMINAL IS ON THE PROWL!
IF THOU WISHEST TO GO SO BADLY, THEN GO BY THYSELF! I'LL STAND GUARD!
WHA?!
rmb rmb rmb rmb
I SEE WHAT'S GOING ON HERE!
YOU JUST WANT TO KEEP DARLING ALL TO YOURSELF!
N-NONSENSE!
TIS A MERE TRIFLE! PROTECTING MY MASTER IS OF COURSE MY TOP PRIORITY!!
rmb rmb rmb rmb
SLAP SLAP SLAP SLAP SLAP SLAP
flail flail flail flail flail flail flail flail
STEP RIGHT UP, LADIES AND GENTLEMEN!! COME TEST YOUR STRENGTH!!
AKAMATA
HUH?
I KNOW THAT VOICE...

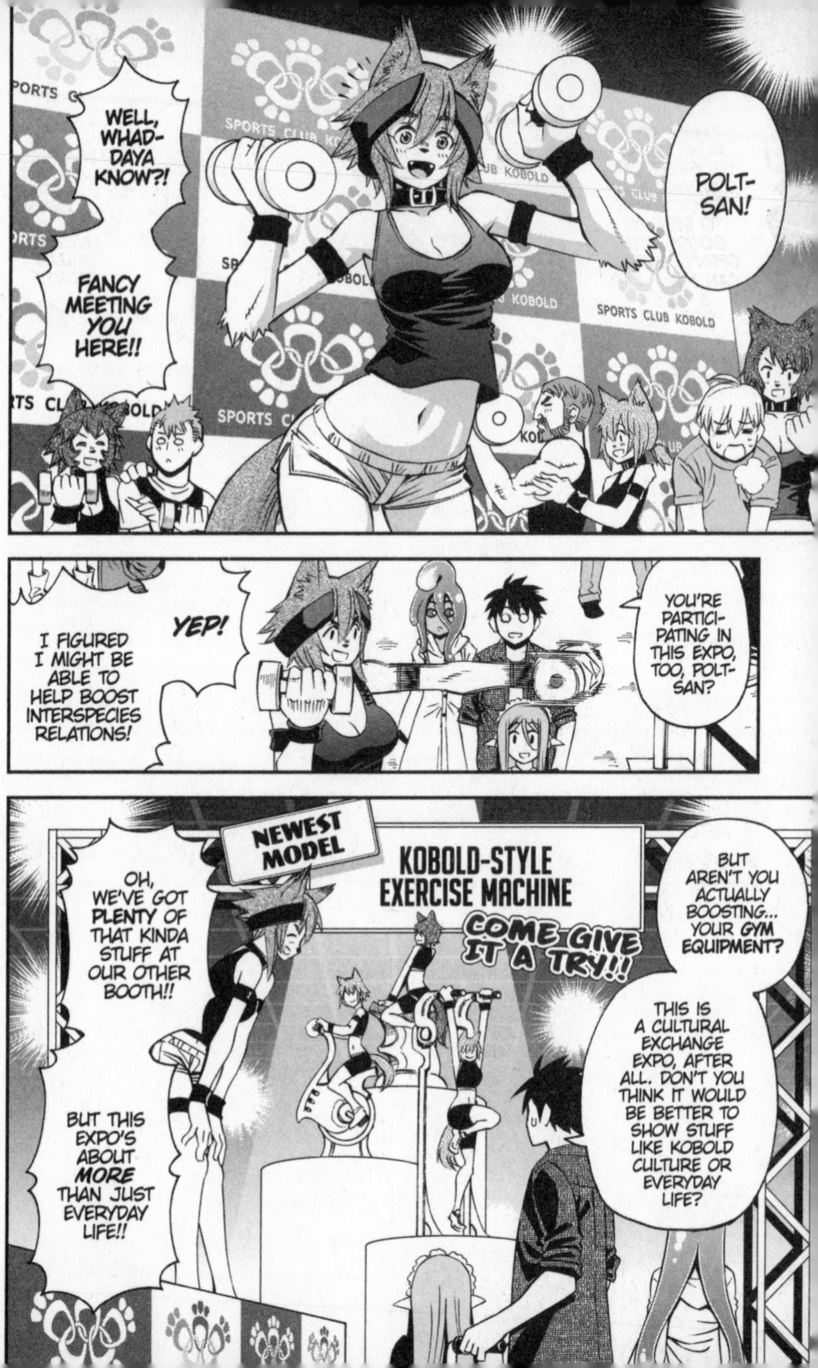
SPORTS CLUB KOBOLD
POLT-SAN!
WELL, WHAD-DAYA KNOW?!
FANCY MEETING YOU HERE!!
YOU'RE PARTICI-PATING IN THIS EXPO, TOO, POLT-SAN?
YEP!
I FIGURED I MIGHT BE ABLE TO HELP BOOST INTERSPECIES RELATIONS!
NEWEST MODEL
KOBOLD-STYLE EXERCISE MACHINE
COME GIVE IT A TRY!!
BUT AREN'T YOU ACTUALLY BOOSTING... YOUR GYM EQUIPMENT?
THIS IS A CULTURAL EXCHANGE EXPO, AFTER ALL. DON'T YOU THINK IT WOULD BE BETTER TO SHOW STUFF LIKE KOBOLD CULTURE OR EVERYDAY LIFE?
OH, WE'VE GOT PLENTY OF THAT KINDA STUFF AT OUR OTHER BOOTH!!
BUT THIS EXPO'S ABOUT MORE THAN JUST EVERYDAY LIFE!!

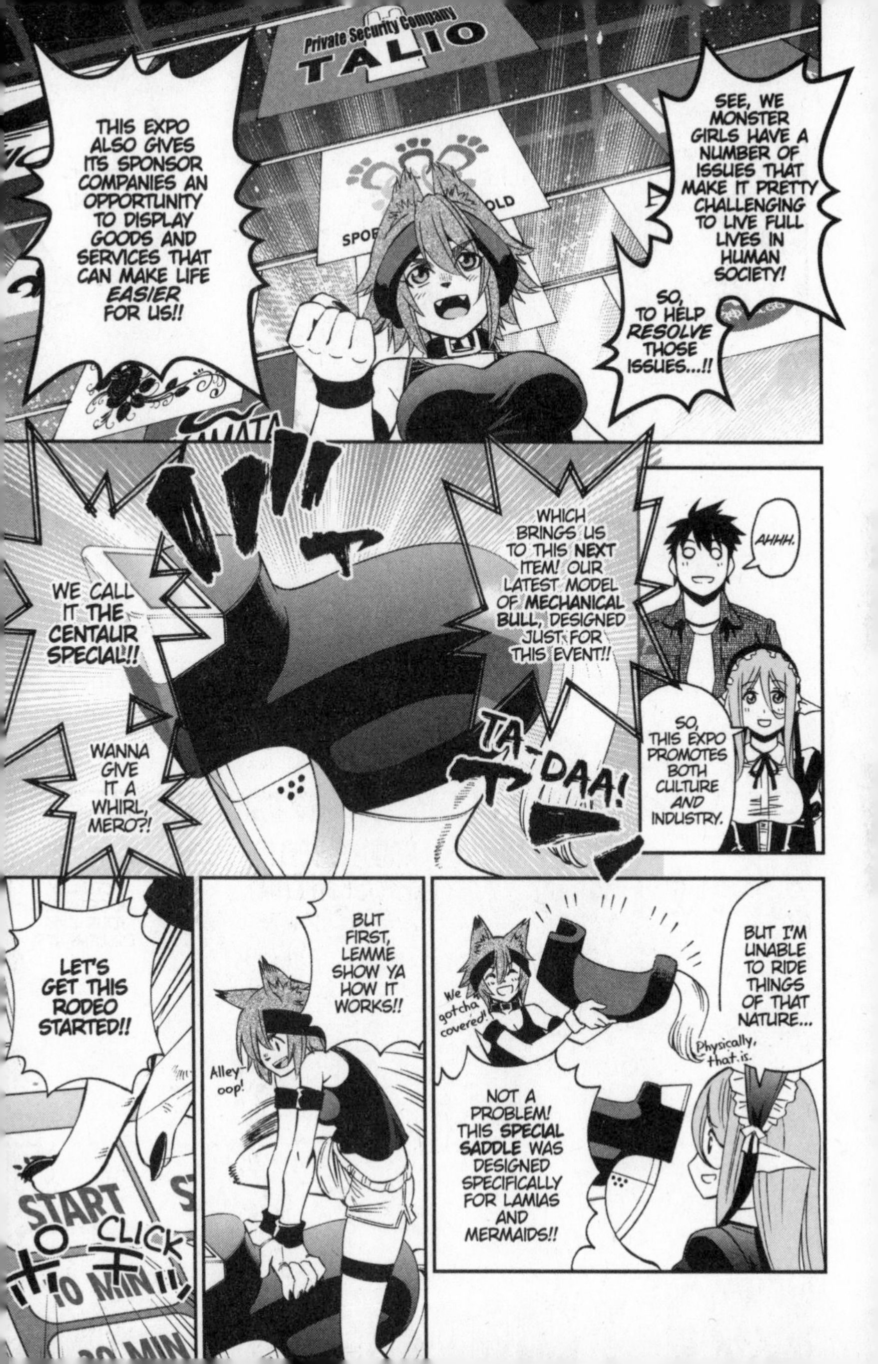
Private Security Company
TALIO
SEE, WE MONSTER GIRLS HAVE A NUMBER OF ISSUES THAT MAKE IT PRETTY CHALLENGING TO LIVE FULL LIVES IN HUMAN SOCIETY!
SO, TO HELP RESOLVE THOSE ISSUES...!!
THIS EXPO ALSO GIVES ITS SPONSOR COMPANIES AN OPPORTUNITY TO DISPLAY GOODS AND SERVICES THAT CAN MAKE LIFE EASIER FOR US!!
AHHH.
SO, THIS EXPO PROMOTES BOTH CULTURE AND INDUSTRY.
WHICH BRINGS US TO THIS NEXT ITEM! OUR LATEST MODEL OF MECHANICAL BULL, DESIGNED JUST FOR THIS EVENT!!
TA-DAA!
WE CALL IT THE CENTAUR SPECIAL!!
WANNA GIVE IT A WHIRL, MERO?!
BUT I'M UNABLE TO RIDE THINGS OF THAT NATURE...
Physically, that is.
We gotcha covered!
NOT A PROBLEM! THIS SPECIAL SADDLE WAS DESIGNED SPECIFICALLY FOR LAMIAS AND MERMAIDS!!
BUT FIRST, LEMME SHOW YA HOW IT WORKS!!
Alley-oop!
LET'S GET THIS RODEO STARTED!!
START
CLICK
10 MIN

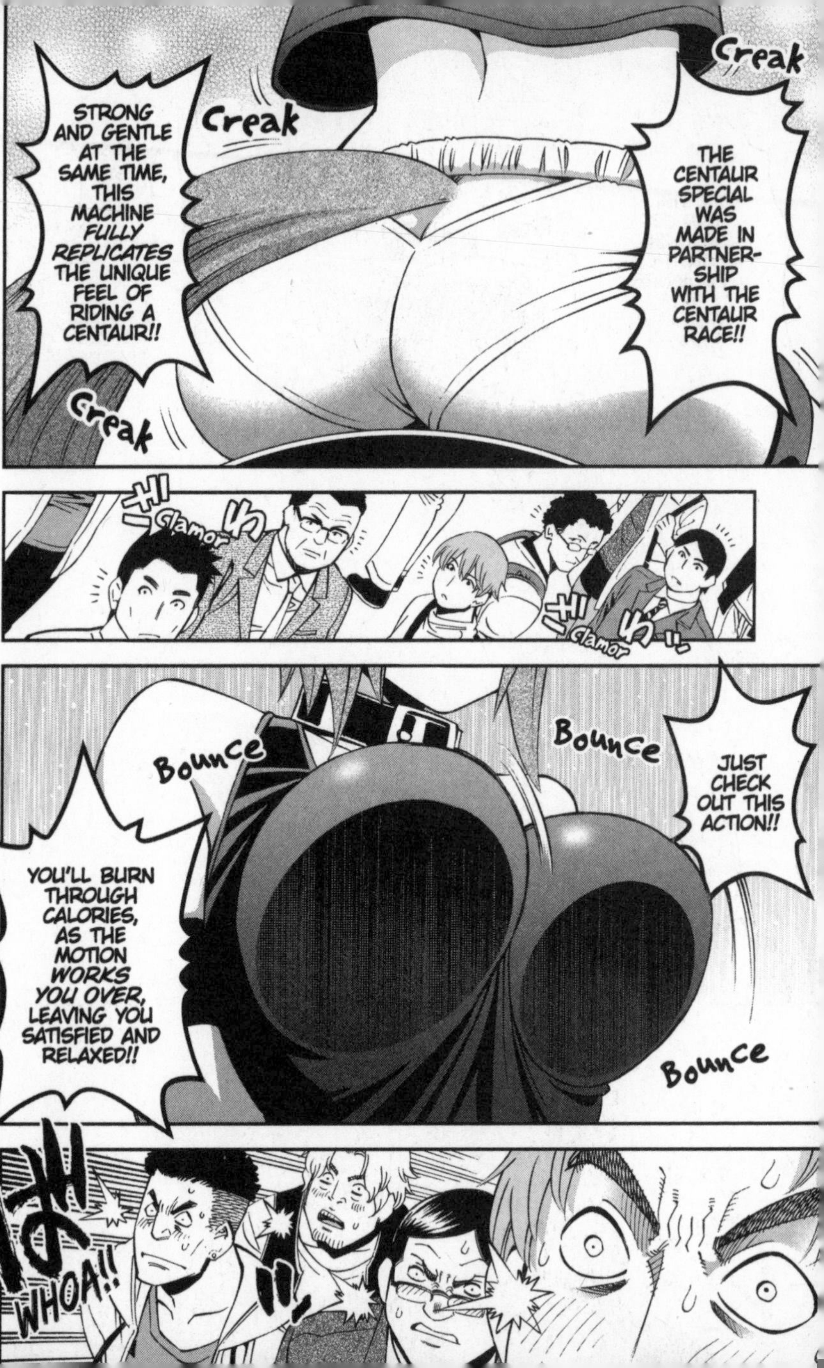
Creak
THE CENTAUR SPECIAL WAS MADE IN PARTNER-SHIP WITH THE CENTAUR RACE!!
Creak
STRONG AND GENTLE AT THE SAME TIME, THIS MACHINE *FULLY* REPLICATES THE UNIQUE FEEL OF RIDING A CENTAUR!!
Creak
Clamor
Clamor
JUST CHECK OUT THIS ACTION!!
Bounce
Bounce
YOU'LL BURN THROUGH CALORIES, AS THE MOTION *WORKS* YOU OVER, LEAVING YOU SATISFIED AND RELAXED!!
Bounce
WHOA!!

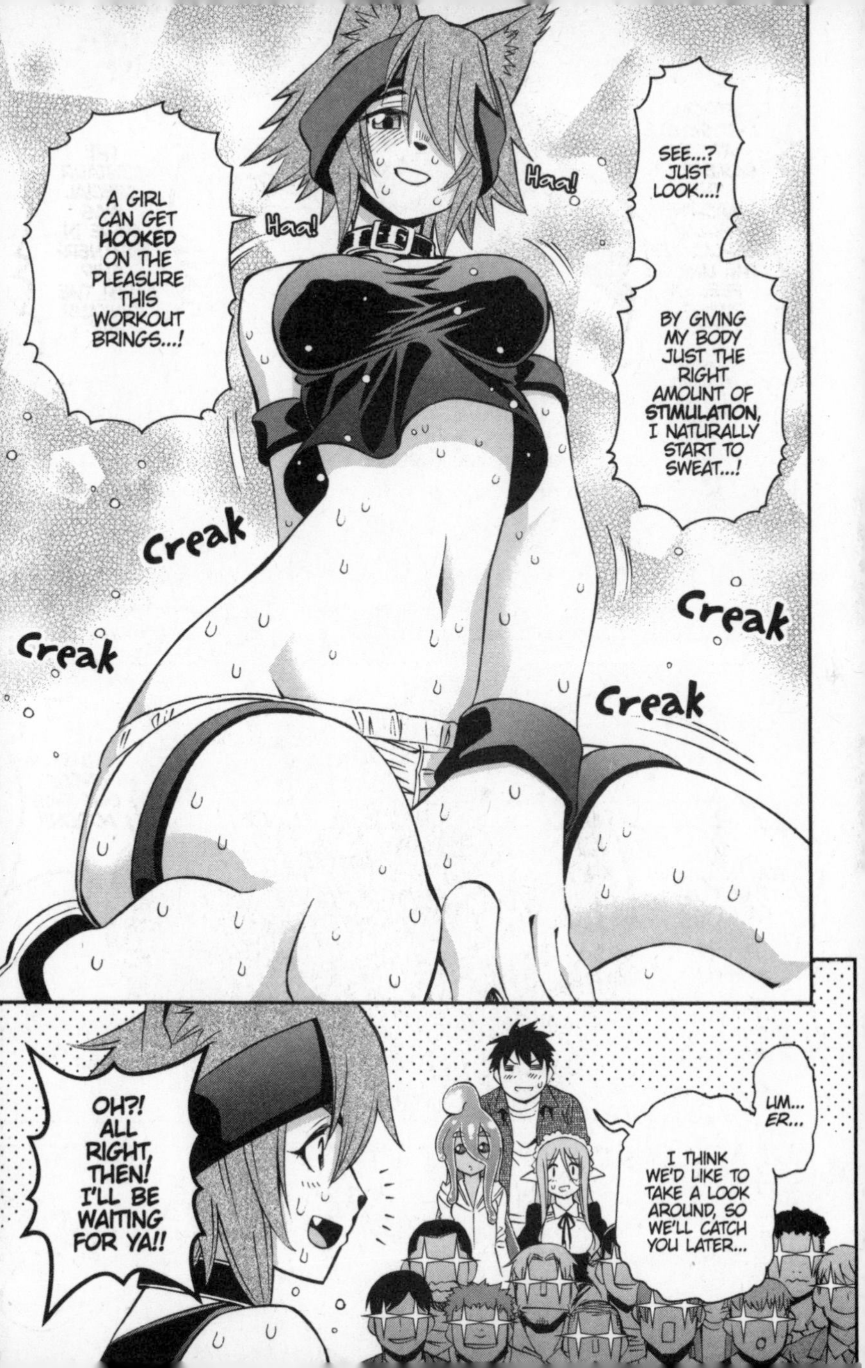
SEE...? JUST LOOK...!
BY GIVING MY BODY JUST THE RIGHT AMOUNT OF STIMULATION, I NATURALLY START TO SWEAT...!
Haa!
Haa!
A GIRL CAN GET HOOKED ON THE PLEASURE THIS WORKOUT BRINGS...!
Creak
Creak
Creak
Creak
UM... ER...
I THINK WE'D LIKE TO TAKE A LOOK AROUND, SO WE'LL CATCH YOU LATER...
OH?! ALL RIGHT, THEN! I'LL BE WAITING FOR YA!!

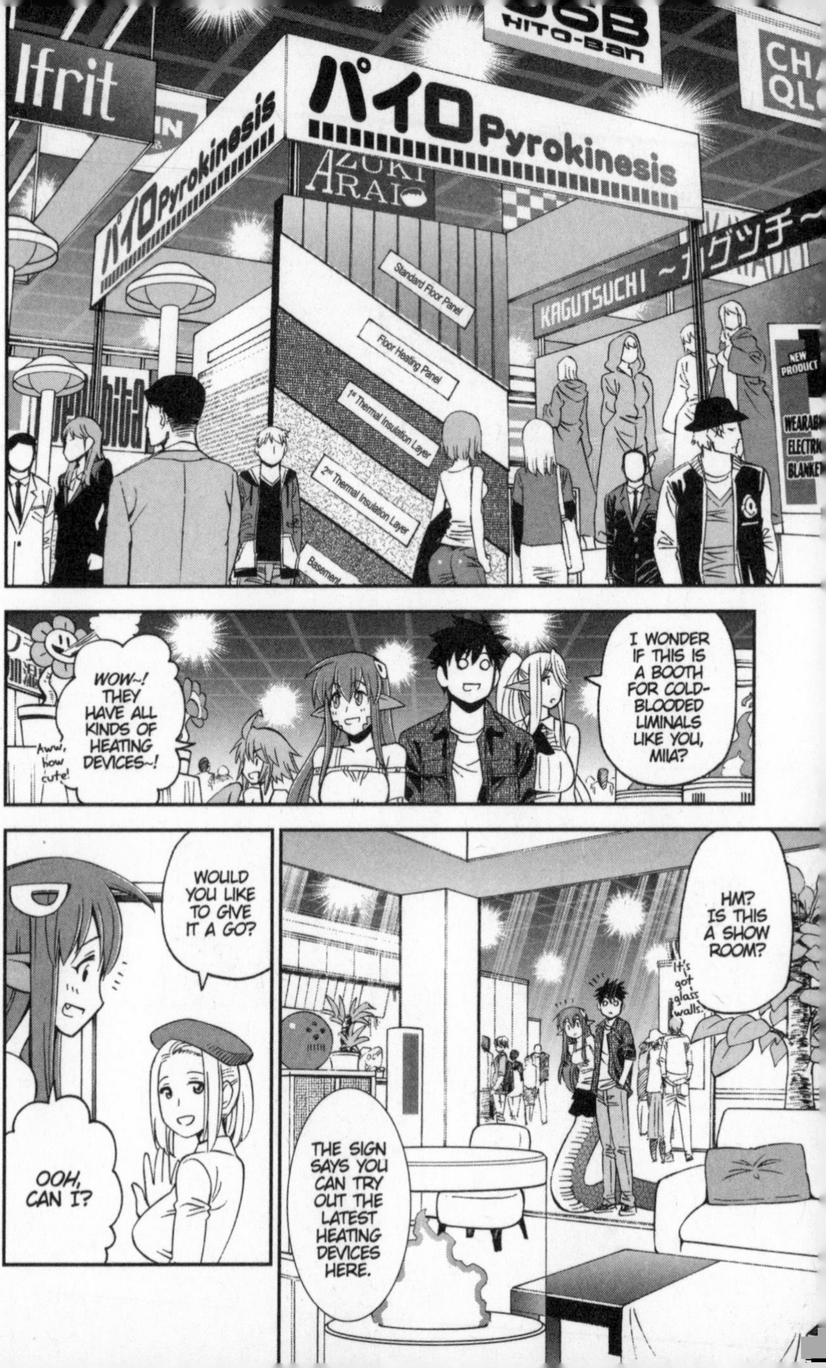
HITO-Ban
パイロ Pyrokinesis
Ifrit
パイロ Pyrokinesis
AZUKI ARAI
KAGUTSUCHI
NEW PRODUCT
Standard Floor Panel
Floor Heating Panel
1st Thermal Insulation Layer
2nd Thermal Insulation Layer
Basement
I WONDER IF THIS IS A BOOTH FOR COLD-BLOODED LIMINALS LIKE YOU, MIIA?
WOW~! THEY HAVE ALL KINDS OF HEATING DEVICES~!
Aww, how cute!
HM? IS THIS A SHOW ROOM?
It's got glass walls.
THE SIGN SAYS YOU CAN TRY OUT THE LATEST HEATING DEVICES HERE.
WOULD YOU LIKE TO GIVE IT A GO?
OOH, CAN I?

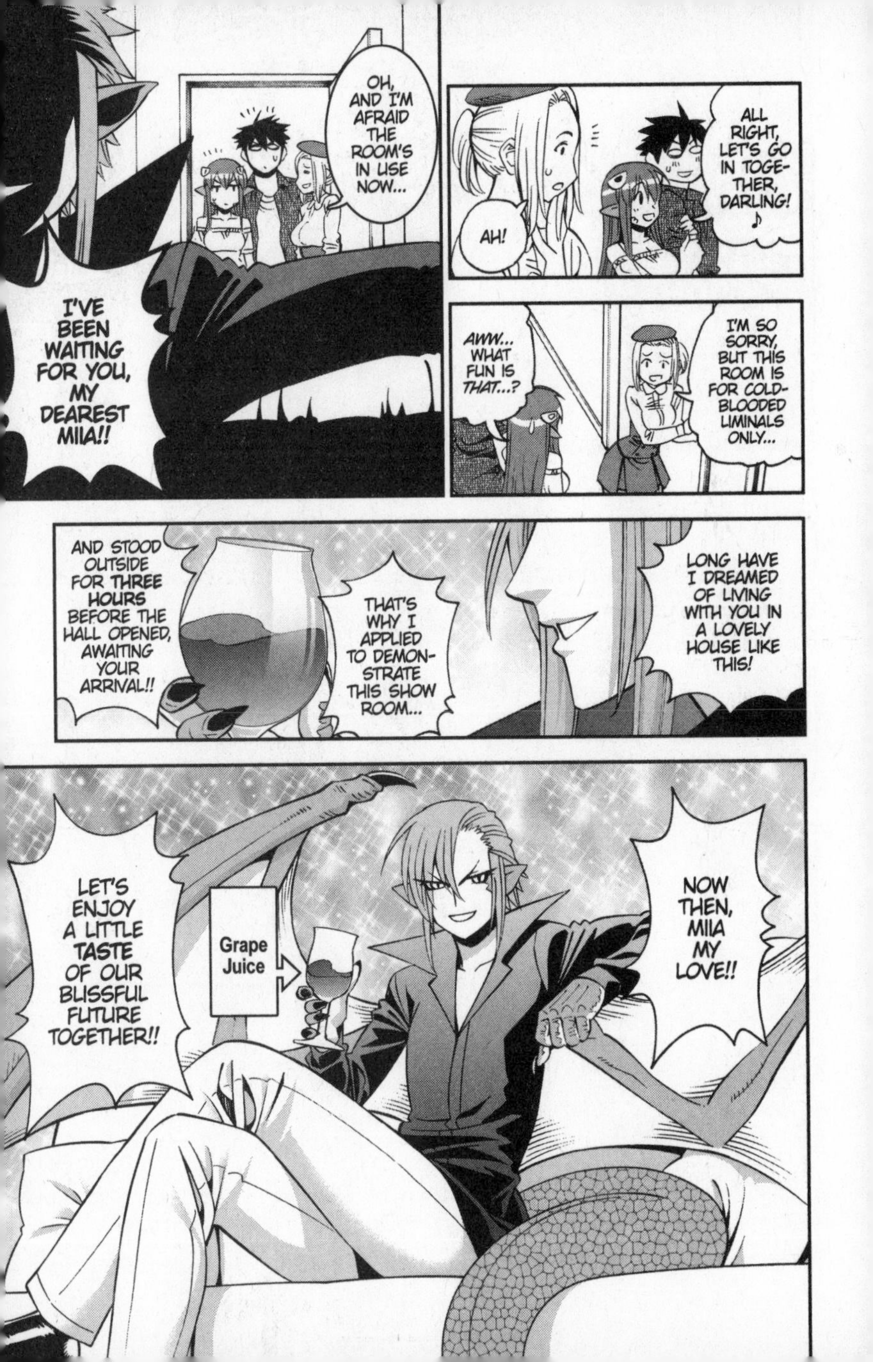

ALL RIGHT, LET'S GO IN TOGETHER, DARLING! ♪
AH!
I'M SO SORRY, BUT THIS ROOM IS FOR COLD-BLOODED LIMINALS ONLY...
AWW... WHAT FUN IS THAT...?
OH, AND I'M AFRAID THE ROOM'S IN USE NOW...
I'VE BEEN WAITING FOR YOU, MY DEAREST MIIA!!
LONG HAVE I DREAMED OF LIVING WITH YOU IN A LOVELY HOUSE LIKE THIS!
THAT'S WHY I APPLIED TO DEMONSTRATE THIS SHOW ROOM...
AND STOOD OUTSIDE FOR THREE HOURS BEFORE THE HALL OPENED, AWAITING YOUR ARRIVAL!!
NOW THEN, MIIA MY LOVE!!
Grape Juice
LET'S ENJOY A LITTLE TASTE OF OUR BLISSFUL FUTURE TOGETHER!!

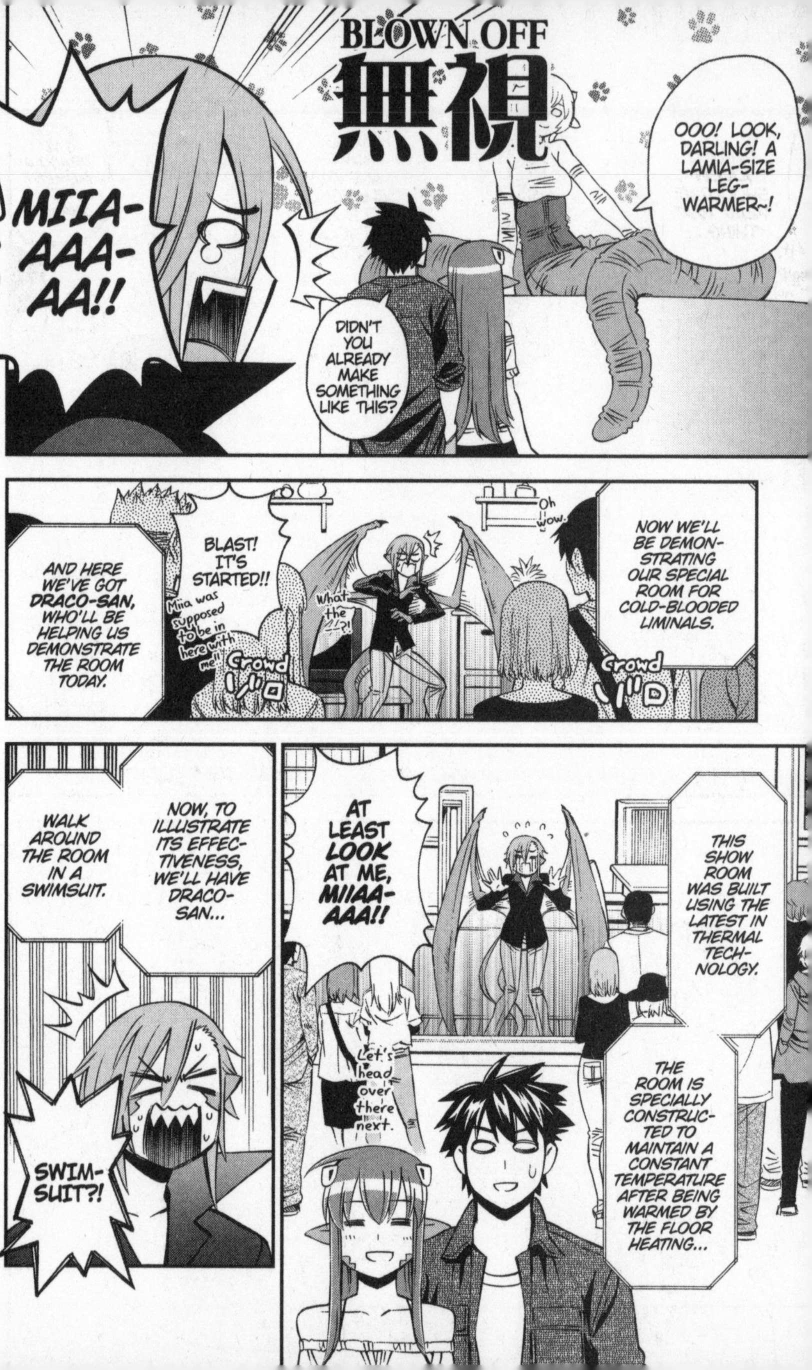
BLOWN OFF
無視
OOO! LOOK, DARLING! A LAMIA-SIZE LEG-WARMER~!
DIDN'T YOU ALREADY MAKE SOMETHING LIKE THIS?
MIIA-AAAA-AA!!
NOW WE'LL BE DEMONSTRATING OUR SPECIAL ROOM FOR COLD-BLOODED LIMINALS.
Oh wow.
Crowd
BLAST! IT'S STARTED!!
What the -!?
Miia was supposed to be in here with me!
Crowd
AND HERE WE'VE GOT DRACO-SAN, WHO'LL BE HELPING US DEMONSTRATE THE ROOM TODAY.
THIS SHOW ROOM WAS BUILT USING THE LATEST IN THERMAL TECHNOLOGY.
AT LEAST LOOK AT ME, MIIAA-AAA!!
THE ROOM IS SPECIALLY CONSTRUCTED TO MAINTAIN A CONSTANT TEMPERATURE AFTER BEING WARMED BY THE FLOOR HEATING...
Let's head over there next.
NOW, TO ILLUSTRATE ITS EFFECTIVENESS, WE'LL HAVE DRACO-SAN...
WALK AROUND THE ROOM IN A SWIMSUIT.
SWIM-SUIT?!

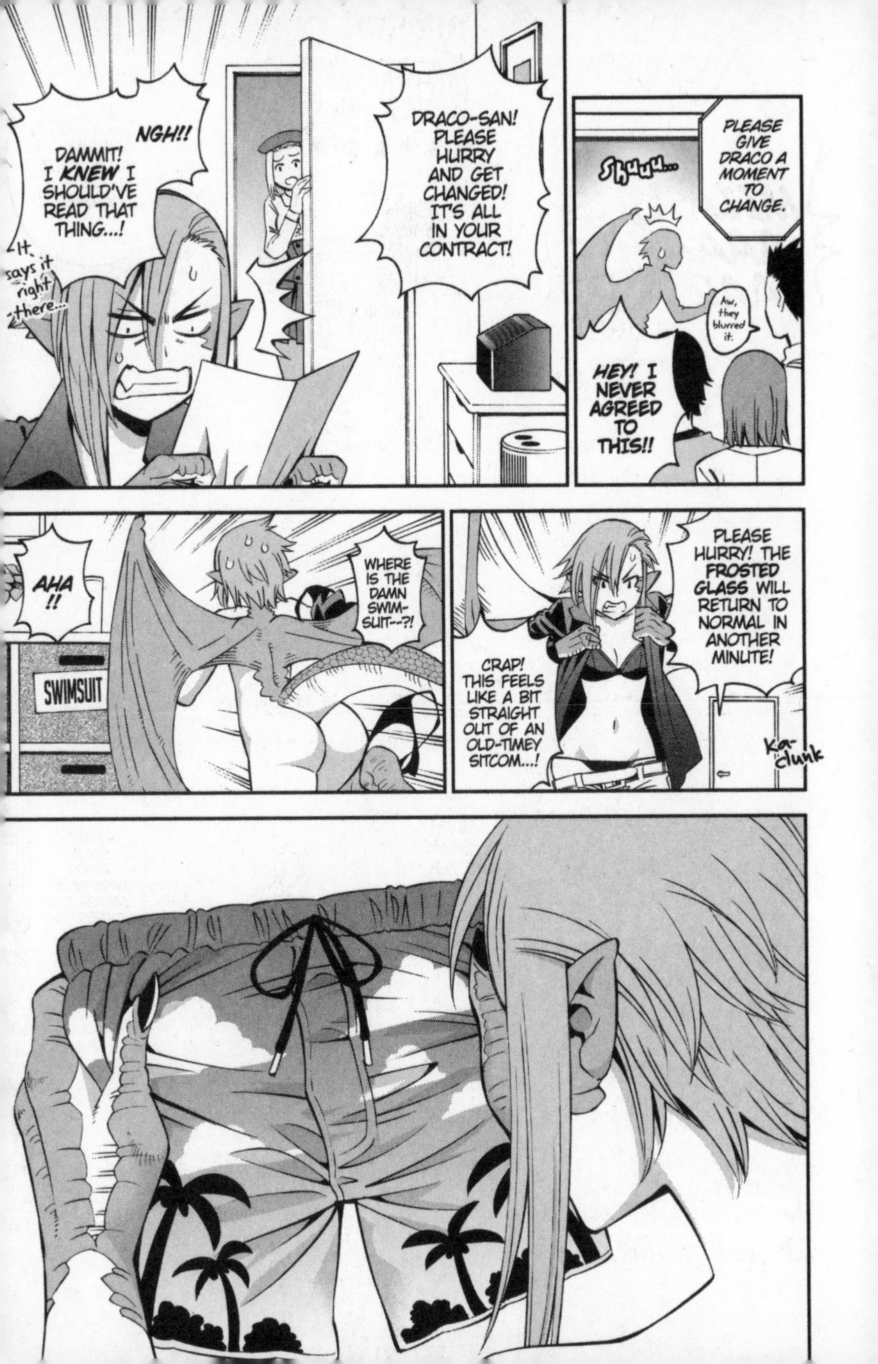
PLEASE GIVE DRACO A MOMENT TO CHANGE.
Shuuu...
Aw, they blurred it.
HEY! I NEVER AGREED TO THIS!!
DRACO-SAN! PLEASE HURRY AND GET CHANGED! IT'S ALL IN YOUR CONTRACT!
NGH!!
DAMMIT! I KNEW I SHOULD'VE READ THAT THING...!
It says it right there...
PLEASE HURRY! THE FROSTED GLASS WILL RETURN TO NORMAL IN ANOTHER MINUTE!
CRAP! THIS FEELS LIKE A BIT STRAIGHT OUT OF AN OLD-TIMEY SITCOM...!
Ka-clunk
WHERE IS THE DAMN SWIM-SUIT--?!
AHA!!
SWIMSUIT

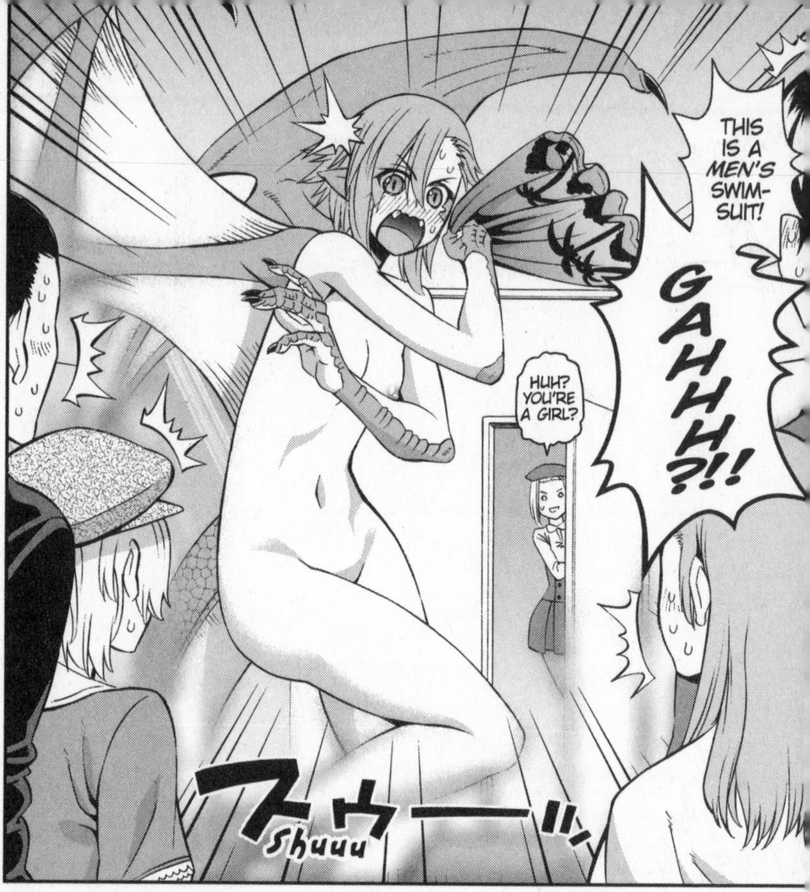
THIS IS A MEN'S SWIM-SUIT!
GAHHHH?!!
HUH? YOU'RE A GIRL?
Shuuu

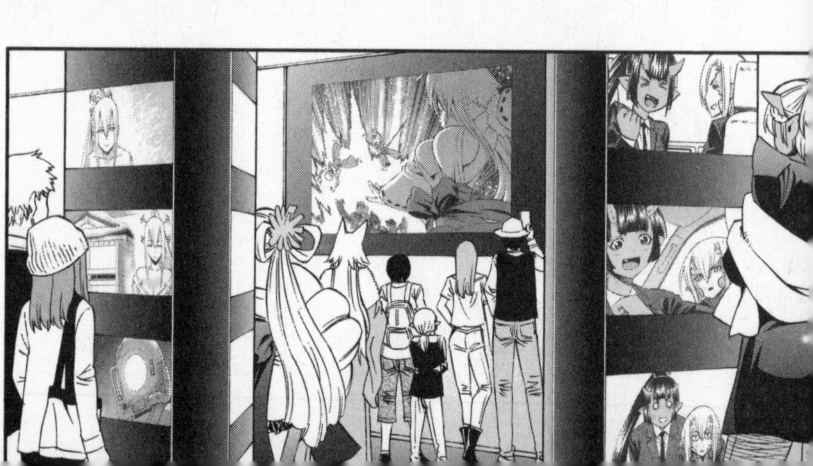

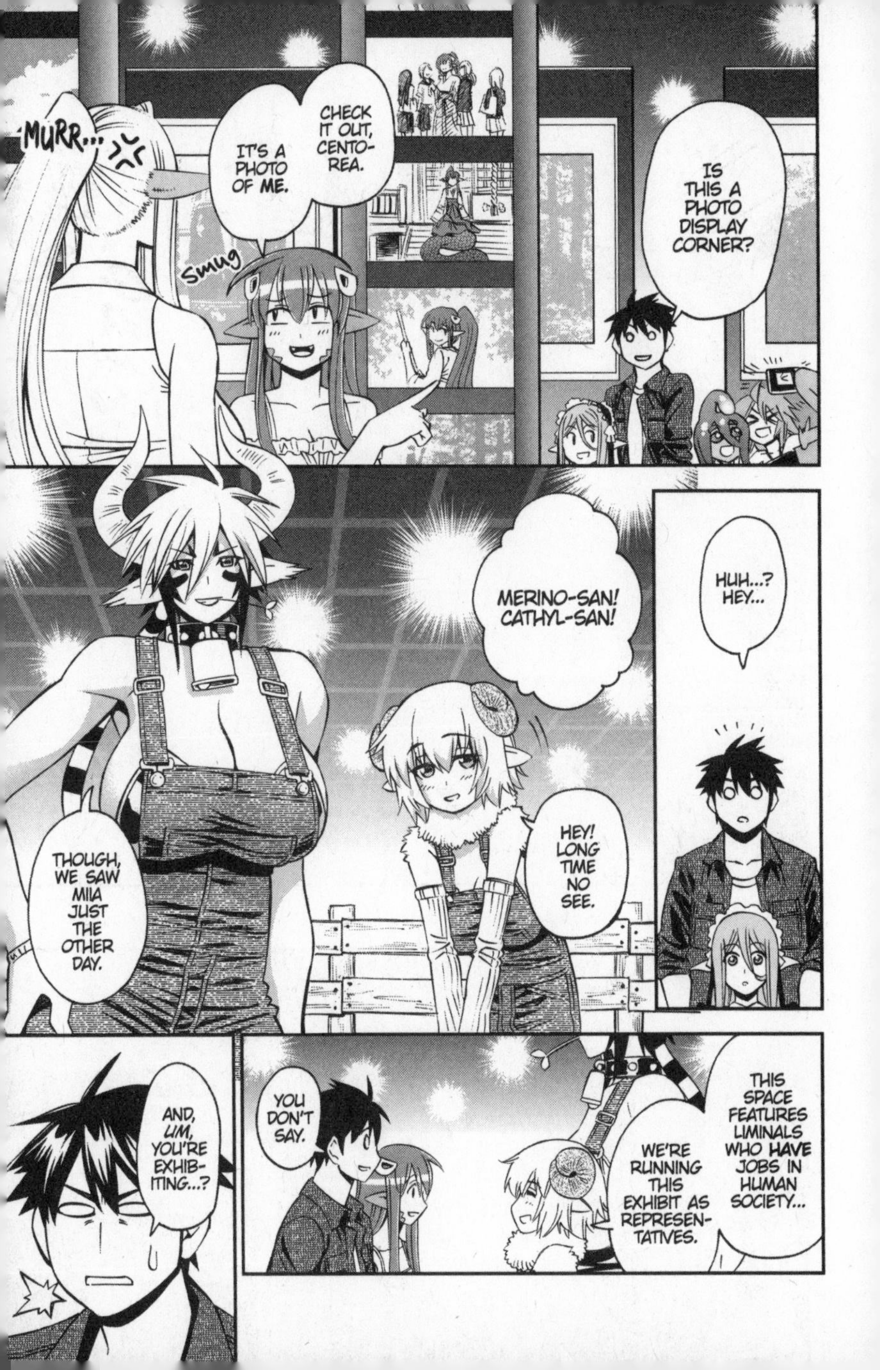
IS THIS A PHOTO DISPLAY CORNER?
CHECK IT OUT, CENTOREA.
IT'S A PHOTO OF ME.
Smug
MURR...
HUH...? HEY...
MERINO-SAN! CATHYL-SAN!
HEY! LONG TIME NO SEE.
THOUGH, WE SAW MIIA JUST THE OTHER DAY.
THIS SPACE FEATURES LIMINALS WHO HAVE JOBS IN HUMAN SOCIETY...
WE'RE RUNNING THIS EXHIBIT AS REPRESENTATIVES.
YOU DON'T SAY.
AND, UM, YOU'RE EXHIBITING...?

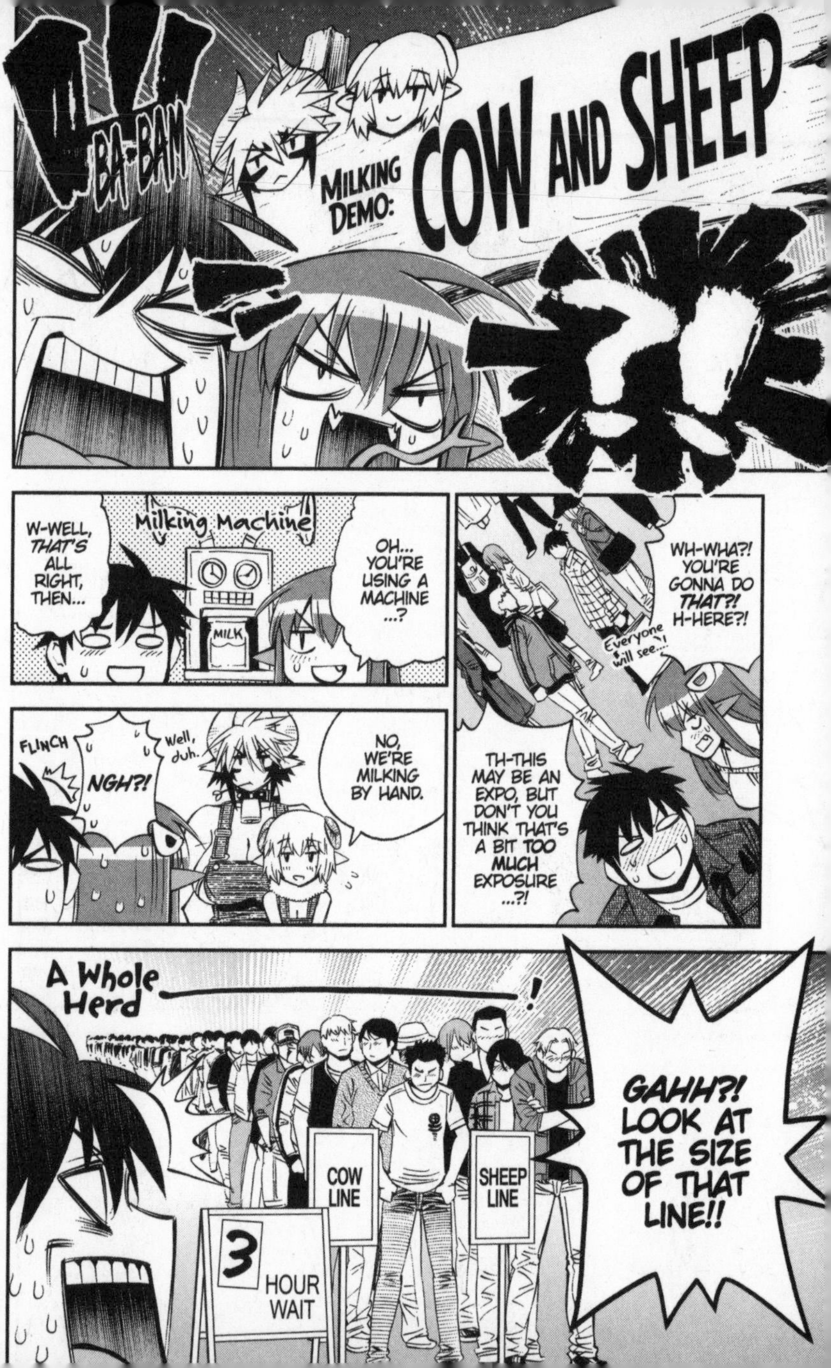
MILKING DEMO: COW AND SHEEP
BA-BAM
?!
WH-WHA?! YOU'RE GONNA DO THAT?! H-HERE?!
Everyone will see...!
TH-THIS MAY BE AN EXPO, BUT DON'T YOU THINK THAT'S A BIT TOO MUCH EXPOSURE ...?!
OH... YOU'RE USING A MACHINE ...?
Milking Machine
MILK
W-WELL, THAT'S ALL RIGHT, THEN...
NO, WE'RE MILKING BY HAND.
Well, duh.
NGH?!
FLINCH
GAHH?! LOOK AT THE SIZE OF THAT LINE!!
A Whole Herd—!
SHEEP LINE
COW LINE
3 HOUR WAIT

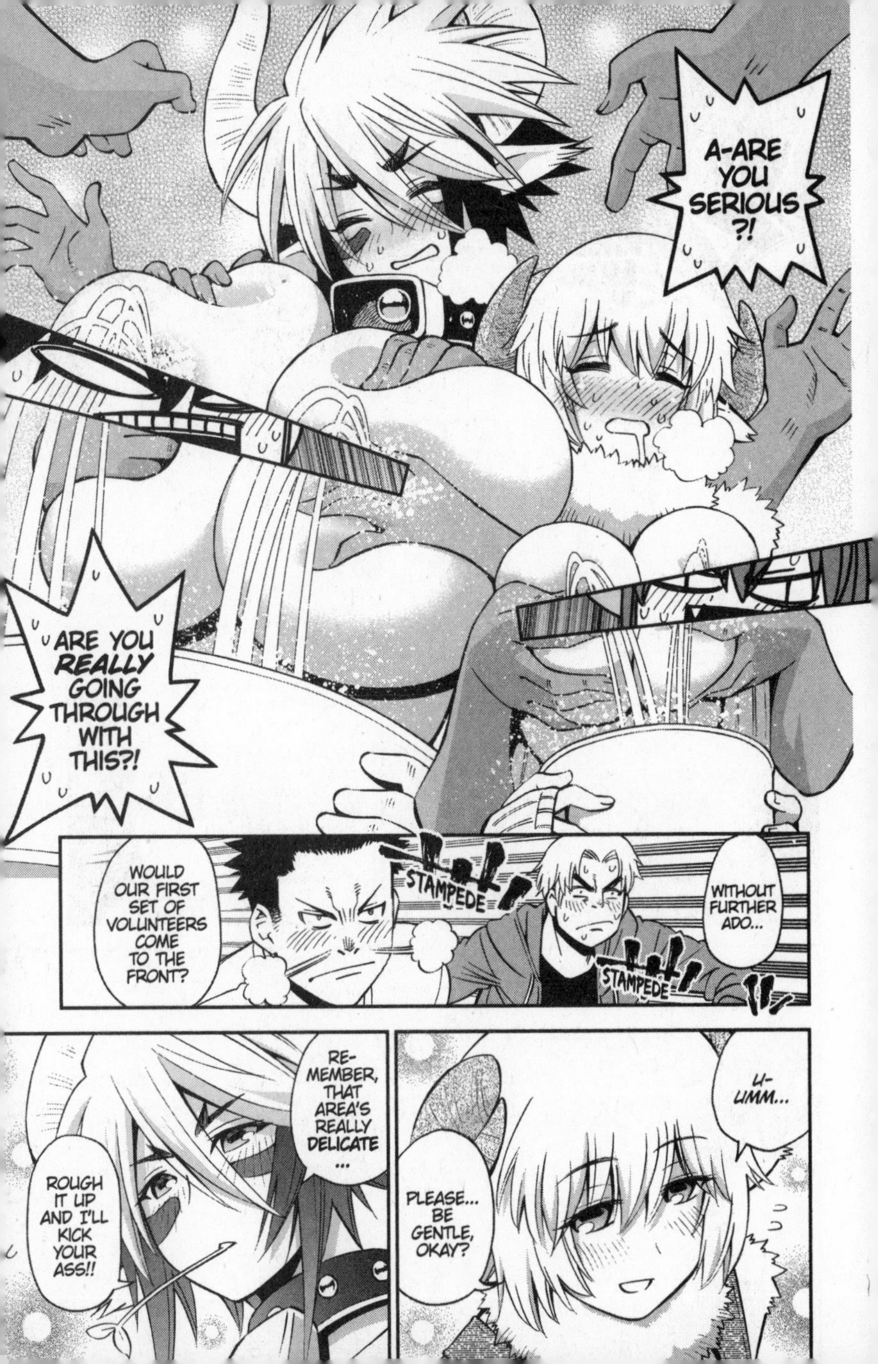
A-ARE YOU SERIOUS ?!
ARE YOU *REALLY* GOING THROUGH WITH THIS?!
WITHOUT FURTHER ADO...
STAMPEDE
STAMPEDE
WOULD OUR FIRST SET OF VOLUNTEERS COME TO THE FRONT?
U-UMM...
PLEASE... BE GENTLE, OKAY?
RE-MEMBER, THAT AREA'S REALLY DELICATE ...
ROUGH IT UP AND I'LL KICK YOUR ASS!!

MOO

BAA

I JUST SAID NOT TO ROUGH HER UP!!

THAT'S RIGHT. PLEASE BE GENTLE WHEN YOU MILK HER.

HOW TO MILK

STEP 1
Squeeze the base of the teat between your extended thumb and first finger, so that the milk doesn't flow back up into the udder.

STEP 2
Squeeze your fingers one at a time from the index to the pinky.

STEP 3
Tug down to draw the milk out.

Repeat steps 1-3. If you have troub In steps 1-2, the milk can get com animal gets restless and steps in th this happen you will need to discar

They're real animals...

How did they get them all this way...?

MAYBE THIS IS THE STUFF POLT WAS TALKING ABOUT?

WHAT'S OVER HERE?

LENDING A HAND
This new tech
3137 units
Military t
51 people
O more

Spectacles for
Spec...

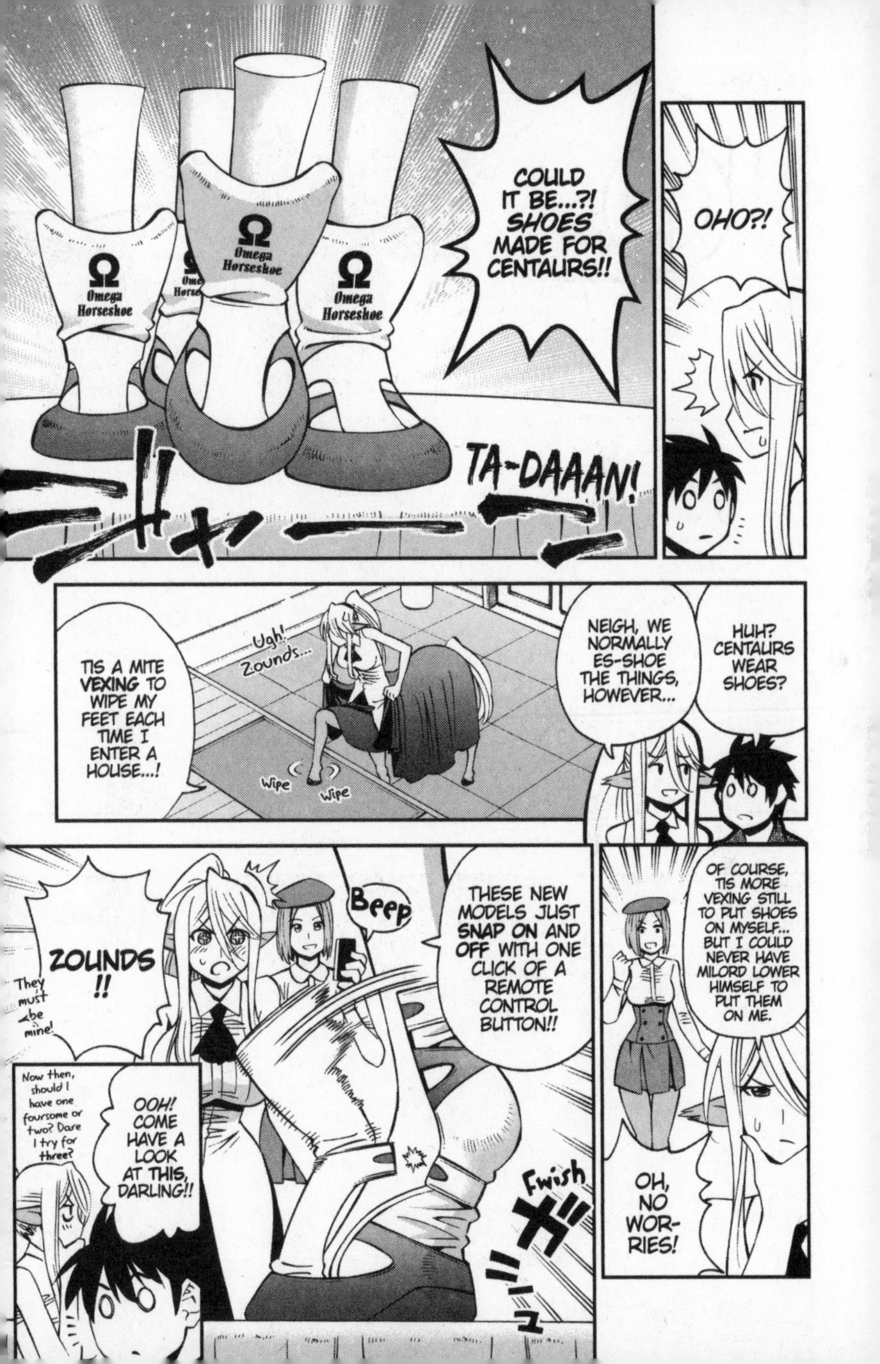
OHO?!
COULD IT BE...?! SHOES MADE FOR CENTAURS!!
Omega Horseshoe
Omega Horseshoe
Omega Horseshoe
TA-DAAAN!
HUH? CENTAURS WEAR SHOES?
NEIGH, WE NORMALLY ES-SHOE THE THINGS, HOWEVER...
Ugh! Zounds...
TIS A MITE VEXING TO WIPE MY FEET EACH TIME I ENTER A HOUSE...!
Wipe
Wipe
OF COURSE, TIS MORE VEXING STILL TO PUT SHOES ON MYSELF... BUT I COULD NEVER HAVE MILORD LOWER HIMSELF TO PUT THEM ON ME.
OH, NO WOR-RIES!
THESE NEW MODELS JUST SNAP ON AND OFF WITH ONE CLICK OF A REMOTE CONTROL BUTTON!!
Beep
ZOUNDS!!
They must be mine!
OOH! COME HAVE A LOOK AT THIS, DARLING!!
Now then, should I have one foursome or two? Dare I try for three?
Fwish

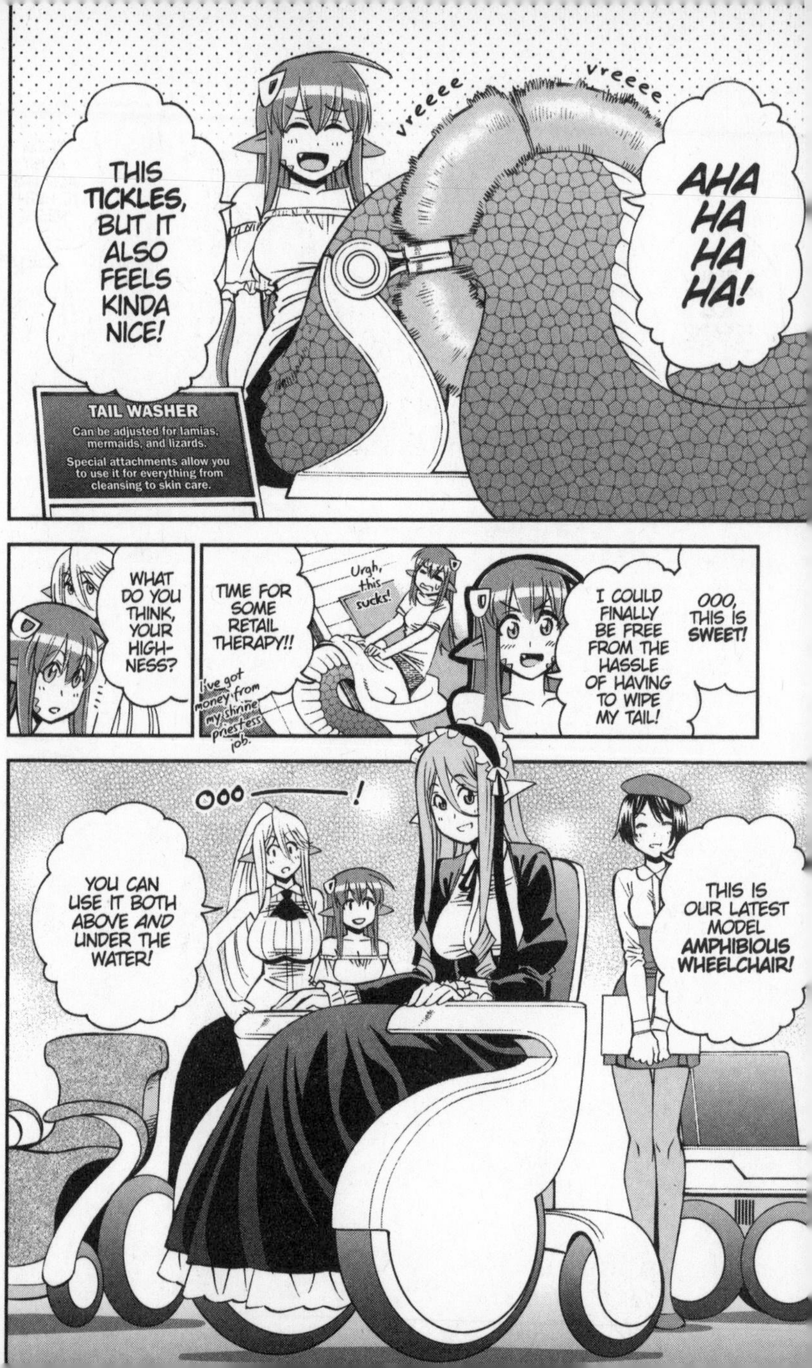
Vreeeee
AHA HA HA HA!
vreeee
THIS TICKLES, BUT IT ALSO FEELS KINDA NICE!
TAIL WASHER
Can be adjusted for lamias, mermaids, and lizards.
Special attachments allow you to use it for everything from cleansing to skin care.
OOO, THIS IS SWEET!
I COULD FINALLY BE FREE FROM THE HASSLE OF HAVING TO WIPE MY TAIL!
Urgh, this sucks!
TIME FOR SOME RETAIL THERAPY!!
I've got money from my shrine priestess job.
WHAT DO YOU THINK, YOUR HIGHNESS?
THIS IS OUR LATEST MODEL AMPHIBIOUS WHEELCHAIR!
OOO——!
YOU CAN USE IT BOTH ABOVE AND UNDER THE WATER!

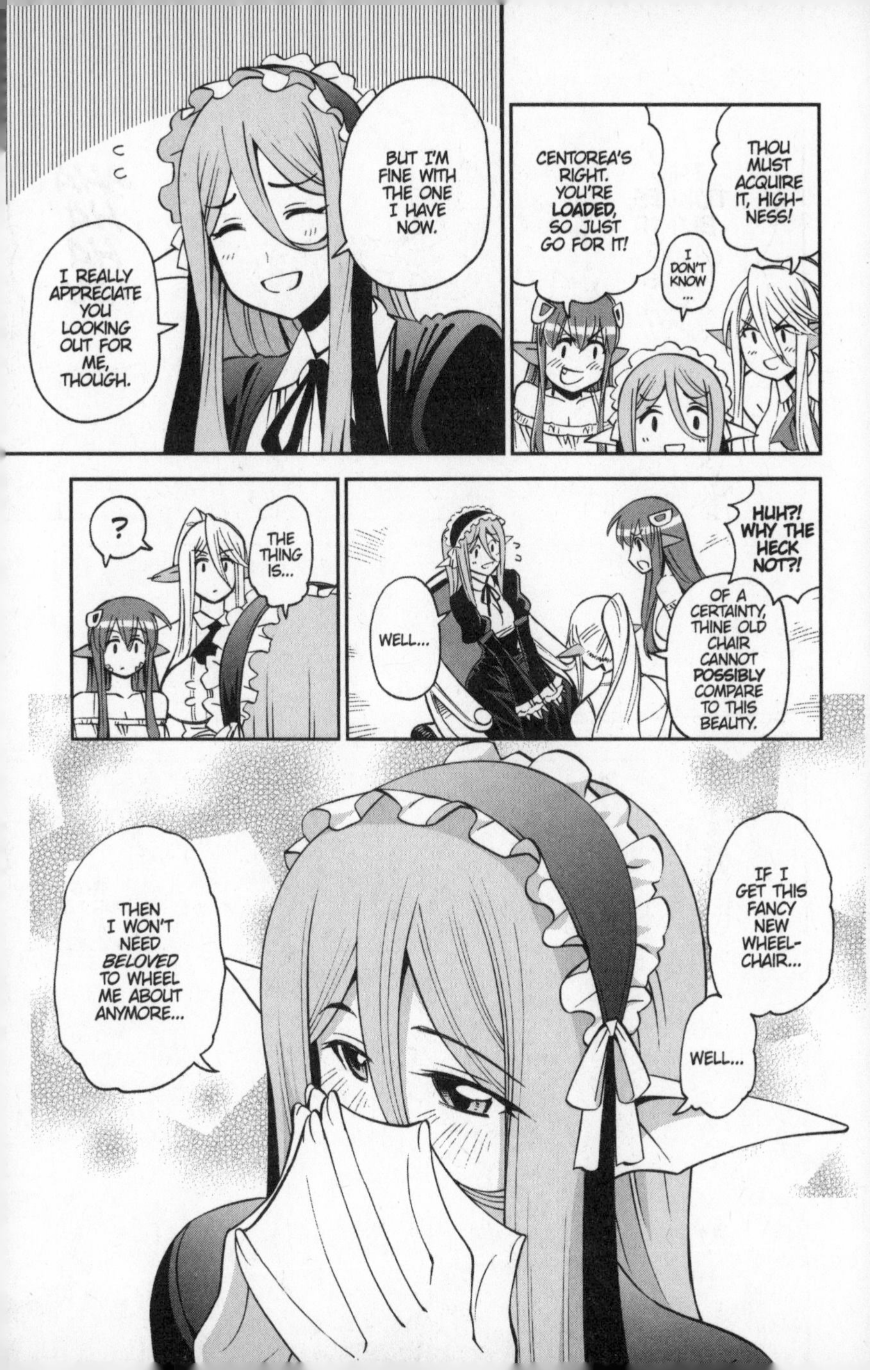
THOU MUST ACQUIRE IT, HIGHNESS!
CENTOREA'S RIGHT. YOU'RE **LOADED**, SO JUST GO FOR IT!
I DON'T KNOW...
BUT I'M FINE WITH THE ONE I HAVE NOW.
I REALLY APPRECIATE YOU LOOKING OUT FOR ME, THOUGH.
HUH?! WHY THE HECK NOT?!
OF A CERTAINTY, THINE OLD CHAIR CANNOT POSSIBLY COMPARE TO THIS BEAUTY.
WELL...
THE THING IS...
?
IF I GET THIS FANCY NEW WHEEL-CHAIR...
WELL...
THEN I WON'T NEED *BELOVED* TO WHEEL ME ABOUT ANYMORE...

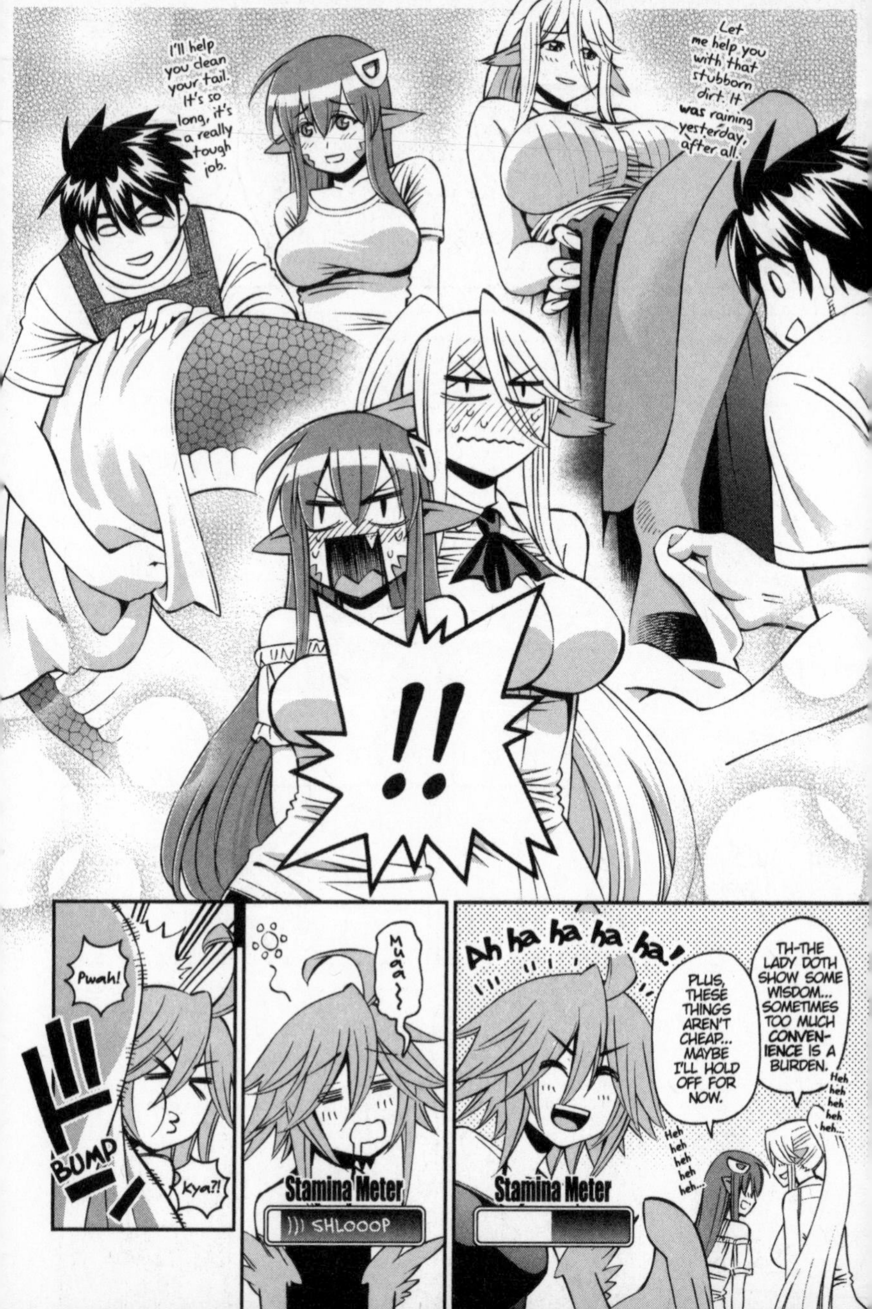
Let me help you with that stubborn dirt. It was raining yesterday, after all.
I'll help you clean your tail. It's so long, it's a really tough job.
!!
TH-THE LADY DOTH SHOW SOME WISDOM... SOMETIMES TOO MUCH CONVEN-IENCE IS A BURDEN.
Ah ha ha ha ha!
PLUS, THESE THINGS AREN'T CHEAP... MAYBE I'LL HOLD OFF FOR NOW.
Heh heh heh heh heh...
Heh heh heh heh heh...
Stamina Meter
Muaa~
Stamina Meter
SHLOOOP
Pwah!
BUMP
Kya?!

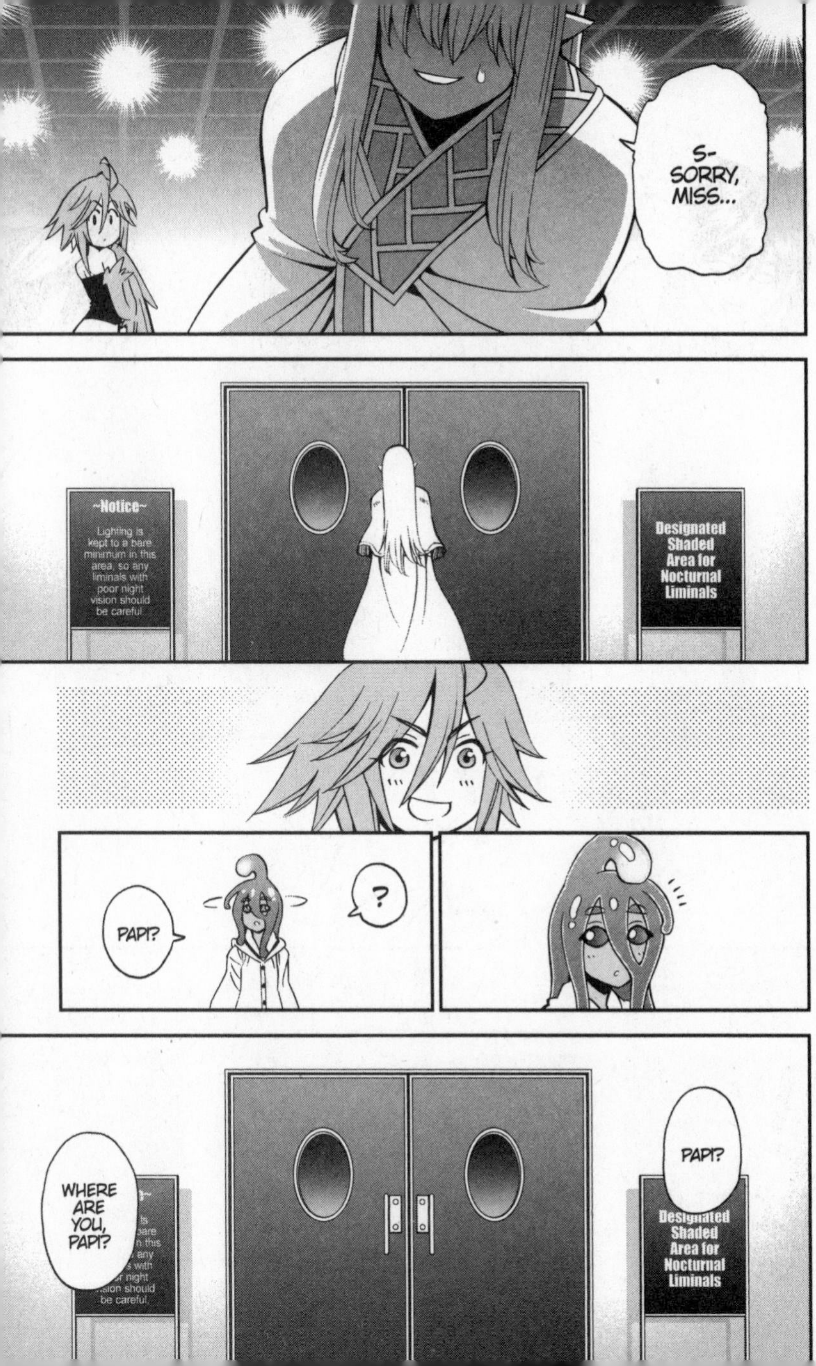
S-SORRY, MISS...
Designated Shaded Area for Nocturnal Liminals
~Notice~
Lighting is kept to a bare minimum in this area, so any liminals with poor night vision should be careful.
?
PAPI?
PAPI?
Designated Shaded Area for Nocturnal Liminals
WHERE ARE YOU, PAPI?
be careful.

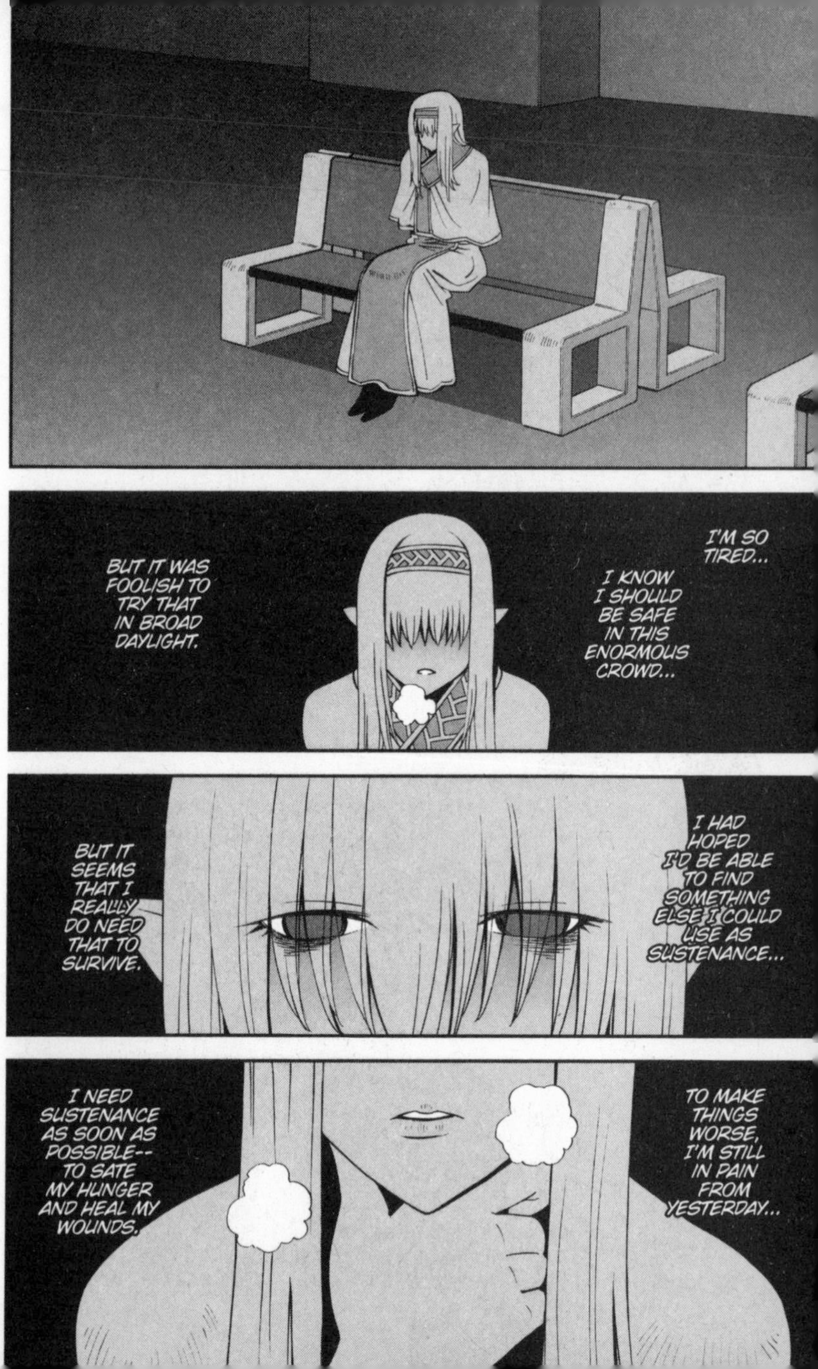
I'M SO TIRED...
I KNOW I SHOULD BE SAFE IN THIS ENORMOUS CROWD...
BUT IT WAS FOOLISH TO TRY THAT IN BROAD DAYLIGHT.
I HAD HOPED I'D BE ABLE TO FIND SOMETHING ELSE I COULD USE AS SUSTENANCE...
BUT IT SEEMS THAT I REALLY DO NEED THAT TO SURVIVE.
TO MAKE THINGS WORSE, I'M STILL IN PAIN FROM YESTERDAY...
I NEED SUSTENANCE AS SOON AS POSSIBLE-- TO SATE MY HUNGER AND HEAL MY WOUNDS.

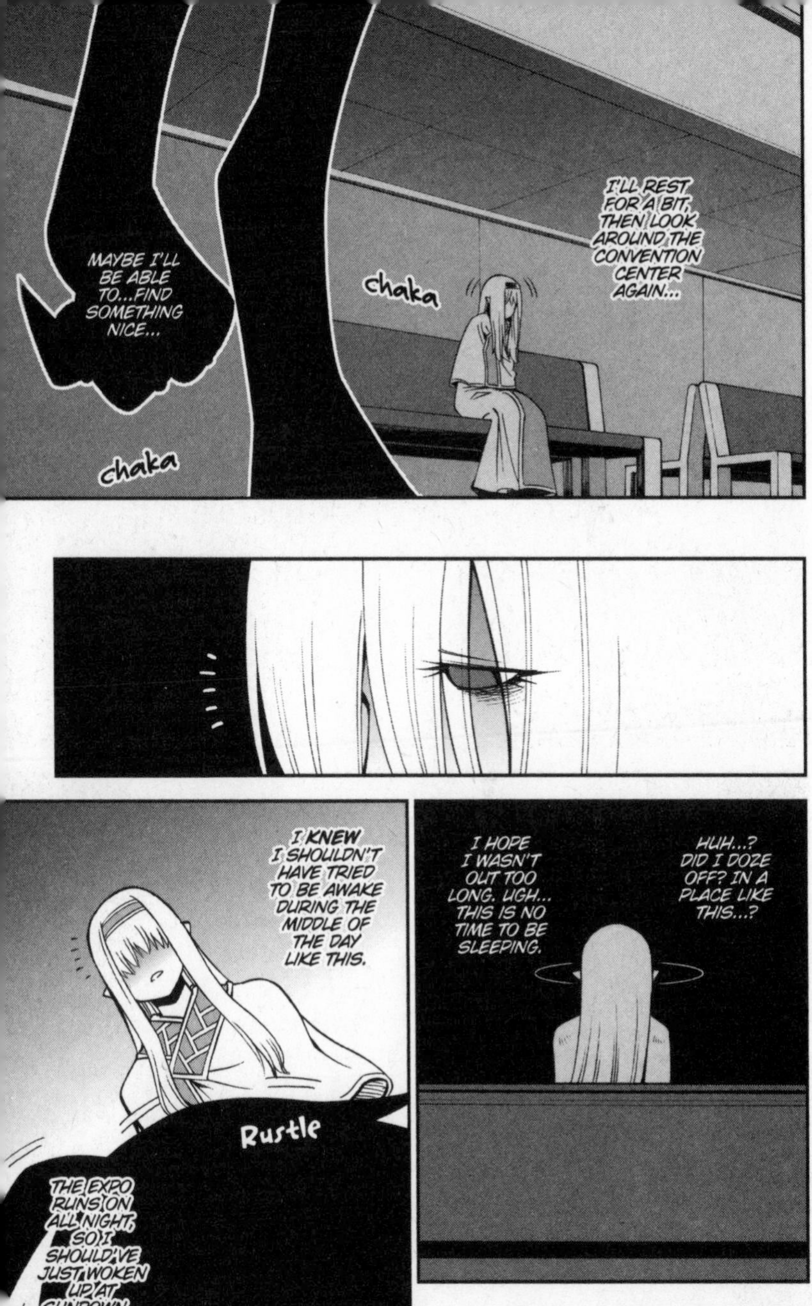
I'LL REST FOR A BIT, THEN LOOK AROUND THE CONVENTION CENTER AGAIN...
chaka
MAYBE I'LL BE ABLE TO...FIND SOMETHING NICE...
chaka
HUH...? DID I DOZE OFF? IN A PLACE LIKE THIS...?
I HOPE I WASN'T OUT TOO LONG. UGH... THIS IS NO TIME TO BE SLEEPING.
I KNEW I SHOULDN'T HAVE TRIED TO BE AWAKE DURING THE MIDDLE OF THE DAY LIKE THIS.
Rustle
THE EXPO RUNS ON ALL NIGHT, SO I SHOULD'VE JUST WOKEN UP AT SUNDOWN...

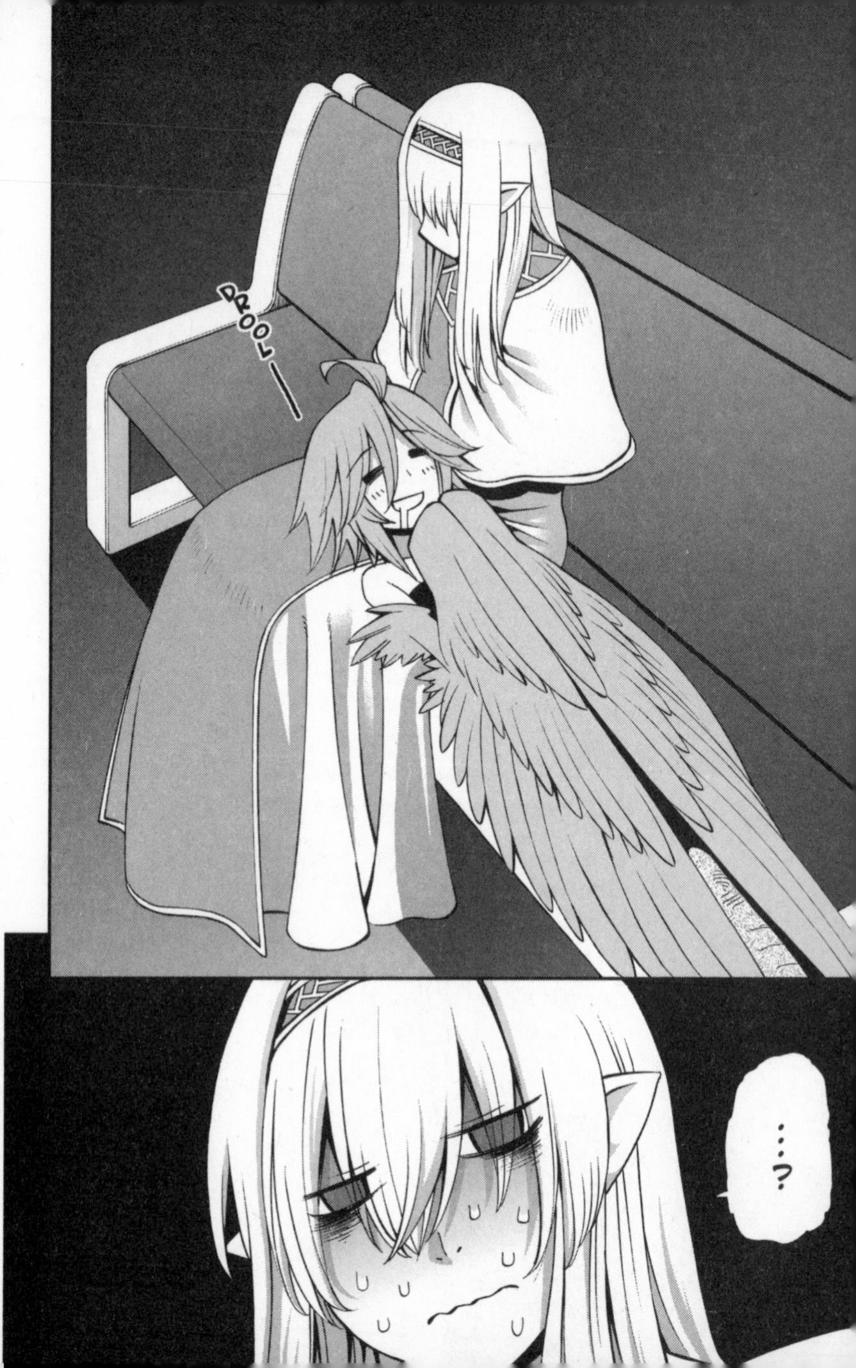
DROOL—
...?

Monster Musume

Everyday Life with Monster Girls

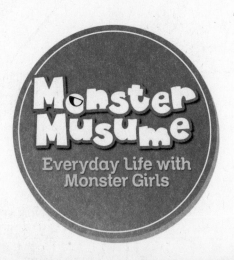

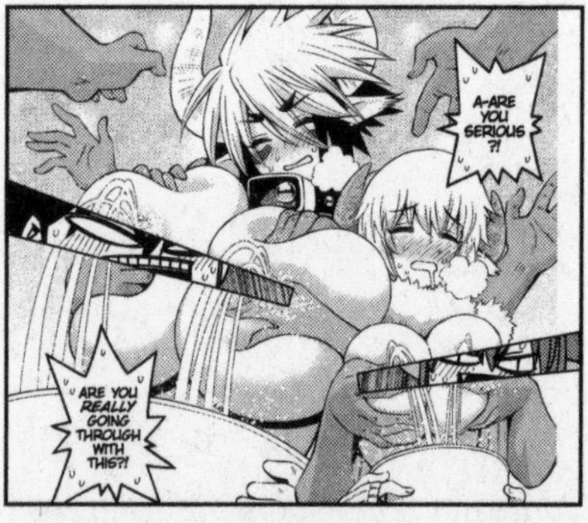
A-ARE YOU SERIOUS?!
ARE YOU REALLY GOING THROUGH WITH THIS?!

Chapter 49

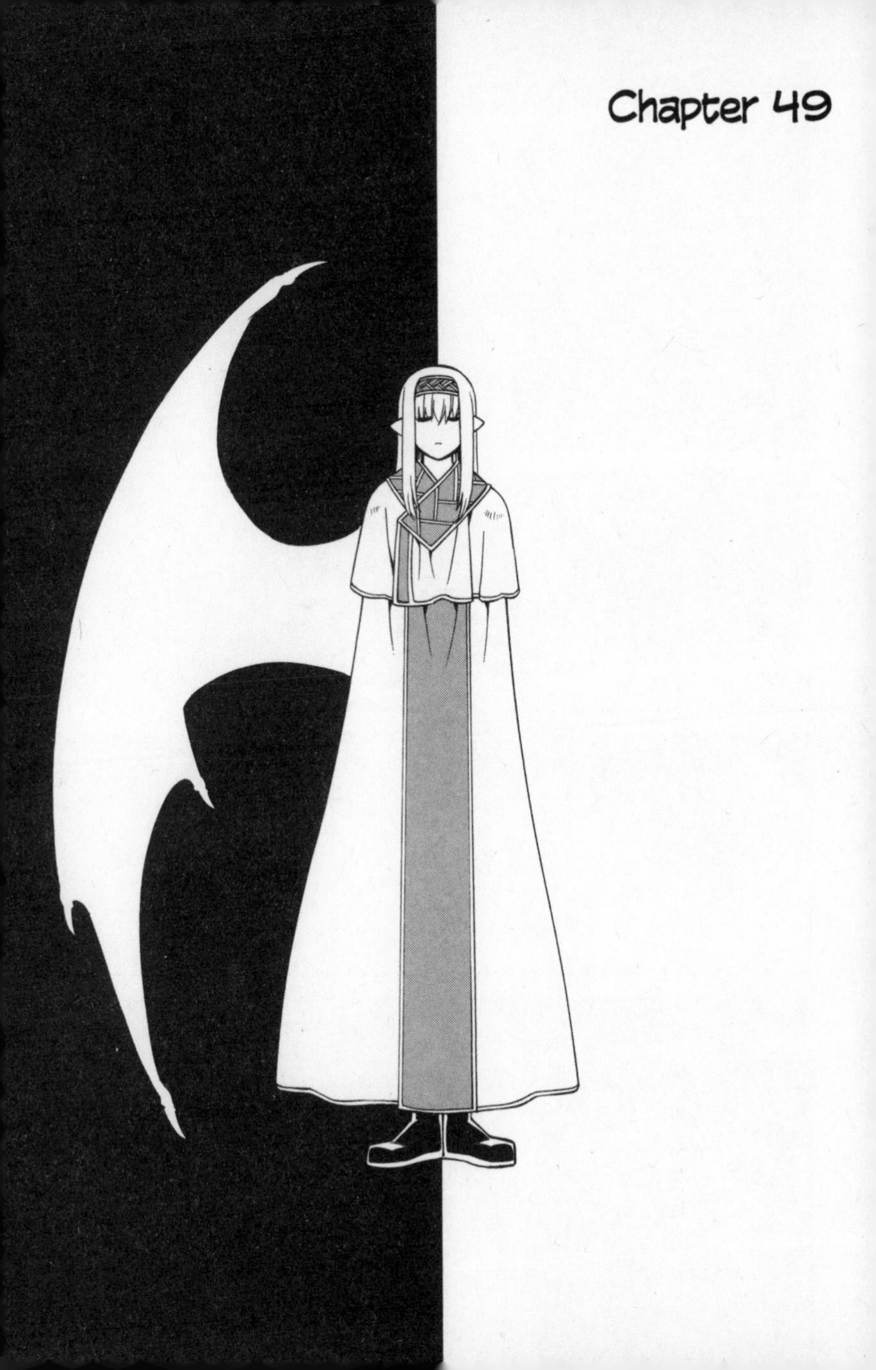

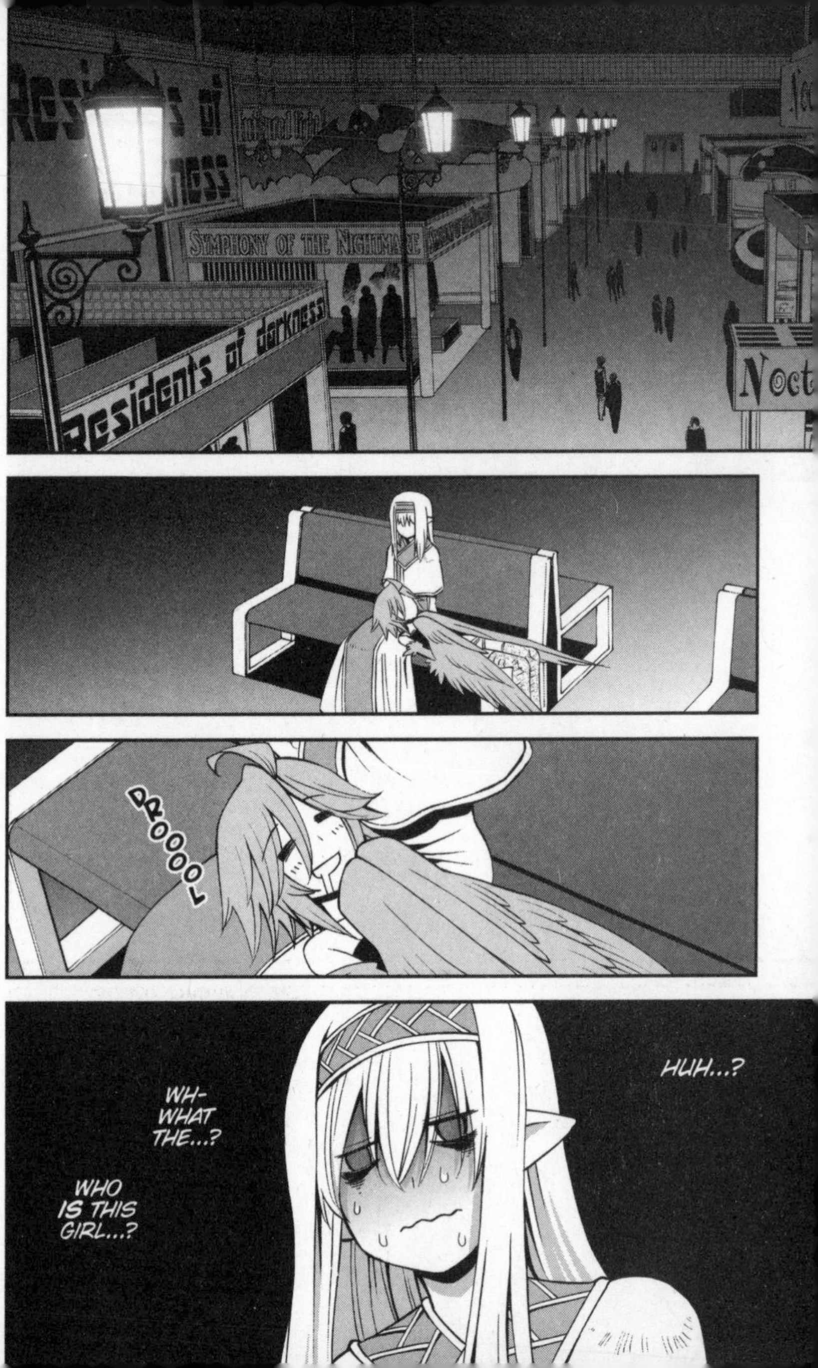
SYMPHONY OF THE NIGHTMARE
Residents of darkness
DROOOOOL
HUH...?
WH-WHAT THE...?
WHO IS THIS GIRL...?

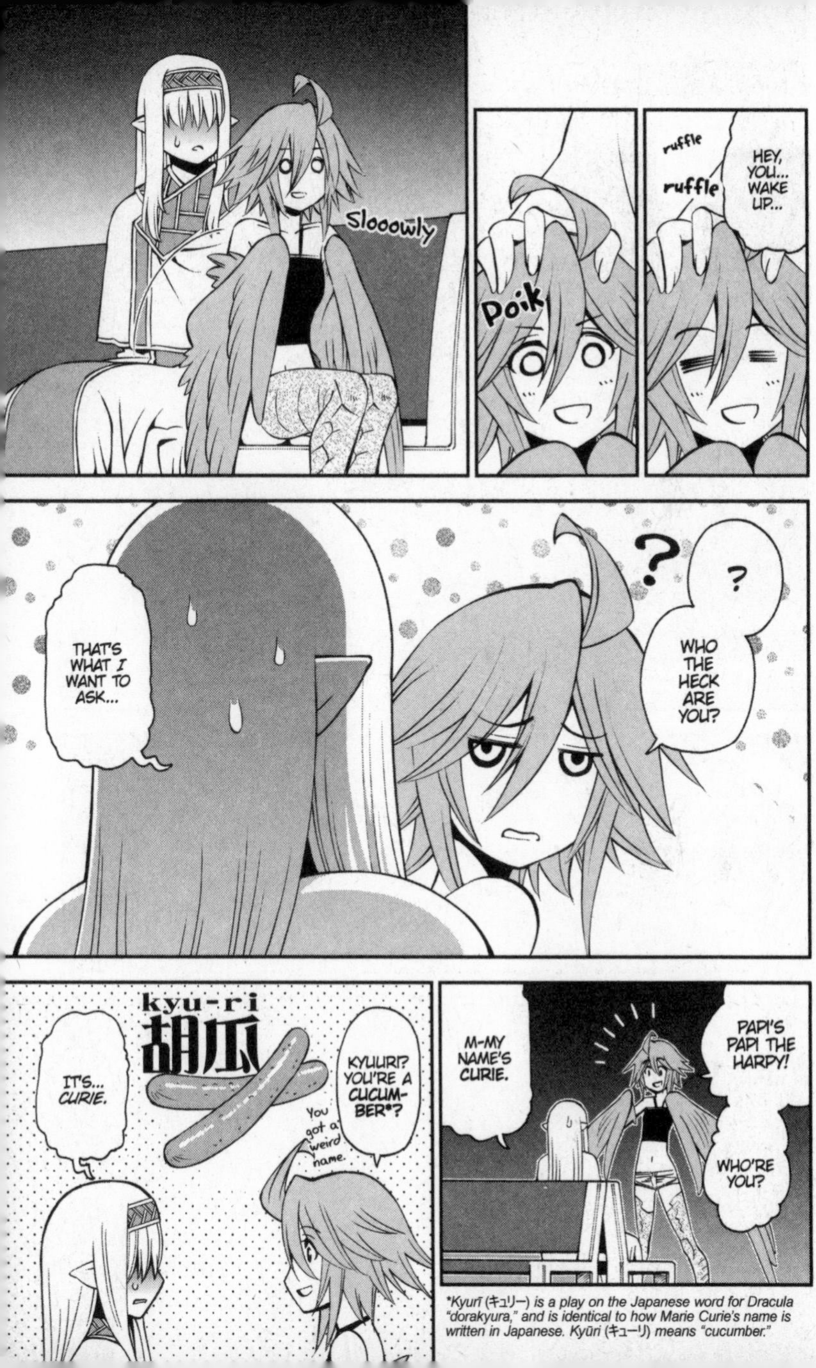
ruffle
ruffle
HEY, YOU... WAKE UP...
Poik
Slooowly
?
?
WHO THE HECK ARE YOU?
THAT'S WHAT *I* WANT TO ASK...
PAPI'S PAPI THE HARPY!
WHO'RE YOU?
M-MY NAME'S CURIE.
KYUURI? YOU'RE A CUCUM-BER*?
You got a weird name.
kyu-ri
胡瓜
IT'S... CURIE.

*Kyurī (キュリー) is a play on the Japanese word for Dracula "dorakyura," and is identical to how Marie Curie's name is written in Japanese. Kyūri (キューリ) means "cucumber."

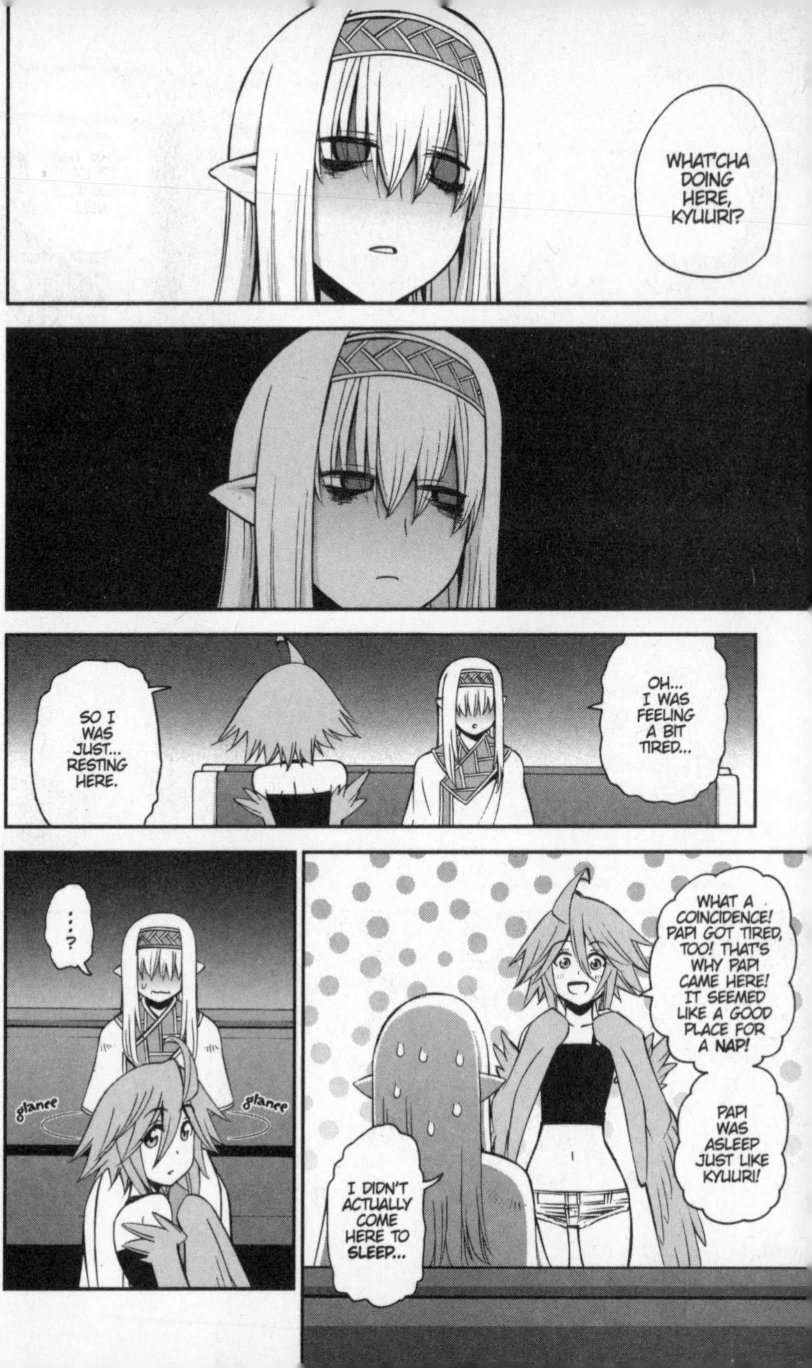
WHAT'CHA DOING HERE, KYUURI?
OH... I WAS FEELING A BIT TIRED...
SO I WAS JUST... RESTING HERE.
WHAT A COINCIDENCE! PAPI GOT TIRED, TOO! THAT'S WHY PAPI CAME HERE! IT SEEMED LIKE A GOOD PLACE FOR A NAP!
PAPI WAS ASLEEP JUST LIKE KYUURI!
I DIDN'T ACTUALLY COME HERE TO SLEEP...
...?
glance
glance

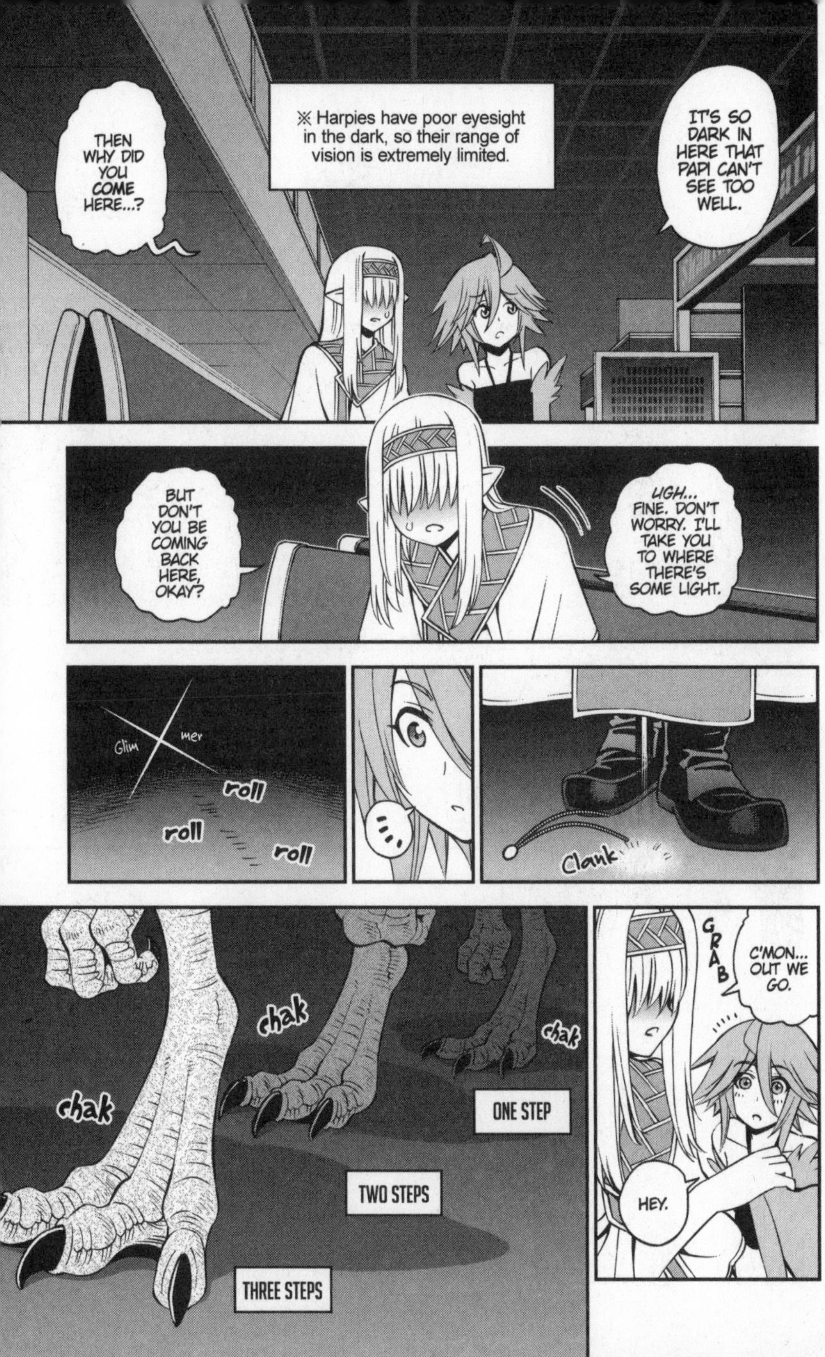
IT'S SO DARK IN HERE THAT PAPI CAN'T SEE TOO WELL.
※ Harpies have poor eyesight in the dark, so their range of vision is extremely limited.
THEN WHY DID YOU COME HERE...?
UGH... FINE. DON'T WORRY. I'LL TAKE YOU TO WHERE THERE'S SOME LIGHT.
BUT DON'T YOU BE COMING BACK HERE, OKAY?
Clank
...
Glim mer
roll
roll
roll
GRAB
C'MON... OUT WE GO.
HEY.
chak
chak
chak
ONE STEP
TWO STEPS
THREE STEPS

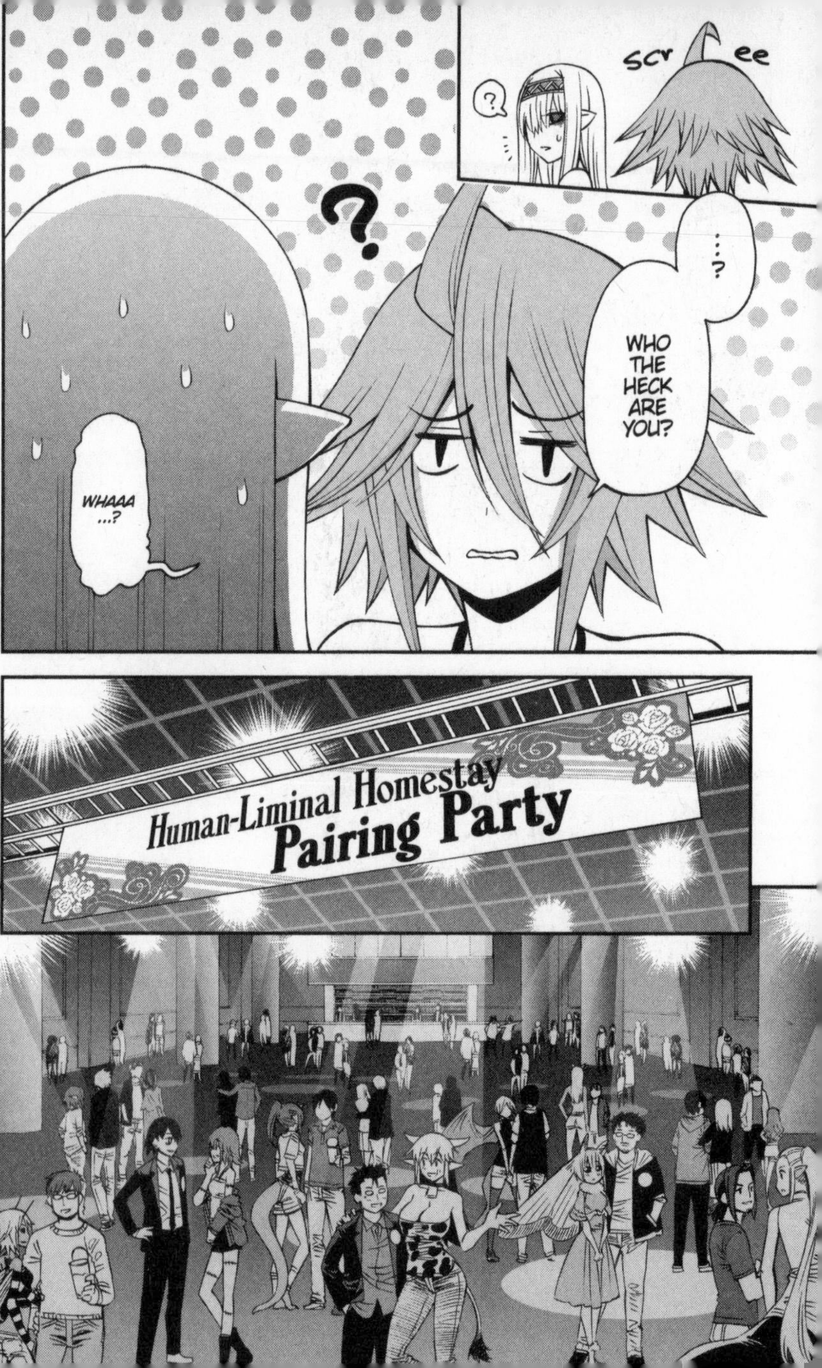
Scr ee
?
?
...?
WHO THE HECK ARE YOU?
WHAAA ...?
Human-Liminal Homestay Pairing Party

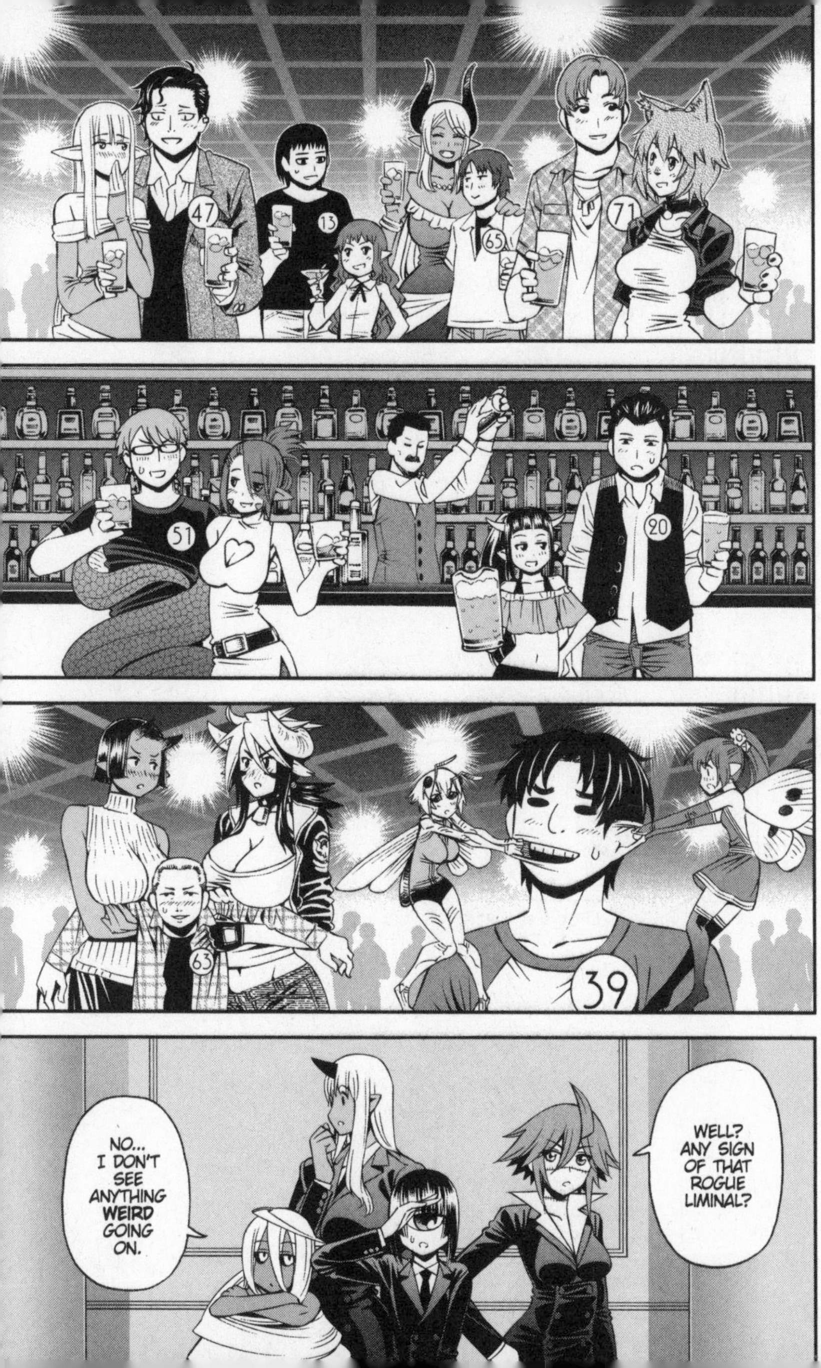
71
65
13
47
20
51
39
63
WELL? ANY SIGN OF THAT ROGUE LIMINAL?
NO... I DON'T SEE ANYTHING WEIRD GOING ON.

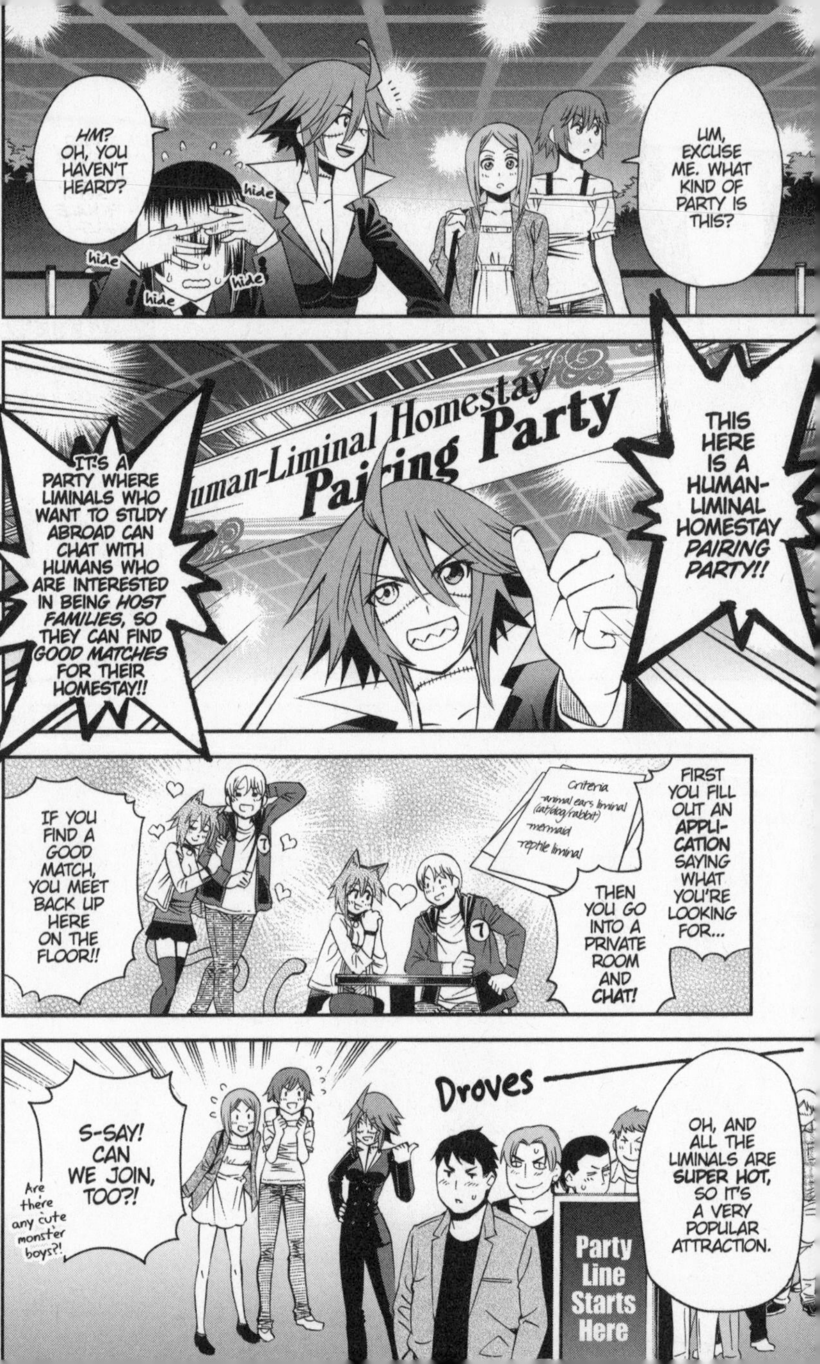
UM, EXCUSE ME. WHAT KIND OF PARTY IS THIS?
HM? OH, YOU HAVEN'T HEARD?
hide hide hide hide
THIS HERE IS A HUMAN-LIMINAL HOMESTAY PAIRING PARTY!!
uman-Liminal Homestay
Pai ing Party
IT'S A PARTY WHERE LIMINALS WHO WANT TO STUDY ABROAD CAN CHAT WITH HUMANS WHO ARE INTERESTED IN BEING HOST FAMILIES, SO THEY CAN FIND GOOD MATCHES FOR THEIR HOMESTAY!!
FIRST YOU FILL OUT AN APPLICATION SAYING WHAT YOU'RE LOOKING FOR...
Criteria
-animal ears liminal (cat/dog/rabbit)
-mermaid
-reptile liminal
THEN YOU GO INTO A PRIVATE ROOM AND CHAT!
IF YOU FIND A GOOD MATCH, YOU MEET BACK UP HERE ON THE FLOOR!!
OH, AND ALL THE LIMINALS ARE SUPER HOT, SO IT'S A VERY POPULAR ATTRACTION.
Party Line Starts Here
Droves
S-SAY! CAN WE JOIN, TOO?!
Are there any cute monster boys?!

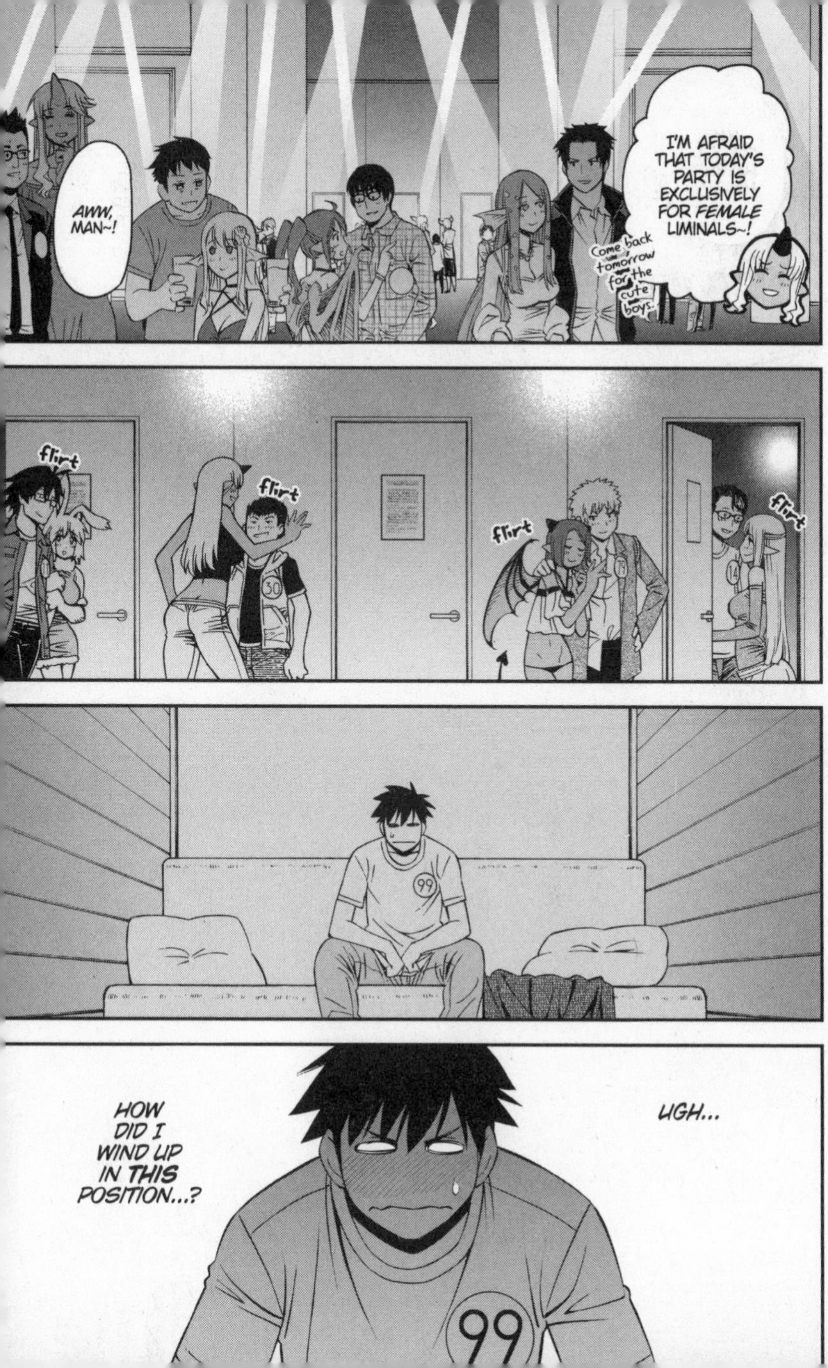
I'M AFRAID THAT TODAY'S PARTY IS EXCLUSIVELY FOR *FEMALE* LIMINALS~!
Come back tomorrow for the cute boys.
AWW, MAN~!
flirt
flirt
flirt
flirt
UGH...
HOW DID I WIND UP IN **THIS** POSITION...?

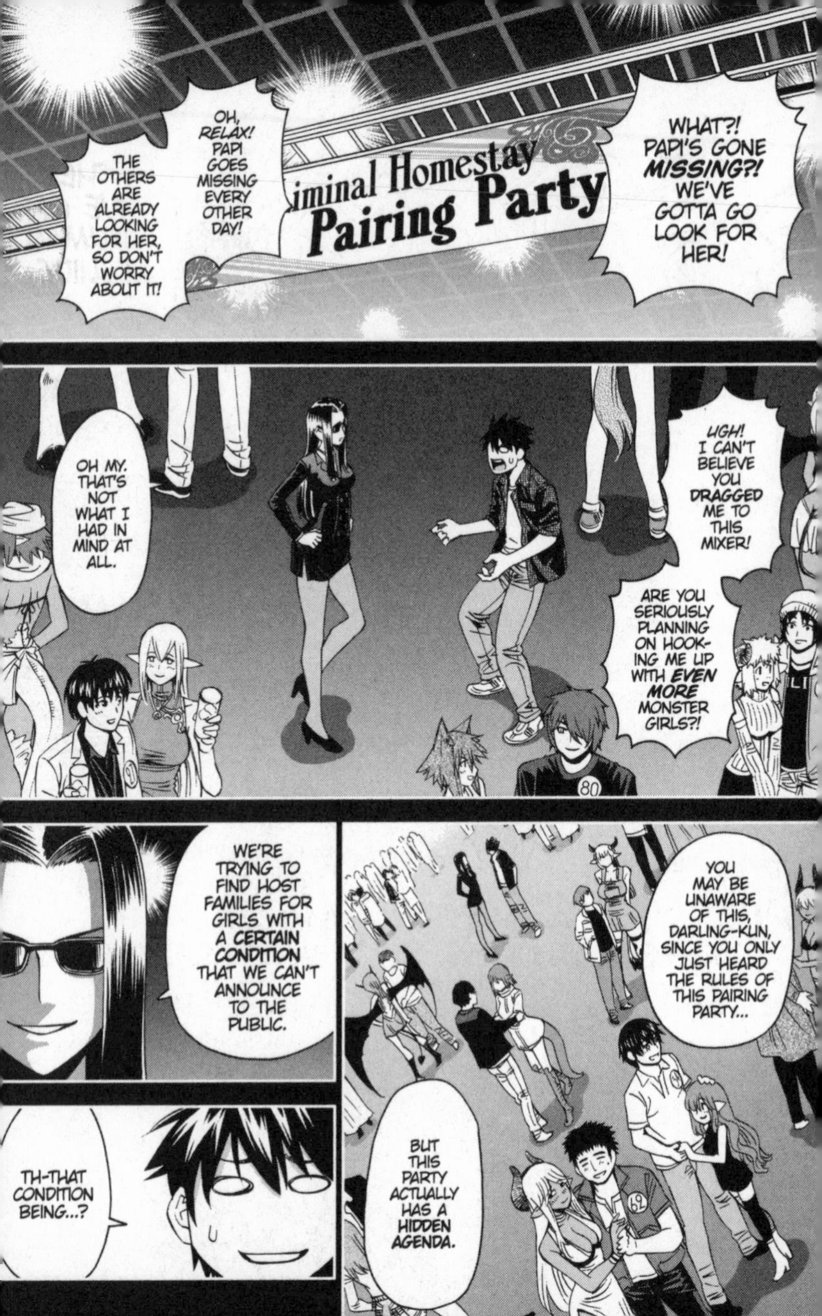
iminal Homestay Pairing Party
WHAT?! PAPI'S GONE *MISSING?!* WE'VE GOTTA GO LOOK FOR HER!
OH, *RELAX!* PAPI GOES MISSING EVERY OTHER DAY!
THE OTHERS ARE ALREADY LOOKING FOR HER, SO DON'T WORRY ABOUT IT!
UGH! I CAN'T BELIEVE YOU **DRAGGED** ME TO THIS MIXER!
ARE YOU SERIOUSLY PLANNING ON HOOKING ME UP WITH ***EVEN MORE*** MONSTER GIRLS?!
OH MY. THAT'S NOT WHAT I HAD IN MIND AT ALL.
YOU MAY BE UNAWARE OF THIS, DARLING-KUN, SINCE YOU ONLY JUST HEARD THE RULES OF THIS PAIRING PARTY...
BUT THIS PARTY ACTUALLY HAS A HIDDEN AGENDA.
WE'RE TRYING TO FIND HOST FAMILIES FOR GIRLS WITH **A CERTAIN CONDITION** THAT WE CAN'T ANNOUNCE TO THE PUBLIC.
TH-THAT CONDITION BEING...?

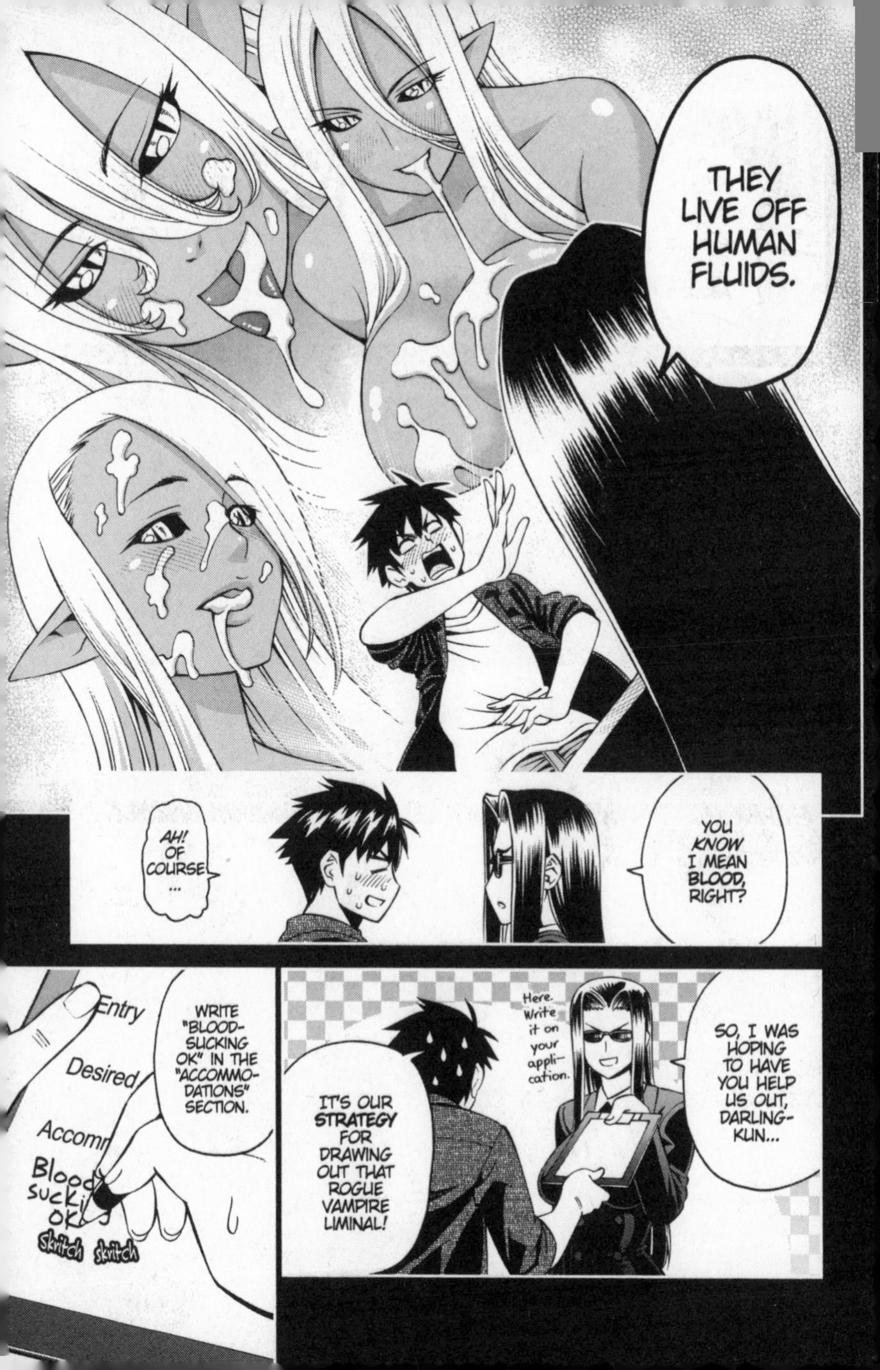
THEY LIVE OFF HUMAN FLUIDS.
YOU KNOW I MEAN BLOOD, RIGHT?
AH! OF COURSE...
SO, I WAS HOPING TO HAVE YOU HELP US OUT, DARLING-KUN...
Here. Write it on your application.
IT'S OUR STRATEGY FOR DRAWING OUT THAT ROGUE VAMPIRE LIMINAL!
WRITE "BLOOD-SUCKING OK" IN THE "ACCOMMODATIONS" SECTION.
Entry
Desired
Skritch skritch

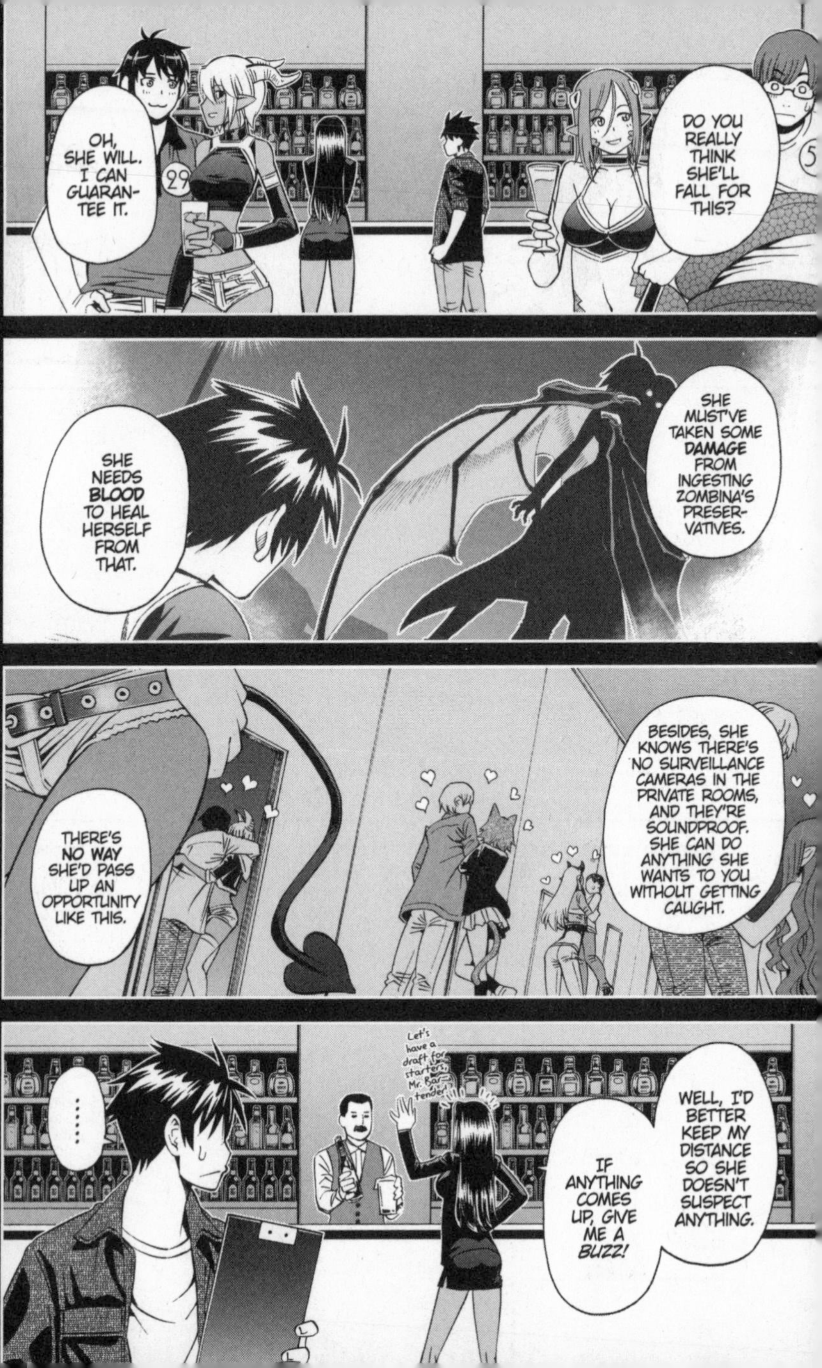
DO YOU REALLY THINK SHE'LL FALL FOR THIS?
OH, SHE WILL. I CAN GUARANTEE IT.
SHE MUST'VE TAKEN SOME **DAMAGE** FROM INGESTING ZOMBINA'S PRESERVATIVES.
SHE NEEDS **BLOOD** TO HEAL HERSELF FROM THAT.
BESIDES, SHE KNOWS THERE'S NO SURVEILLANCE CAMERAS IN THE PRIVATE ROOMS, AND THEY'RE SOUNDPROOF. SHE CAN DO ANYTHING SHE WANTS TO YOU WITHOUT GETTING CAUGHT.
THERE'S **NO WAY** SHE'D PASS UP AN OPPORTUNITY LIKE THIS.
WELL, I'D BETTER KEEP MY DISTANCE SO SHE DOESN'T SUSPECT ANYTHING.
IF ANYTHING COMES UP, GIVE ME A *BUZZ!*
Let's have a draft for starters, Mr. Bartender!
......

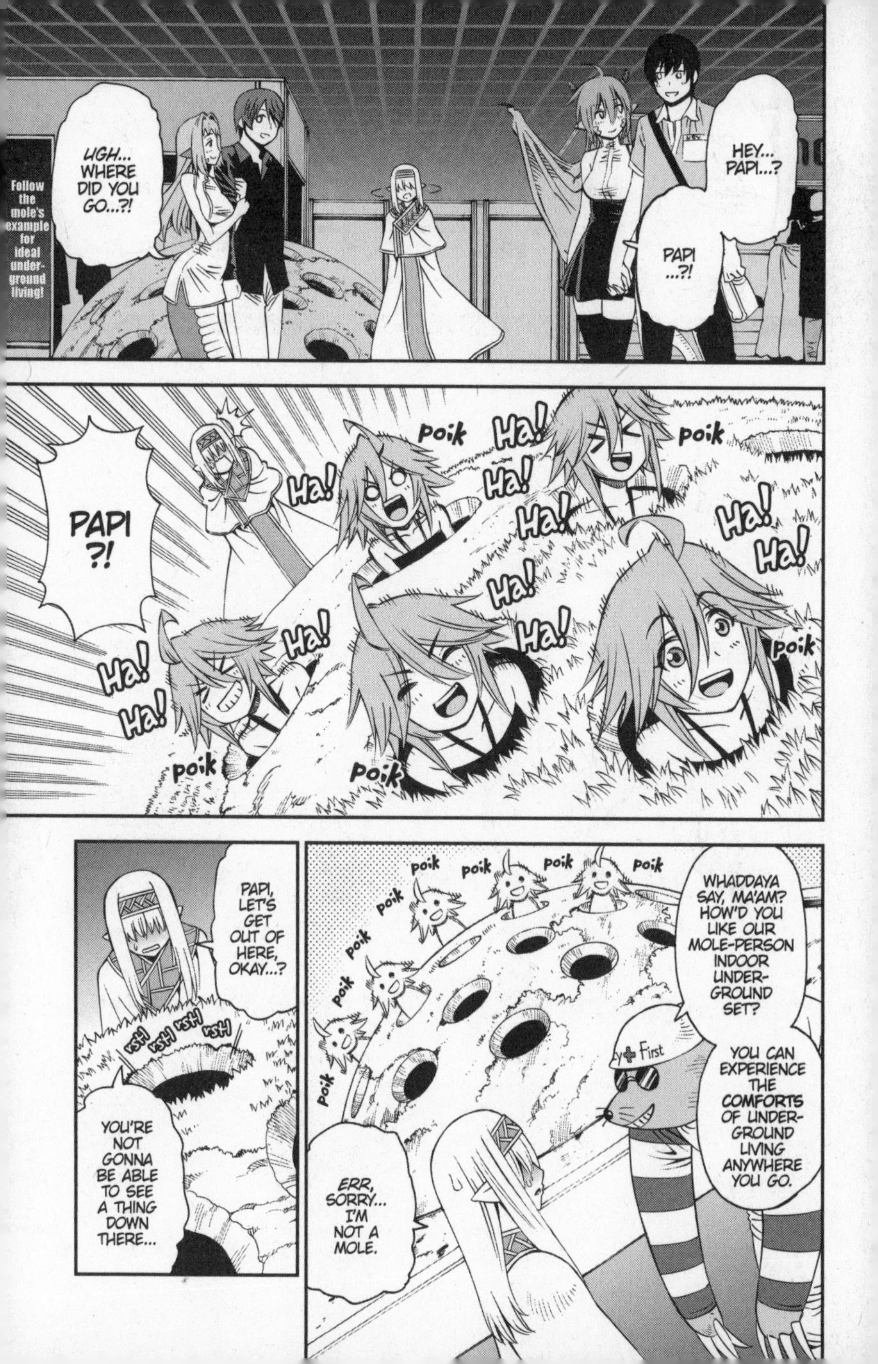
HEY... PAPI...?
PAPI ...?!
UGH... WHERE DID YOU GO...?!
Follow the mole's example for ideal under-ground living!
poik
Ha!
Ha!
poik
Ha!
Ha!
Ha!
Ha!
Ha!
Ha!
poik
Ha!
poik
Ha!
Ha!
Ha!
poik
PAPI ?!
poik
poik
poik
poik
poik
poik
poik
poik
WHADDAYA SAY, MA'AM? HOW'D YOU LIKE OUR MOLE-PERSON INDOOR UNDER-GROUND SET?
YOU CAN EXPERIENCE THE COMFORTS OF UNDER-GROUND LIVING ANYWHERE YOU GO.
y First
ERR, SORRY... I'M NOT A MOLE.
PAPI, LET'S GET OUT OF HERE, OKAY...?
Hsh Hsh Hsh Hsh
YOU'RE NOT GONNA BE ABLE TO SEE A THING DOWN THERE...

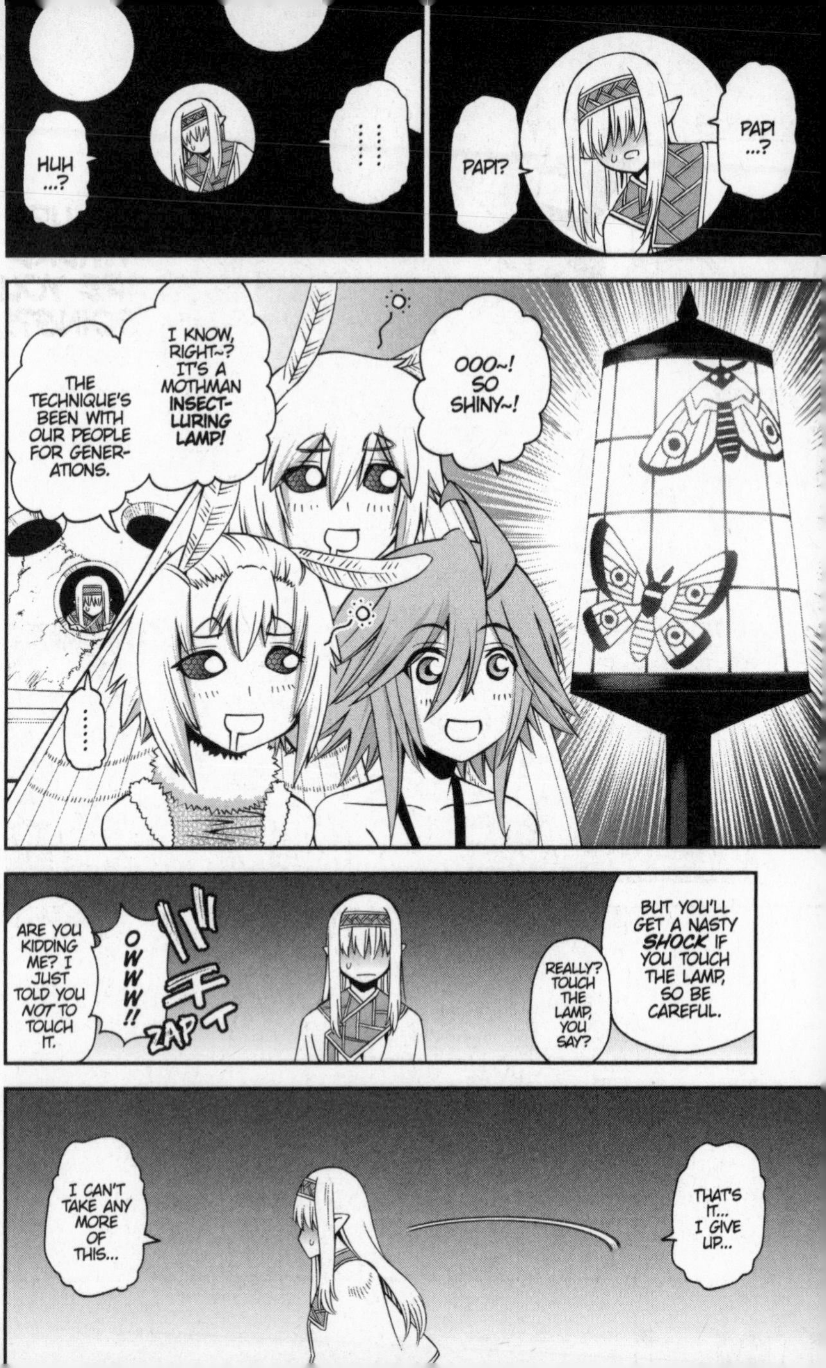
PAPI ...?
PAPI?
......
HUH ...?
OOO~! SO SHINY~!
I KNOW, RIGHT~? IT'S A MOTHMAN INSECT-LURING LAMP!
THE TECHNIQUE'S BEEN WITH OUR PEOPLE FOR GENERATIONS.
......
BUT YOU'LL GET A NASTY SHOCK IF YOU TOUCH THE LAMP, SO BE CAREFUL.
REALLY? TOUCH THE LAMP, YOU SAY?
ZAP
OWWW!!
ARE YOU KIDDING ME? I JUST TOLD YOU NOT TO TOUCH IT.
THAT'S IT... I GIVE UP...
I CAN'T TAKE ANY MORE OF THIS...

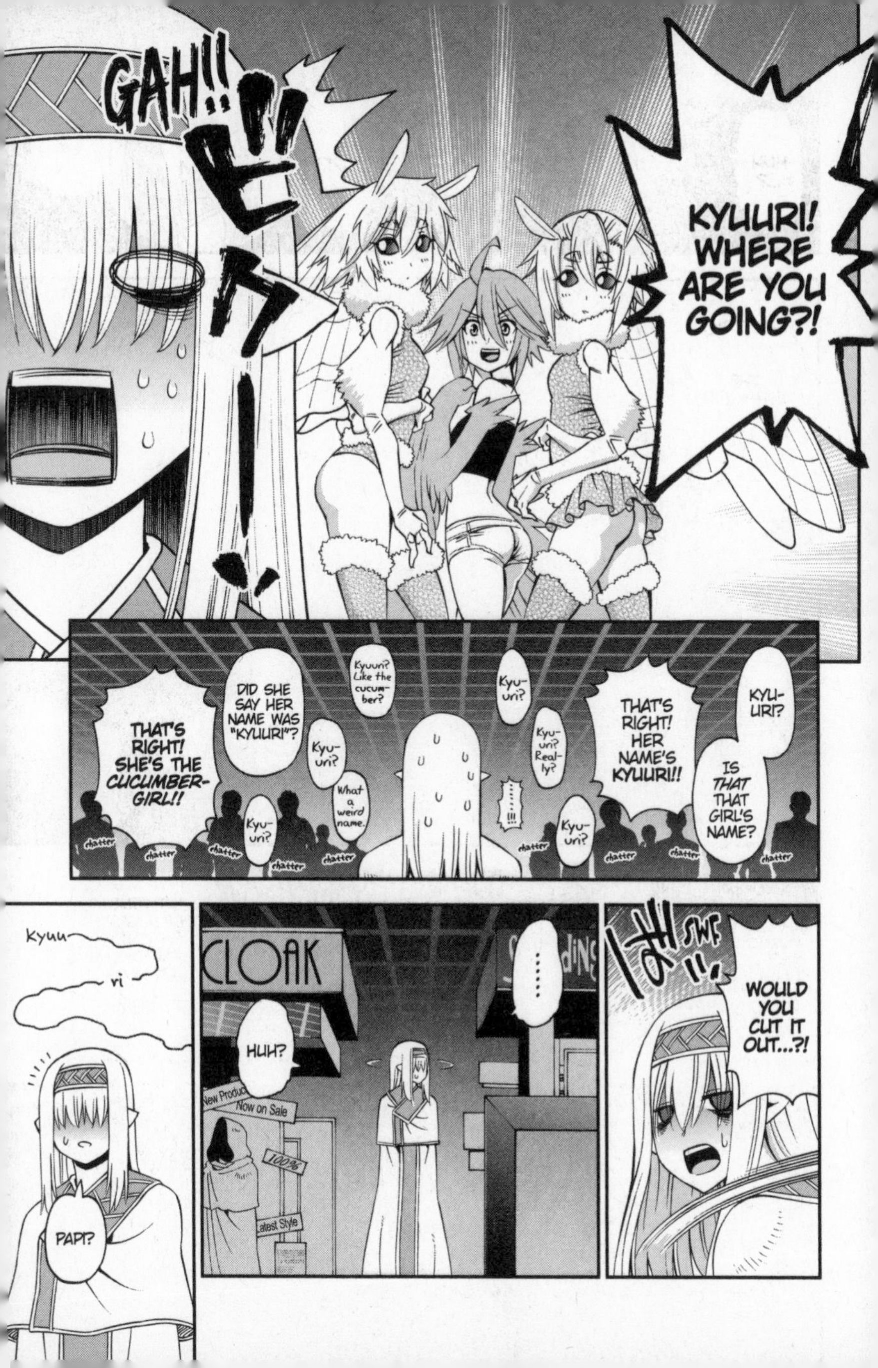
KYUURI! WHERE ARE YOU GOING?!
GAH!!
KYU-URI?
IS THAT THAT GIRL'S NAME?
THAT'S RIGHT! HER NAME'S KYUURI!!
Kyu-uri? Real-ly?
Kyu-uri?
......!!!
Kyu-uri?
Kyuuri? Like the cucumber?
DID SHE SAY HER NAME WAS "KYUURI"?
Kyu-uri?
What a weird name.
Kyu-uri?
THAT'S RIGHT! SHE'S THE CUCUMBER-GIRL!!
chatter
chatter
chatter
chatter
chatter
chatter
chatter
chatter
chatter
chatter
SWE!!
WOULD YOU CUT IT OUT...?!
CLOAK
......
HUH?
New Product Now on Sale
100%
Latest Style
Kyuu
ri
PAPI?

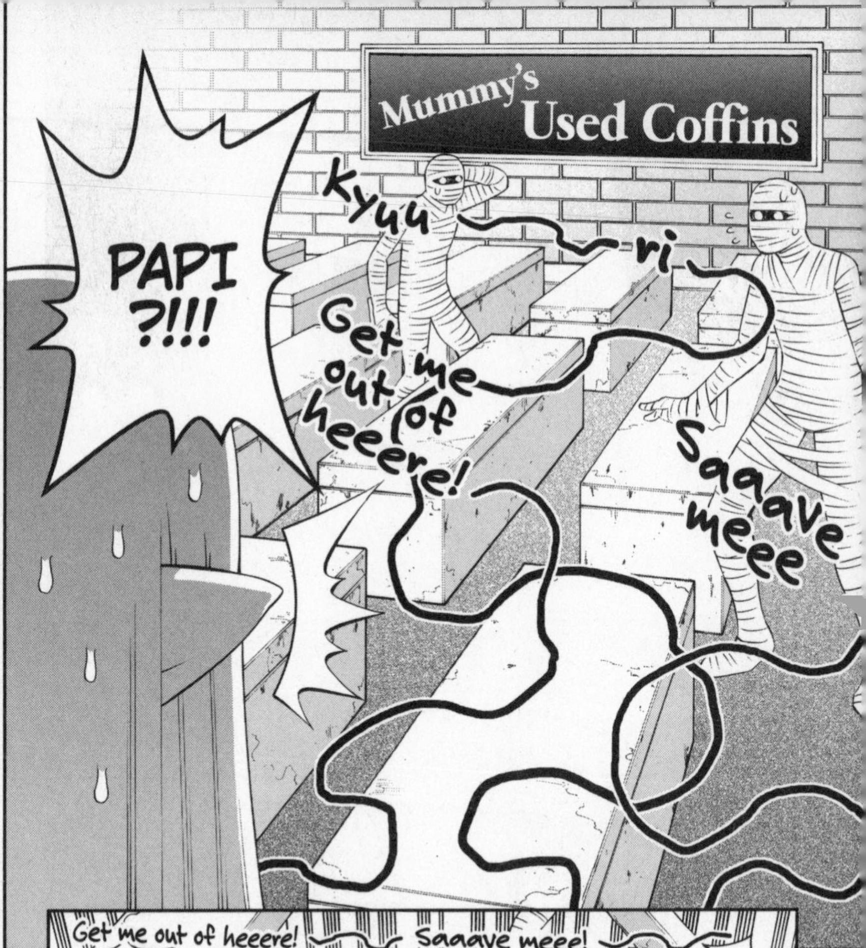
Mummy's Used Coffins
Kyuu~~ri
Saaave meee
Get me out of heeere!
PAPI ?!!!

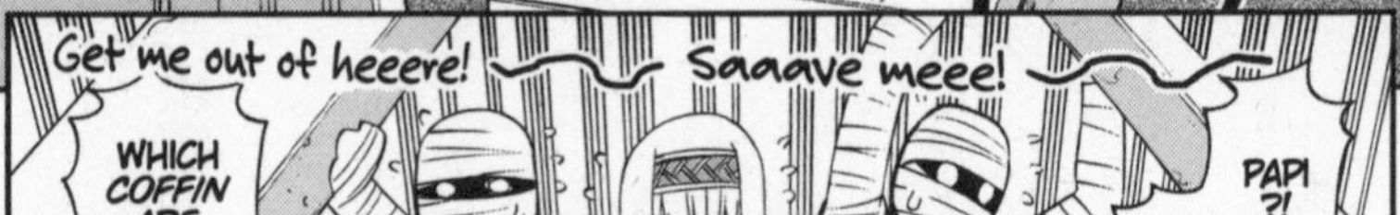
Get me out of heeere!~~Saaave meee!
PAPI ?!
PAPI ?!
?
WHICH COFFIN ARE YOU IN?!

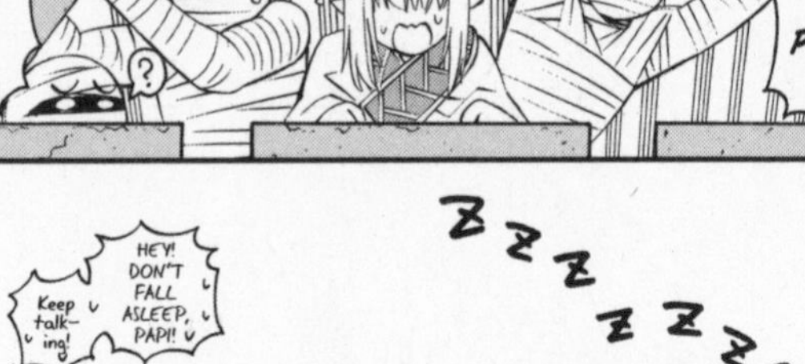
Z Z Z Z Z Z Z
HEY! DON'T FALL ASLEEP, PAPI!
Keep talk-ing!

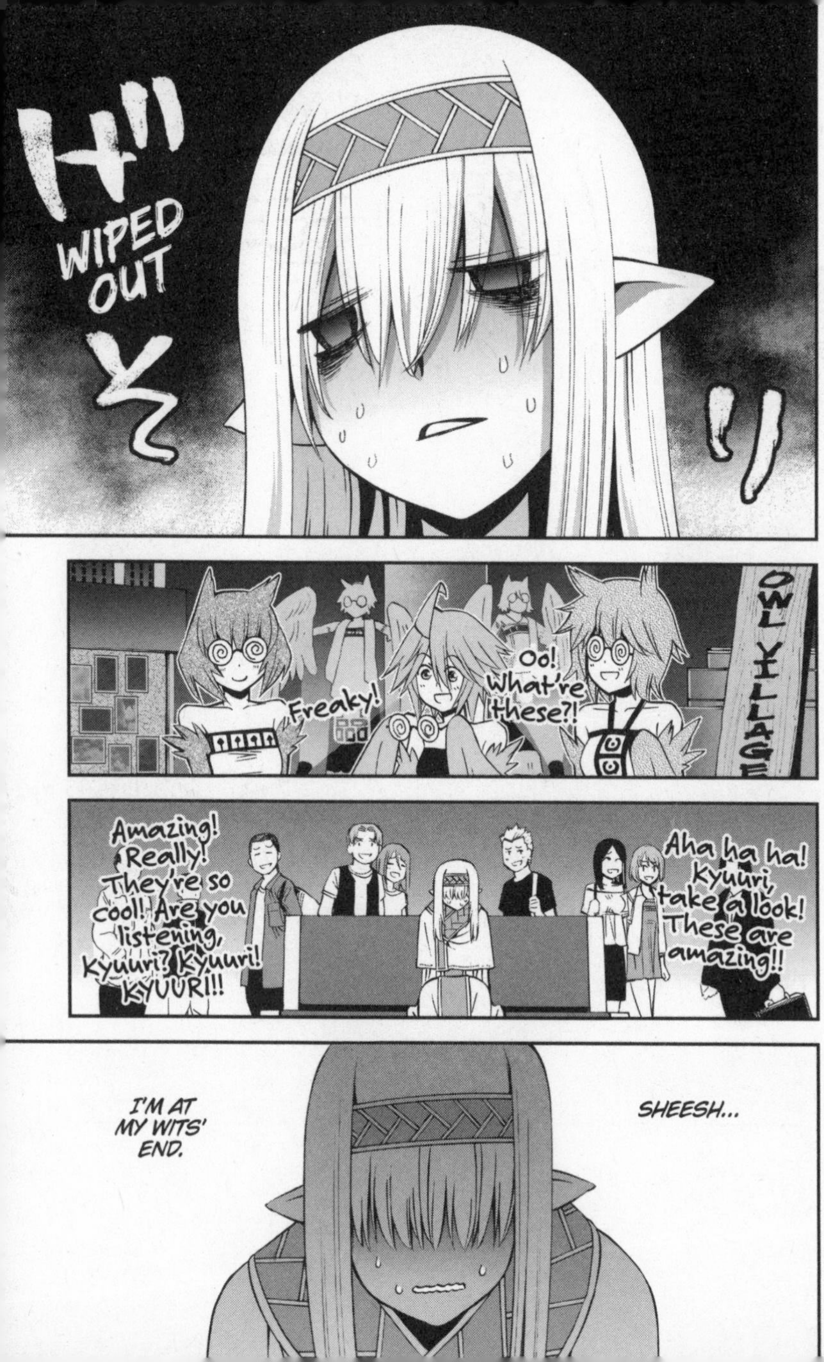
WIPED OUT
OWL VILLAGE
Oo! What're these?!
Freaky!
Aha ha ha! Kyuuri, take a look! These are amazing!!
Amazing! Really! They're so cool! Are you listening, Kyuuri? Kyuuri! KYUURI!!
SHEESH...
I'M AT MY WITS' END.

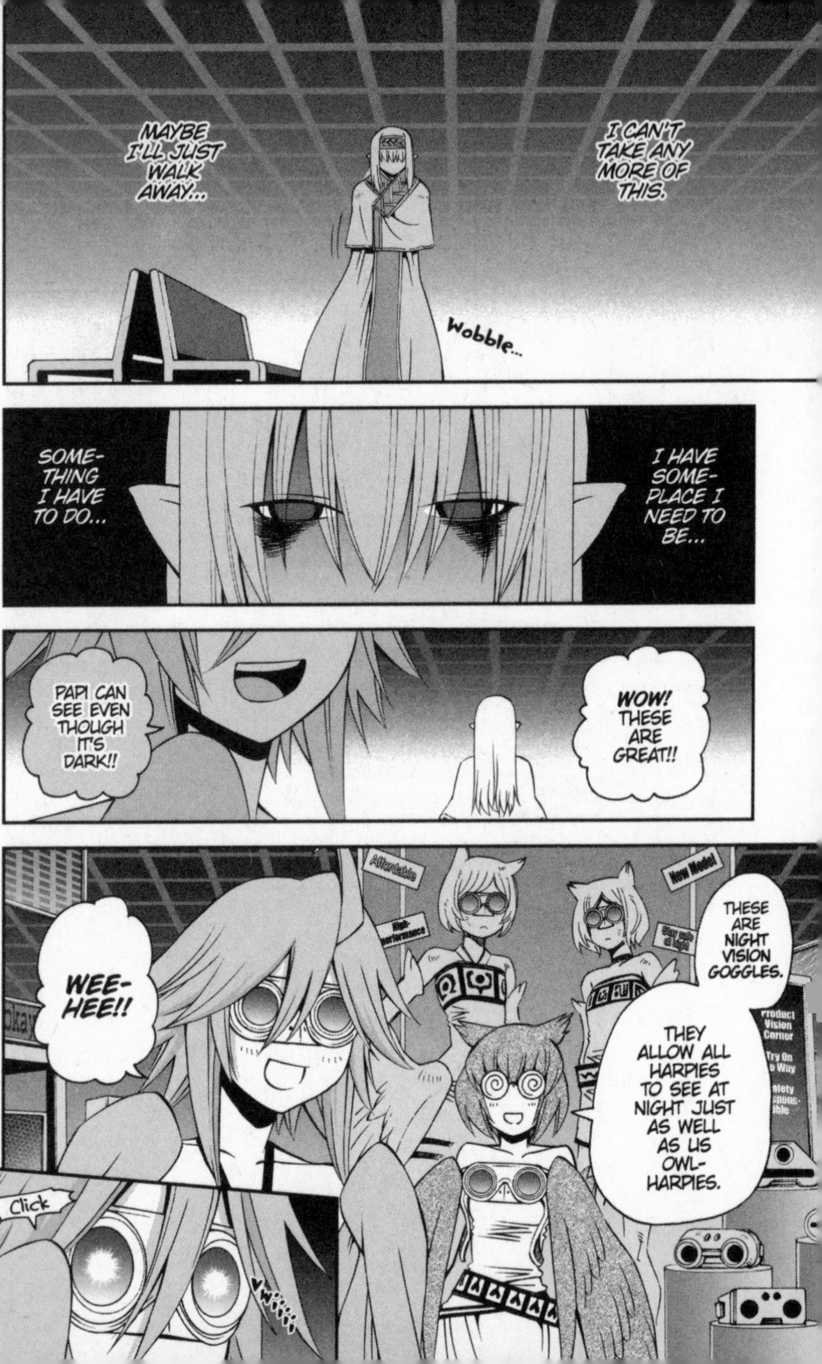
I CAN'T TAKE ANY MORE OF THIS.
MAYBE I'LL JUST WALK AWAY...
Wobble...
I HAVE SOMEPLACE I NEED TO BE...
SOMETHING I HAVE TO DO...
WOW! THESE ARE GREAT!!
PAPI CAN SEE EVEN THOUGH IT'S DARK!!
New Model
Affordable
High-performance
THESE ARE NIGHT VISION GOGGLES.
THEY ALLOW ALL HARPIES TO SEE AT NIGHT JUST AS WELL AS US OWL-HARPIES.
WEE-HEE!!
Click

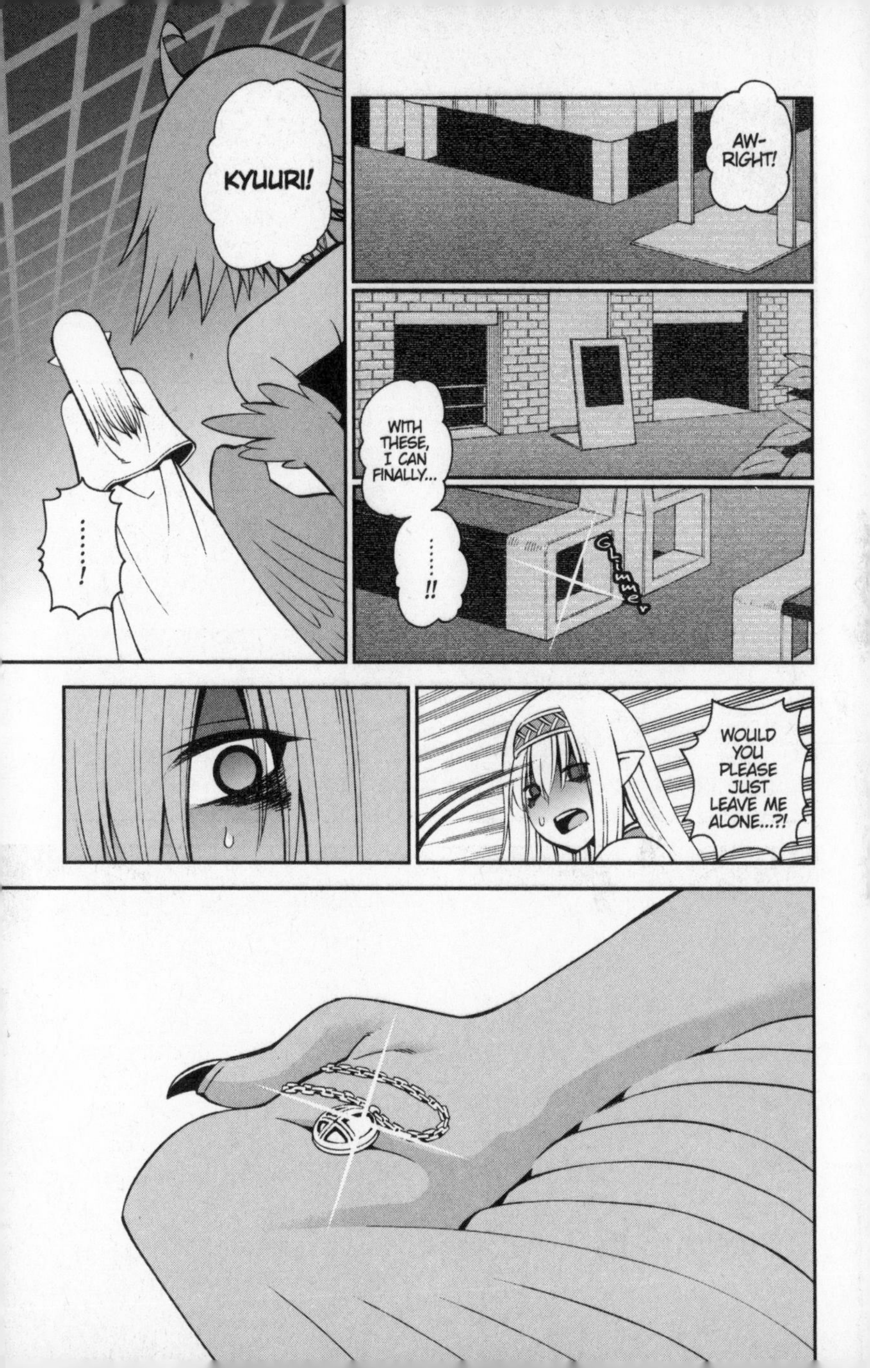
AW-RIGHT!
WITH THESE, I CAN FINALLY...
......!!
Glimmer
KYUURI!
......!
WOULD YOU PLEASE JUST LEAVE ME ALONE...?!

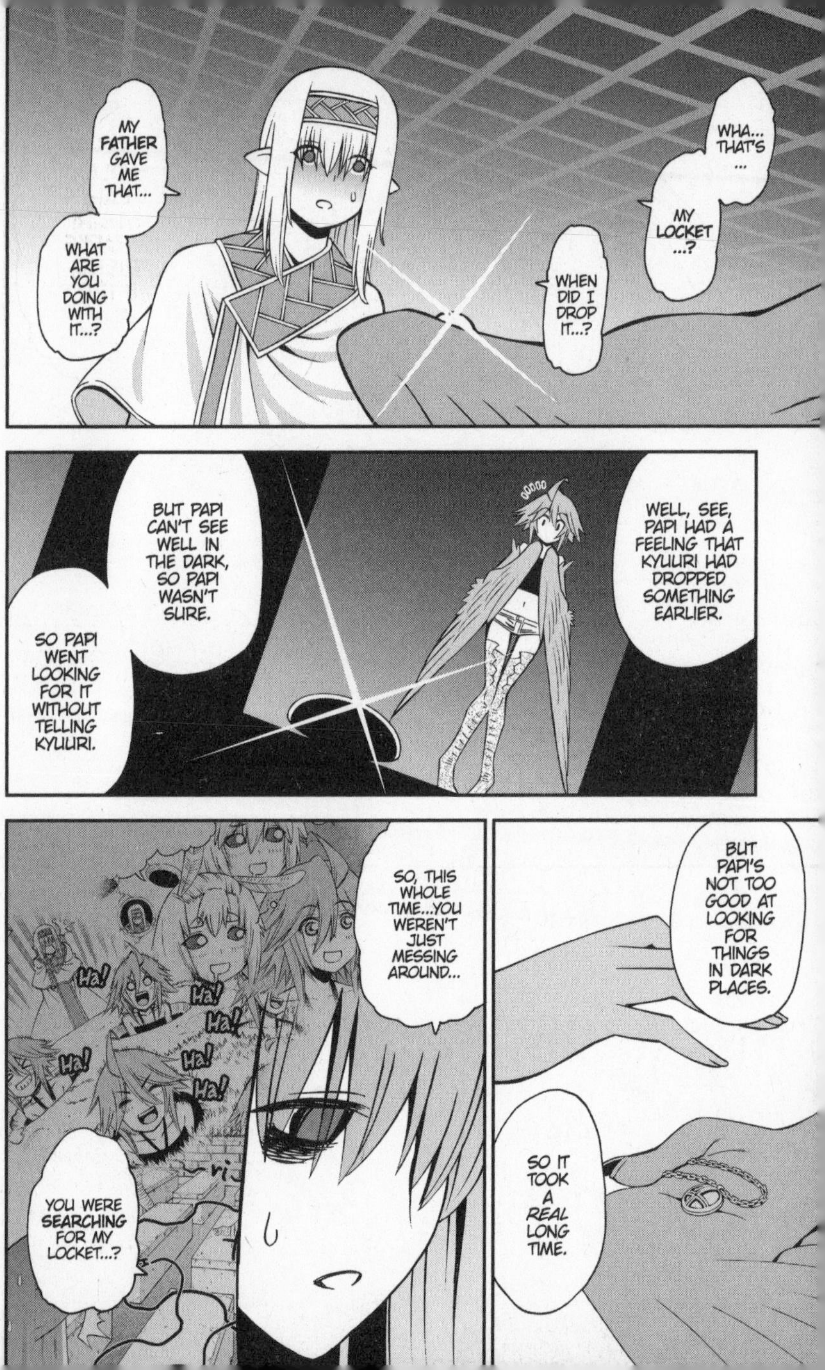
WHA... THAT'S ...
MY LOCKET ...?
WHEN DID I DROP IT...?
MY FATHER GAVE ME THAT...
WHAT ARE YOU DOING WITH IT...?
WELL, SEE, PAPI HAD A FEELING THAT KYUURI HAD DROPPED SOMETHING EARLIER.
BUT PAPI CAN'T SEE WELL IN THE DARK, SO PAPI WASN'T SURE.
SO PAPI WENT LOOKING FOR IT WITHOUT TELLING KYUURI.
BUT PAPI'S NOT TOO GOOD AT LOOKING FOR THINGS IN DARK PLACES.
SO IT TOOK A REAL LONG TIME.
SO, THIS WHOLE TIME...YOU WEREN'T JUST MESSING AROUND...
YOU WERE SEARCHING FOR MY LOCKET...?
Ha! Ha! Ha! Ha! Ha! Ha!

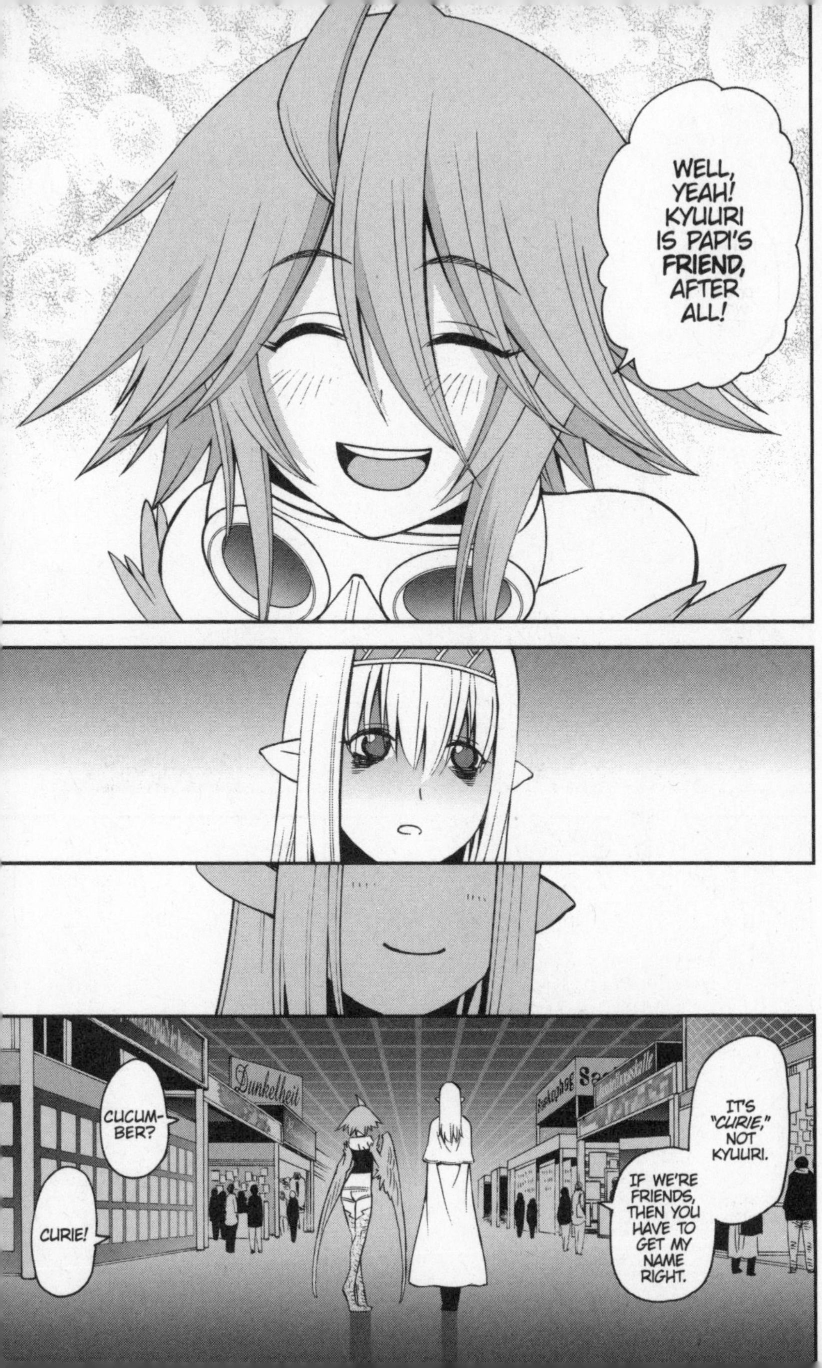
WELL, YEAH! KYUURI IS PAPI'S FRIEND, AFTER ALL!
IT'S "CURIE," NOT KYUURI.
IF WE'RE FRIENDS, THEN YOU HAVE TO GET MY NAME RIGHT.
Dunkelheit
CUCUMBER?
CURIE!

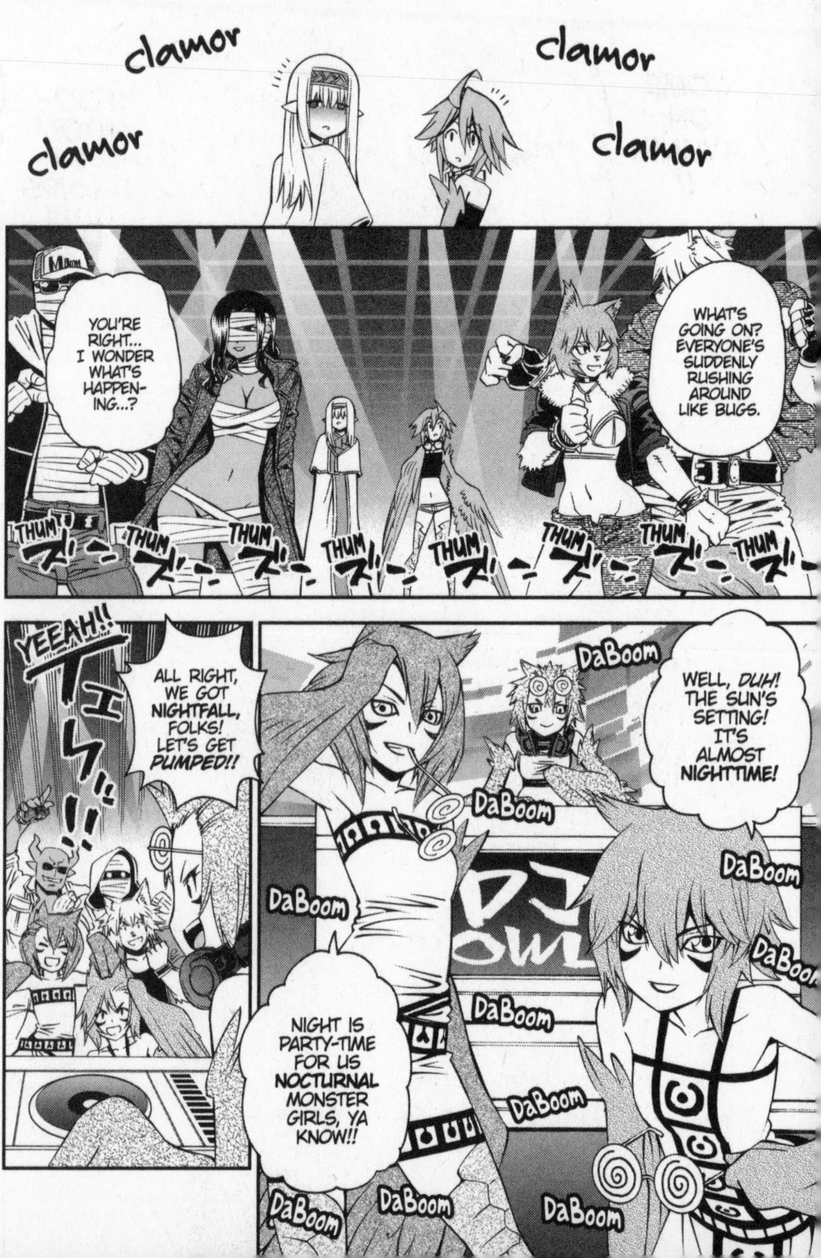
clamor
clamor
clamor
clamor
WHAT'S GOING ON? EVERYONE'S SUDDENLY RUSHING AROUND LIKE BUGS.
YOU'RE RIGHT... I WONDER WHAT'S HAPPENING...?
THUM
THUM
THUM
THUM
THUM
THUM
THUM
THUM
DaBoom
WELL, *DUH!* THE SUN'S SETTING! IT'S ALMOST **NIGHTTIME!**
DaBoom
DaBoom
DaBoom
DaBoom
NIGHT IS PARTY-TIME FOR US **NOCTURNAL** MONSTER GIRLS, YA KNOW!!
DaBoom
DaBoom
DaBoom
DaBoom
YEEAH!!
ALL RIGHT, WE GOT **NIGHTFALL,** FOLKS! LET'S GET ***PUMPED!!***

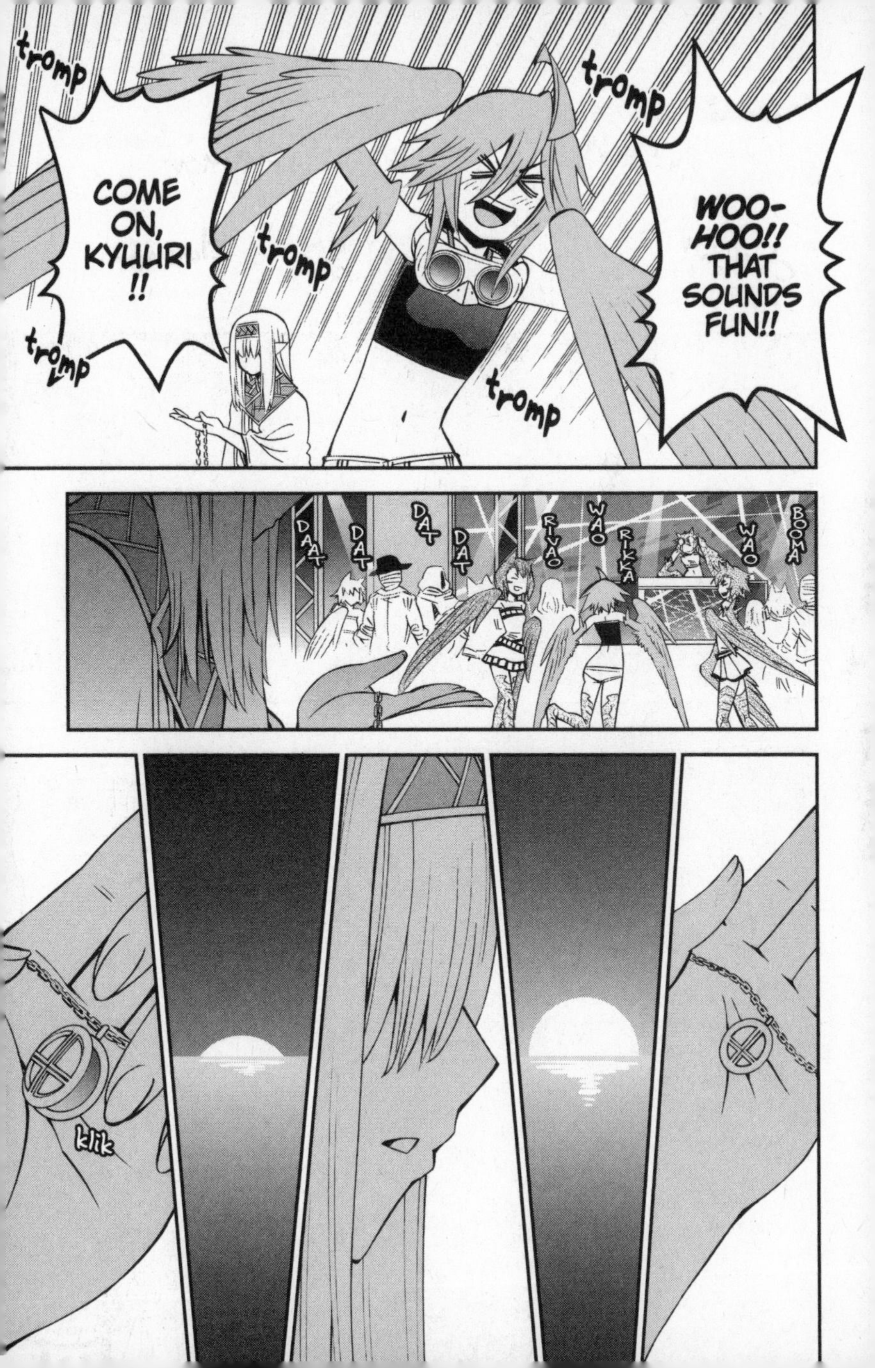
tromp
WOO-HOO!! THAT SOUNDS FUN!!
tromp
tromp
COME ON, KYUURI!!
tromp
tromp
BOOMA
WAO
RIKKA
WAO
RIVAO
DAT
DAT
DAT
DAAT
klik

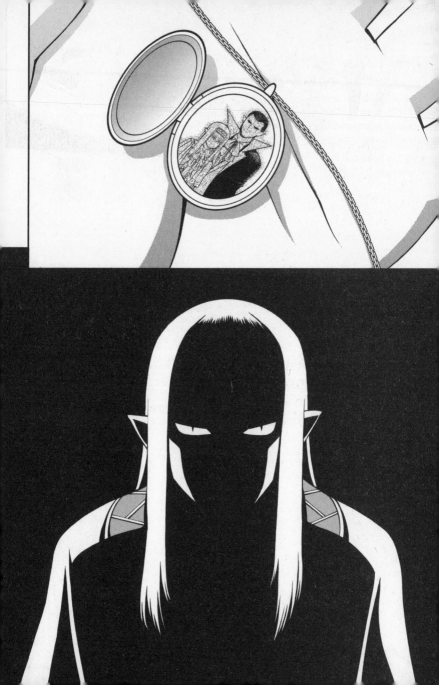

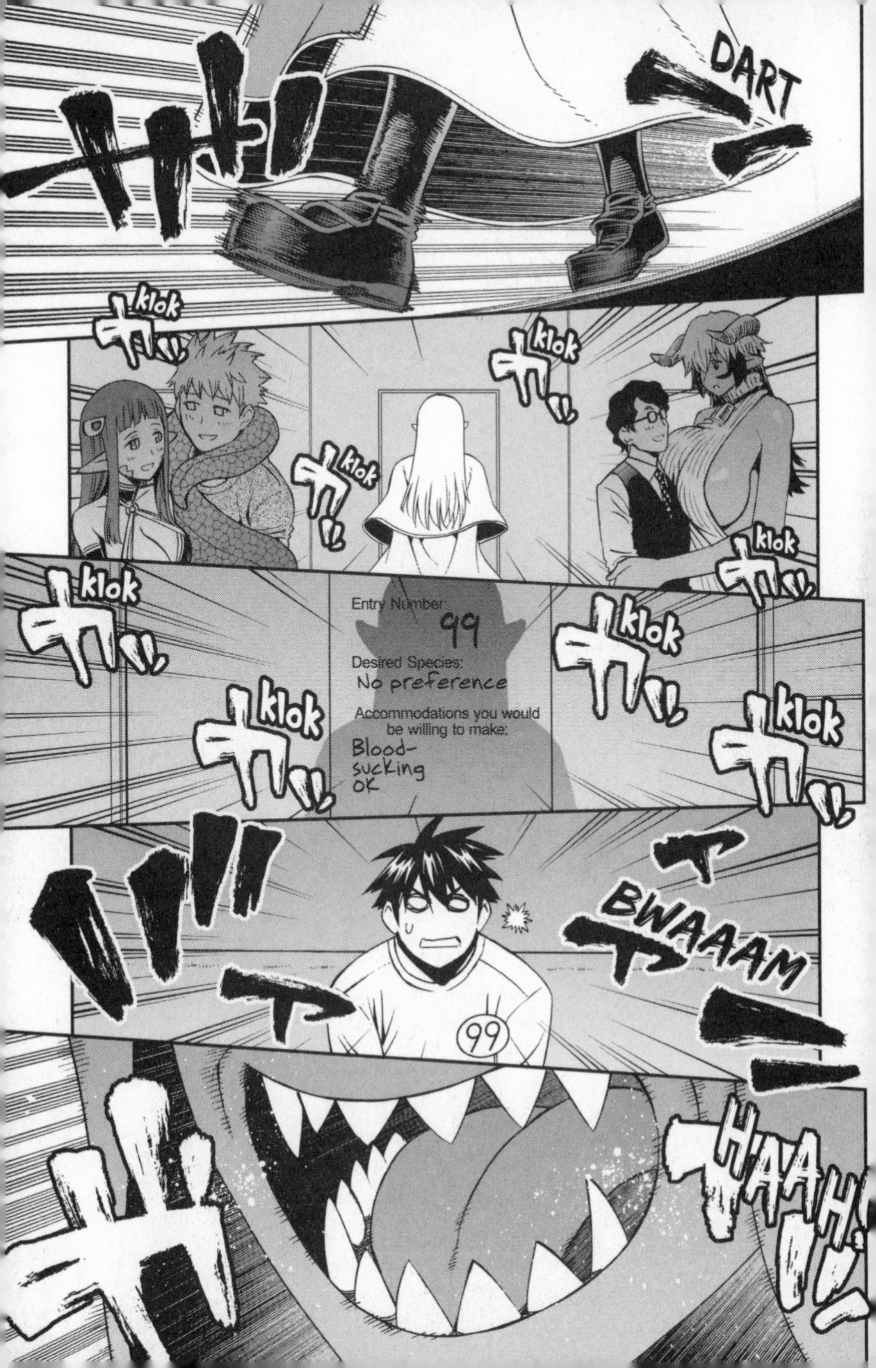
DART
klok
klok
klok
klok
klok
klok
Entry Number
99
Desired Species:
No preference
Accommodations you would be willing to make:
Blood-sucking OK
klok
klok
BWAAAM
HAAH!

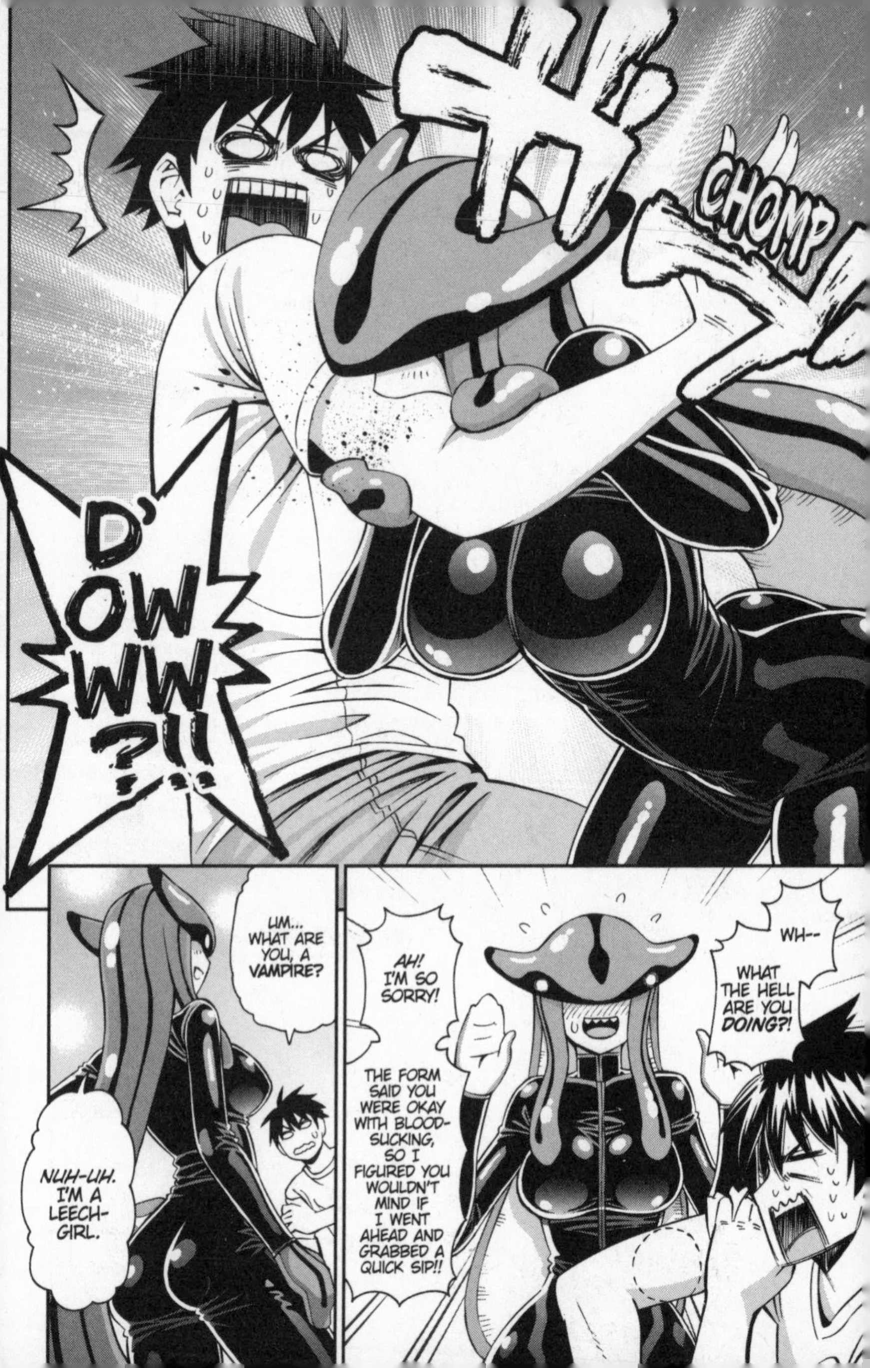
CHOMP
D'OWWWW?!!
WH--
WHAT THE HELL ARE YOU DOING?!
AH! I'M SO SORRY!
THE FORM SAID YOU WERE OKAY WITH BLOOD-SUCKING, SO I FIGURED YOU WOULDN'T MIND IF I WENT AHEAD AND GRABBED A QUICK SIP!!
UM... WHAT ARE YOU, A VAMPIRE?
NUH-UH. I'M A LEECH-GIRL.

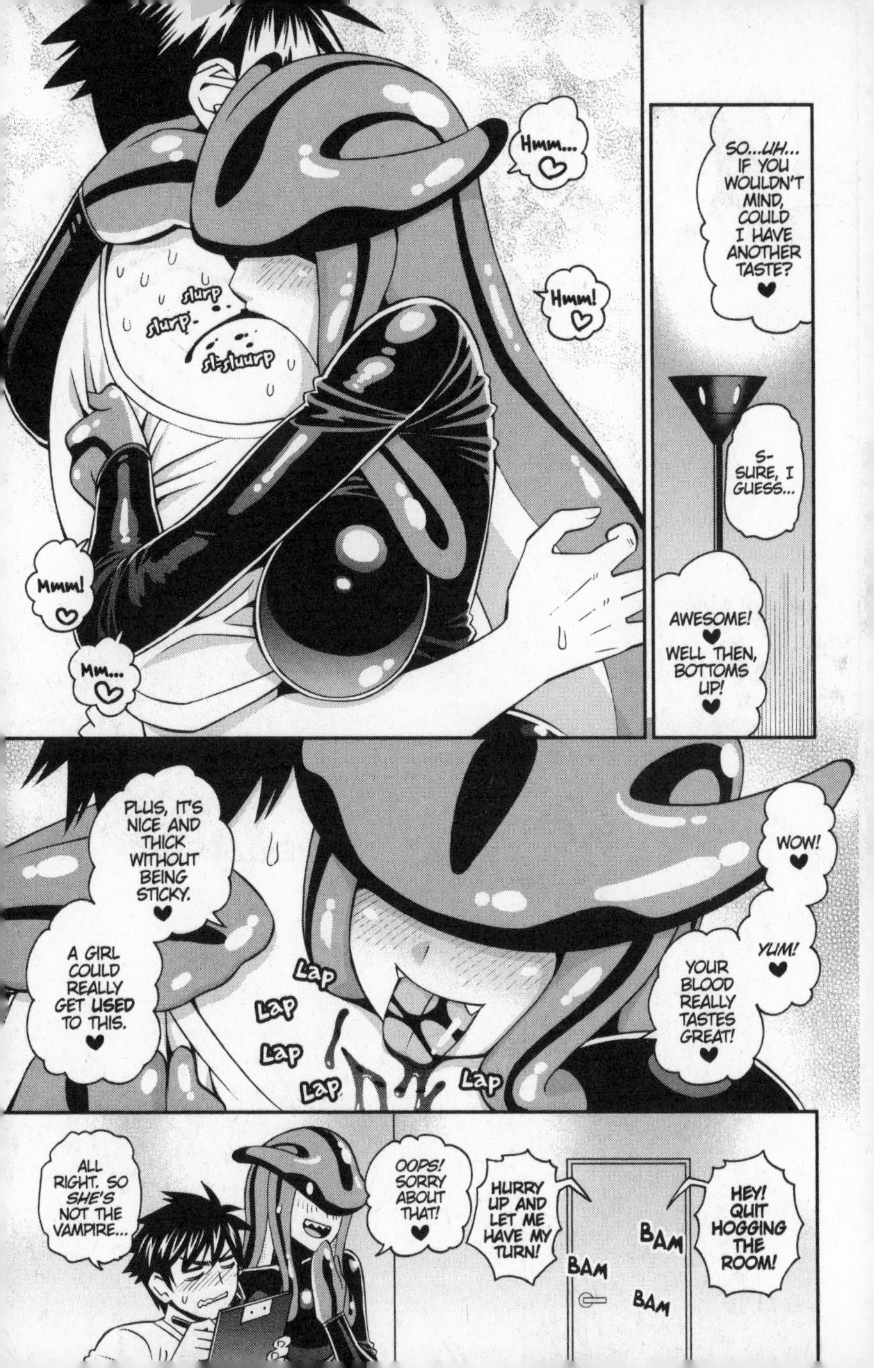
SO...UH... IF YOU WOULDN'T MIND, COULD I HAVE ANOTHER TASTE? ♥
S-SURE, I GUESS...
AWESOME! ♥ WELL THEN, BOTTOMS UP! ♥
Hmm... ♥
Hmm! ♥
slurp
slurp
sl-sluurp
Mmm! ♥
Mm... ♥
WOW! ♥
YUM! ♥
YOUR BLOOD REALLY TASTES GREAT! ♥
Lap
Lap
Lap
Lap
Lap
PLUS, IT'S NICE AND THICK WITHOUT BEING STICKY. ♥
A GIRL COULD REALLY GET USED TO THIS. ♥
HEY! QUIT HOGGING THE ROOM!
BAM
BAM
BAM
HURRY UP AND LET ME HAVE MY TURN!
OOPS! SORRY ABOUT THAT! ♥
ALL RIGHT. SO *SHE'S* NOT THE VAMPIRE...

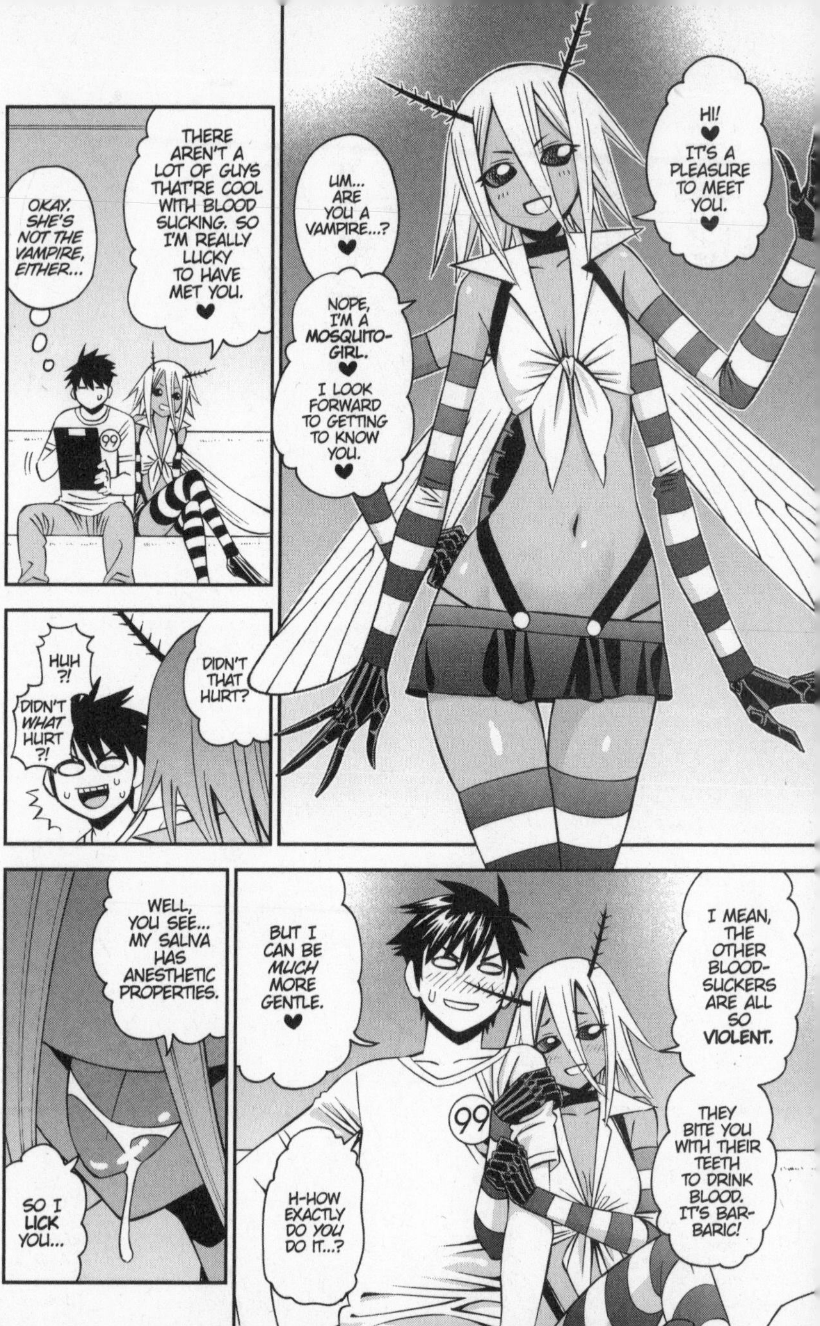
HI! ♥ IT'S A PLEASURE TO MEET YOU. ♥
UM... ARE YOU A VAMPIRE...? ♥
NOPE, I'M A MOSQUITO-GIRL. ♥ I LOOK FORWARD TO GETTING TO KNOW YOU. ♥
THERE AREN'T A LOT OF GUYS THAT'RE COOL WITH BLOOD SUCKING. SO I'M REALLY LUCKY TO HAVE MET YOU. ♥
OKAY. SHE'S NOT THE VAMPIRE, EITHER...
DIDN'T THAT HURT?
HUH?! DIDN'T *WHAT* HURT?!
I MEAN, THE OTHER BLOOD-SUCKERS ARE ALL SO **VIOLENT**.
THEY BITE YOU WITH THEIR TEETH TO DRINK BLOOD. IT'S BAR-BARIC!
BUT I CAN BE *MUCH* MORE GENTLE. ♥
H-HOW EXACTLY DO *YOU* DO IT...?
WELL, YOU SEE... MY SALIVA HAS ANESTHETIC PROPERTIES.
SO I LICK YOU...

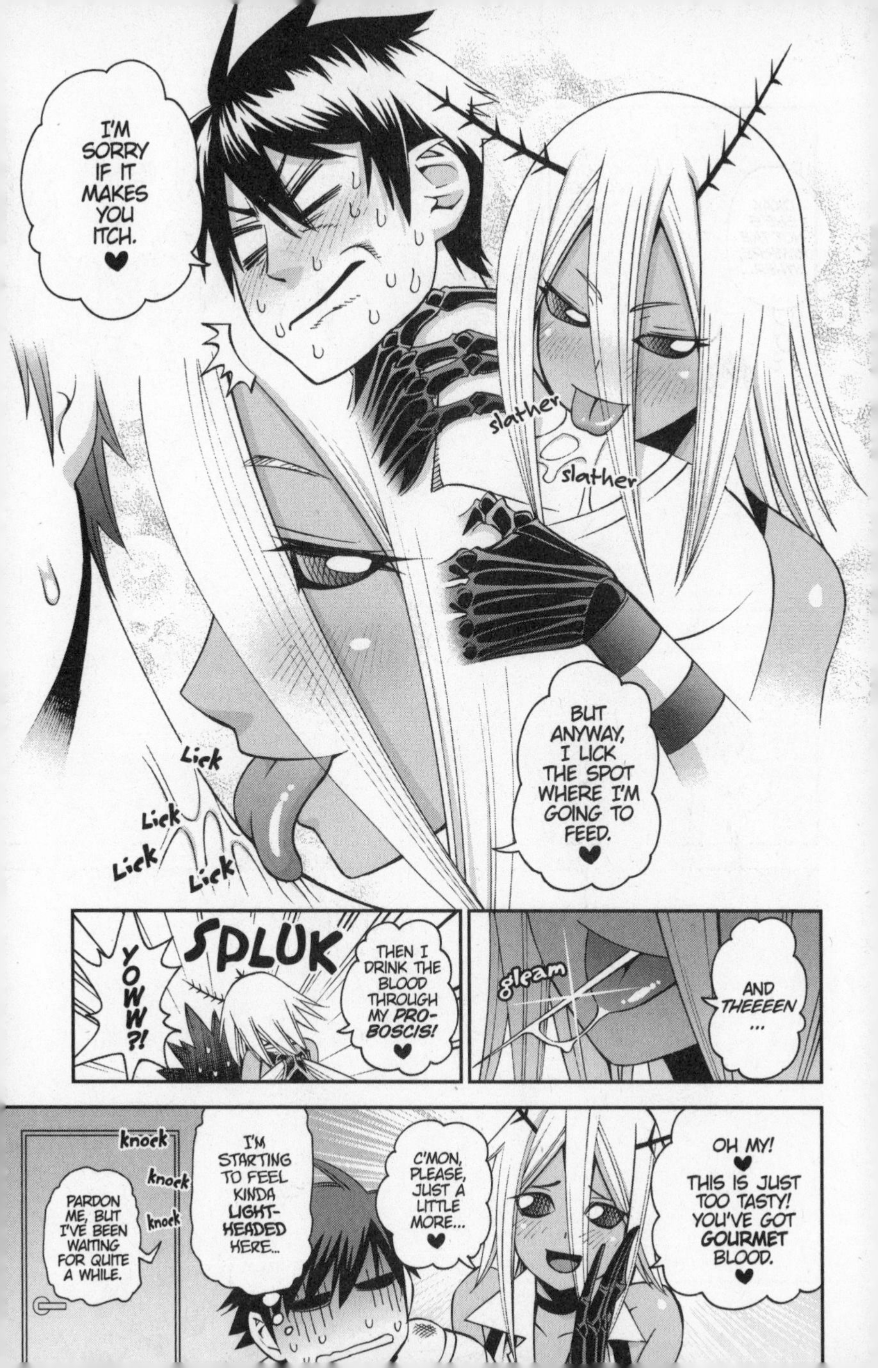
I'M SORRY IF IT MAKES YOU ITCH. ♥
slather
slather
BUT ANYWAY, I LICK THE SPOT WHERE I'M GOING TO FEED. ♥
Lick
Lick
Lick
Lick
gleam
AND THEEEEN...
THEN I DRINK THE BLOOD THROUGH MY PRO-BOSCIS! ♥
SPLUK
YOWW?!
OH MY! ♥ THIS IS JUST TOO TASTY! YOU'VE GOT GOURMET BLOOD. ♥
C'MON, PLEASE, JUST A LITTLE MORE... ♥
I'M STARTING TO FEEL KINDA LIGHT-HEADED HERE...
knock
knock
knock
PARDON ME, BUT I'VE BEEN WAITING FOR QUITE A WHILE.

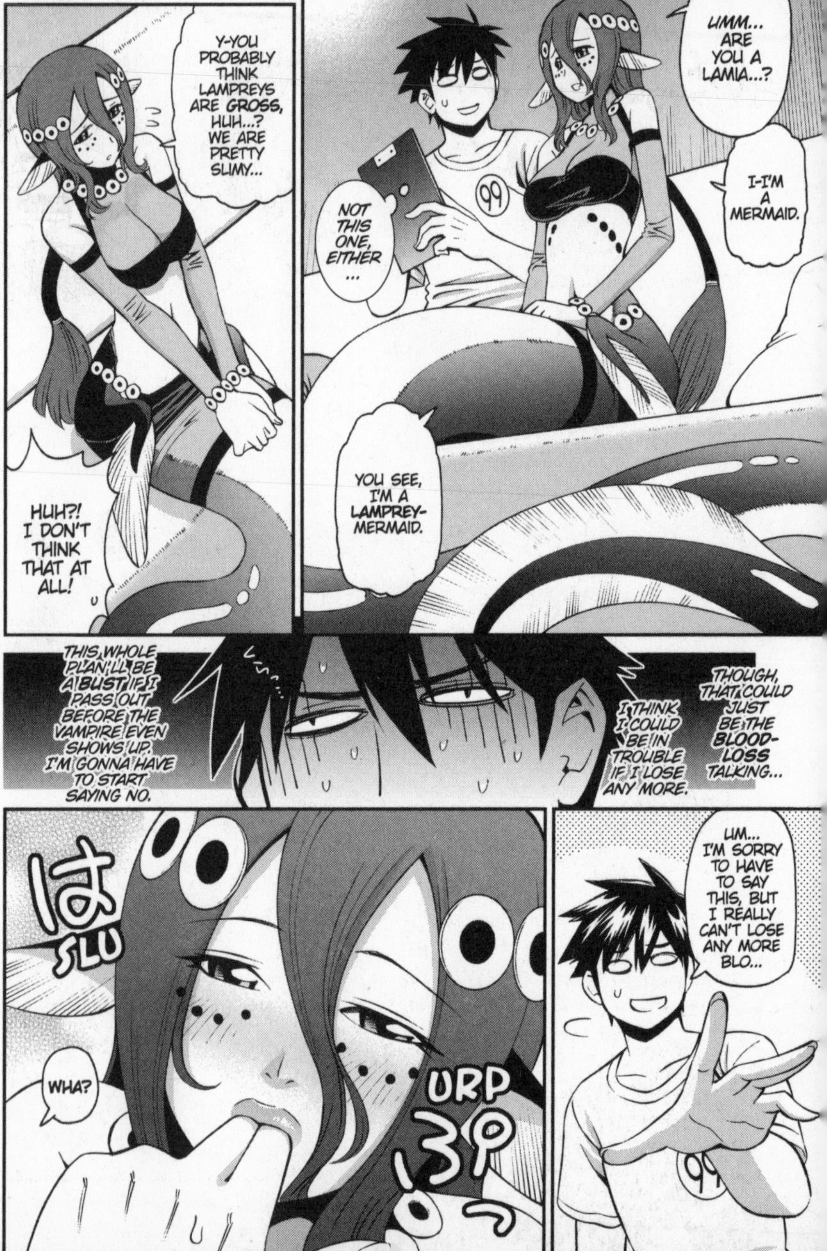
UMM... ARE YOU A LAMIA...?
I-I'M A MERMAID.
NOT THIS ONE, EITHER...
YOU SEE, I'M A LAMPREY-MERMAID.
Y-YOU PROBABLY THINK LAMPREYS ARE GROSS, HUH...? WE ARE PRETTY SLIMY...
HUH?! I DON'T THINK THAT AT ALL!
THOUGH, THAT COULD JUST BE THE BLOOD-LOSS TALKING...
I THINK I COULD BE IN TROUBLE IF I LOSE ANY MORE.
THIS WHOLE PLAN'LL BE A BUST IF I PASS OUT BEFORE THE VAMPIRE EVEN SHOWS UP. I'M GONNA HAVE TO START SAYING NO.
UM... I'M SORRY TO HAVE TO SAY THIS, BUT I REALLY CAN'T LOSE ANY MORE BLO...
URP
ぷっ
は
SLU
WHA?

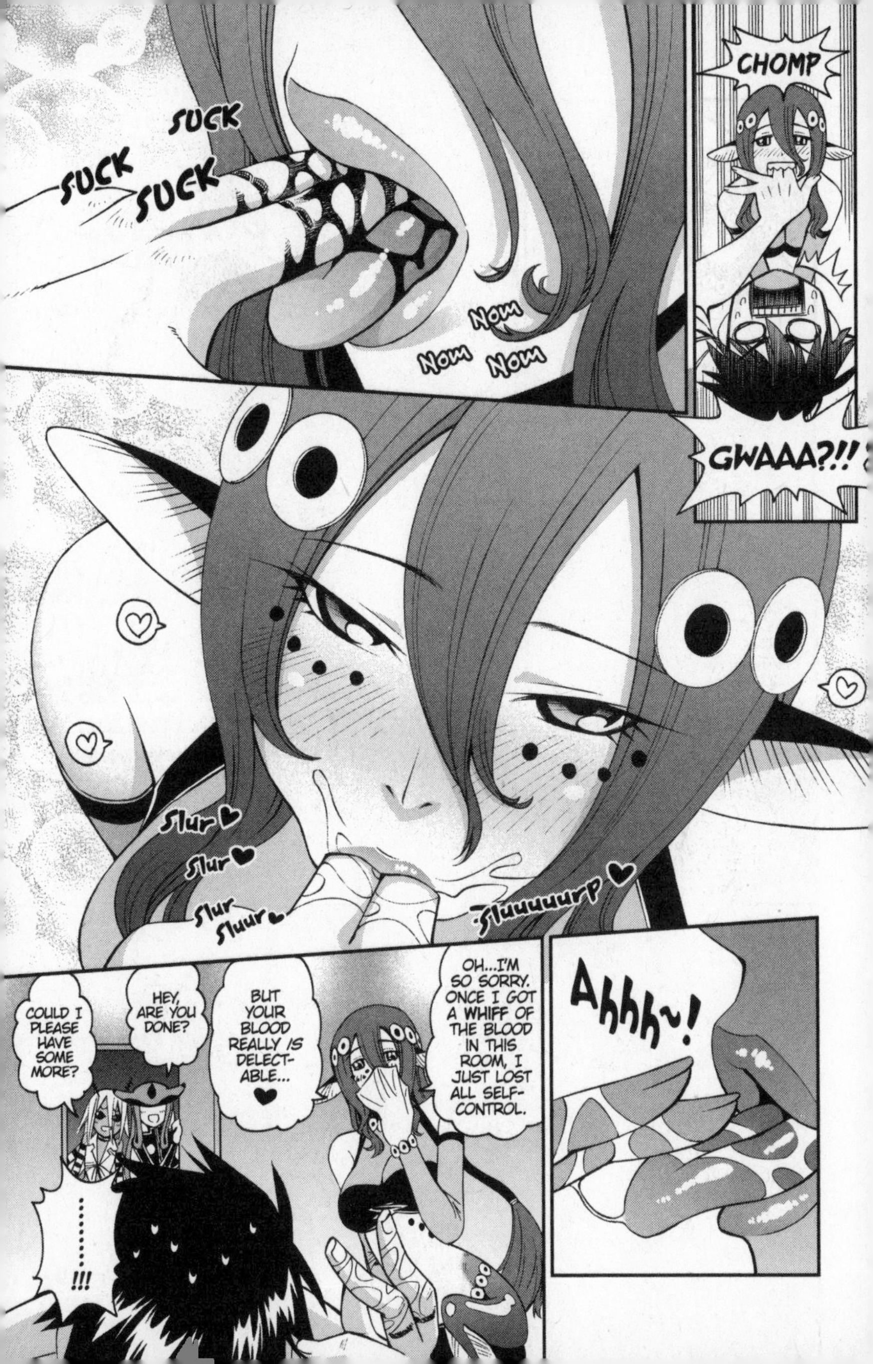
CHOMP
GWAAA?!!
SUCK
SUCK
SUCK
Nom
Nom Nom
Slur ♥
Slur ♥
Slur Sluur ♥
Sluuuuurp ♥
Ahhh~!
OH...I'M SO SORRY. ONCE I GOT A WHIFF OF THE BLOOD IN THIS ROOM, I JUST LOST ALL SELF-CONTROL.
BUT YOUR BLOOD REALLY IS DELECTABLE... ♥
HEY, ARE YOU DONE?
COULD I PLEASE HAVE SOME MORE?
......!!!

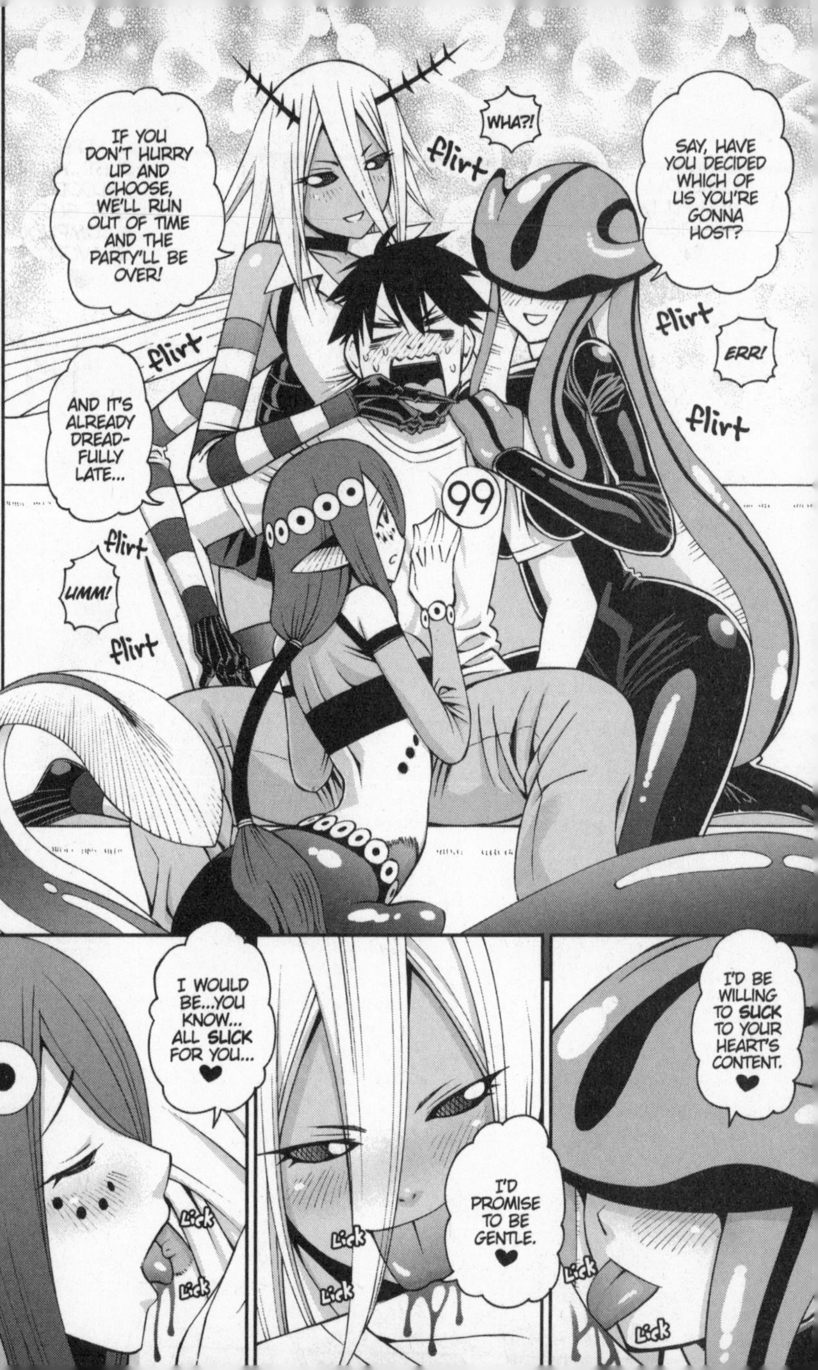
SAY, HAVE YOU DECIDED WHICH OF US YOU'RE GONNA HOST?
WHA?!
flirt
IF YOU DON'T HURRY UP AND CHOOSE, WE'LL RUN OUT OF TIME AND THE PARTY'LL BE OVER!
flirt
ERR!
flirt
flirt
AND IT'S ALREADY DREAD-FULLY LATE...
flirt
UMM!
flirt
I'D BE WILLING TO SUCK TO YOUR HEART'S CONTENT. ♥
Lick
Lick
I'D PROMISE TO BE GENTLE. ♥
Lick
Lick
I WOULD BE...YOU KNOW... ALL SLICK FOR YOU... ♥
Lick
Lick

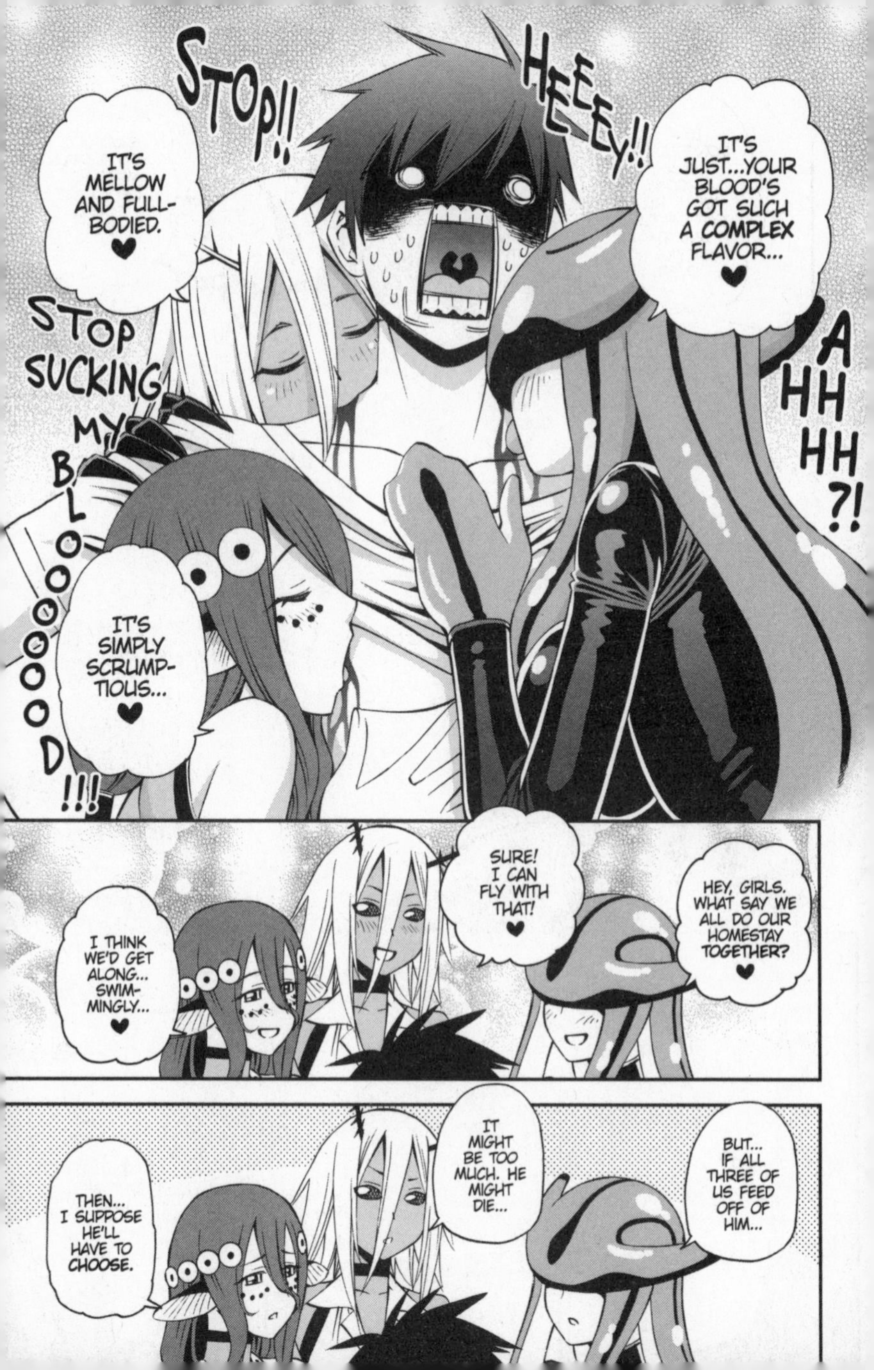
HEEEY!!
IT'S JUST...YOUR BLOOD'S GOT SUCH A **COMPLEX** FLAVOR... ♥
AHHHH?!
STOP!!
IT'S MELLOW AND FULL-BODIED. ♥
STOP SUCKING MY BLOOOOOOD!!!
IT'S SIMPLY SCRUMPTIOUS... ♥
HEY, GIRLS. WHAT SAY WE ALL DO OUR HOMESTAY TOGETHER? ♥
SURE! I CAN FLY WITH THAT! ♥
I THINK WE'D GET ALONG... SWIMMINGLY... ♥
BUT... IF ALL THREE OF US FEED OFF OF HIM...
IT MIGHT BE TOO MUCH. HE MIGHT DIE...
THEN... I SUPPOSE HE'LL HAVE TO CHOOSE.

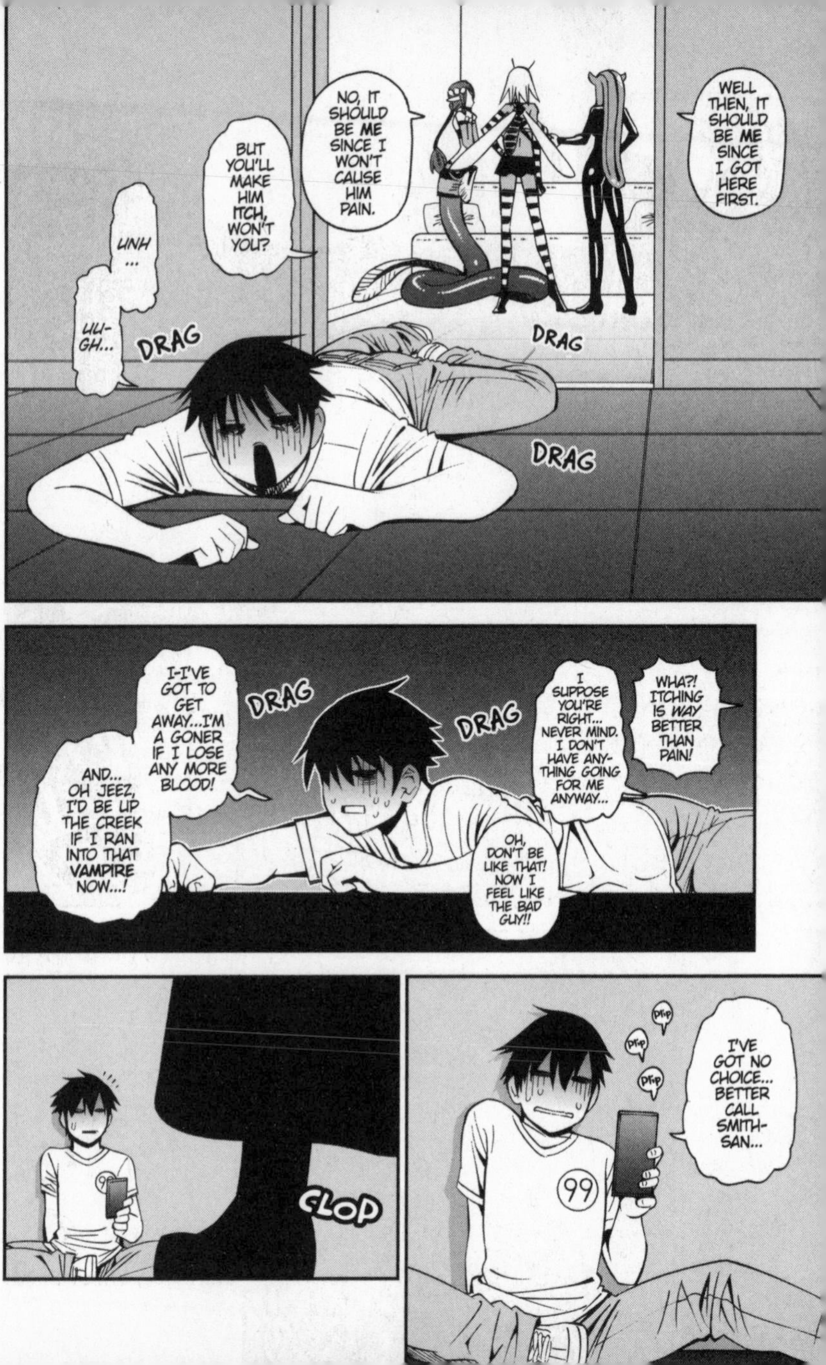
WELL THEN, IT SHOULD BE ME SINCE I GOT HERE FIRST.
NO, IT SHOULD BE ME SINCE I WON'T CAUSE HIM PAIN.
BUT YOU'LL MAKE HIM ITCH, WON'T YOU?
UNH ...
ULI-GH...
DRAG
DRAG
DRAG
WHA?! ITCHING IS *WAY* BETTER THAN PAIN!
I SUPPOSE YOU'RE RIGHT... NEVER MIND. I DON'T HAVE ANY-THING GOING FOR ME ANYWAY...
OH, DON'T BE LIKE THAT! NOW I FEEL LIKE THE BAD GUY!!
DRAG
DRAG
I-I'VE GOT TO GET AWAY...I'M A GONER IF I LOSE ANY MORE BLOOD!
AND... OH JEEZ, I'D BE UP THE CREEK IF I RAN INTO THAT VAMPIRE NOW...!
I'VE GOT NO CHOICE... BETTER CALL SMITH-SAN...
CLOP

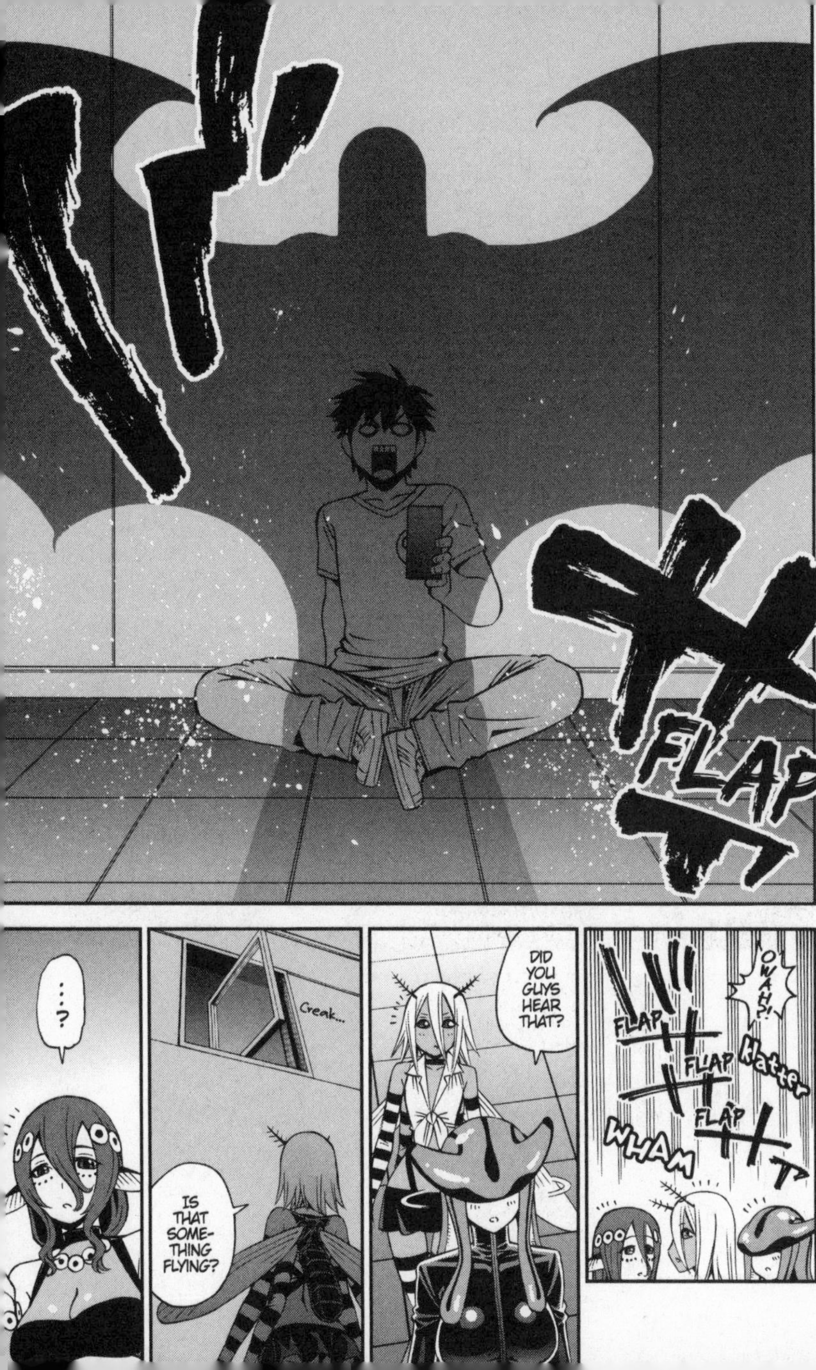
FLAP
OWAH?!
FLAP FLAP FLAP
Klatter
WHAM
DID YOU GUYS HEAR THAT?
Creak...
IS THAT SOME-THING FLYING?
...?

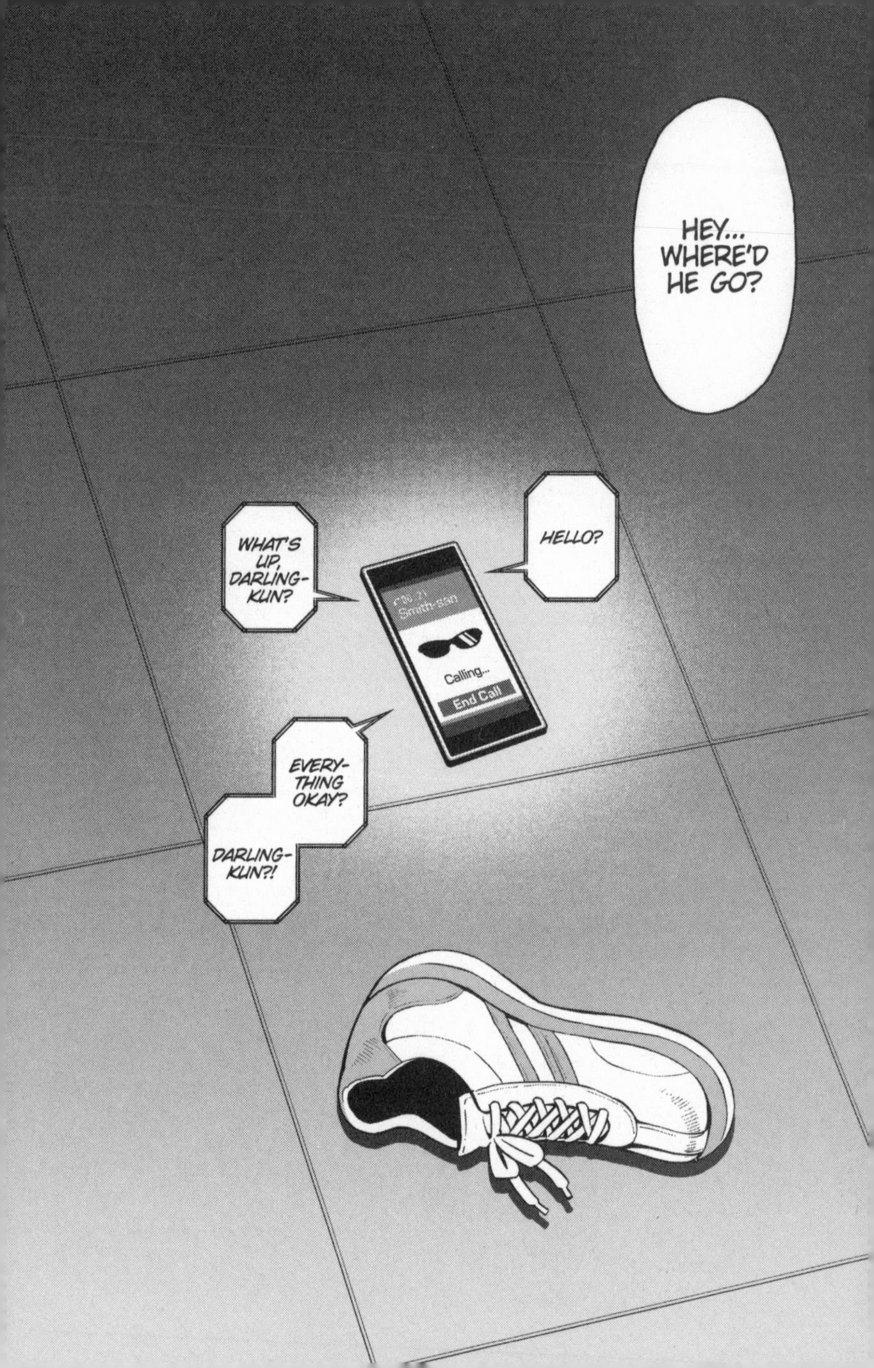
HEY... WHERE'D HE GO?
HELLO?
WHAT'S UP, DARLING-KUN?
Smith-san
Calling...
End Call
EVERYTHING OKAY?
DARLING-KUN?!

Monster Musume

Everyday Life with Monster Girls

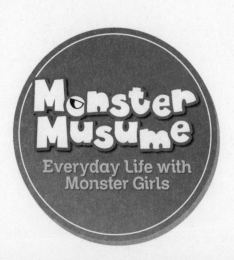

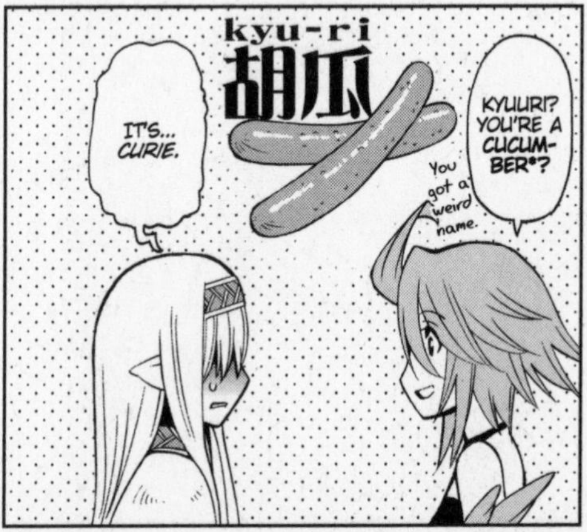
kyu-ri
胡瓜
KYUURI? YOU'RE A CUCUM-BER*?
You got a weird name.
IT'S... CURIE.

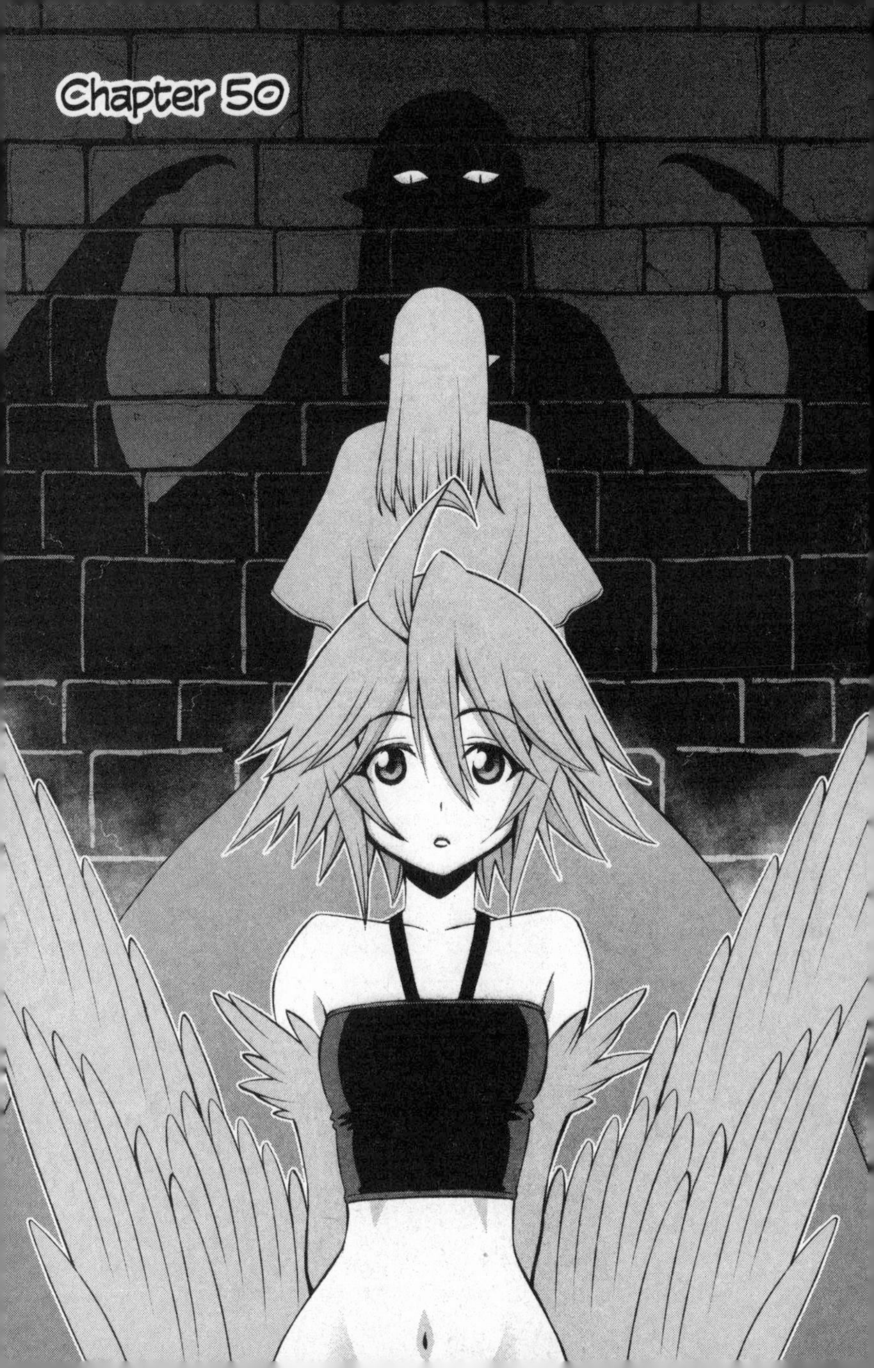
Chapter 50

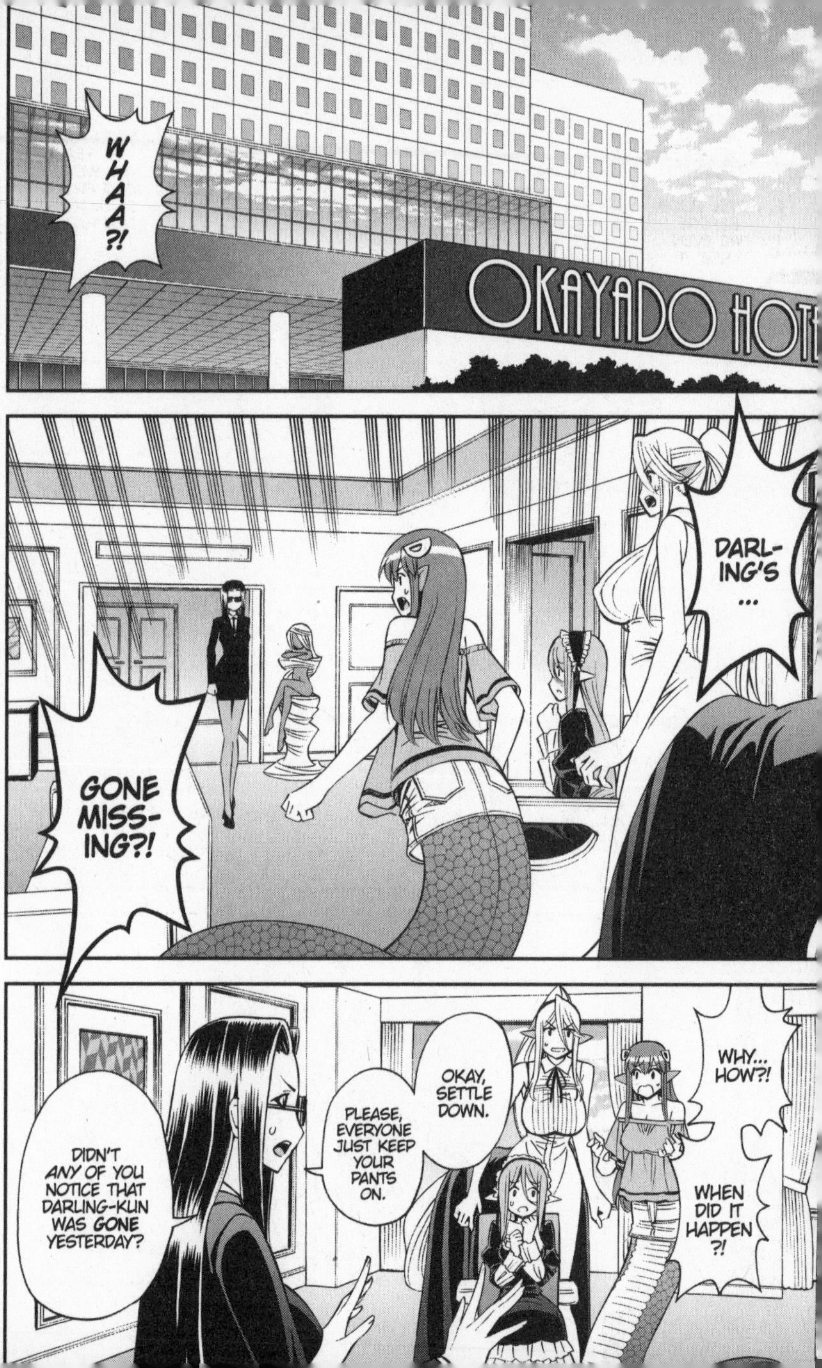
OKAYADO HOTE
WHAAA?!
DARLING'S ...
GONE MISSING?!
WHY... HOW?!
WHEN DID IT HAPPEN ?!
OKAY, SETTLE DOWN.
PLEASE, EVERYONE JUST KEEP YOUR PANTS ON.
DIDN'T ANY OF YOU NOTICE THAT DARLING-KUN WAS GONE YESTERDAY?

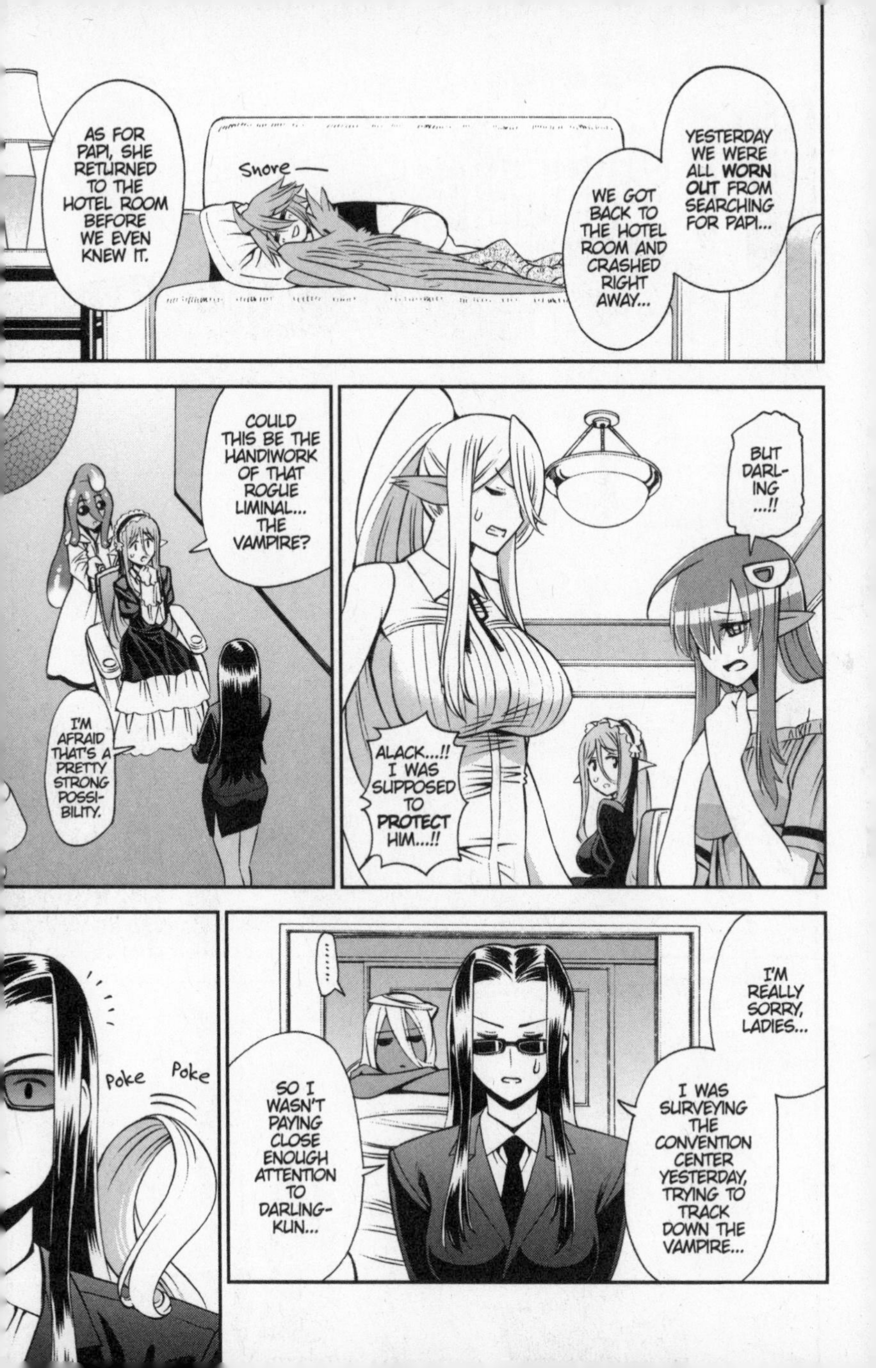
YESTERDAY WE WERE ALL **WORN OUT** FROM SEARCHING FOR PAPI...
WE GOT BACK TO THE HOTEL ROOM AND CRASHED RIGHT AWAY...
Snore—
AS FOR PAPI, SHE RETURNED TO THE HOTEL ROOM BEFORE WE EVEN KNEW IT.
BUT DARLING...!!
ALACK...!! I WAS SUPPOSED TO **PROTECT** HIM...!!
COULD THIS BE THE HANDIWORK OF THAT ROGUE LIMINAL... THE VAMPIRE?
I'M AFRAID THAT'S A PRETTY STRONG POSSIBILITY.
I'M REALLY SORRY, LADIES...
I WAS SURVEYING THE CONVENTION CENTER YESTERDAY, TRYING TO TRACK DOWN THE VAMPIRE...
SO I WASN'T PAYING CLOSE ENOUGH ATTENTION TO DARLING-KUN...
......
Poke Poke

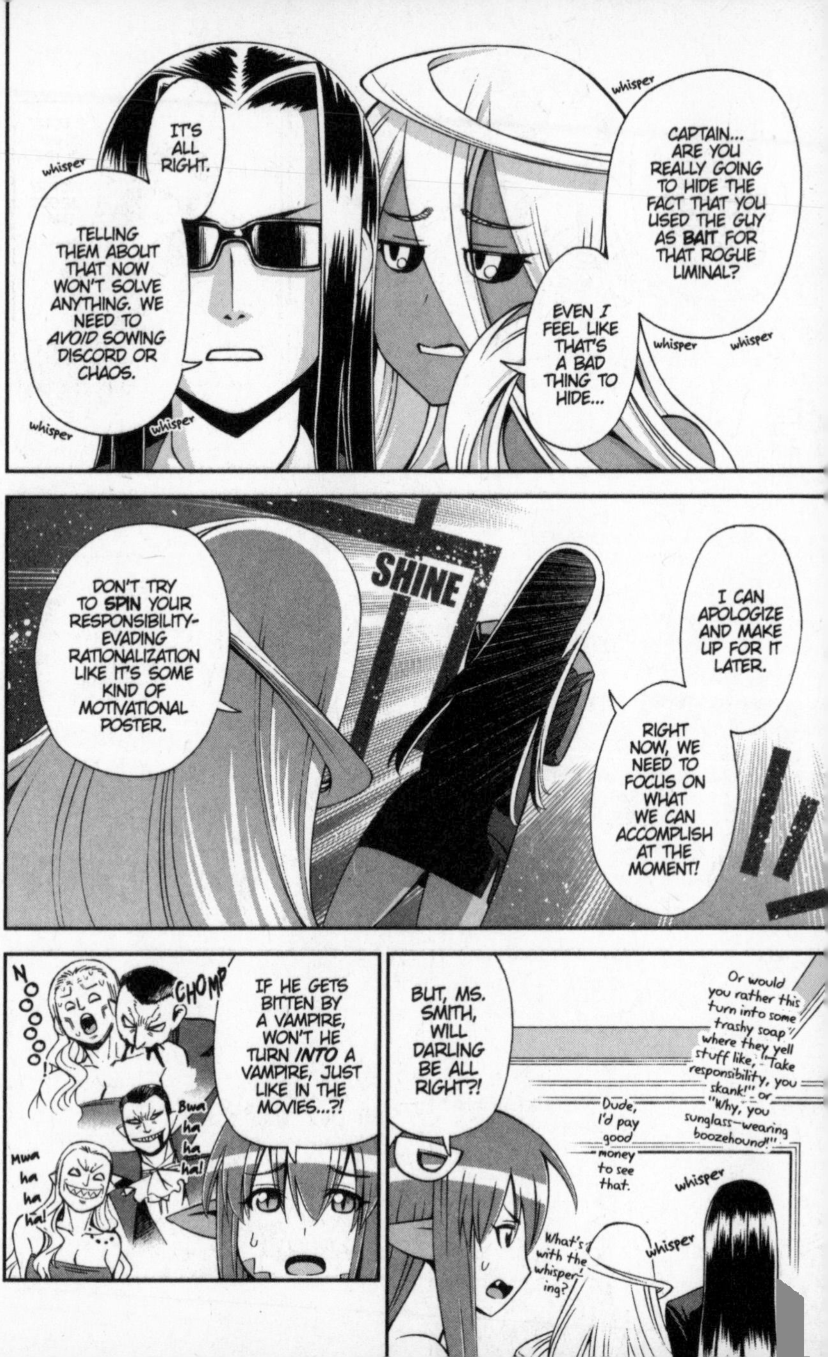
whisper
CAPTAIN... ARE YOU REALLY GOING TO HIDE THE FACT THAT YOU USED THE GUY AS BAIT FOR THAT ROGUE LIMINAL?
whisper whisper
EVEN I FEEL LIKE THAT'S A BAD THING TO HIDE...
IT'S ALL RIGHT.
whisper
TELLING THEM ABOUT THAT NOW WON'T SOLVE ANYTHING. WE NEED TO AVOID SOWING DISCORD OR CHAOS.
whisper whisper
I CAN APOLOGIZE AND MAKE UP FOR IT LATER.
RIGHT NOW, WE NEED TO FOCUS ON WHAT WE CAN ACCOMPLISH AT THE MOMENT!
SHINE
DON'T TRY TO SPIN YOUR RESPONSIBILITY-EVADING RATIONALIZATION LIKE IT'S SOME KIND OF MOTIVATIONAL POSTER.
Or would you rather this turn into some trashy soap where they yell stuff like, "Take responsibility, you skank!" or "Why, you sunglass-wearing boozehound!"
Dude, I'd pay good money to see that.
whisper
BUT, MS. SMITH, WILL DARLING BE ALL RIGHT?!
whisper
What's with the whispering?
IF HE GETS BITTEN BY A VAMPIRE, WON'T HE TURN INTO A VAMPIRE, JUST LIKE IN THE MOVIES...?!
CHOMP
NOOOOOO!
Bwa ha ha ha ha!
Mwa ha ha ha!

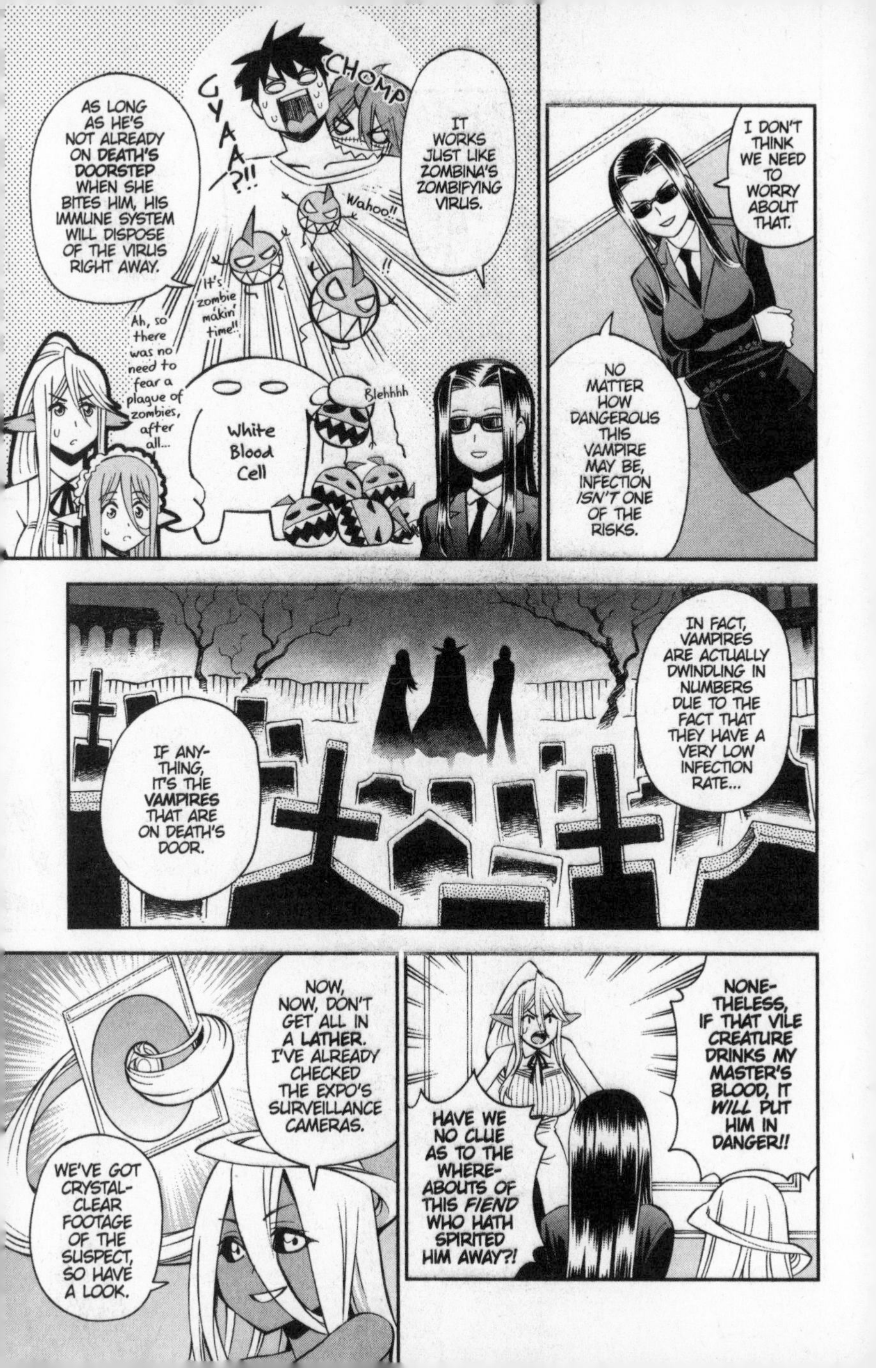
I DON'T THINK WE NEED TO WORRY ABOUT THAT.
NO MATTER HOW DANGEROUS THIS VAMPIRE MAY BE, INFECTION *ISN'T* ONE OF THE RISKS.
CHOMP
IT WORKS JUST LIKE ZOMBINA'S ZOMBIFYING VIRUS.
GYAAA?!!
Wahoo!!
!!
AS LONG AS HE'S NOT ALREADY ON **DEATH'S DOORSTEP** WHEN SHE BITES HIM, HIS IMMUNE SYSTEM WILL DISPOSE OF THE VIRUS RIGHT AWAY.
It's zombie makin' time!!
Ah, so there was no need to fear a plague of zombies, after all...
White Blood Cell
Blehhhh
IN FACT, VAMPIRES ARE ACTUALLY DWINDLING IN NUMBERS DUE TO THE FACT THAT THEY HAVE A VERY LOW INFECTION RATE...
IF ANY-THING, IT'S THE **VAMPIRES** THAT ARE ON DEATH'S DOOR.
NONE-THELESS, IF THAT VILE CREATURE DRINKS MY MASTER'S BLOOD, IT *WILL* PUT HIM IN DANGER!!
HAVE WE NO CLUE AS TO THE WHERE-ABOUTS OF THIS *FIEND* WHO HATH SPIRITED HIM AWAY?!
NOW, NOW, DON'T GET ALL IN A LATHER. I'VE ALREADY CHECKED THE EXPO'S SURVEILLANCE CAMERAS.
WE'VE GOT CRYSTAL-CLEAR FOOTAGE OF THE SUSPECT, SO HAVE A LOOK.

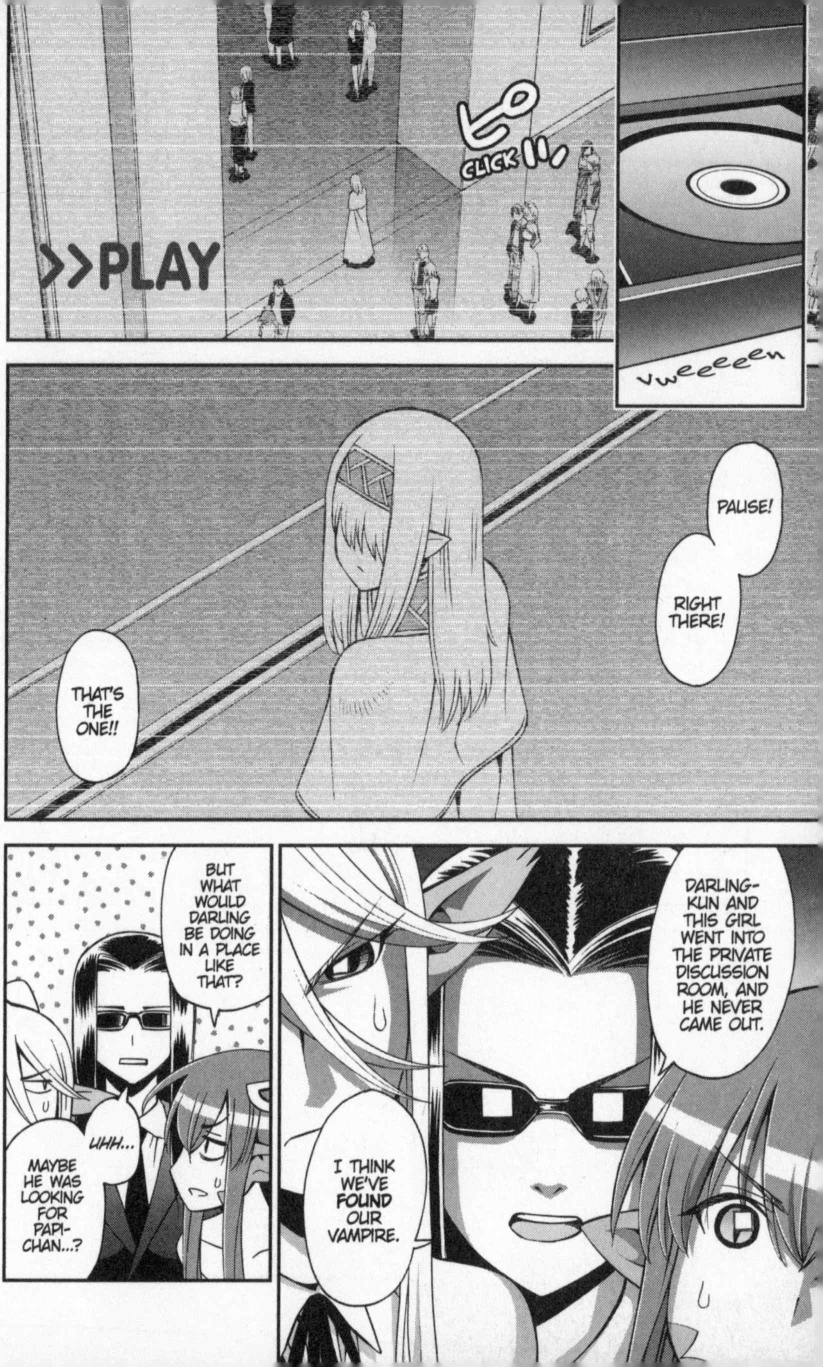
VWEEEEEN
CLICK
>>PLAY
PAUSE!
RIGHT THERE!
THAT'S THE ONE!!
DARLING-KUN AND THIS GIRL WENT INTO THE PRIVATE DISCUSSION ROOM, AND HE NEVER CAME OUT.
I THINK WE'VE FOUND OUR VAMPIRE.
BUT WHAT WOULD DARLING BE DOING IN A PLACE LIKE THAT?
UHH...
MAYBE HE WAS LOOKING FOR PAPI-CHAN...?

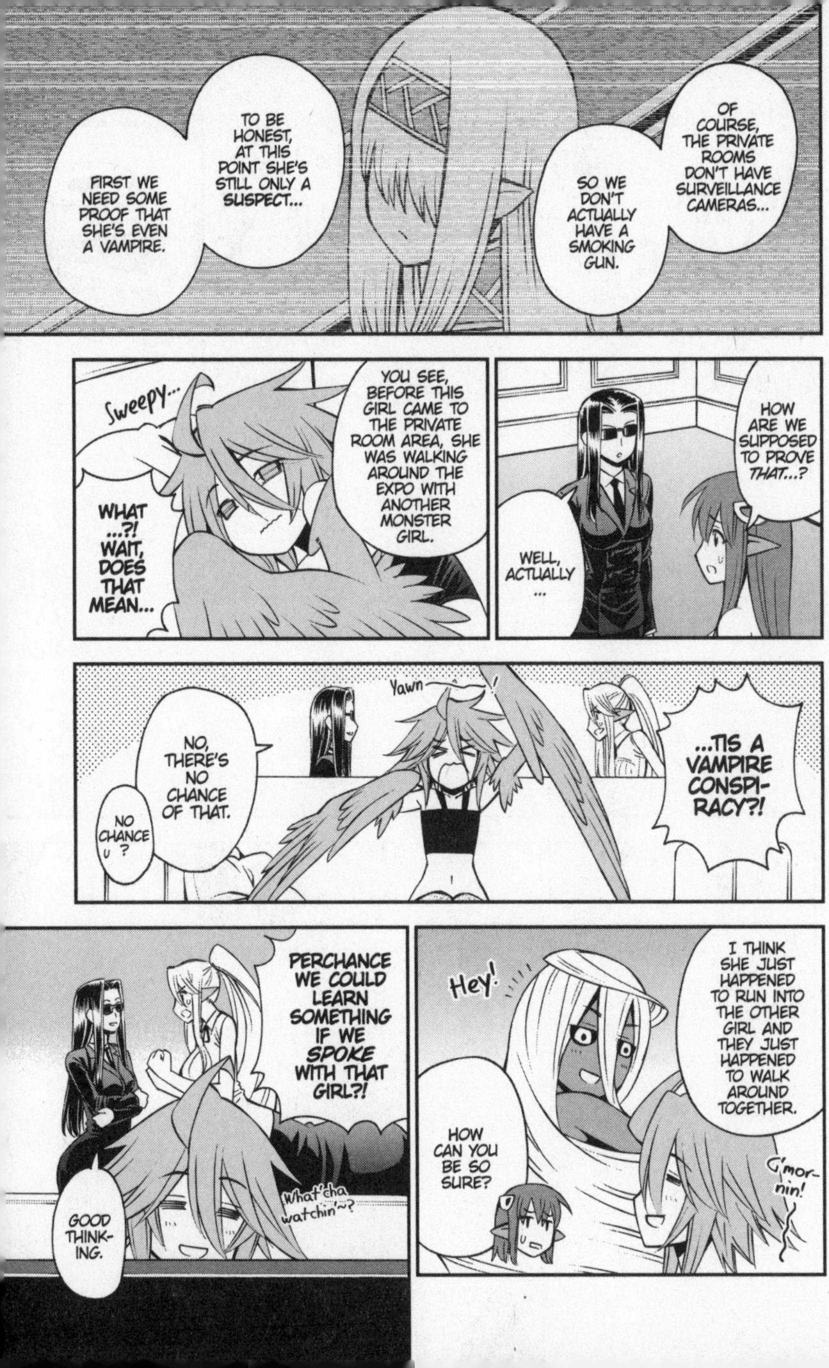
OF COURSE, THE PRIVATE ROOMS DON'T HAVE SURVEILLANCE CAMERAS...
SO WE DON'T ACTUALLY HAVE A SMOKING GUN.
TO BE HONEST, AT THIS POINT SHE'S STILL ONLY A SUSPECT...
FIRST WE NEED SOME PROOF THAT SHE'S EVEN A VAMPIRE.
HOW ARE WE SUPPOSED TO PROVE THAT...?
WELL, ACTUALLY ...
YOU SEE, BEFORE THIS GIRL CAME TO THE PRIVATE ROOM AREA, SHE WAS WALKING AROUND THE EXPO WITH ANOTHER MONSTER GIRL.
Sweepy...
WHAT ...?! WAIT, DOES THAT MEAN...
...TIS A VAMPIRE CONSPIRACY?!
Yawn
NO, THERE'S NO CHANCE OF THAT.
NO CHANCE ?
I THINK SHE JUST HAPPENED TO RUN INTO THE OTHER GIRL AND THEY JUST HAPPENED TO WALK AROUND TOGETHER.
Hey!
HOW CAN YOU BE SO SURE?
G'mornin!
PERCHANCE WE COULD LEARN SOMETHING IF WE SPOKE WITH THAT GIRL?!
What'cha watchin'~?
GOOD THINKING.

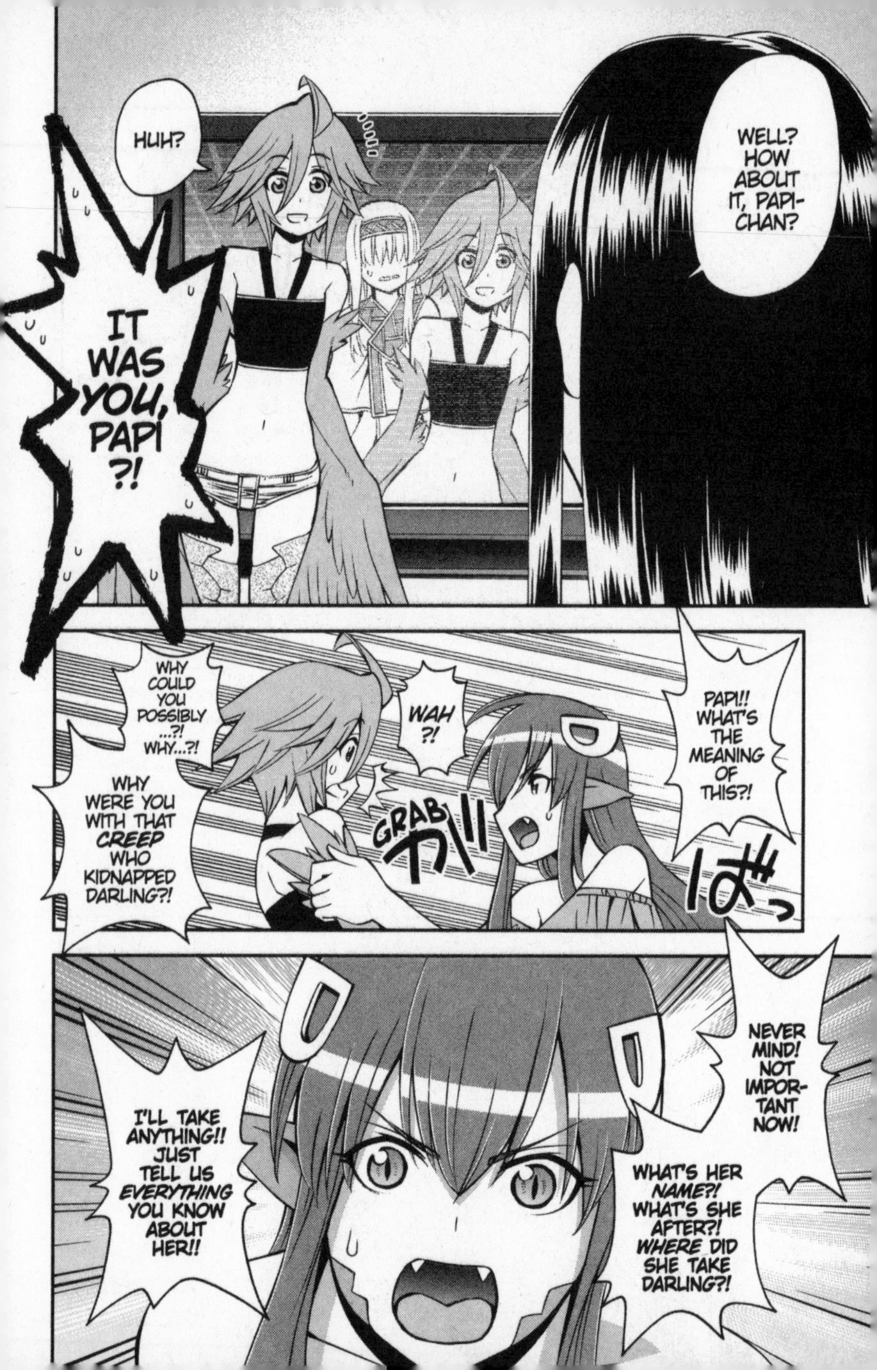
WELL? HOW ABOUT IT, PAPI-CHAN?
HUH?
IT WAS *YOU*, PAPI?!
PAPI!! WHAT'S THE MEANING OF THIS?!
ばっ
WAH?!
GRAB
WHY COULD YOU POSSIBLY ...?! WHY...?!
WHY WERE YOU WITH THAT *CREEP* WHO KIDNAPPED DARLING?!
NEVER MIND! NOT IMPORTANT NOW!
WHAT'S HER *NAME*?! WHAT'S SHE AFTER?! *WHERE* DID SHE TAKE DARLING?!
I'LL TAKE ANYTHING!! JUST TELL US *EVERYTHING* YOU KNOW ABOUT HER!!

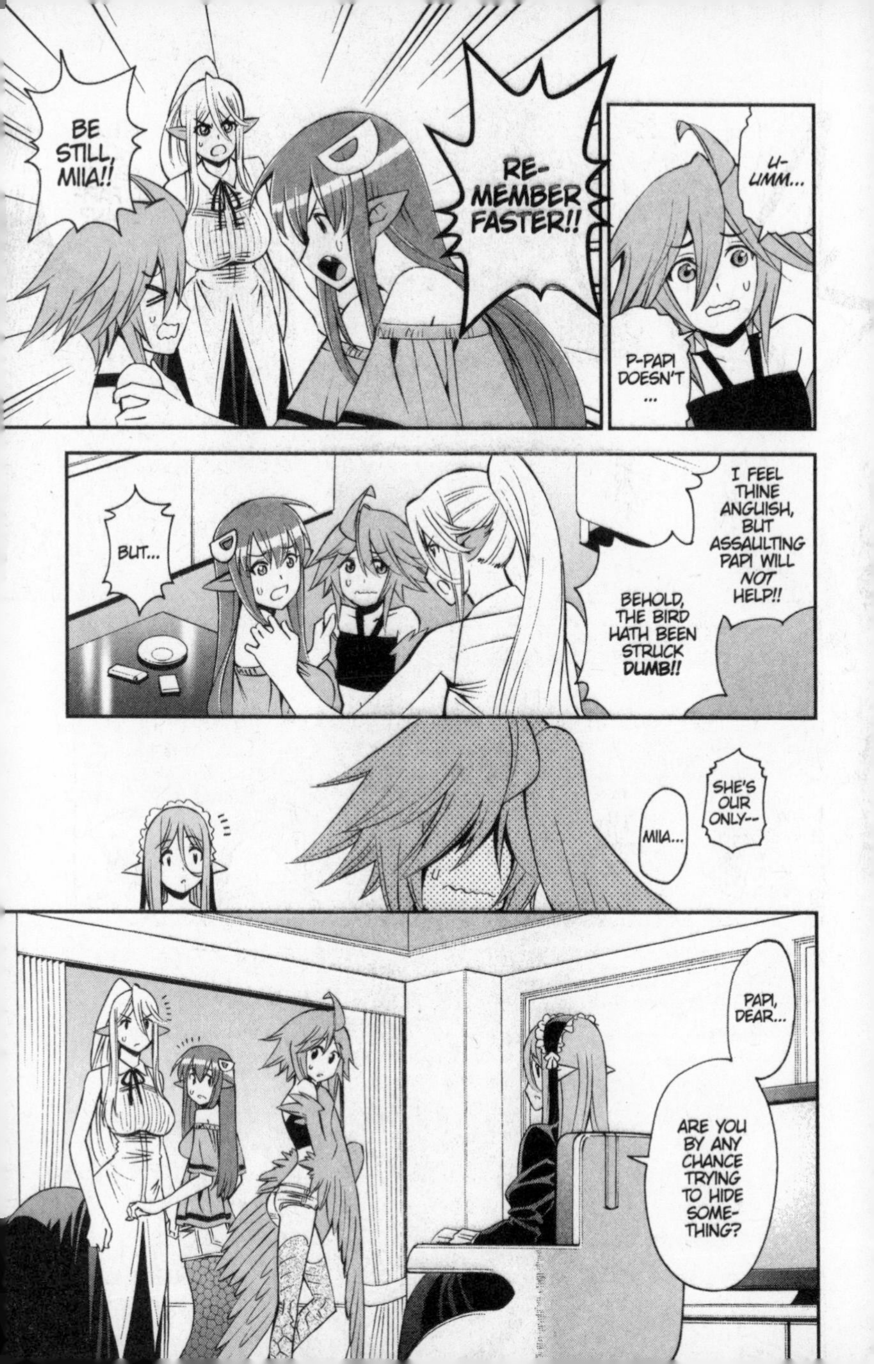
U-UMM...
P-PAPI DOESN'T ...
RE-MEMBER FASTER!!
BE STILL, MIIA!!
I FEEL THINE ANGUISH, BUT ASSAULTING PAPI WILL NOT HELP!!
BEHOLD, THE BIRD HATH BEEN STRUCK DUMB!!
BUT...
SHE'S OUR ONLY--
MIIA...
PAPI, DEAR...
ARE YOU BY ANY CHANCE TRYING TO HIDE SOME-THING?

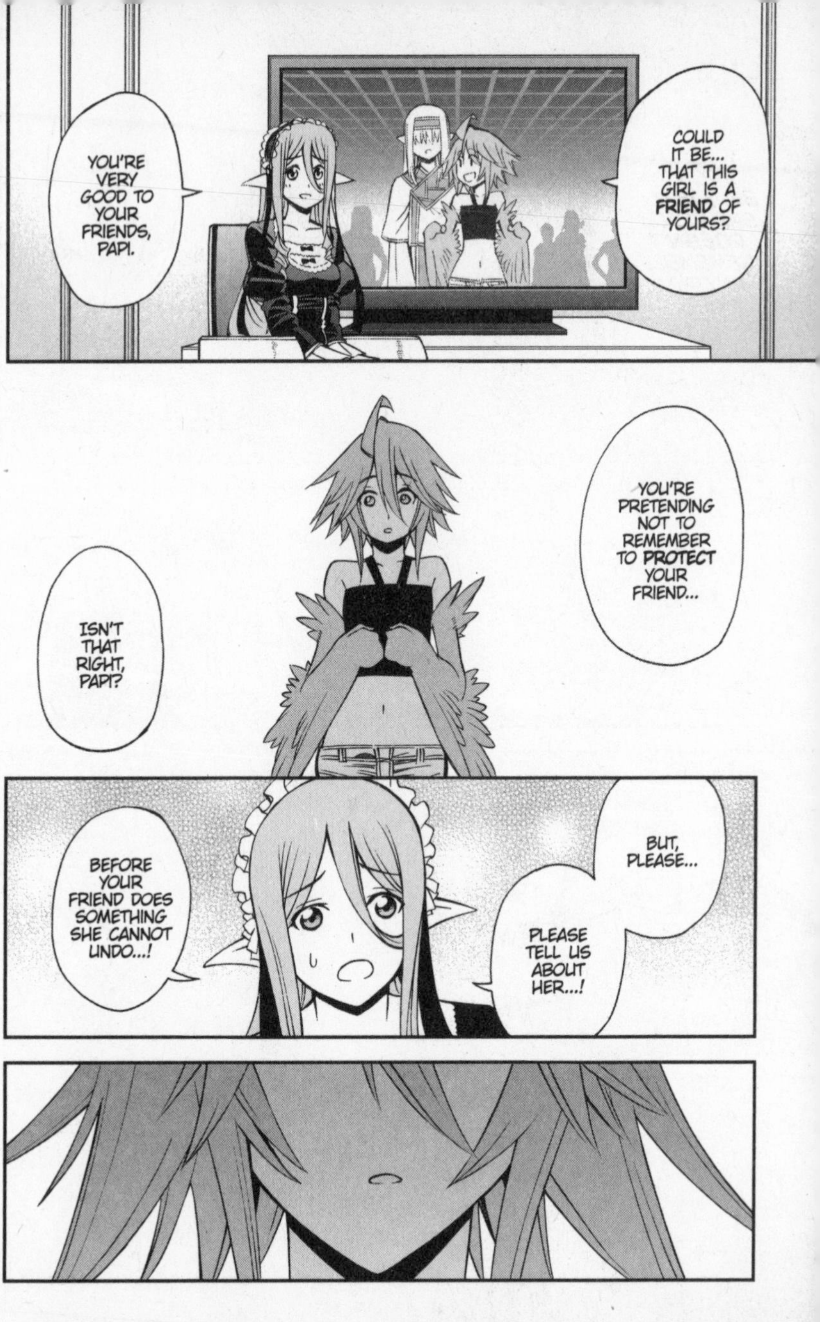
COULD IT BE... THAT THIS GIRL IS A FRIEND OF YOURS?
YOU'RE VERY GOOD TO YOUR FRIENDS, PAPI.
YOU'RE PRETENDING NOT TO REMEMBER TO PROTECT YOUR FRIEND...
ISN'T THAT RIGHT, PAPI?
BUT, PLEASE...
PLEASE TELL US ABOUT HER...!
BEFORE YOUR FRIEND DOES SOMETHING SHE CANNOT UNDO...!

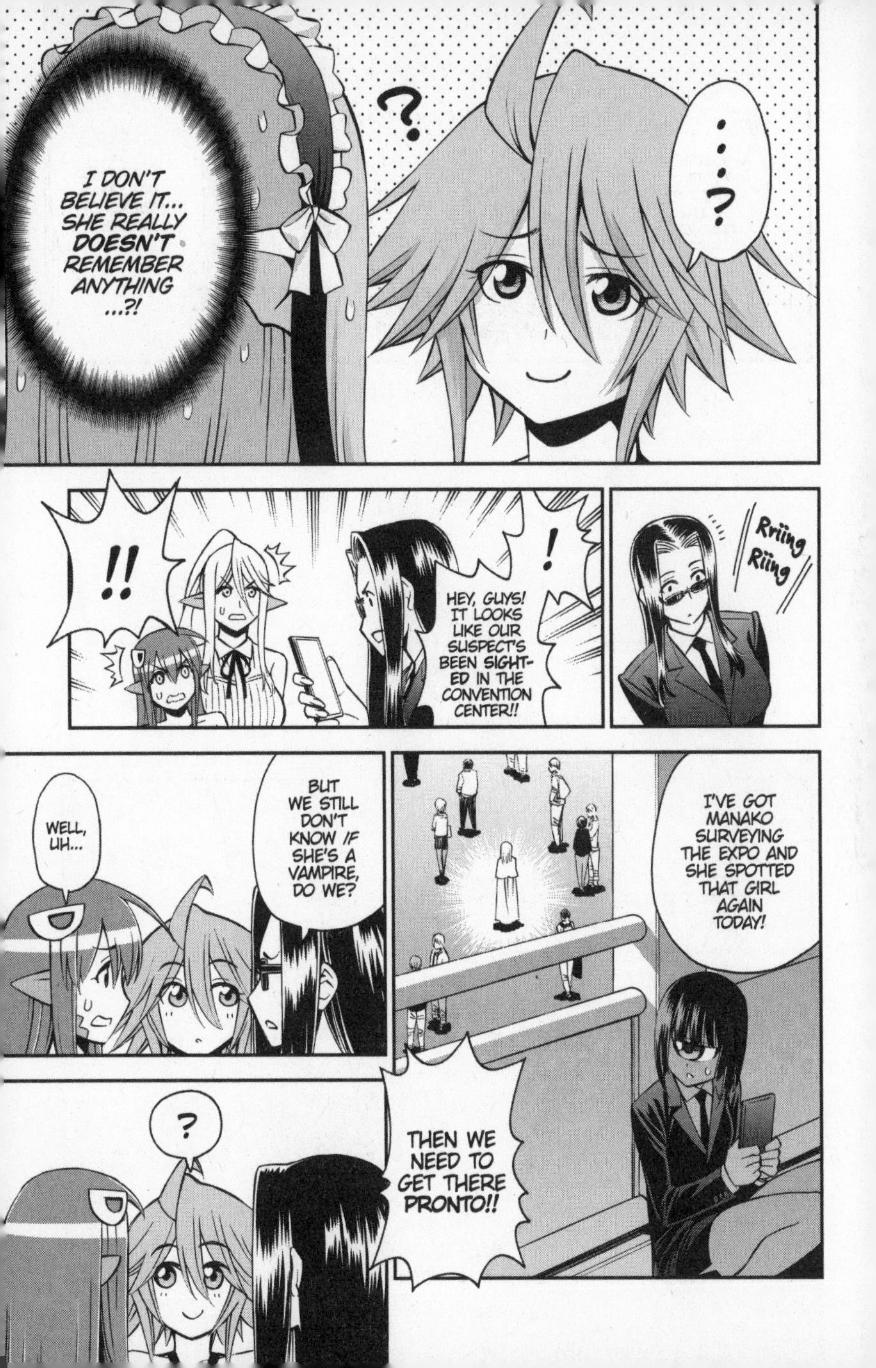
...?
?
I DON'T BELIEVE IT... SHE REALLY DOESN'T REMEMBER ANYTHING ...?!
Rriing Riing
!
HEY, GUYS! IT LOOKS LIKE OUR SUSPECT'S BEEN SIGHTED IN THE CONVENTION CENTER!!
!!
I'VE GOT MANAKO SURVEYING THE EXPO AND SHE SPOTTED THAT GIRL AGAIN TODAY!
BUT WE STILL DON'T KNOW IF SHE'S A VAMPIRE, DO WE?
WELL, UH...
THEN WE NEED TO GET THERE PRONTO!!
?

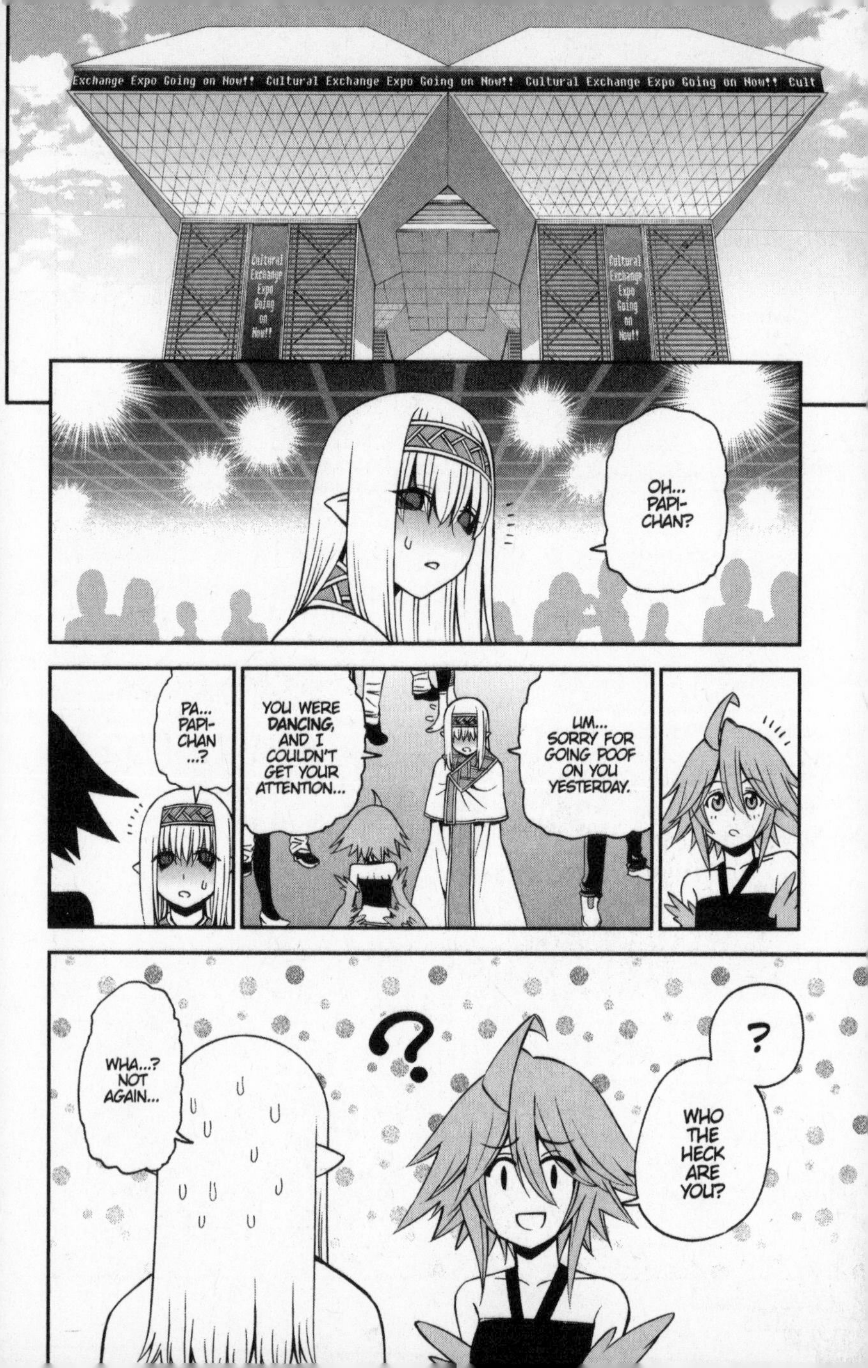
Exchange Expo Going on Now!! Cultural Exchange Expo Going on Now!! Cultural Exchange Expo Going on Now!! Cult
Cultural Exchange Expo Going on Now!!
Cultural Exchange Expo Going on Now!!
OH... PAPI-CHAN?
UM... SORRY FOR GOING POOF ON YOU YESTERDAY.
YOU WERE DANCING, AND I COULDN'T GET YOUR ATTENTION...
PA... PAPI-CHAN ...?
?
WHO THE HECK ARE YOU?
WHA...? NOT AGAIN...

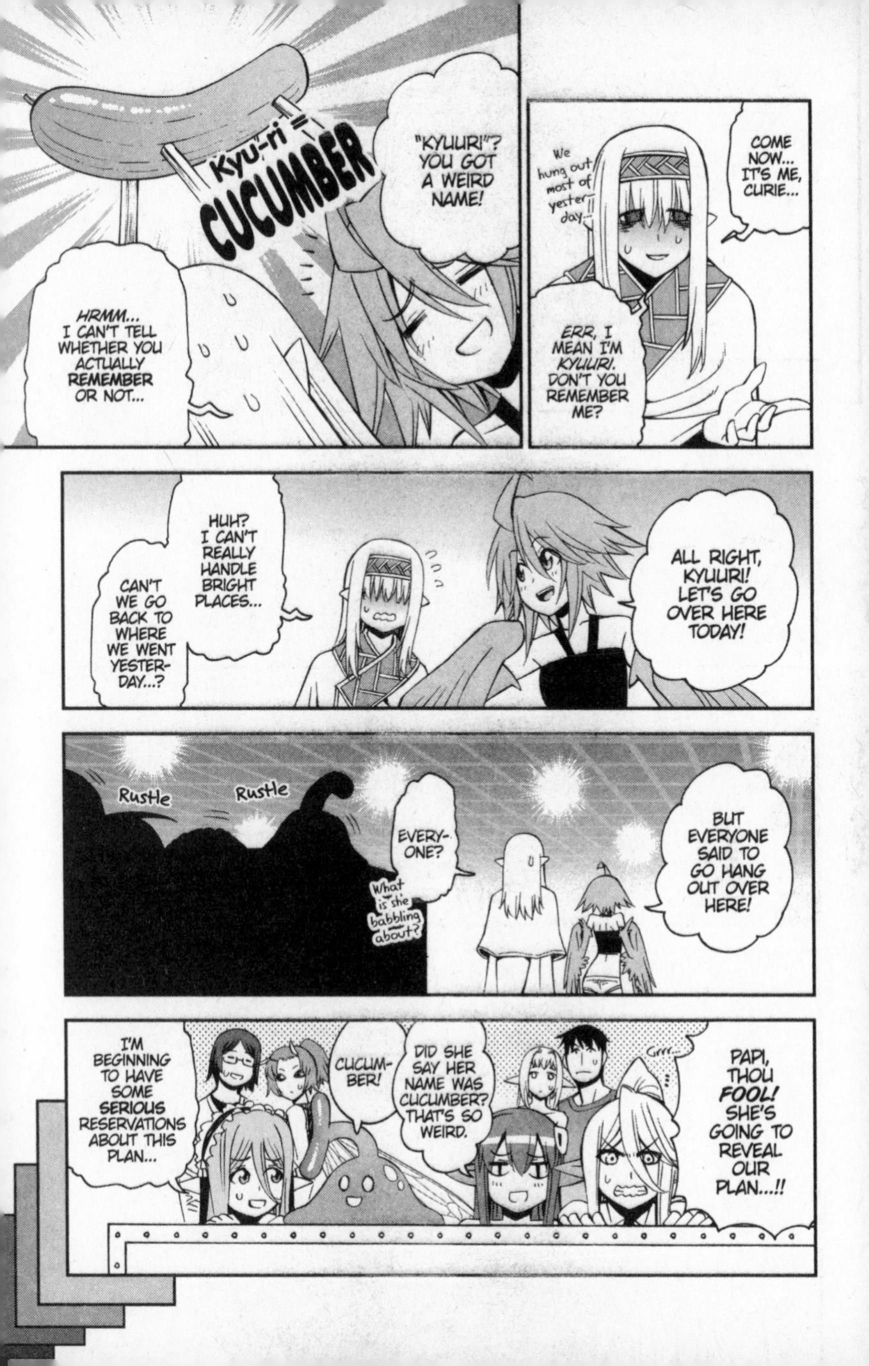
COME NOW... IT'S ME, CURIE...
We hung out most of yester-day...
ERR, I MEAN I'M KYUURI. DON'T YOU REMEMBER ME?
"KYUURI"? YOU GOT A WEIRD NAME!
Kyu-ri = CUCUMBER
HRMM... I CAN'T TELL WHETHER YOU ACTUALLY REMEMBER OR NOT...
ALL RIGHT, KYUURI! LET'S GO OVER HERE TODAY!
HUH? I CAN'T REALLY HANDLE BRIGHT PLACES...
CAN'T WE GO BACK TO WHERE WE WENT YESTER-DAY...?
BUT EVERYONE SAID TO GO HANG OUT OVER HERE!
EVERY-ONE?
What is she babbling about?
Rustle
Rustle
PAPI, THOU FOOL! SHE'S GOING TO REVEAL OUR PLAN...!!
Grrr...
DID SHE SAY HER NAME WAS CUCUMBER? THAT'S SO WEIRD.
CUCUM-BER!
I'M BEGINNING TO HAVE SOME SERIOUS RESERVATIONS ABOUT THIS PLAN...

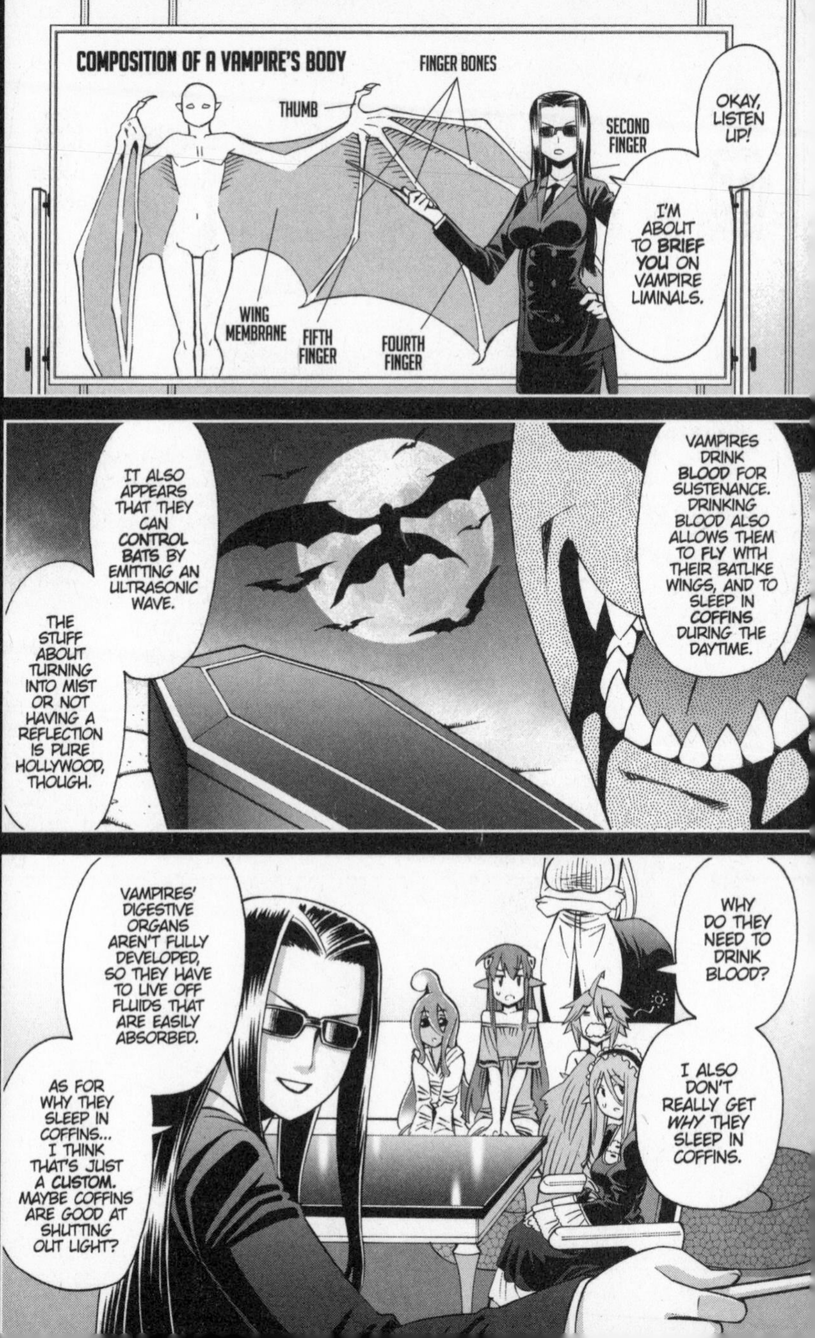
OKAY, LISTEN UP!
I'M ABOUT TO **BRIEF YOU** ON VAMPIRE LIMINALS.
COMPOSITION OF A VAMPIRE'S BODY
FINGER BONES
THUMB
SECOND FINGER
WING MEMBRANE
FIFTH FINGER
FOURTH FINGER
VAMPIRES DRINK **BLOOD** FOR SUSTENANCE. DRINKING BLOOD ALSO ALLOWS THEM TO **FLY** WITH THEIR BATLIKE WINGS, AND TO SLEEP IN **COFFINS** DURING THE DAYTIME.
IT ALSO APPEARS THAT THEY CAN **CONTROL** BATS BY EMITTING AN ULTRASONIC WAVE.
THE STUFF ABOUT TURNING INTO MIST OR NOT HAVING A REFLECTION IS PURE HOLLYWOOD, THOUGH.
WHY DO THEY NEED TO DRINK BLOOD?
I ALSO DON'T REALLY GET *WHY* THEY SLEEP IN COFFINS.
VAMPIRES' DIGESTIVE ORGANS AREN'T FULLY DEVELOPED, SO THEY HAVE TO LIVE OFF FLUIDS THAT ARE EASILY ABSORBED.
AS FOR WHY THEY SLEEP IN COFFINS... I THINK THAT'S JUST A **CUSTOM**. MAYBE COFFINS ARE GOOD AT SHUTTING OUT LIGHT?

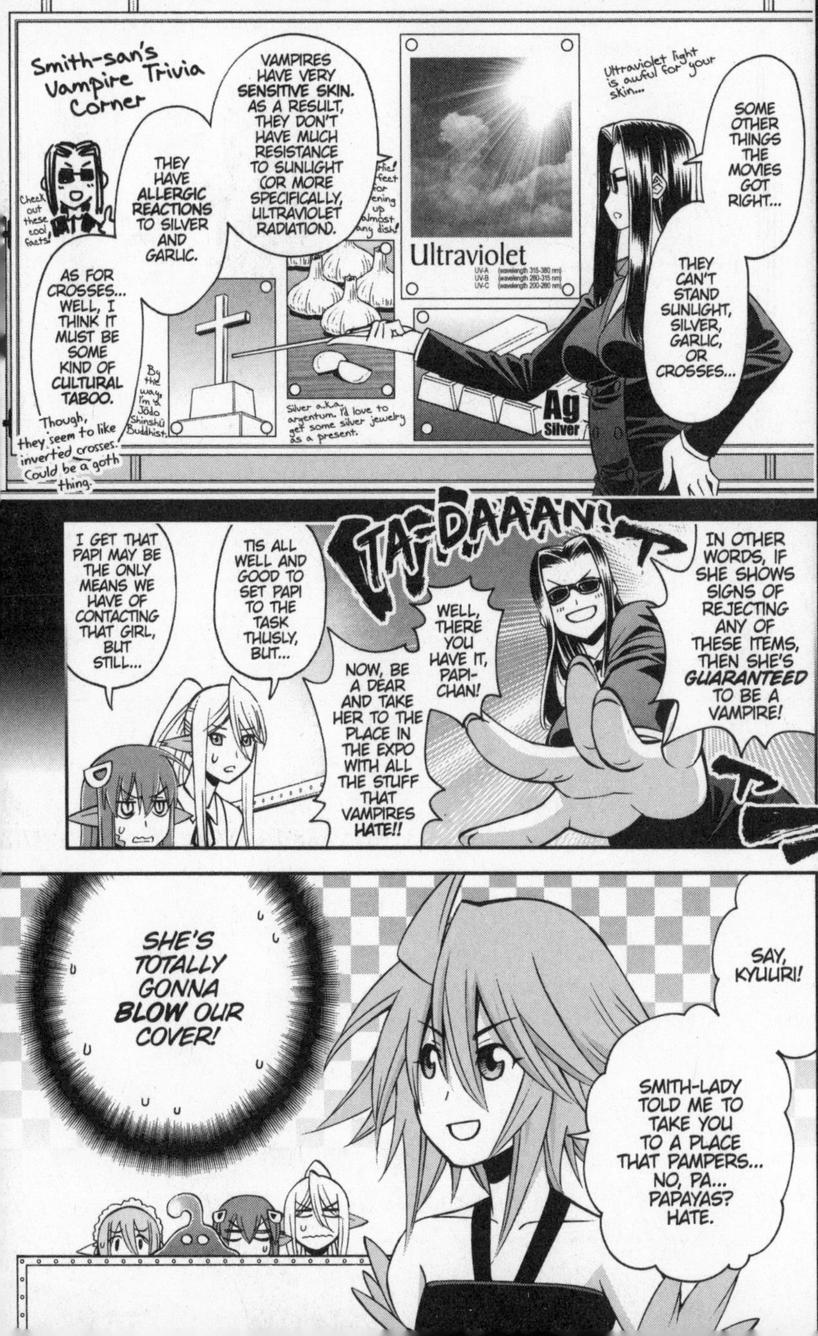
Smith-san's Vampire Trivia Corner
Ultraviolet light is awful for your skin...
SOME OTHER THINGS THE MOVIES GOT RIGHT...
THEY CAN'T STAND SUNLIGHT, SILVER, GARLIC, OR CROSSES...
Ultraviolet
UV-A (wavelength 315-380 nm)
UV-B (wavelength 280-315 nm)
UV-C (wavelength 200-280 nm)
Ag
Silver
Silver a.k.a. argentum. I'd love to get some silver jewelry as a present.
VAMPIRES HAVE VERY SENSITIVE SKIN. AS A RESULT, THEY DON'T HAVE MUCH RESISTANCE TO SUNLIGHT (OR MORE SPECIFICALLY, ULTRAVIOLET RADIATION).
THEY HAVE ALLERGIC REACTIONS TO SILVER AND GARLIC.
Check out these cool facts!
AS FOR CROSSES... WELL, I THINK IT MUST BE SOME KIND OF CULTURAL TABOO.
By the way, I'm a Jōdo Shinshū Buddhist.
Though, they seem to like inverted crosses. Could be a goth thing.
IN OTHER WORDS, IF SHE SHOWS SIGNS OF REJECTING ANY OF THESE ITEMS, THEN SHE'S GUARANTEED TO BE A VAMPIRE!
TA-DAAAN!
WELL, THERE YOU HAVE IT, PAPI-CHAN!
NOW, BE A DEAR AND TAKE HER TO THE PLACE IN THE EXPO WITH ALL THE STUFF THAT VAMPIRES HATE!!
TIS ALL WELL AND GOOD TO SET PAPI TO THE TASK THUSLY, BUT...
I GET THAT PAPI MAY BE THE ONLY MEANS WE HAVE OF CONTACTING THAT GIRL, BUT STILL...
SAY, KYUURI!
SMITH-LADY TOLD ME TO TAKE YOU TO A PLACE THAT PAMPERS... NO, PA... PAPAYAS? HATE.
SHE'S TOTALLY GONNA BLOW OUR COVER!

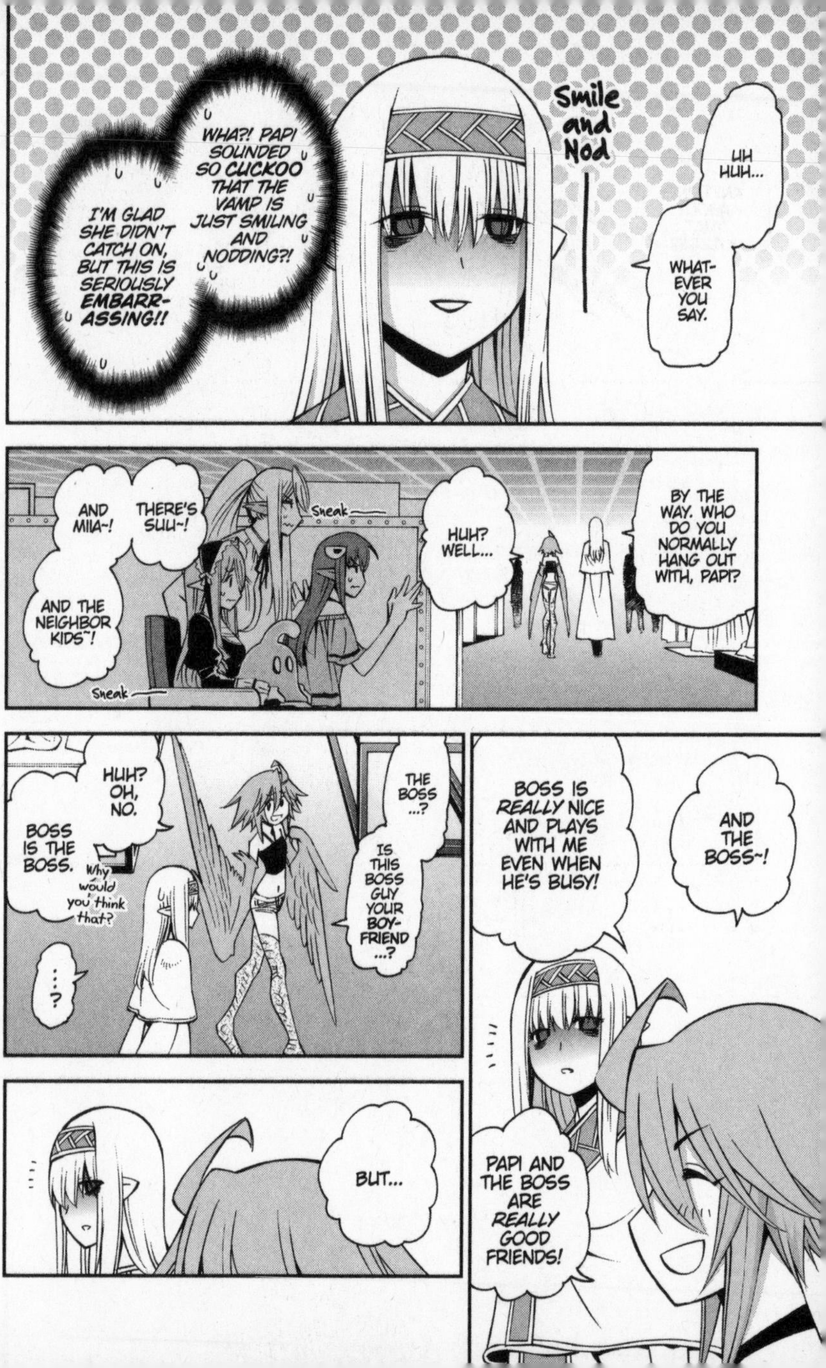

UH HUH...
WHATEVER YOU SAY.
Smile and Nod
WHA?! PAPI SOUNDED SO CUCKOO THAT THE VAMP IS JUST SMILING AND NODDING?!
I'M GLAD SHE DIDN'T CATCH ON, BUT THIS IS SERIOUSLY EMBARRASSING!!
BY THE WAY. WHO DO YOU NORMALLY HANG OUT WITH, PAPI?
HUH? WELL...
Sneak
THERE'S SUU~!
AND MIIA~!
AND THE NEIGHBOR KIDS~!
Sneak
AND THE BOSS~!
BOSS IS REALLY NICE AND PLAYS WITH ME EVEN WHEN HE'S BUSY!
PAPI AND THE BOSS ARE REALLY GOOD FRIENDS!
THE BOSS ...?
IS THIS BOSS GUY YOUR BOYFRIEND ...?
HUH? OH, NO.
BOSS IS THE BOSS.
Why would you think that?
...?
BUT...

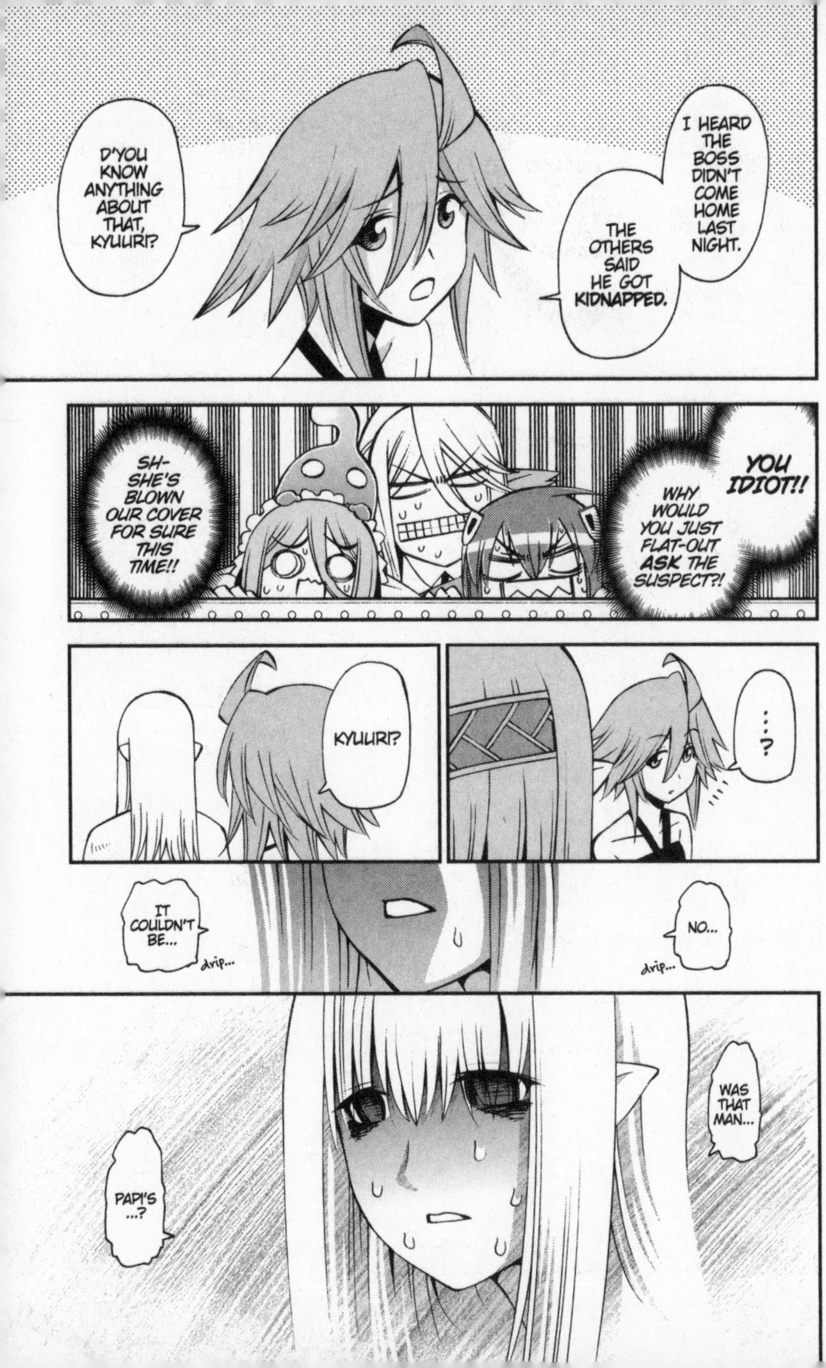
I HEARD THE BOSS DIDN'T COME HOME LAST NIGHT.
THE OTHERS SAID HE GOT KIDNAPPED.
D'YOU KNOW ANYTHING ABOUT THAT, KYUURI?
YOU IDIOT!!
WHY WOULD YOU JUST FLAT-OUT ASK THE SUSPECT?!
SH-SHE'S BLOWN OUR COVER FOR SURE THIS TIME!!
...?
KYUURI?
NO...
drip...
IT COULDN'T BE...
drip...
WAS THAT MAN...
PAPI'S ...?

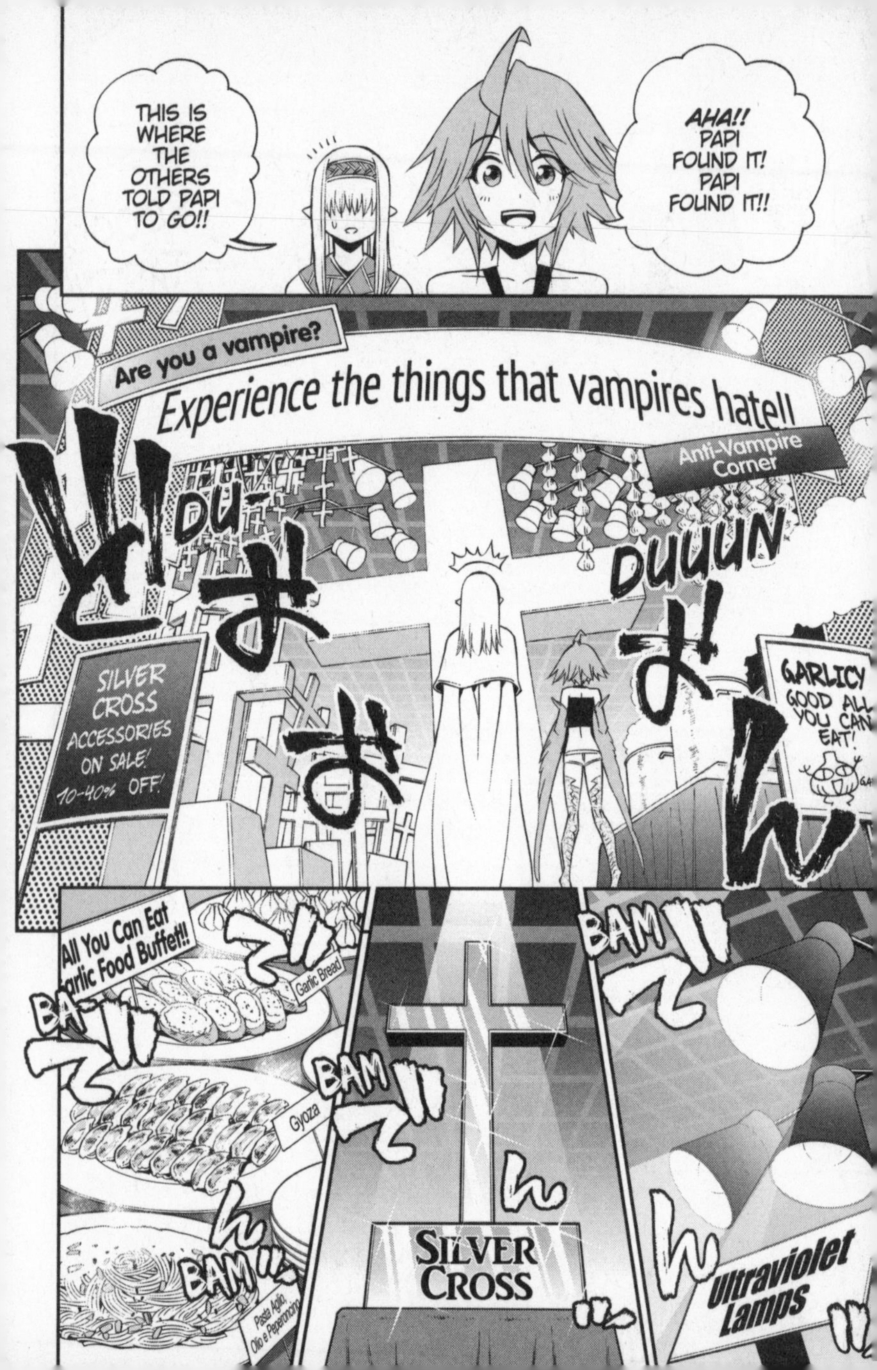
AHA!! PAPI FOUND IT! PAPI FOUND IT!!
THIS IS WHERE THE OTHERS TOLD PAPI TO GO!!
Are you a vampire?
Experience the things that vampires hate!!
Anti-Vampire Corner
DUUUN
DU
GARLICY GOOD ALL YOU CAN EAT!
SILVER CROSS ACCESSORIES ON SALE! 10-40% OFF!
BAM
Ultraviolet Lamps
BAM
SILVER CROSS
All You Can Eat Garlic Food Buffet!!
Garlic Bread
BA-
Gyoza
BAM
Pasta Aglio, Olio e Peperoncino

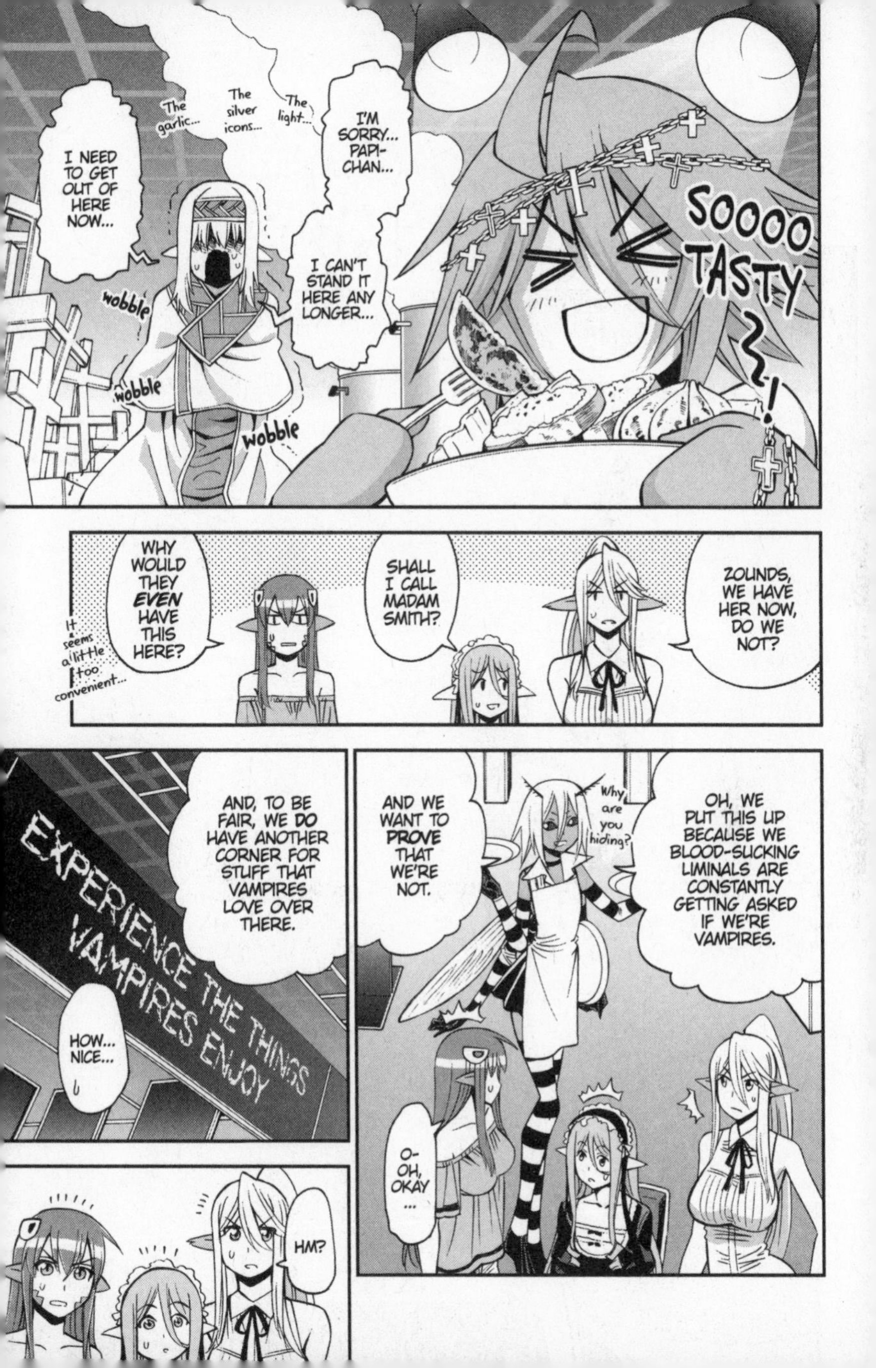
SOOOO TASTY~!
I'M SORRY... PAPI-CHAN...
The light...
The silver icons...
The garlic...
I CAN'T STAND IT HERE ANY LONGER...
I NEED TO GET OUT OF HERE NOW...
wobble
wobble
wobble
ZOUNDS, WE HAVE HER NOW, DO WE NOT?
SHALL I CALL MADAM SMITH?
WHY WOULD THEY EVEN HAVE THIS HERE?
It seems a little too convenient...
OH, WE PUT THIS UP BECAUSE WE BLOOD-SUCKING LIMINALS ARE CONSTANTLY GETTING ASKED IF WE'RE VAMPIRES.
Why are you hiding?
AND WE WANT TO PROVE THAT WE'RE NOT.
O-OH, OKAY...
AND, TO BE FAIR, WE DO HAVE ANOTHER CORNER FOR STUFF THAT VAMPIRES LOVE OVER THERE.
EXPERIENCE THE THINGS VAMPIRES ENJOY
HOW... NICE...
HM?

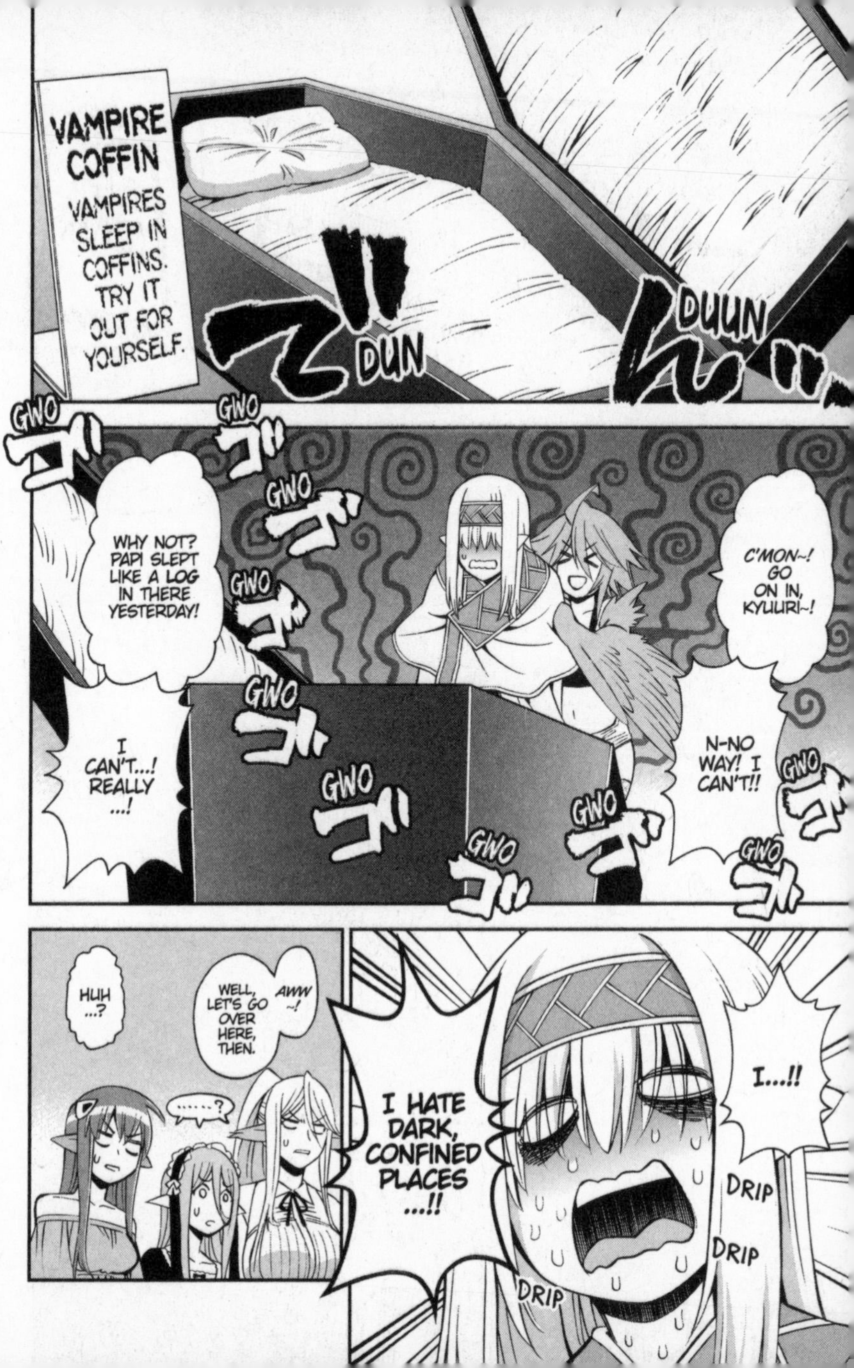
DUUN
DUN
VAMPIRE COFFIN
VAMPIRES SLEEP IN COFFINS. TRY IT OUT FOR YOURSELF.
GWO
C'MON~! GO ON IN, KYUURI~!
GWO
GWO
N-NO WAY! I CAN'T!!
GWO
GWO
GWO
GWO
GWO
GWO
WHY NOT? PAPI SLEPT LIKE A LOG IN THERE YESTERDAY!
GWO
I CAN'T...! REALLY ...!
I...!!
I HATE DARK, CONFINED PLACES ...!!
DRIP
DRIP
DRIP
AWW ~!
WELL, LET'S GO OVER HERE, THEN.
HUH ...?
......?

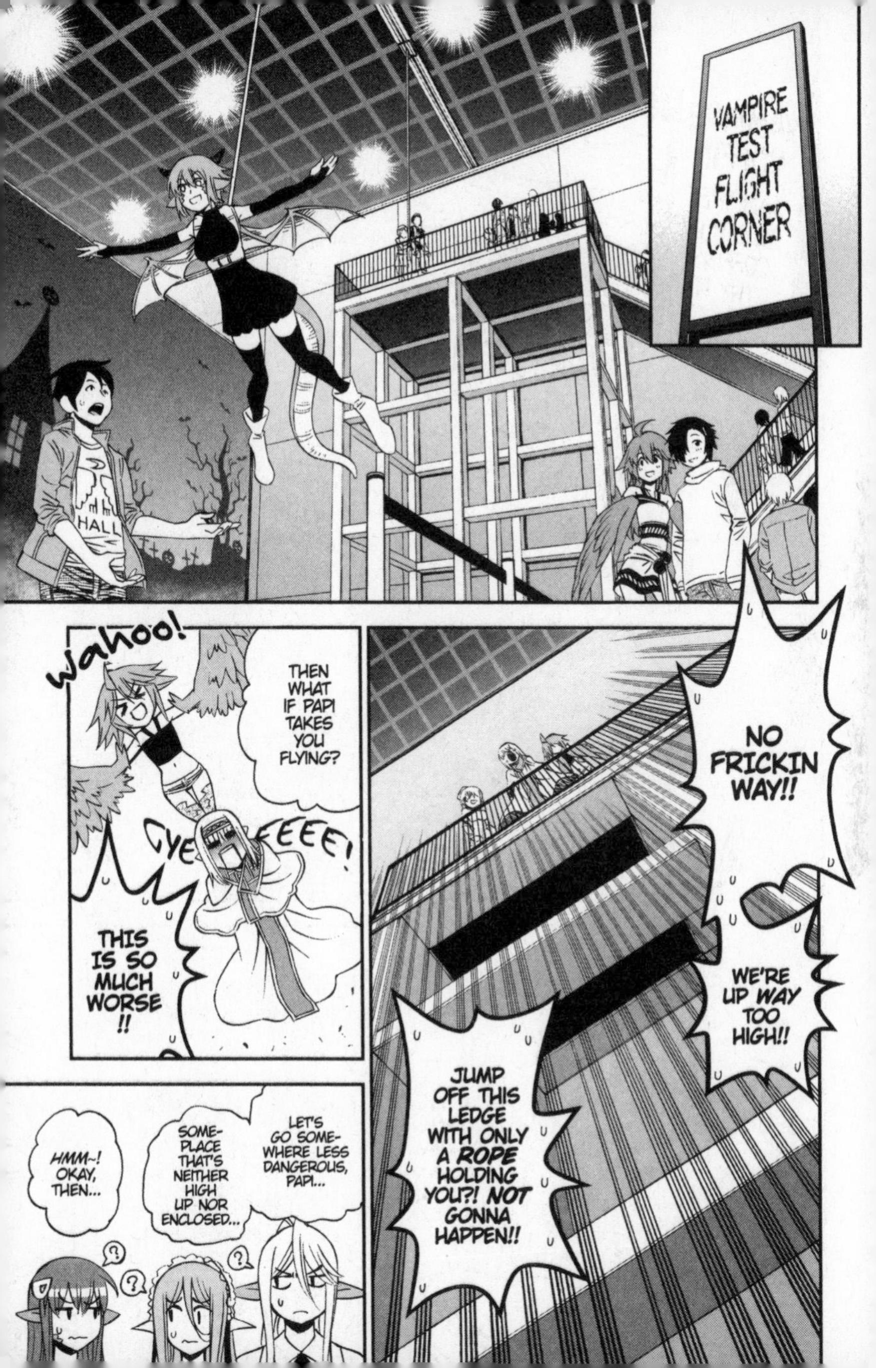
VAMPIRE TEST FLIGHT CORNER
HALL
NO FRICKIN WAY!!
WE'RE UP WAY TOO HIGH!!
JUMP OFF THIS LEDGE WITH ONLY A ROPE HOLDING YOU?! NOT GONNA HAPPEN!!
THEN WHAT IF PAPI TAKES YOU FLYING?
wahoo!
GYEEEEE!
THIS IS SO MUCH WORSE!!
LET'S GO SOME-WHERE LESS DANGEROUS, PAPI...
SOME-PLACE THAT'S NEITHER HIGH UP NOR ENCLOSED...
HMM~! OKAY, THEN...
?
?
?

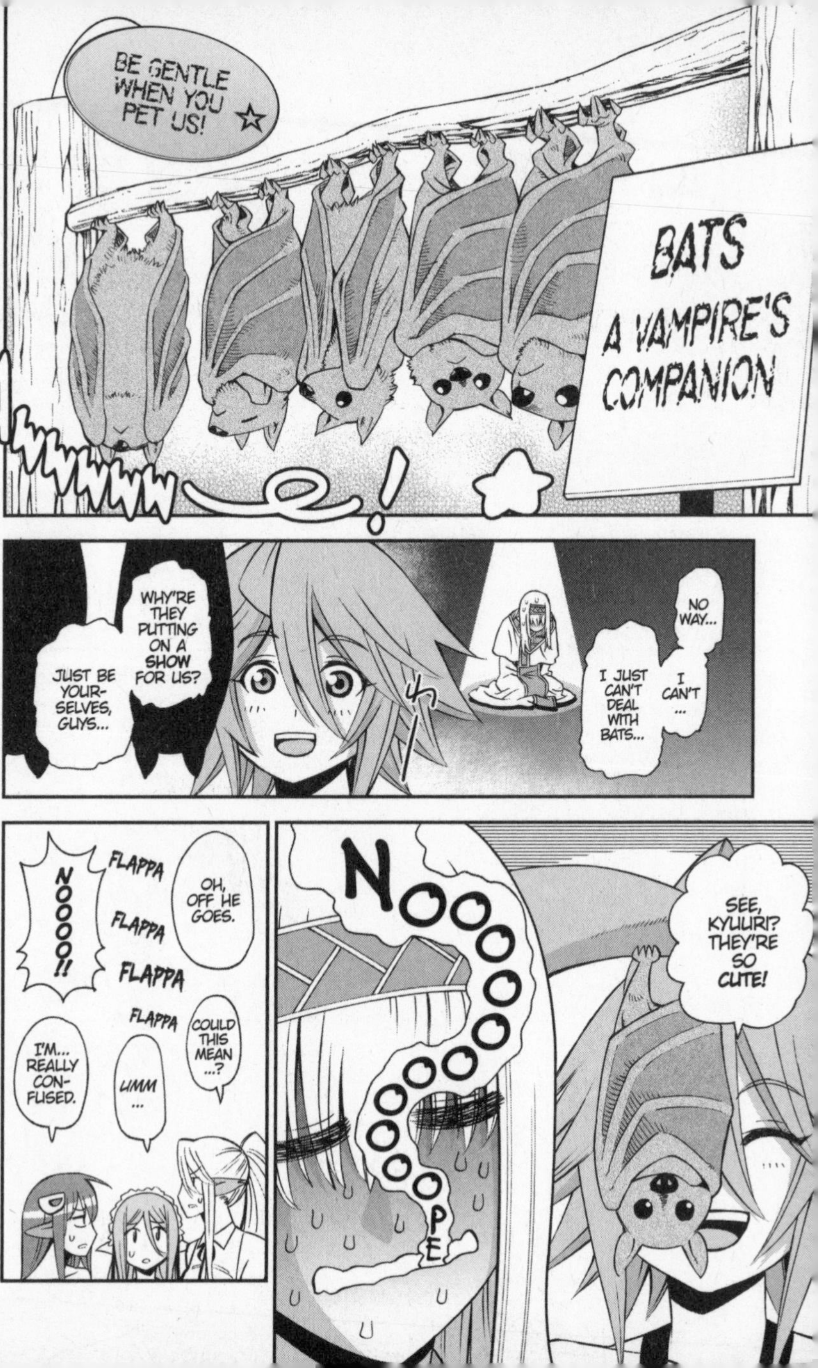
BE GENTLE WHEN YOU PET US! ☆
BATS
A VAMPIRE'S COMPANION
AWWWWWWW~!
NO WAY...
I CAN'T...
I JUST CAN'T DEAL WITH BATS...
WHY'RE THEY PUTTING ON A SHOW FOR US?
JUST BE YOUR-SELVES, GUYS...
SEE, KYUURI? THEY'RE SO CUTE!
NOOOOOOOOOOOOOOOOOPE
OH, OFF HE GOES.
FLAPPA
FLAPPA
FLAPPA
FLAPPA
NOOOOO!!
COULD THIS MEAN ...?
UMM ...
I'M... REALLY CON-FUSED.

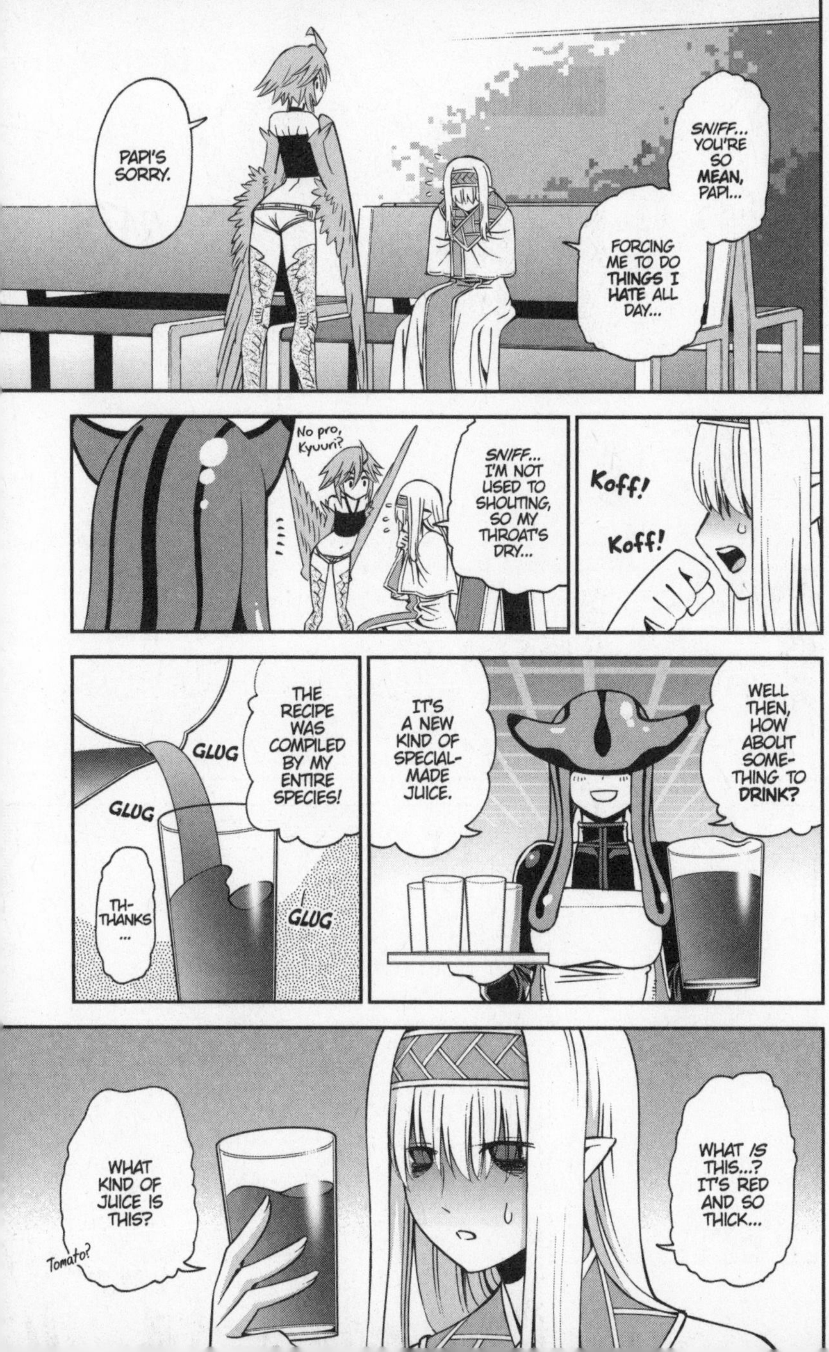
SNIFF... YOU'RE SO MEAN, PAPI...
FORCING ME TO DO THINGS I HATE ALL DAY...
PAPI'S SORRY.
Koff!
Koff!
SNIFF... I'M NOT USED TO SHOUTING, SO MY THROAT'S DRY...
No pro, Kyuuri?
WELL THEN, HOW ABOUT SOMETHING TO DRINK?
IT'S A NEW KIND OF SPECIAL-MADE JUICE.
THE RECIPE WAS COMPILED BY MY ENTIRE SPECIES!
GLUG
GLUG
GLUG
TH-THANKS...
WHAT IS THIS...? IT'S RED AND SO THICK...
WHAT KIND OF JUICE IS THIS?
Tomato?

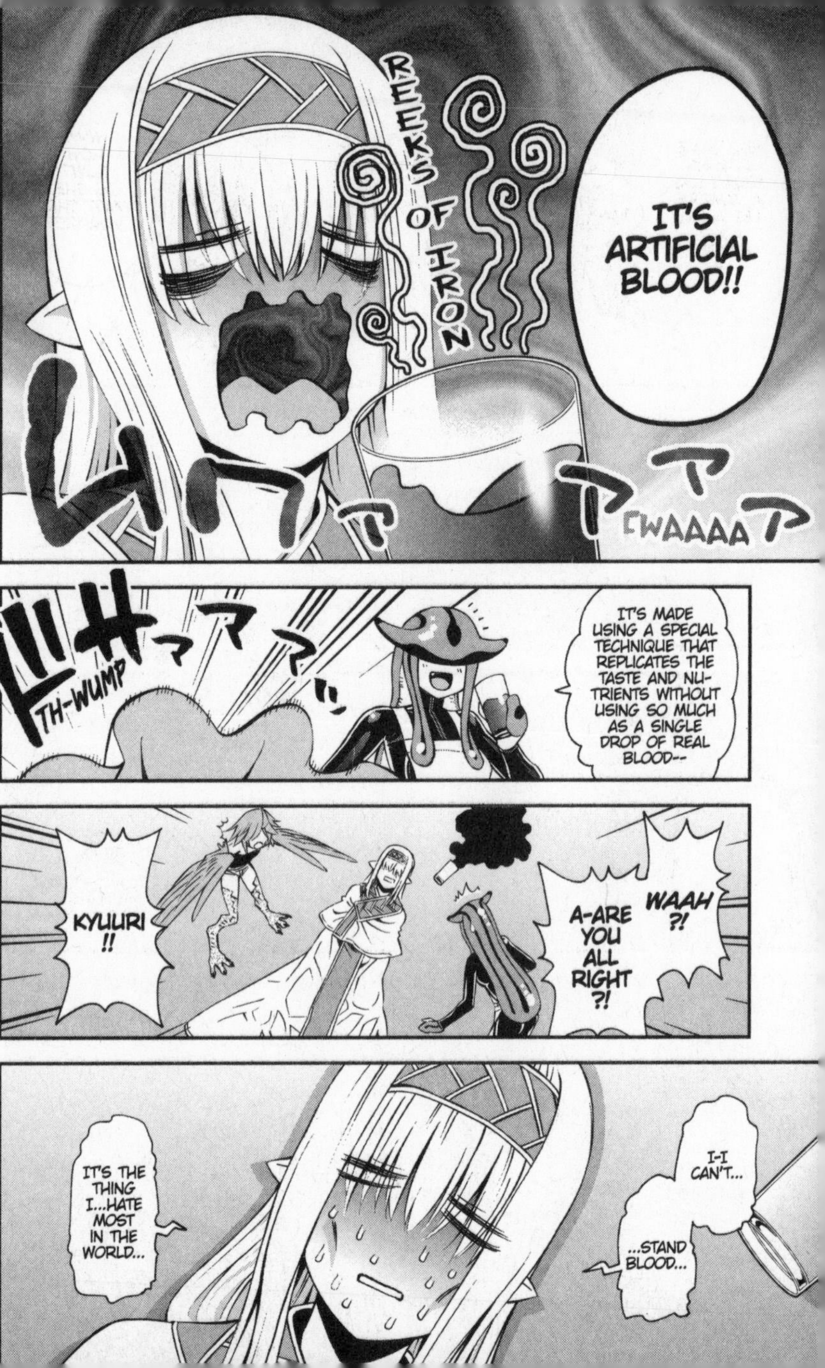
IT'S ARTIFICIAL BLOOD!!
REEKS OF IRON
FWAAAA
IT'S MADE USING A SPECIAL TECHNIQUE THAT REPLICATES THE TASTE AND NU-TRIENTS WITHOUT USING SO MUCH AS A SINGLE DROP OF REAL BLOOD--
TH-WUMP
WAAH ?!
A-ARE YOU ALL RIGHT ?!
KYUURI !!
I-I CAN'T...
...STAND BLOOD...
IT'S THE THING I...HATE MOST IN THE WORLD...

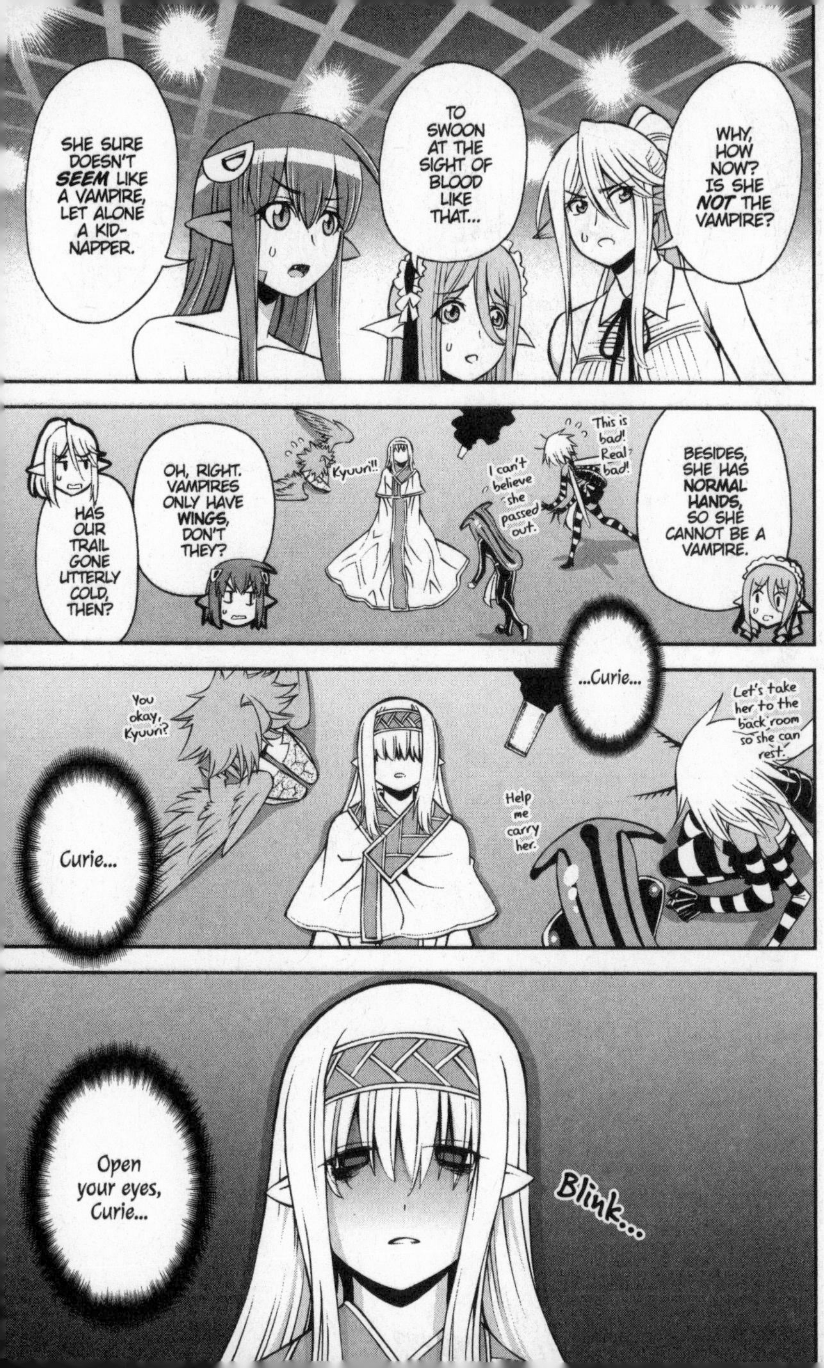
WHY, HOW NOW? IS SHE NOT THE VAMPIRE?
TO SWOON AT THE SIGHT OF BLOOD LIKE THAT...
SHE SURE DOESN'T SEEM LIKE A VAMPIRE, LET ALONE A KID-NAPPER.
BESIDES, SHE HAS NORMAL HANDS, SO SHE CANNOT BE A VAMPIRE.
This is bad! Real bad!
I can't believe she passed out.
Kyuuri!!
OH, RIGHT. VAMPIRES ONLY HAVE WINGS, DON'T THEY?
HAS OUR TRAIL GONE UTTERLY COLD, THEN?
Let's take her to the back room so she can rest.
...Curie...
Help me carry her.
You okay, Kyuuri?
Curie...
Blink...
Open your eyes, Curie...

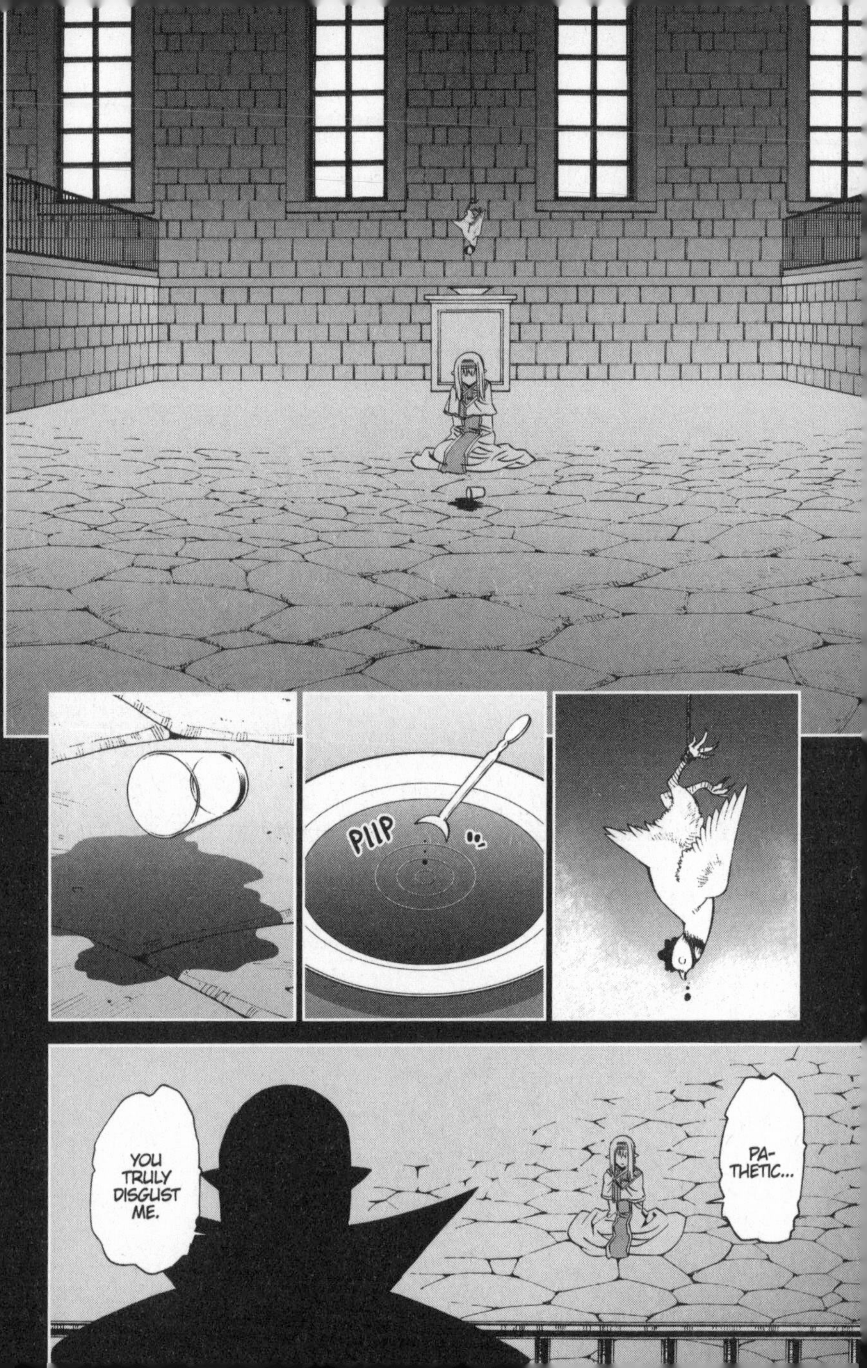
PIIP
PA-THETIC...
YOU TRULY DISGUST ME.

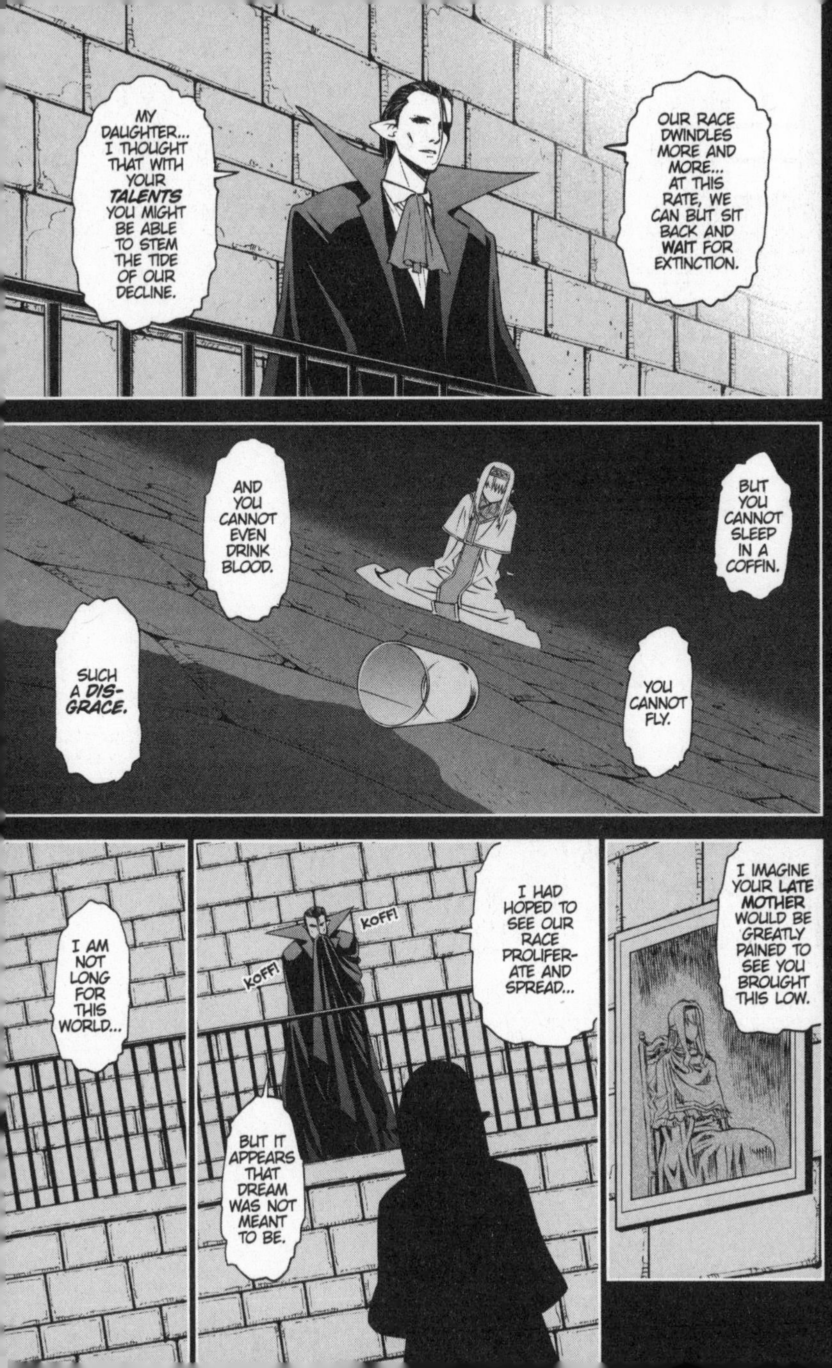
OUR RACE DWINDLES MORE AND MORE... AT THIS RATE, WE CAN BUT SIT BACK AND WAIT FOR EXTINCTION.
MY DAUGHTER... I THOUGHT THAT WITH YOUR ***TALENTS*** YOU MIGHT BE ABLE TO STEM THE TIDE OF OUR DECLINE.
BUT YOU CANNOT SLEEP IN A COFFIN.
AND YOU CANNOT EVEN DRINK BLOOD.
YOU CANNOT FLY.
SUCH A ***DIS-GRACE.***
I IMAGINE YOUR **LATE MOTHER** WOULD BE GREATLY PAINED TO SEE YOU BROUGHT THIS LOW.
I HAD HOPED TO SEE OUR RACE PROLIFER-ATE AND SPREAD...
KOFF!
KOFF!
BUT IT APPEARS THAT DREAM WAS NOT MEANT TO BE.
I AM NOT LONG FOR THIS WORLD...

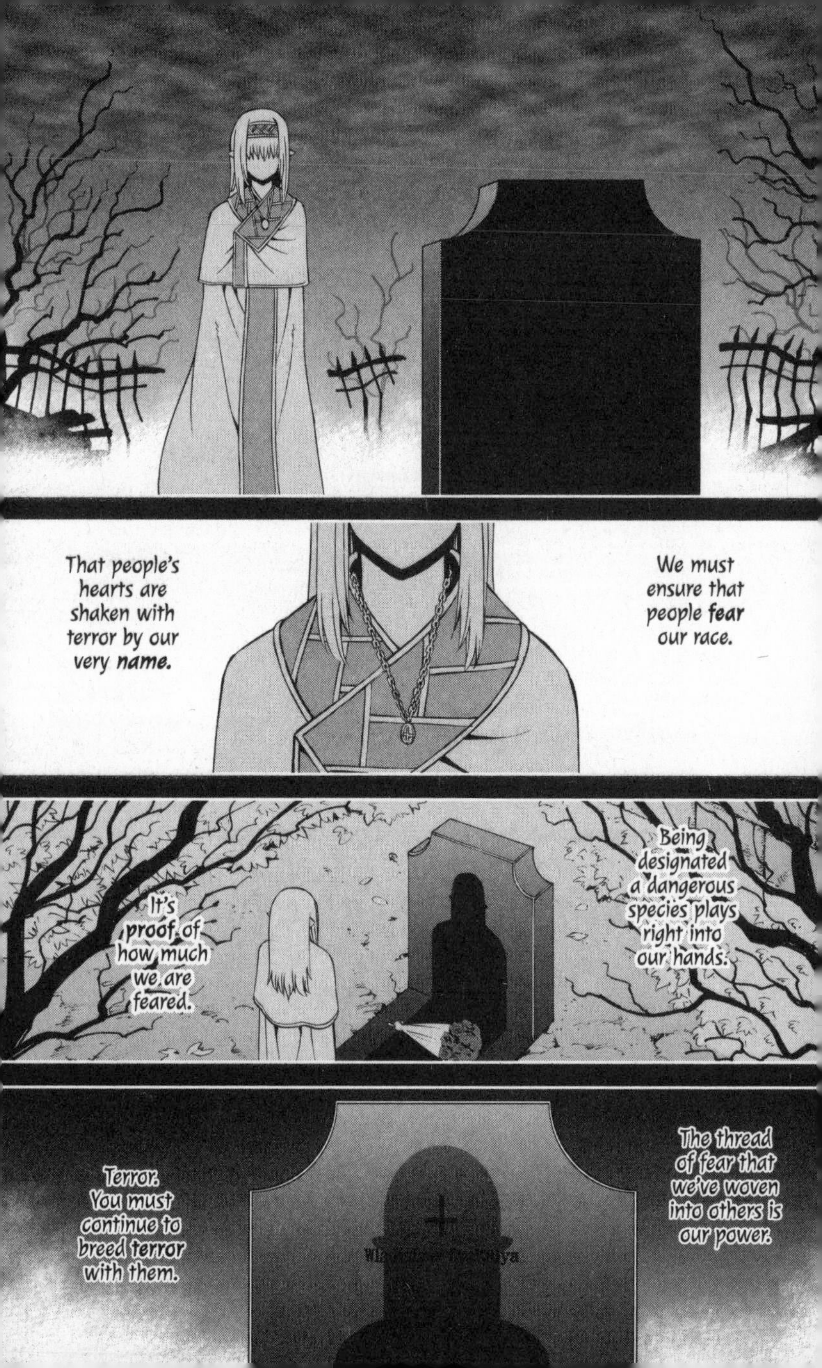
We must ensure that people fear our race.
That people's hearts are shaken with terror by our very name.
Being designated a dangerous species plays right into our hands.
It's proof of how much we are feared.
The thread of fear that we've woven into others is our power.
Terror. You must continue to breed terror with them.

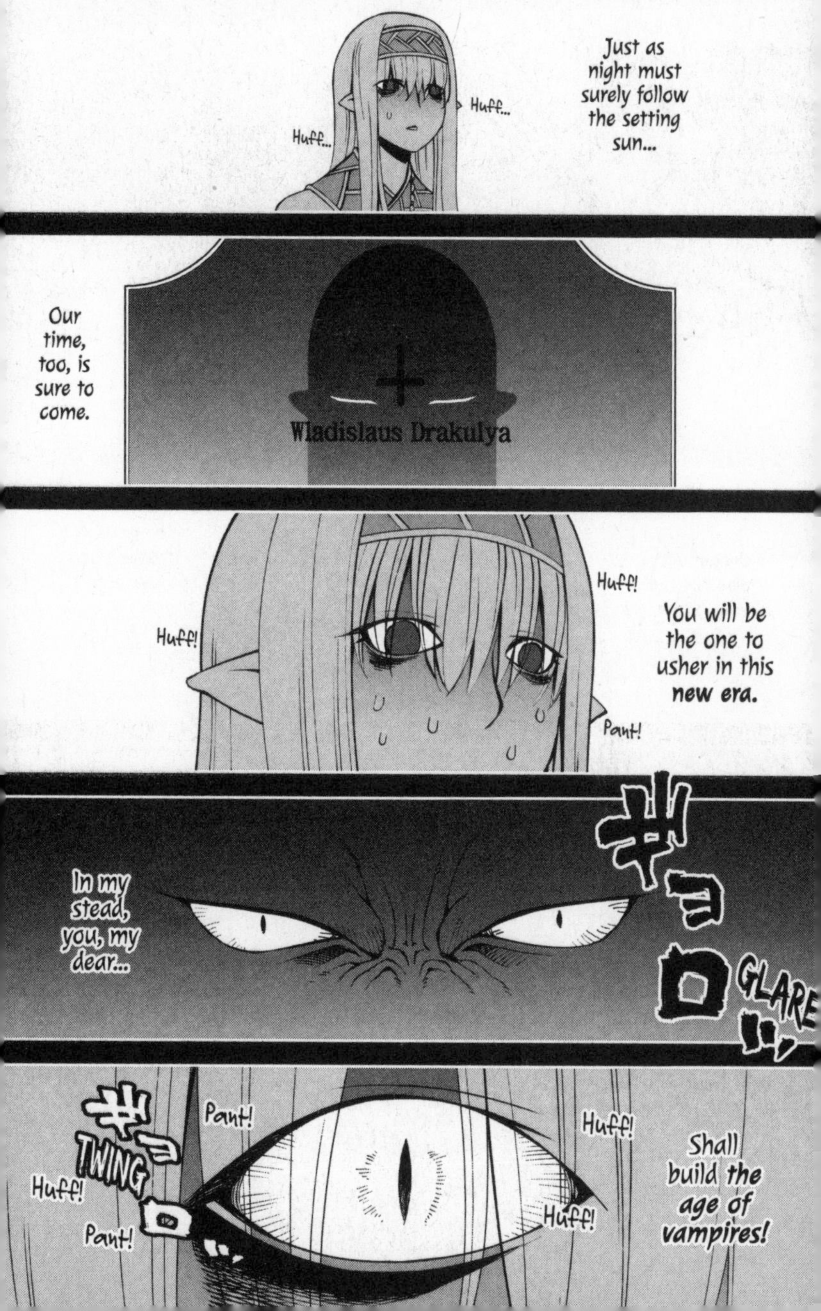

Just as night must surely follow the setting sun...
Huff...
Huff...
Our time, too, is sure to come.
Wladislaus Drakulya
Huff!
You will be the one to usher in this new era.
Huff!
Pant!
ギョロ
GLARE
In my stead, you, my dear...
Huff!
Shall build the age of vampires!
Pant!
ギョロ
TWING
Huff!
Huff!
Pant!

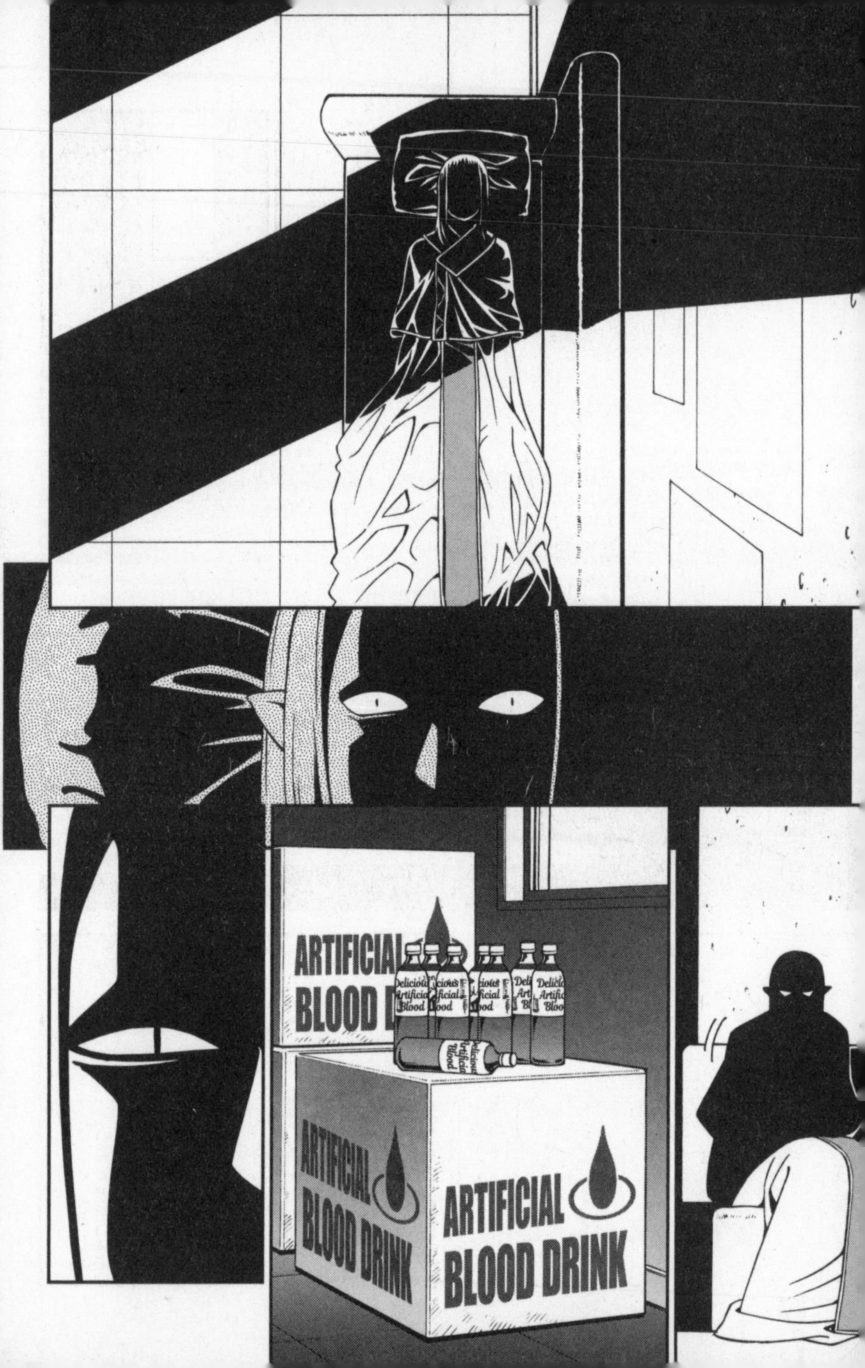
ARTIFICIAL BLOOD DRINK
ARTIFICIAL BLOOD DRINK
Delicious Artificial Blood

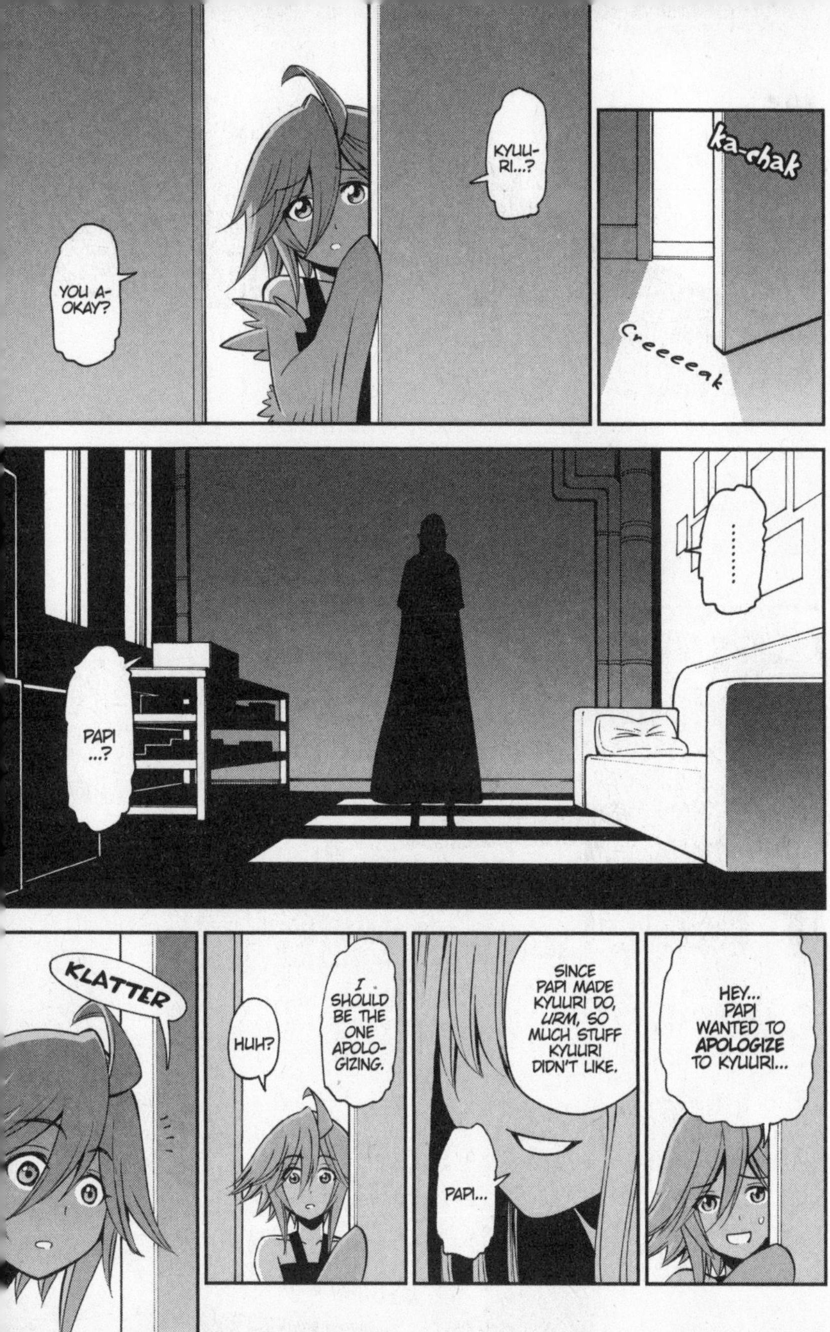

ka-chak
Creeeeeak
KYUU-RI...?
YOU A-OKAY?
......
PAPI ...?
HEY... PAPI WANTED TO APOLOGIZE TO KYUURI...
SINCE PAPI MADE KYUURI DO, *URM*, SO MUCH STUFF KYUURI DIDN'T LIKE.
PAPI...
I SHOULD BE THE ONE APOLOGIZING.
HUH?
KLATTER

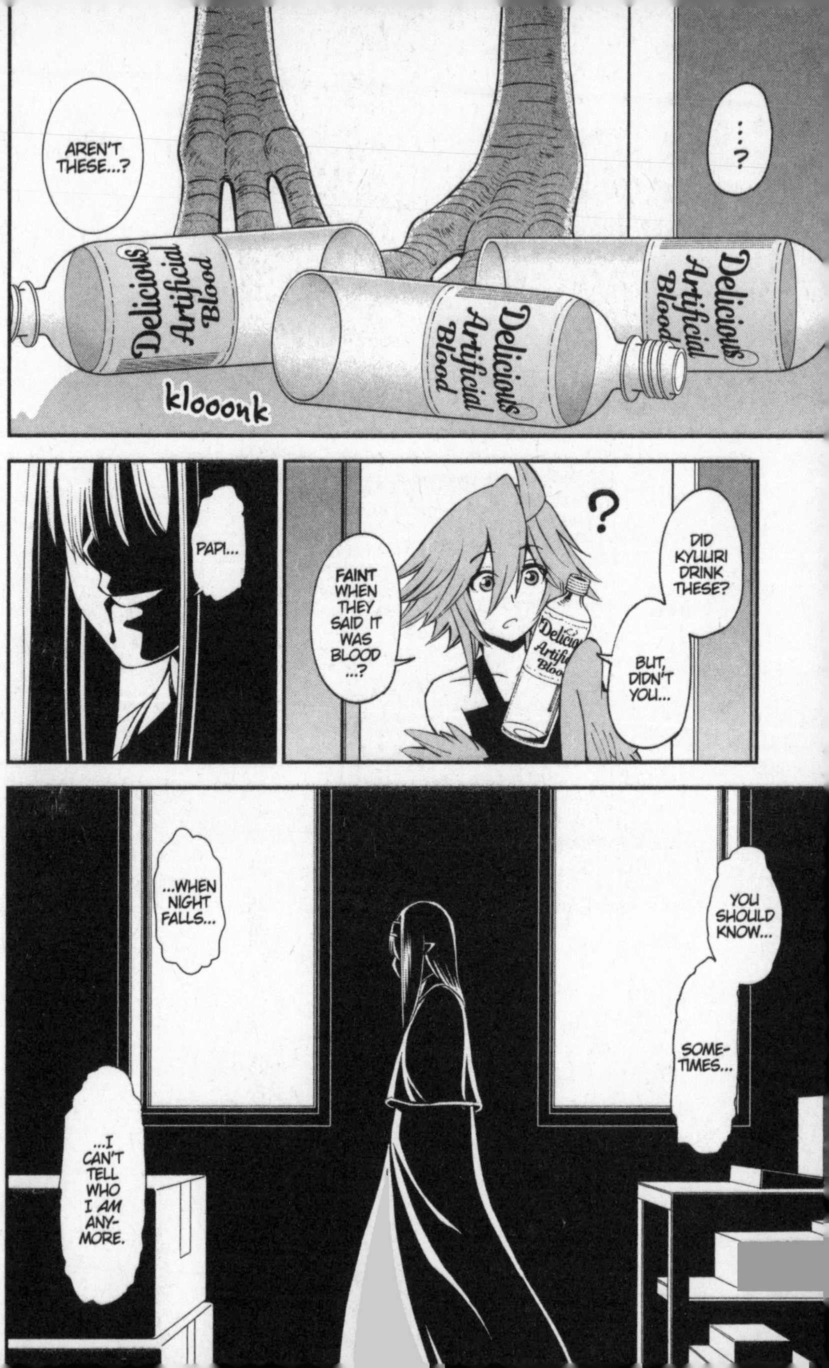
...?
AREN'T THESE...?
Delicious Artificial Blood
Delicious Artificial Blood
Delicious Artificial Blood
kloooonk
?
DID KYUURI DRINK THESE?
BUT, DIDN'T YOU...
FAINT WHEN THEY SAID IT WAS BLOOD ...?
Delicious Artificial Blood
PAPI...
YOU SHOULD KNOW...
...WHEN NIGHT FALLS...
SOME-TIMES...
...I CAN'T TELL WHO I *AM* ANYMORE.

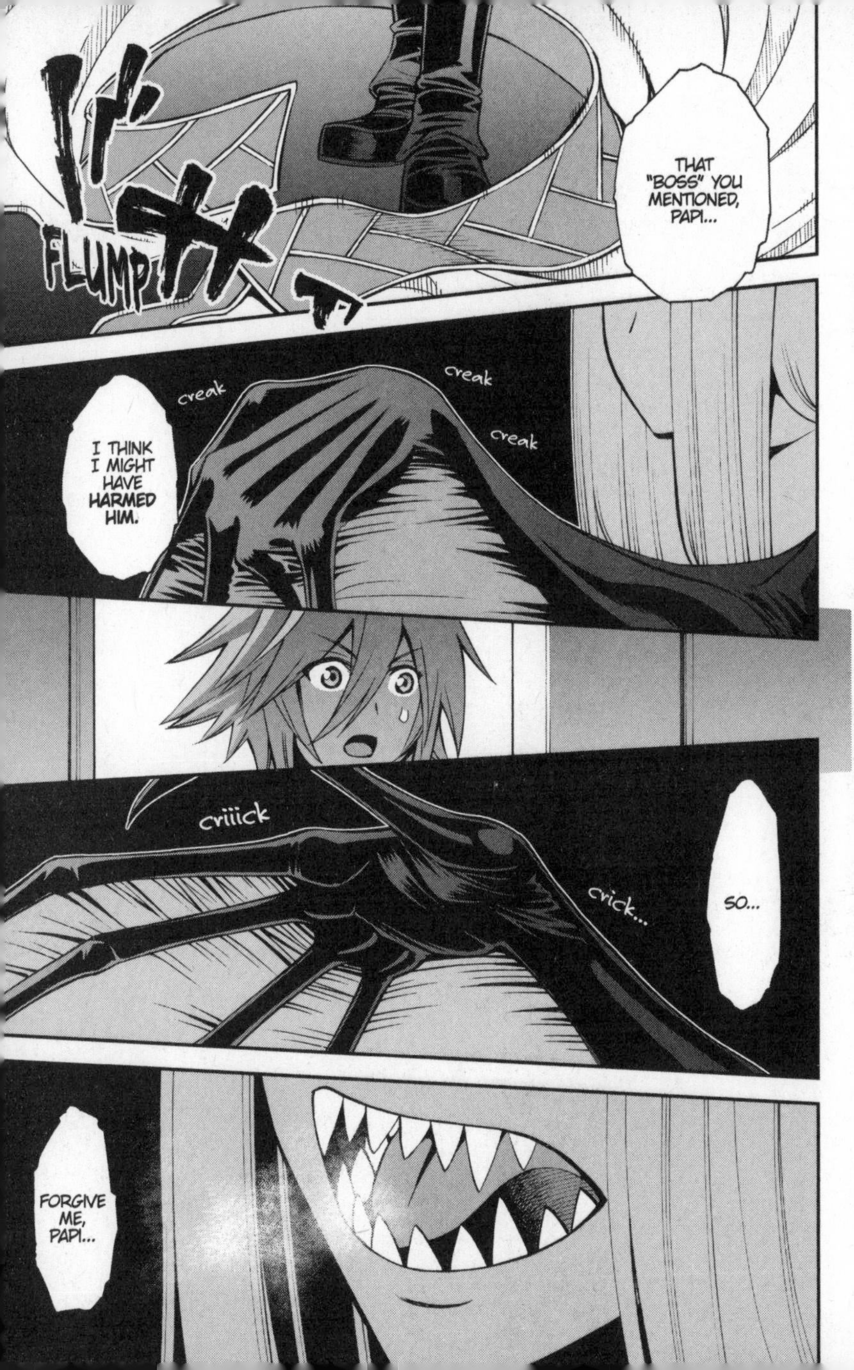
THAT "BOSS" YOU MENTIONED, PAPI...
FLUMP
creak
creak
creak
I THINK I MIGHT HAVE HARMED HIM.
SO...
crick...
criiick
FORGIVE ME, PAPI...

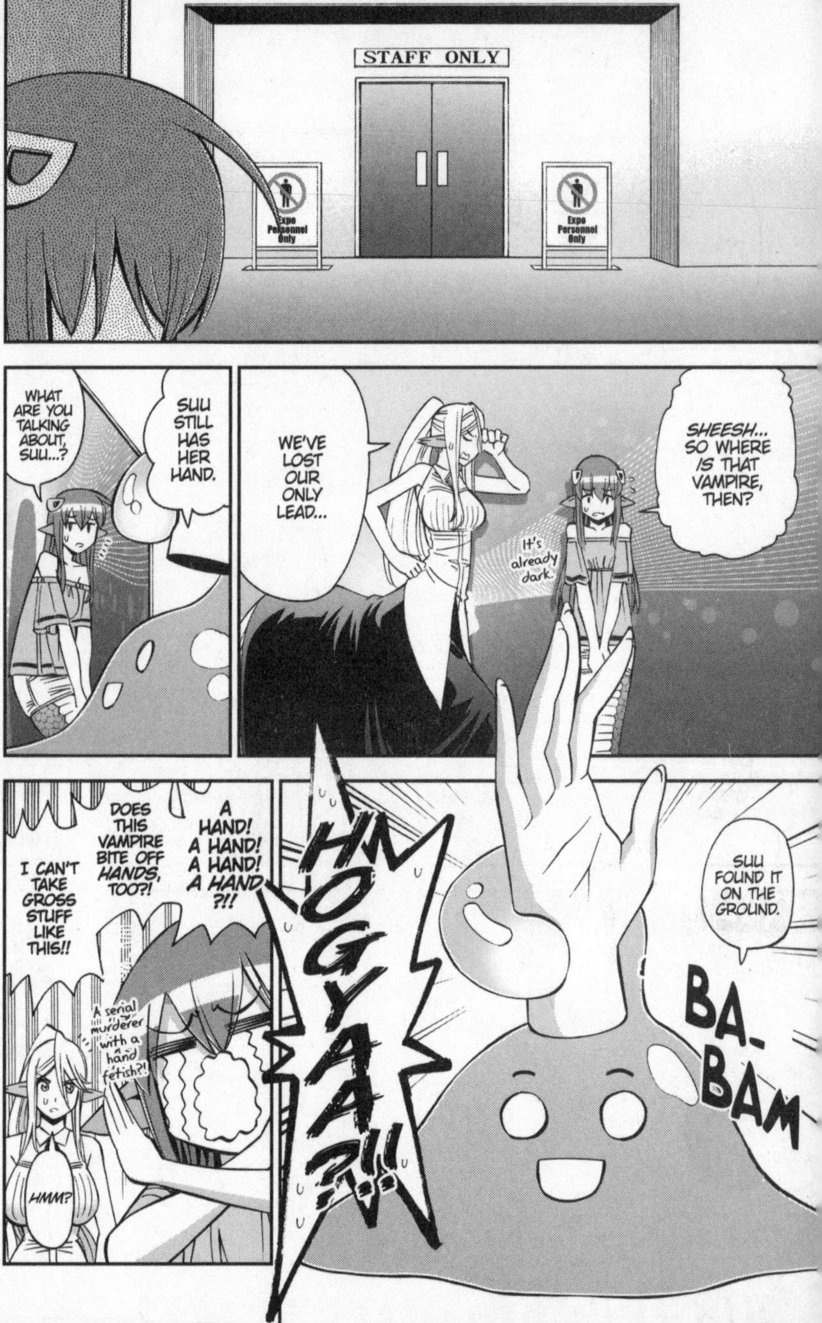
STAFF ONLY
Expo Personnel Only
Expo Personnel Only
SHEESH... SO WHERE IS THAT VAMPIRE, THEN?
It's already dark.
WE'VE LOST OUR ONLY LEAD...
SUU STILL HAS HER HAND.
WHAT ARE YOU TALKING ABOUT, SUU...?
SUU FOUND IT ON THE GROUND.
BA-BAM
HMOGYAA?!!
A HAND! A HAND! A HAND! A HAND?!!
DOES THIS VAMPIRE BITE OFF HANDS, TOO?!
I CAN'T TAKE GROSS STUFF LIKE THIS!!
A serial murderer with a hand fetish?!
HMM?

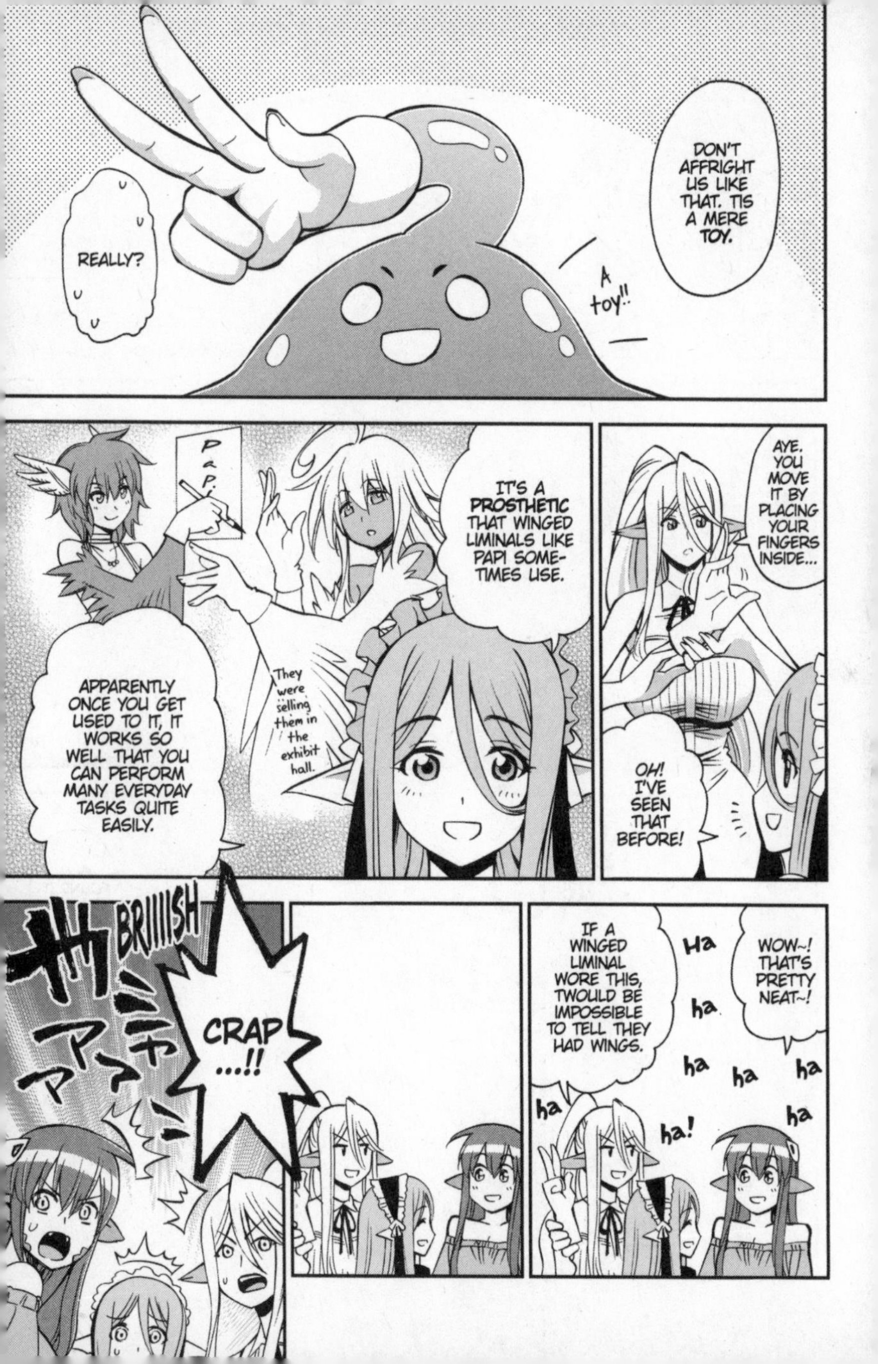

DON'T AFFRIGHT US LIKE THAT. TIS A MERE TOY.
A toy!!
REALLY?
AYE. YOU MOVE IT BY PLACING YOUR FINGERS INSIDE...
OH! I'VE SEEN THAT BEFORE!
IT'S A PROSTHETIC THAT WINGED LIMINALS LIKE PAPI SOME-TIMES USE.
They were selling them in the exhibit hall.
APPARENTLY ONCE YOU GET USED TO IT, IT WORKS SO WELL THAT YOU CAN PERFORM MANY EVERYDAY TASKS QUITE EASILY.
WOW~! THAT'S PRETTY NEAT~!
IF A WINGED LIMINAL WORE THIS, TWOULD BE IMPOSSIBLE TO TELL THEY HAD WINGS.
Ha ha ha ha ha ha ha!
BRIIIISH
CRAP ...!!

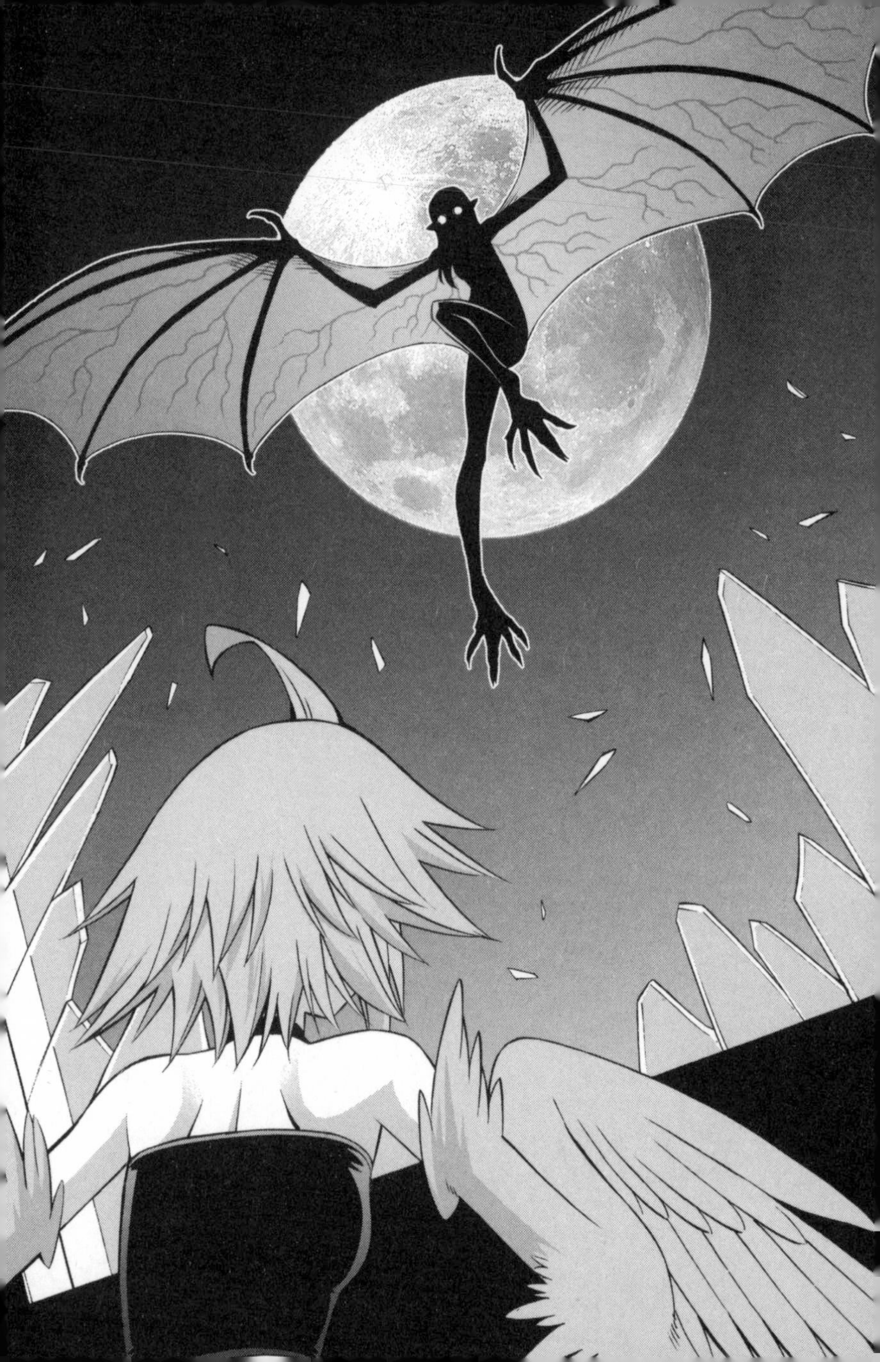

Monster Musume

Everyday Life with Monster Girls

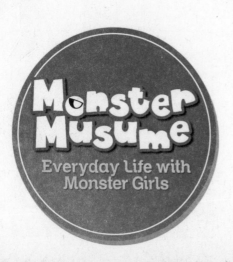

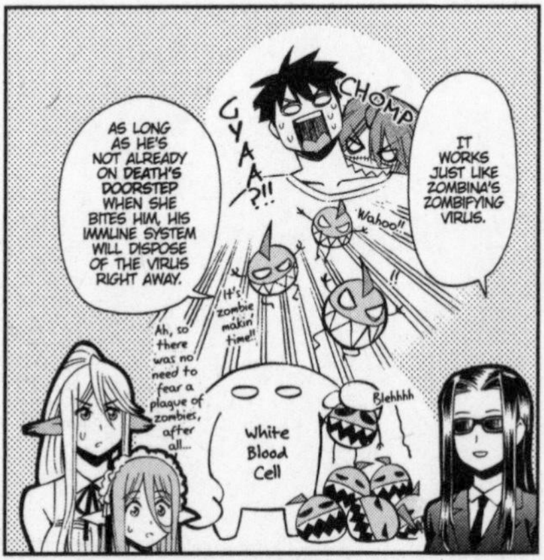
IT WORKS JUST LIKE ZOMBINA'S ZOMBIFYING VIRUS.
CHOMP
GYAA?!!
AS LONG AS HE'S NOT ALREADY ON DEATH'S DOORSTEP WHEN SHE BITES HIM, HIS IMMUNE SYSTEM WILL DISPOSE OF THE VIRUS RIGHT AWAY.
Wahoo!!
!!
It's zombie makin' time!!
Blehhhh
Ah, so there was no need to fear a plague of zombies, after all...
White Blood Cell

Chapter 51

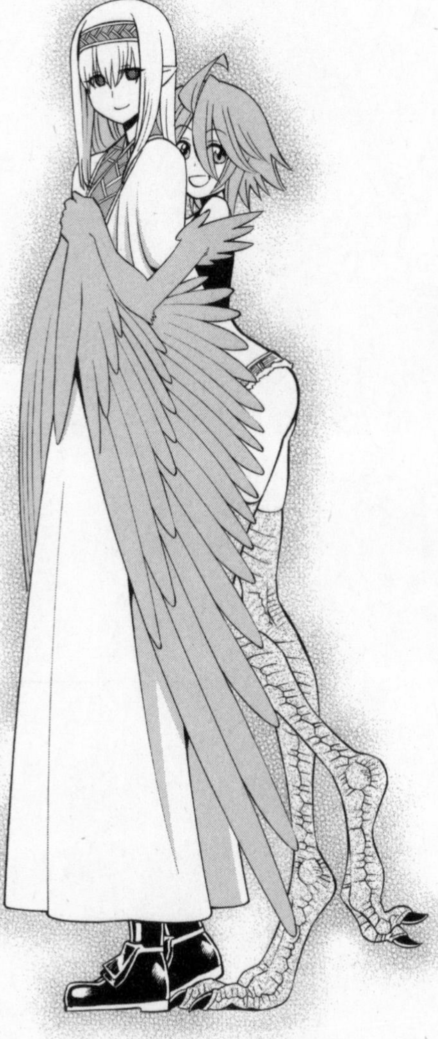

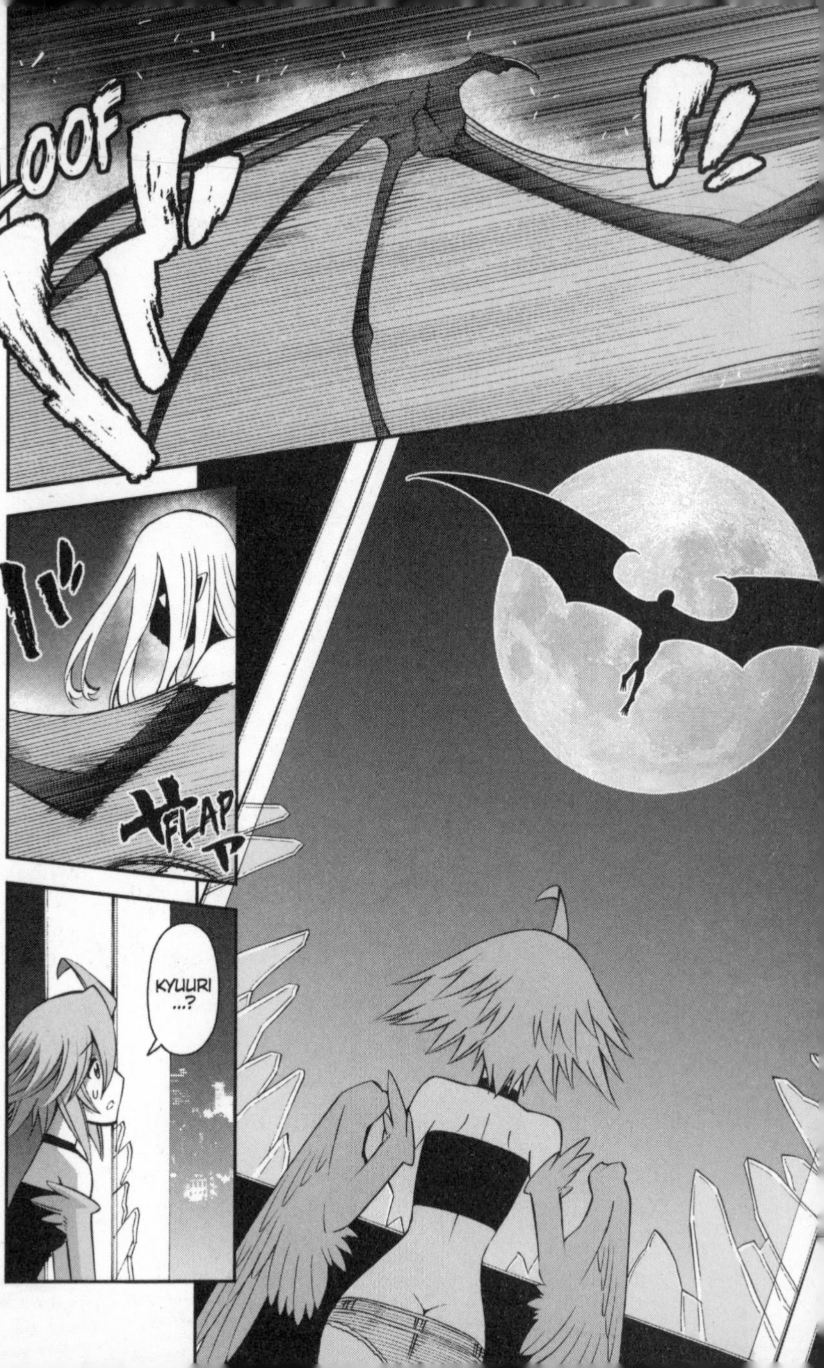
FLOOF
FLAP
KYUURI ...?

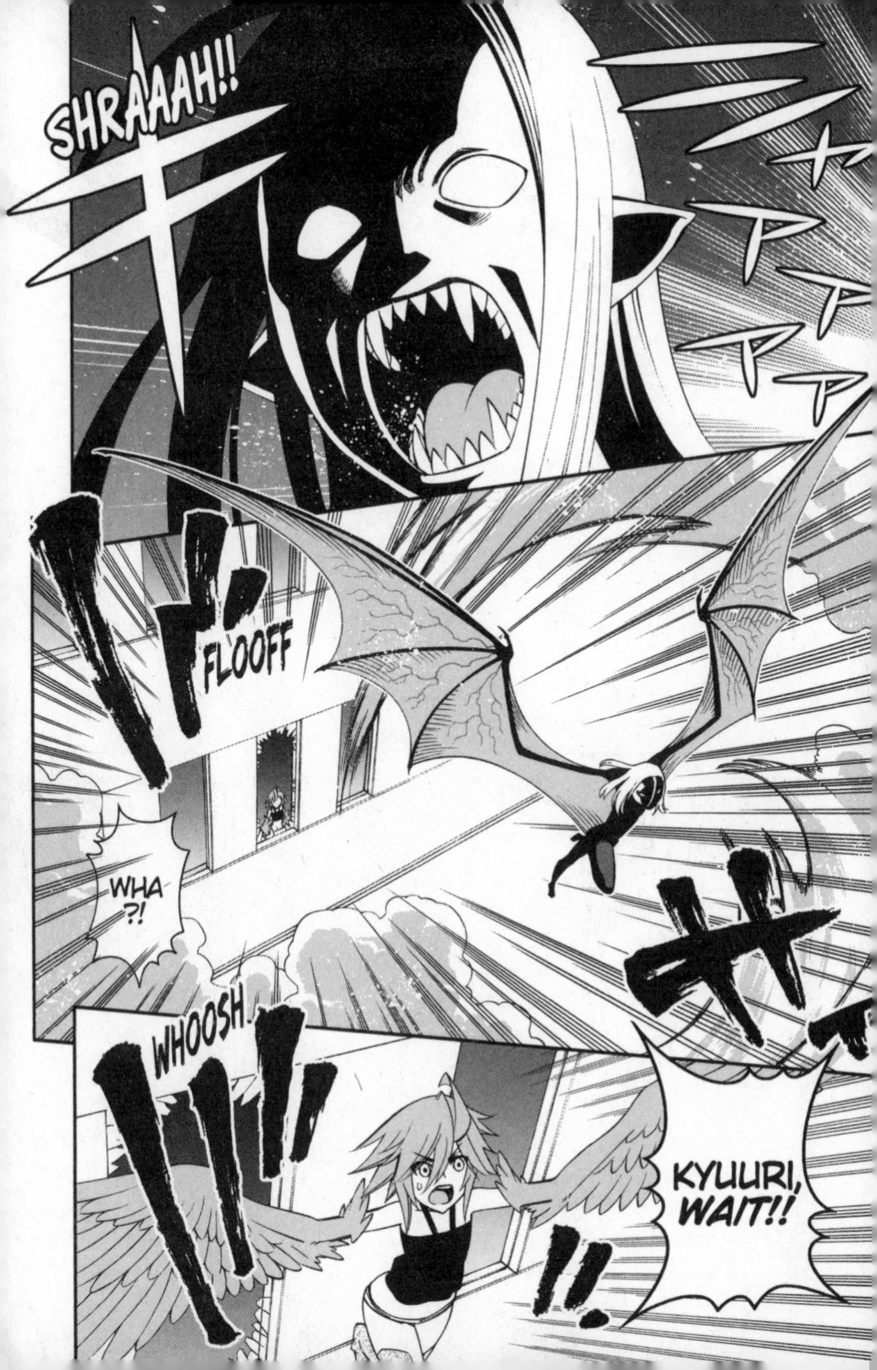
SHRAAAH!!
FLOOFF
WHA?!
WHOOSH
KYUURI, WAIT!!

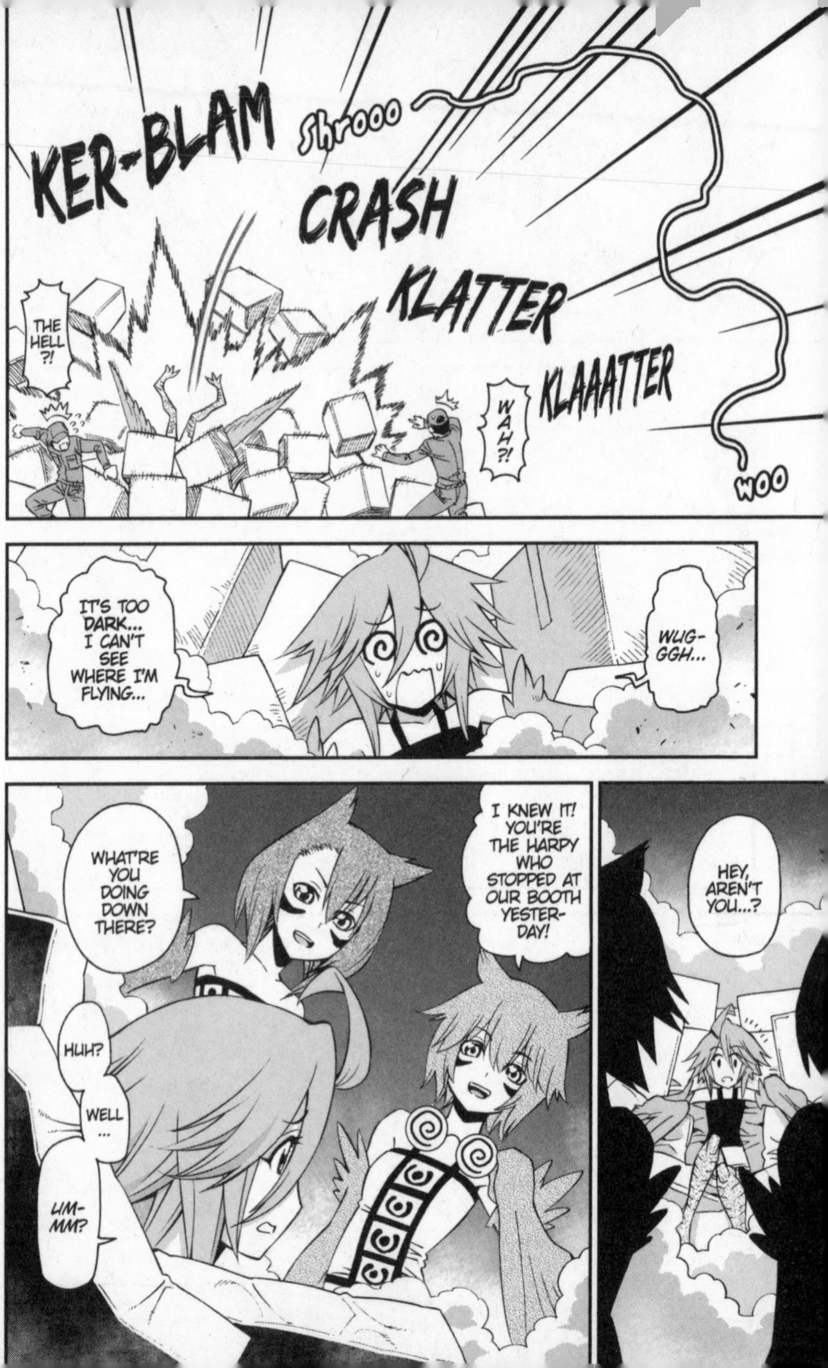
WOO
KLAAATTER
WAH?!
KLATTER
CRASH
Shrooo
KER-BLAM
THE HELL?!
WUG-GGH...
IT'S TOO DARK... I CAN'T SEE WHERE I'M FLYING...
HEY, AREN'T YOU...?
I KNEW IT! YOU'RE THE HARPY WHO STOPPED AT OUR BOOTH YESTER-DAY!
WHAT'RE YOU DOING DOWN THERE?
HUH?
WELL...
UMM-MM?

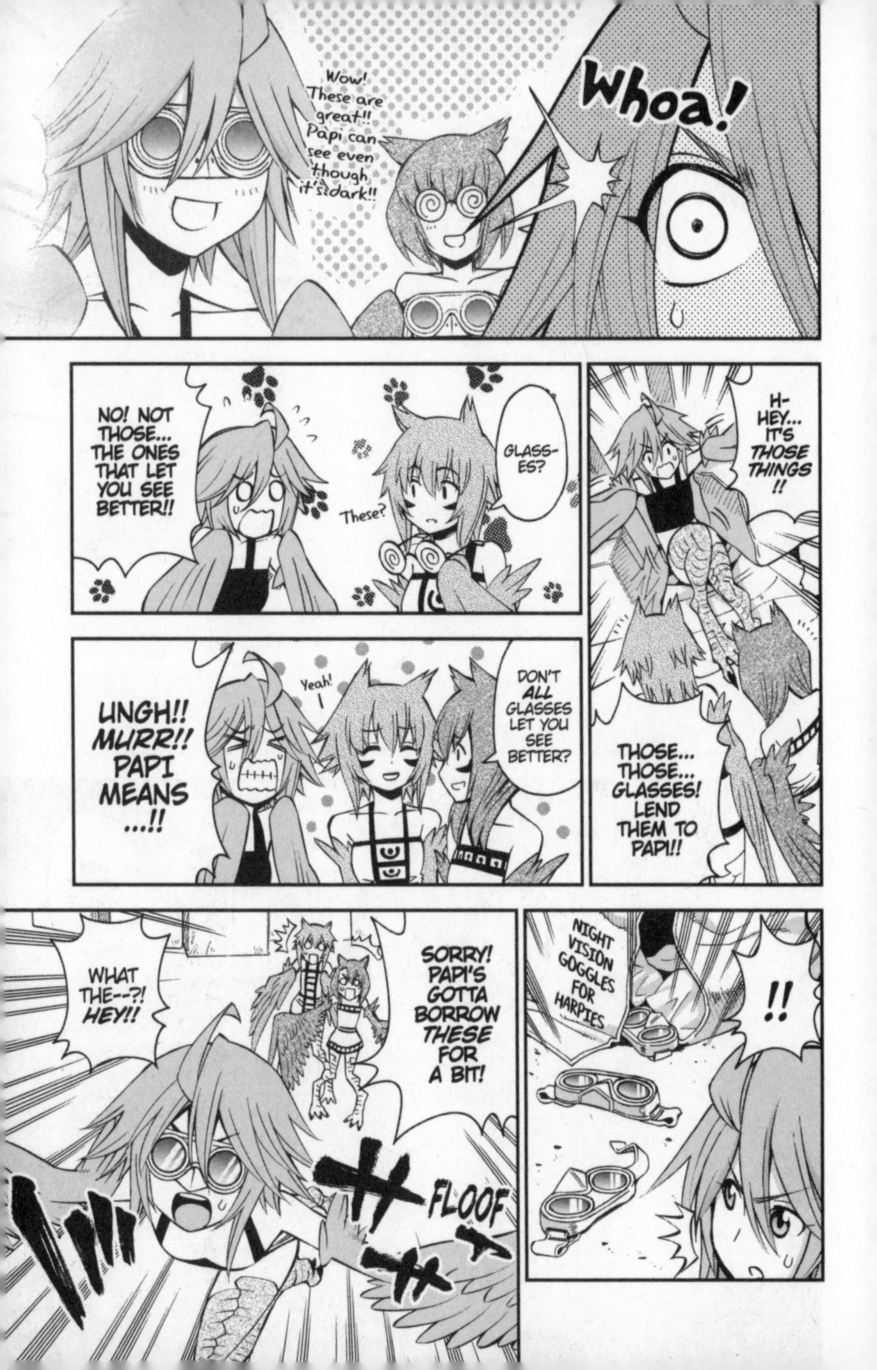
Whoa!
Wow! These are great!! Papi can see even though it's dark!!
H-HEY... IT'S *THOSE THINGS*!!
THOSE... THOSE... GLASSES! LEND THEM TO PAPI!!
GLASSES?
These?
NO! NOT THOSE... THE ONES THAT LET YOU SEE BETTER!!
DON'T *ALL* GLASSES LET YOU SEE BETTER?
Yeah!
UNGH!! *MURR!!* PAPI MEANS ...!!
!!
NIGHT VISION GOGGLES FOR HARPIES
SORRY! PAPI'S GOTTA BORROW *THESE* FOR A BIT!
WHAT THE--?! *HEY!!*
FLOOF

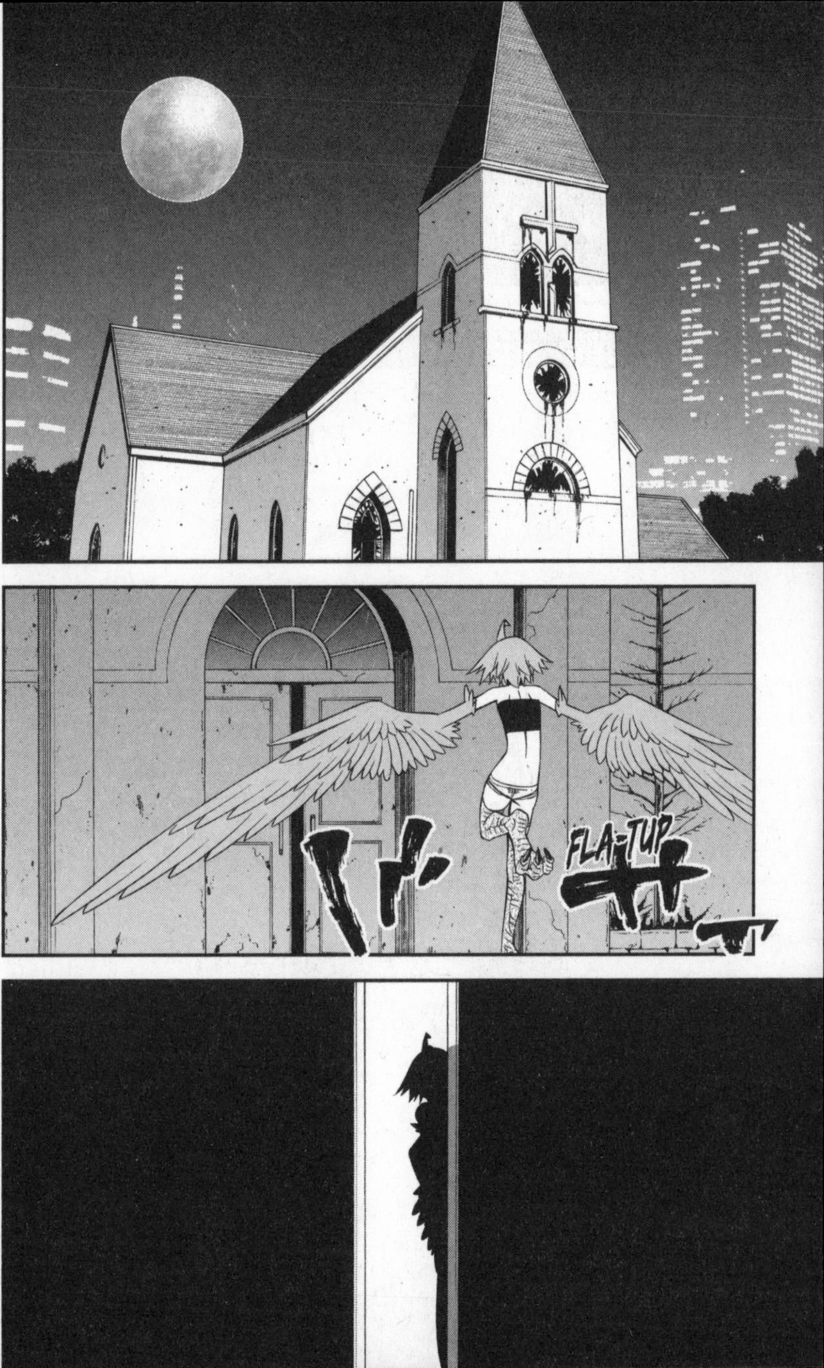
FLA-TUP

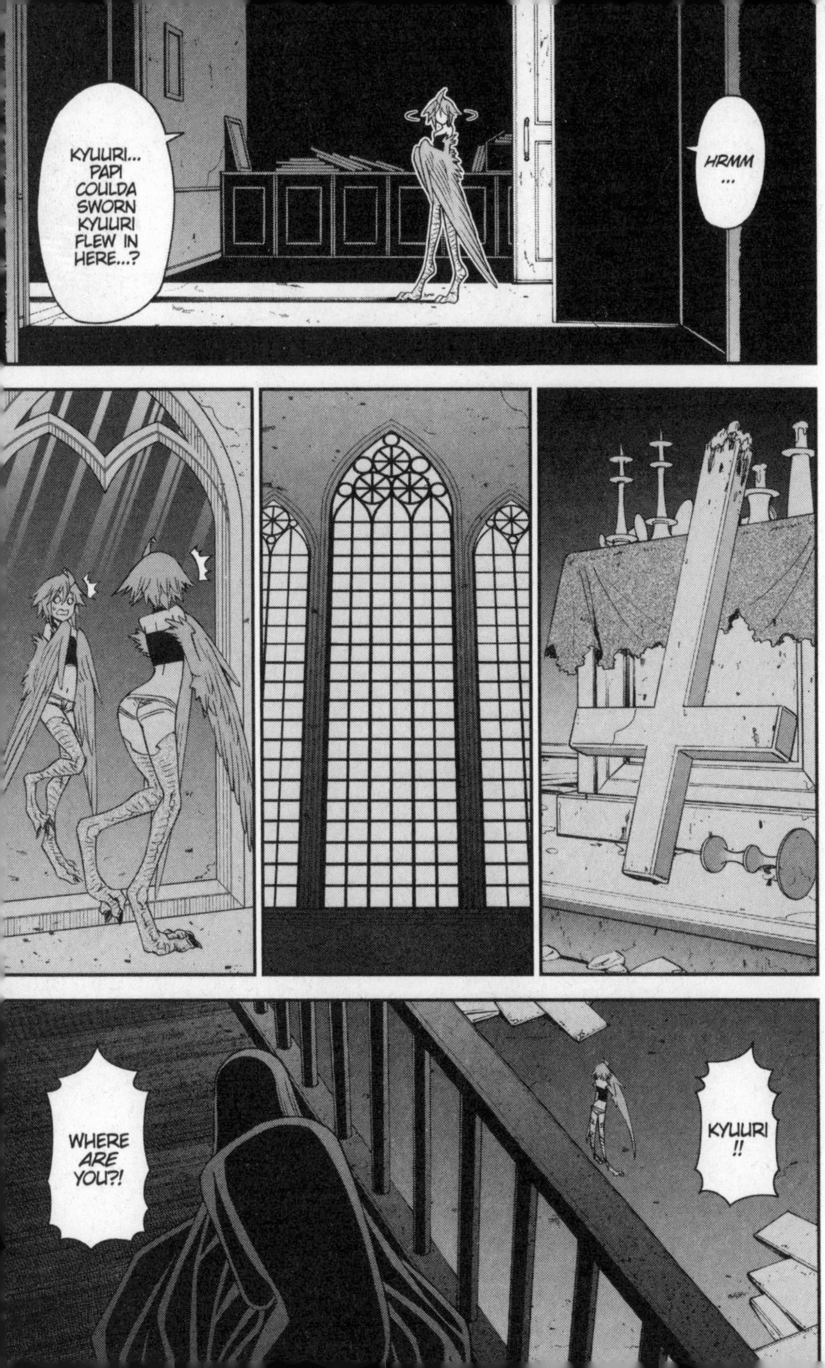
HRMM...
KYUURI... PAPI COULDA SWORN KYUURI FLEW IN HERE...?
KYUURI!!
WHERE ARE YOU?!

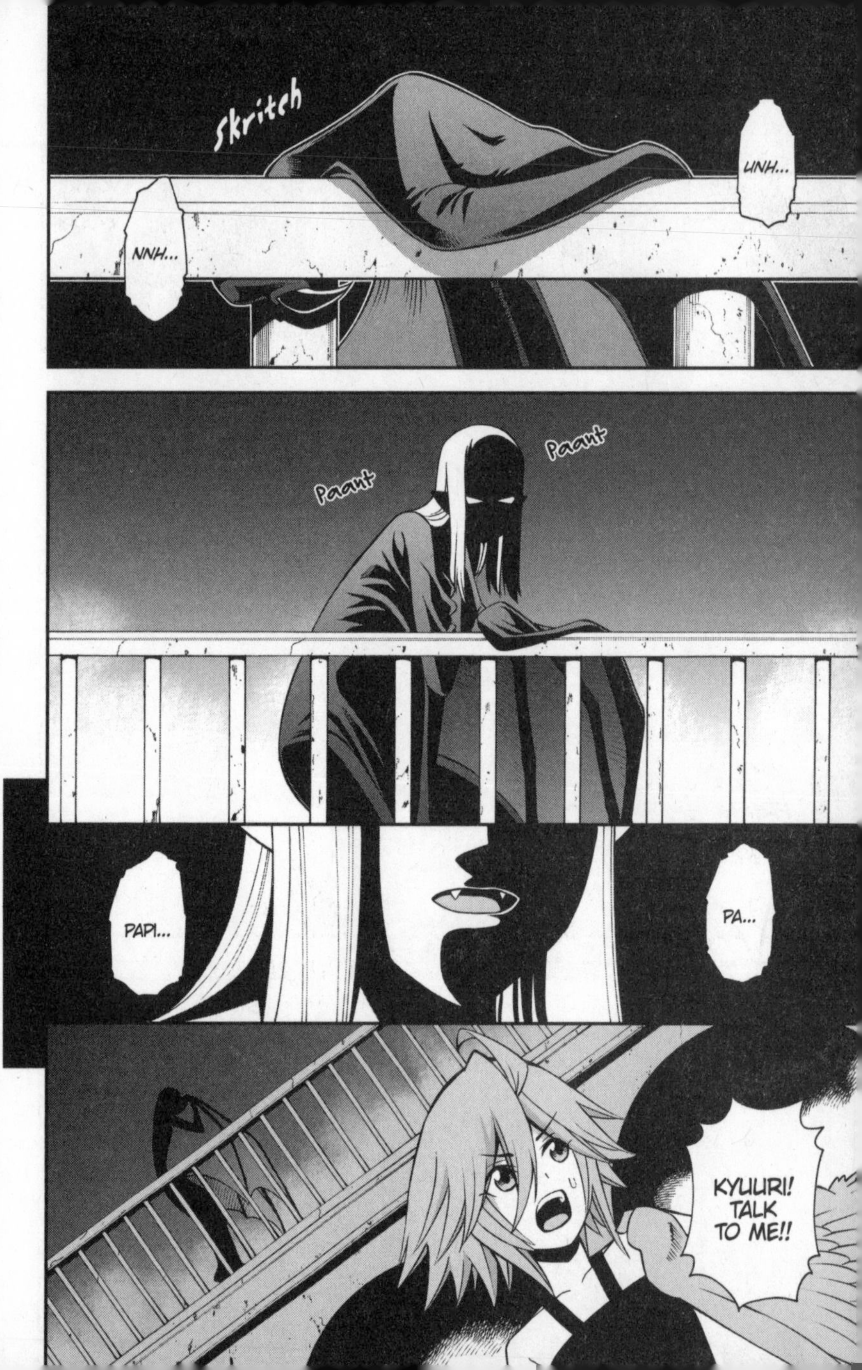
UNH...
Skritch
NNH...
Paant
Paant
PA...
PAPI...
KYUURI! TALK TO ME!!

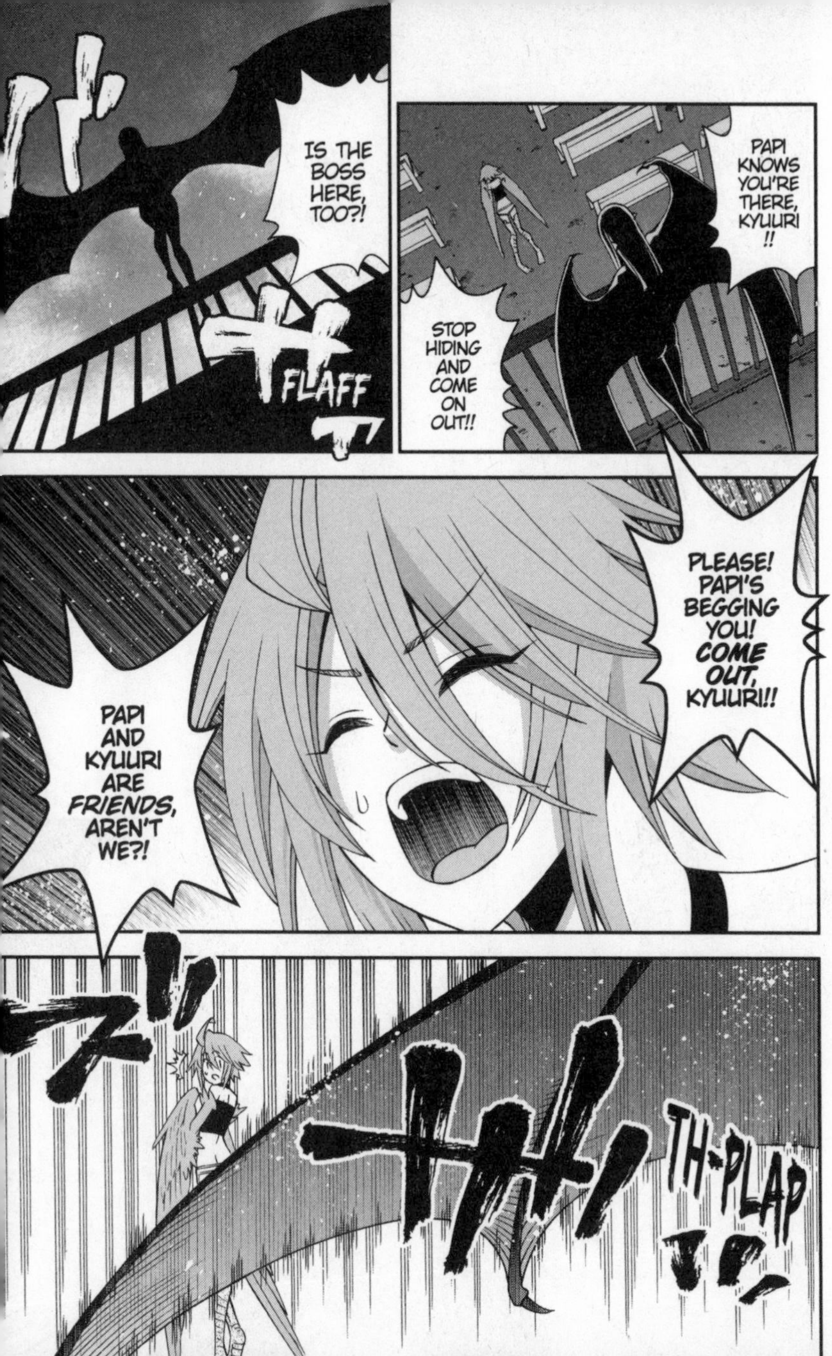
PAPI KNOWS YOU'RE THERE, KYUURI!!
STOP HIDING AND COME ON OUT!!
IS THE BOSS HERE, TOO?!
FLAFF
PLEASE! PAPI'S BEGGING YOU! COME OUT, KYUURI!!
PAPI AND KYUURI ARE FRIENDS, AREN'T WE?!
TH-PLAP

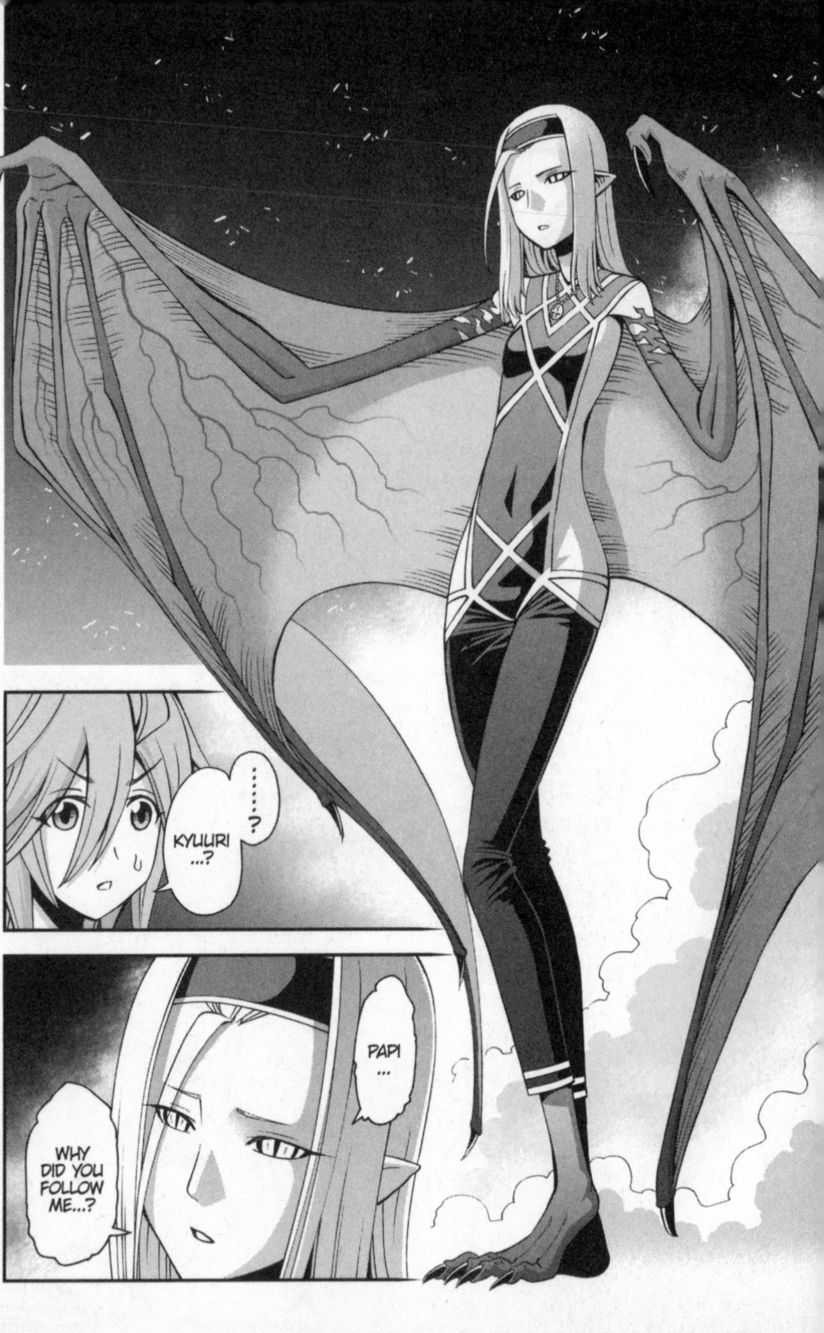
......?
KYUURI ...?
PAPI ...
WHY DID YOU FOLLOW ME...?

STAY BACK!

KYUURI --!

PAPI...

...?!

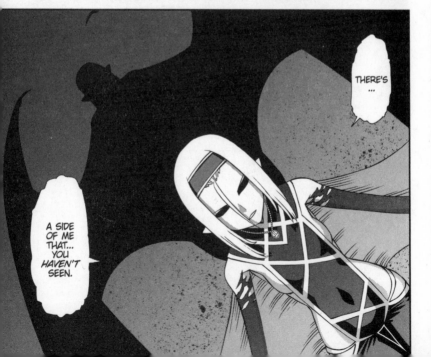

THERE'S ...

A SIDE OF ME THAT... YOU *HAVEN'T* SEEN.

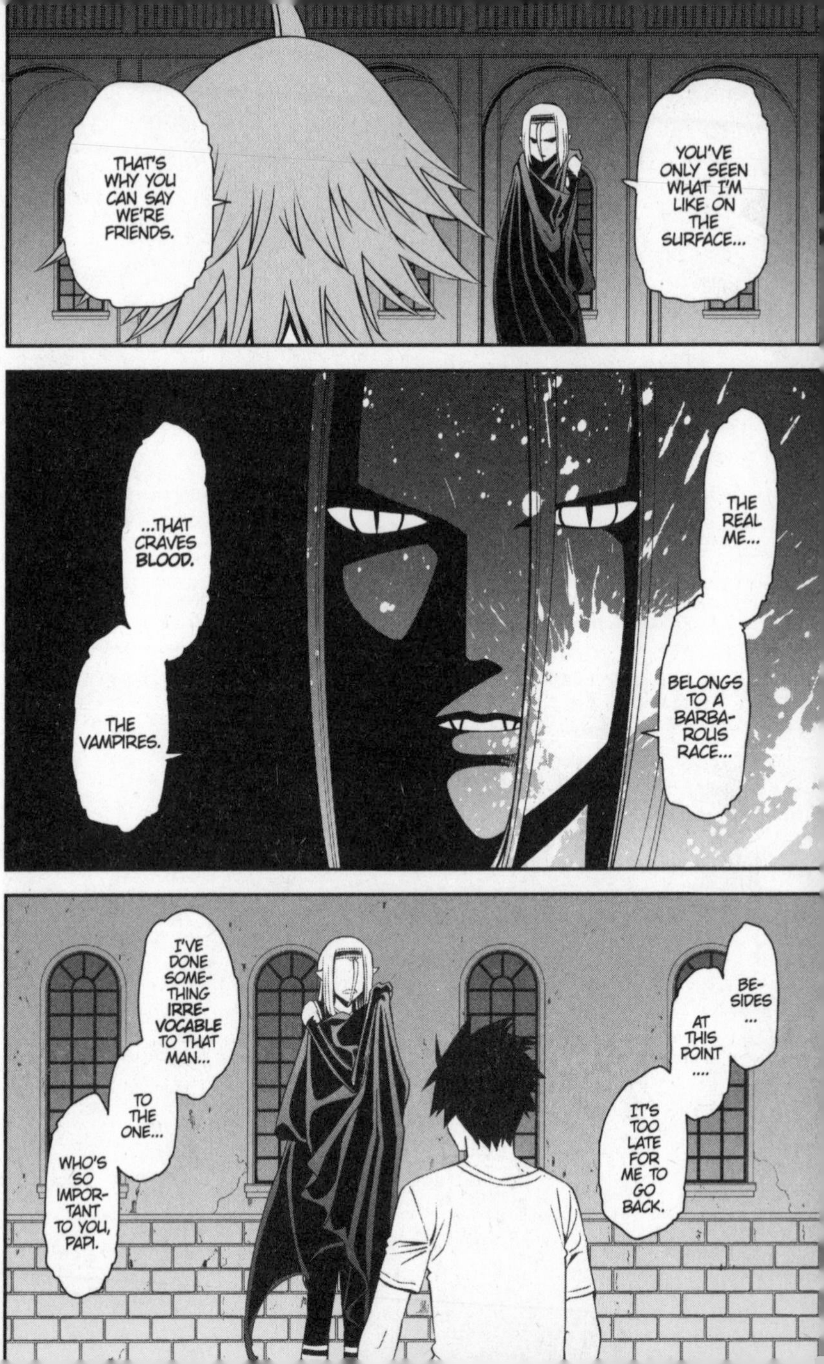
YOU'VE ONLY SEEN WHAT I'M LIKE ON THE SURFACE...
THAT'S WHY YOU CAN SAY WE'RE FRIENDS.
THE REAL ME...
BELONGS TO A BARBA-ROUS RACE...
...THAT CRAVES BLOOD.
THE VAMPIRES.
BE-SIDES...
AT THIS POINT....
IT'S TOO LATE FOR ME TO GO BACK.
I'VE DONE SOME-THING IRRE-VOCABLE TO THAT MAN...
TO THE ONE...
WHO'S SO IMPOR-TANT TO YOU, PAPI.

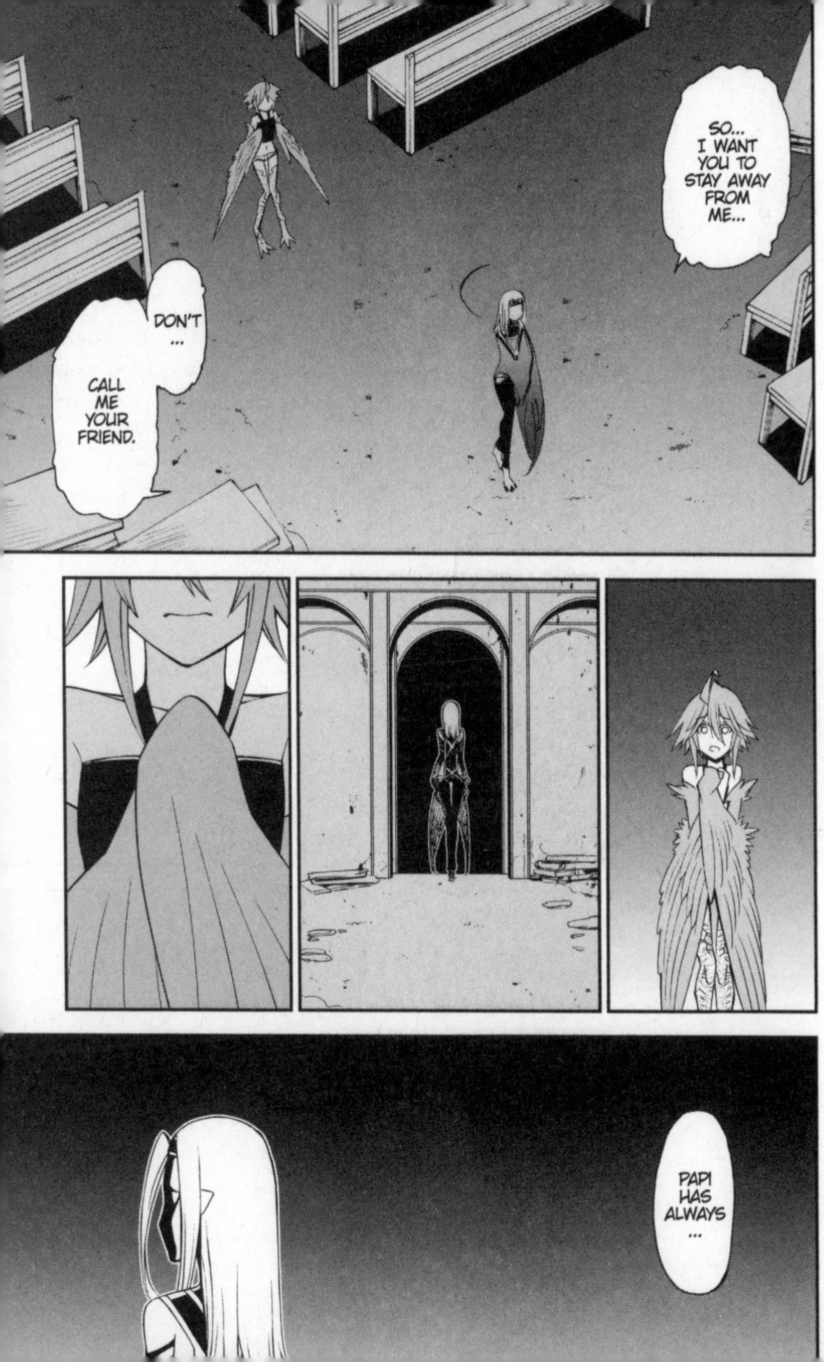
SO... I WANT YOU TO STAY AWAY FROM ME...
DON'T ... CALL ME YOUR FRIEND.
PAPI HAS ALWAYS ...

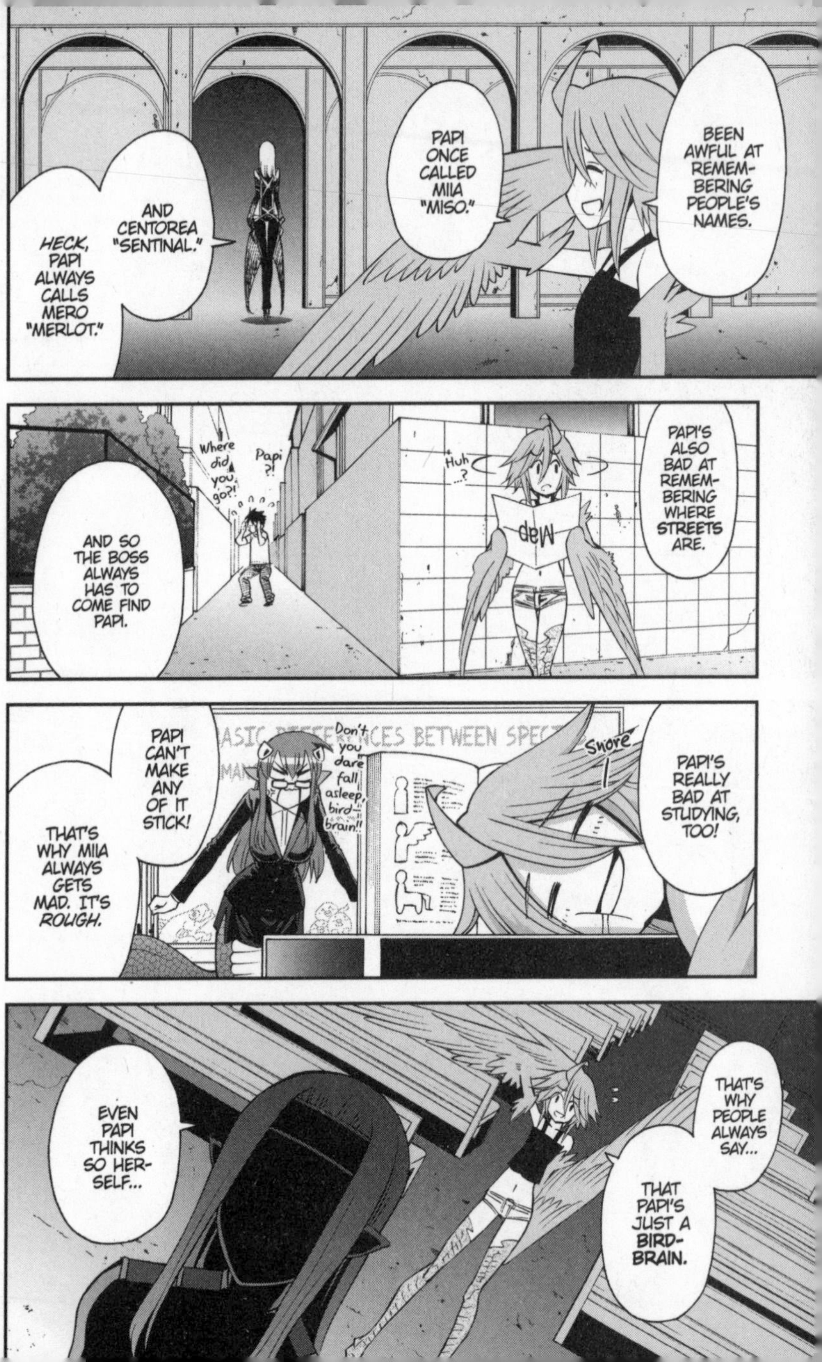
BEEN AWFUL AT REMEMBERING PEOPLE'S NAMES.
PAPI ONCE CALLED MIIA "MISO."
AND CENTOREA "SENTINAL."
HECK, PAPI ALWAYS CALLS MERO "MERLOT."
PAPI'S ALSO BAD AT REMEMBERING WHERE STREETS ARE.
Huh ...?
Map
Papi ?!
Where did you go?!
AND SO THE BOSS ALWAYS HAS TO COME FIND PAPI.
PAPI'S REALLY BAD AT STUDYING, TOO!
Snore
Don't you dare fall asleep, bird-brain!!
PAPI CAN'T MAKE ANY OF IT STICK!
THAT'S WHY MIIA ALWAYS GETS MAD. IT'S *ROUGH.*
THAT'S WHY PEOPLE ALWAYS SAY...
THAT PAPI'S JUST A BIRD-BRAIN.
EVEN PAPI THINKS SO HERSELF...

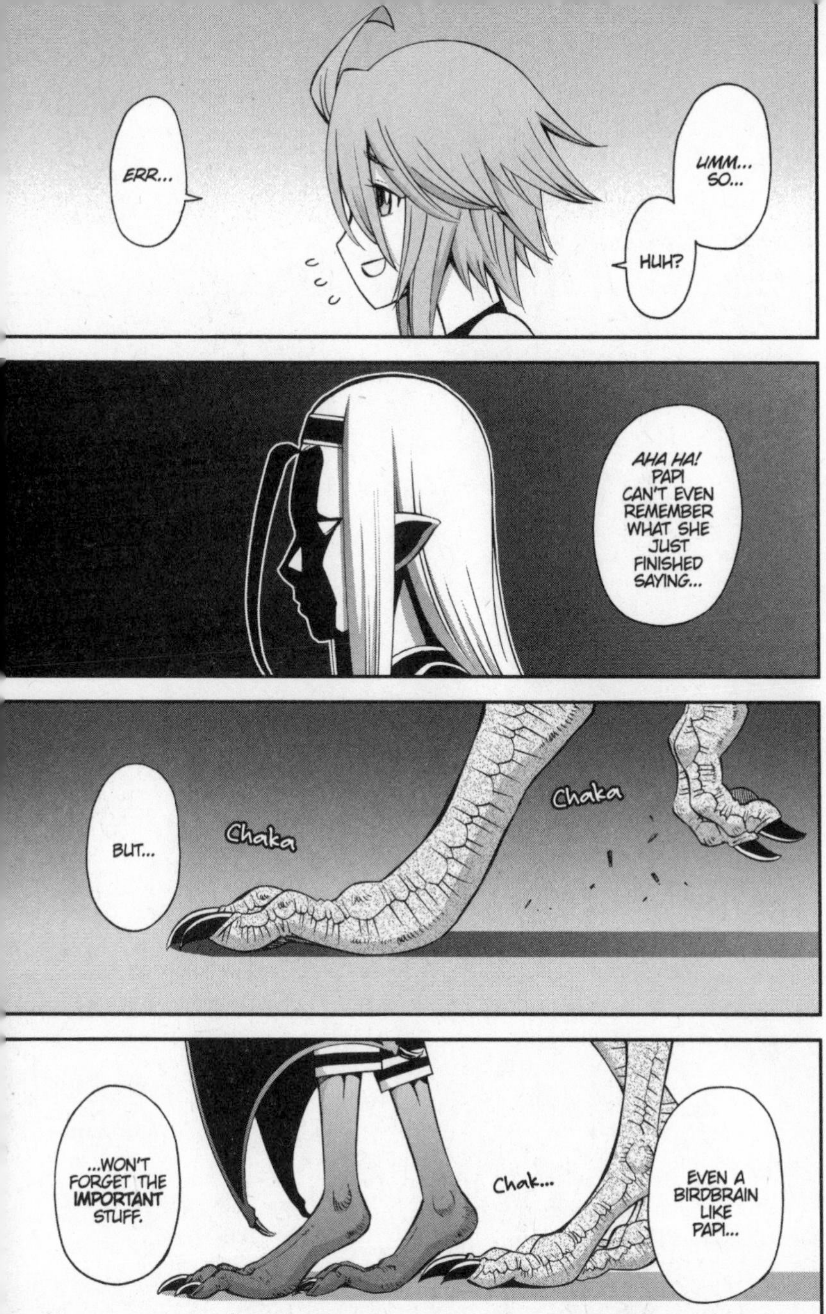
UMM... SO...
HUH?
ERR...
AHA HA! PAPI CAN'T EVEN REMEMBER WHAT SHE JUST FINISHED SAYING...
Chaka
Chaka
BUT...
EVEN A BIRDBRAIN LIKE PAPI...
Chak...
...WON'T FORGET THE IMPORTANT STUFF.

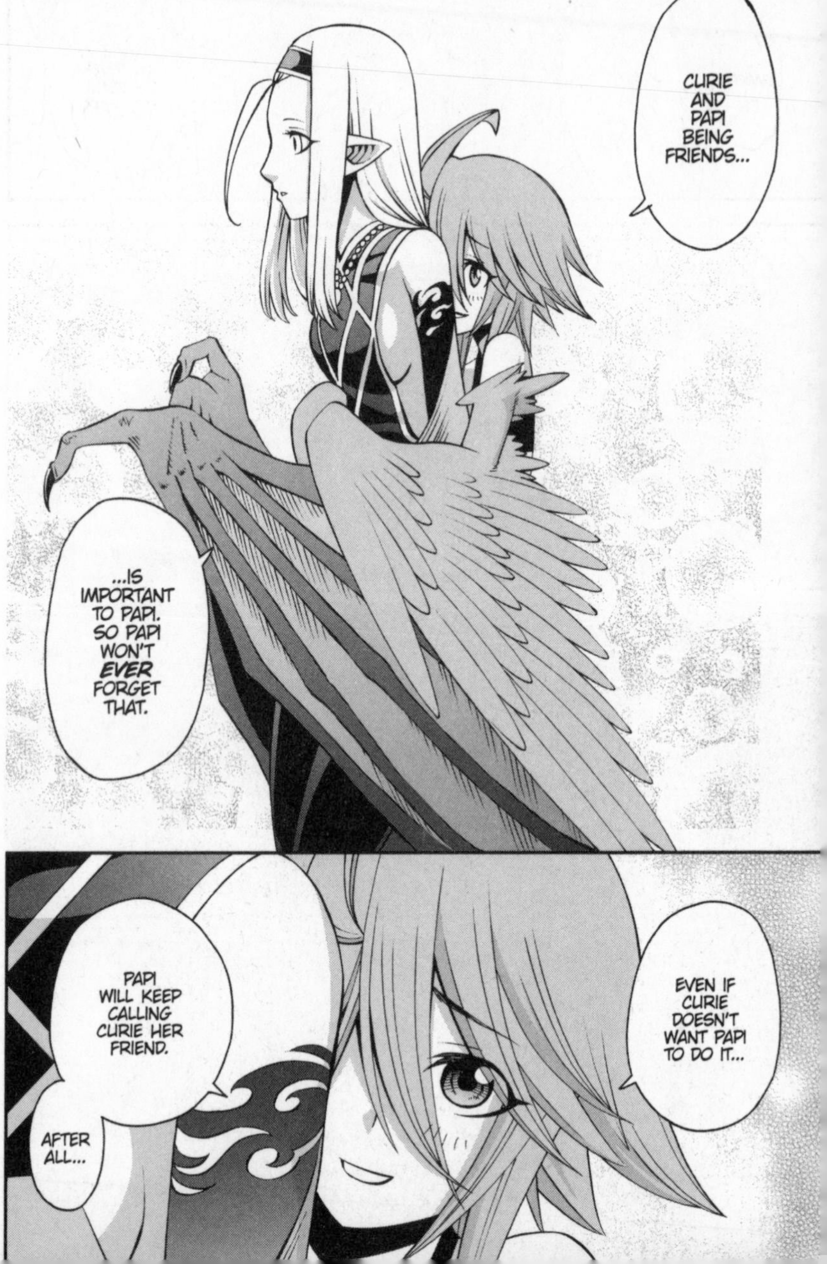
CURIE AND PAPI BEING FRIENDS...
...IS IMPORTANT TO PAPI. SO PAPI WON'T EVER FORGET THAT.
EVEN IF CURIE DOESN'T WANT PAPI TO DO IT...
PAPI WILL KEEP CALLING CURIE HER FRIEND.
AFTER ALL...

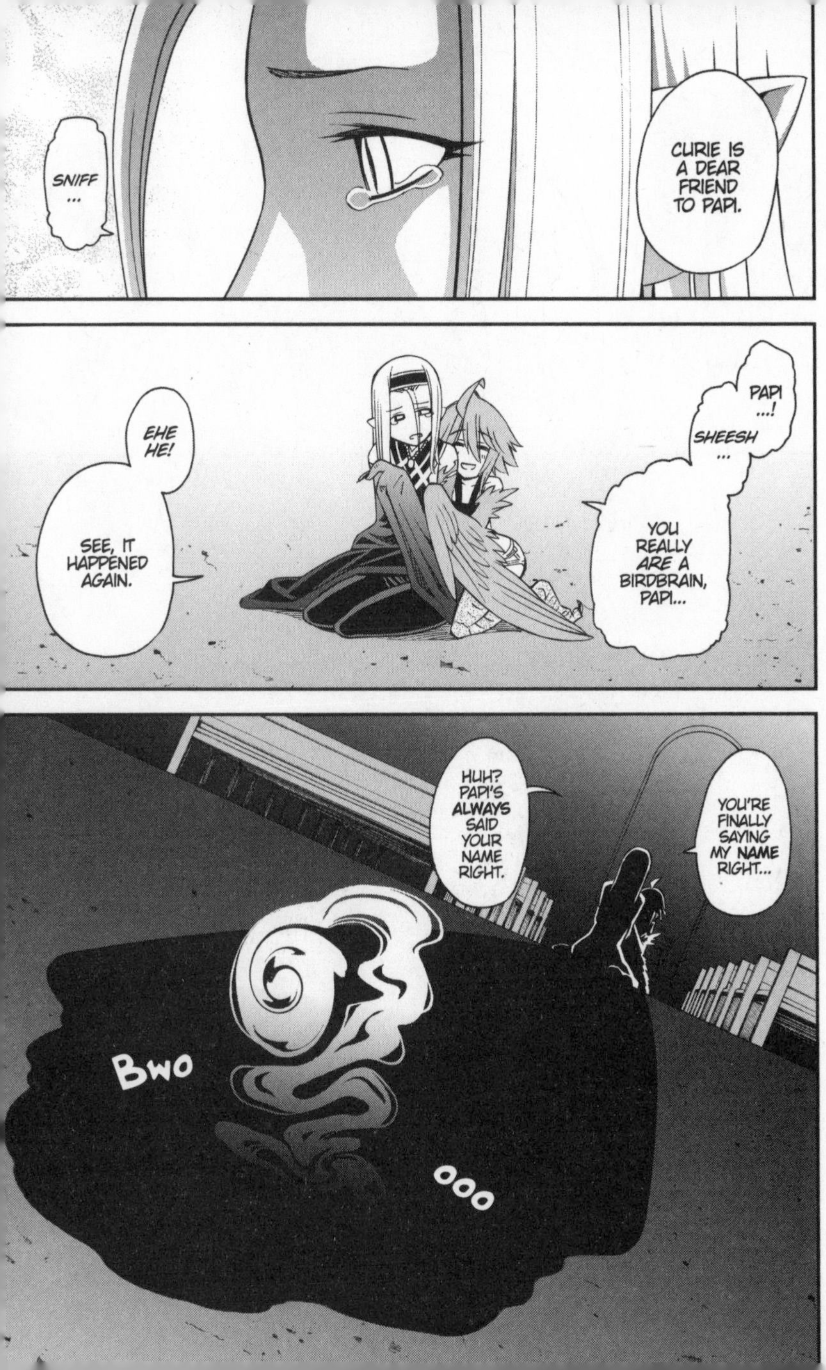
CURIE IS A DEAR FRIEND TO PAPI.
SNIFF ...
PAPI ...!
SHEESH ...
YOU REALLY *ARE* A BIRDBRAIN, PAPI...
EHE HE!
SEE, IT HAPPENED AGAIN.
YOU'RE FINALLY SAYING MY **NAME** RIGHT...
HUH? PAPI'S **ALWAYS** SAID YOUR NAME RIGHT.
BWO
OOO

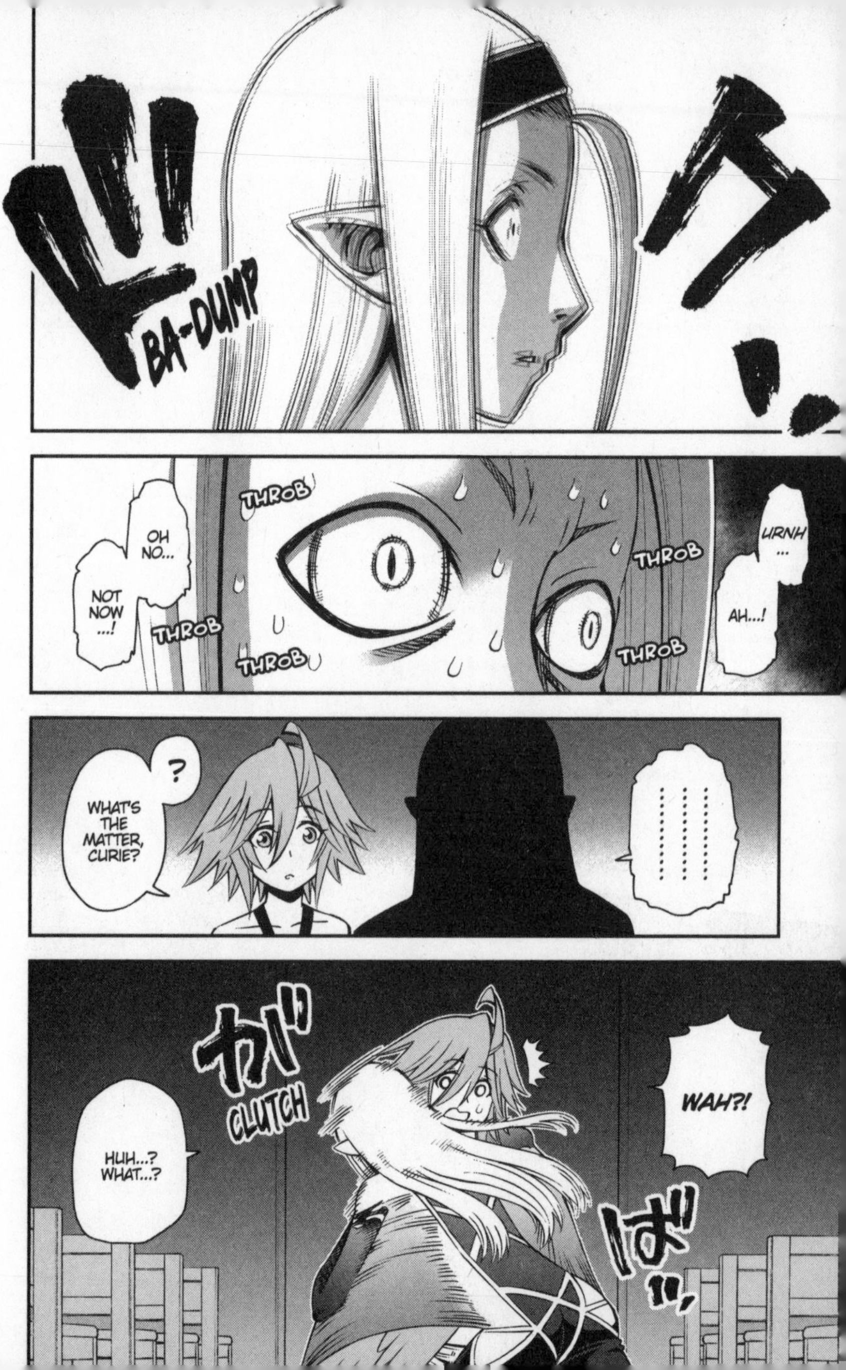
ク…
ド
BA-DUMP
URNH...
AH...!
THROB
THROB
THROB
THROB
THROB
OH NO...
NOT NOW...!
......
?
WHAT'S THE MATTER, CURIE?
WAH?!
ばっ
CLUTCH
HUH...? WHAT...?

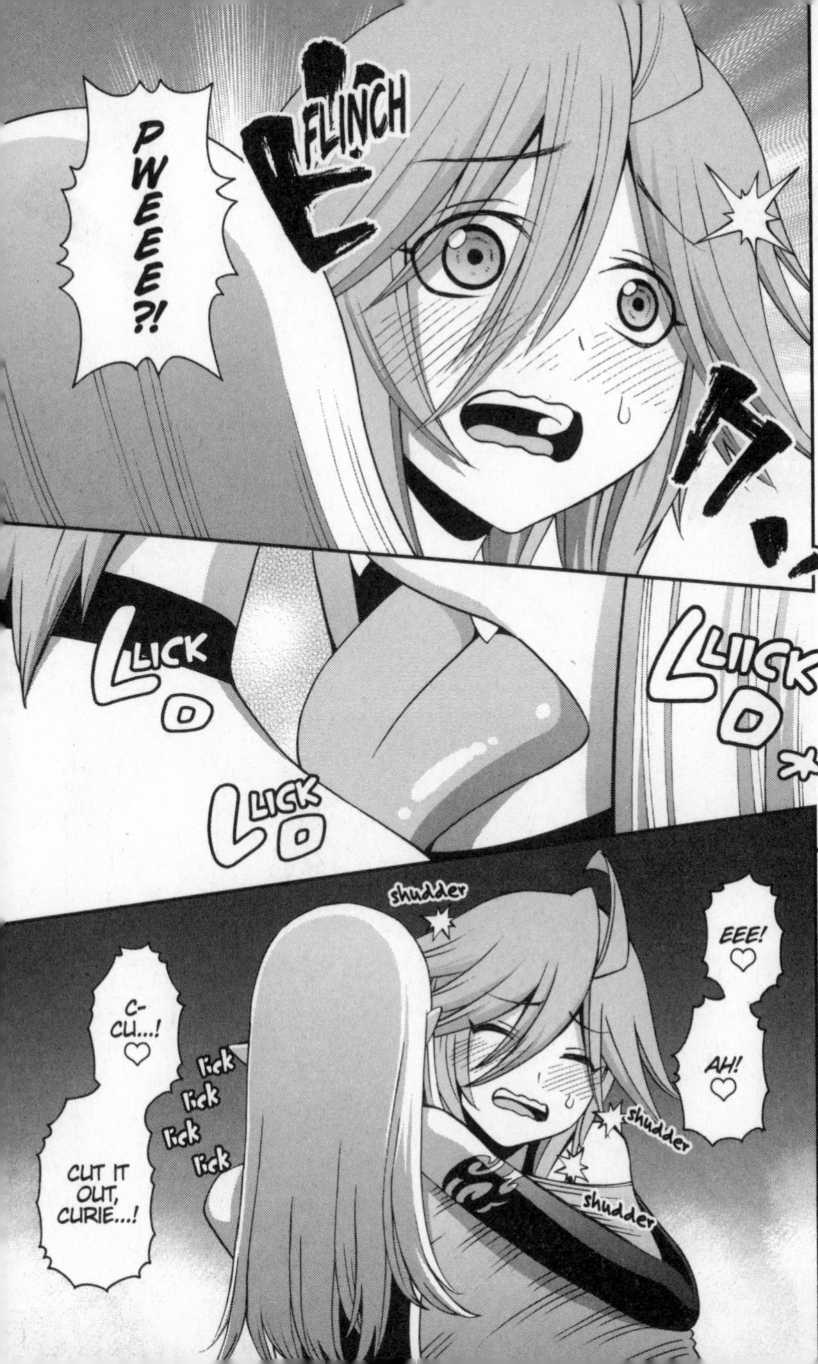
FLINCH
PWEEEE?!
LLIICK
LLICK
LLICK
shudder
EEE! ♡
AH! ♡
shudder
shudder
C-CU...! ♡
lick
lick
lick
lick
CUT IT OUT, CURIE...!

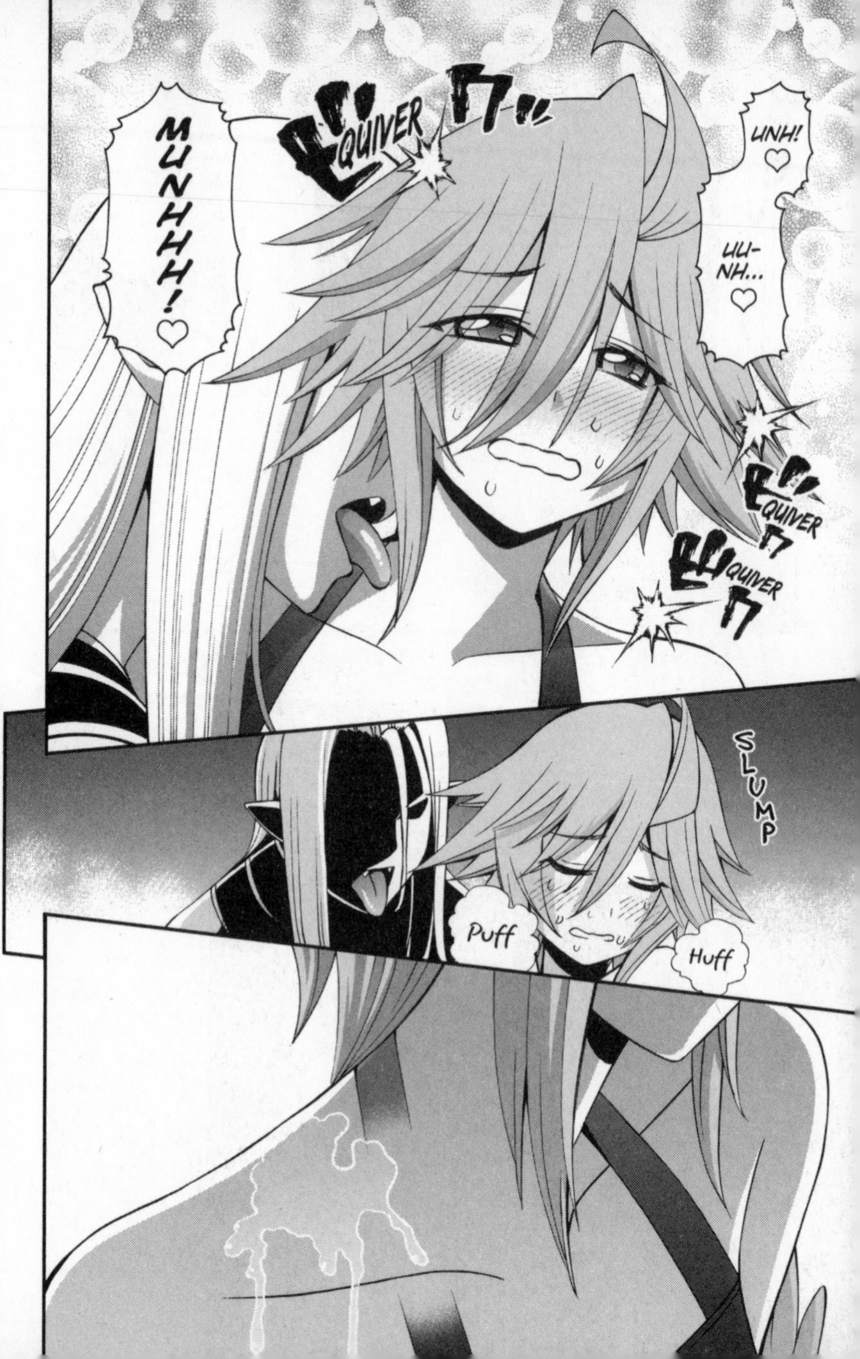
UNH! ♡
QUIVER
MUNHHHH! ♡
UU-NH... ♡
QUIVER
QUIVER
SLUMP
Huff
Puff

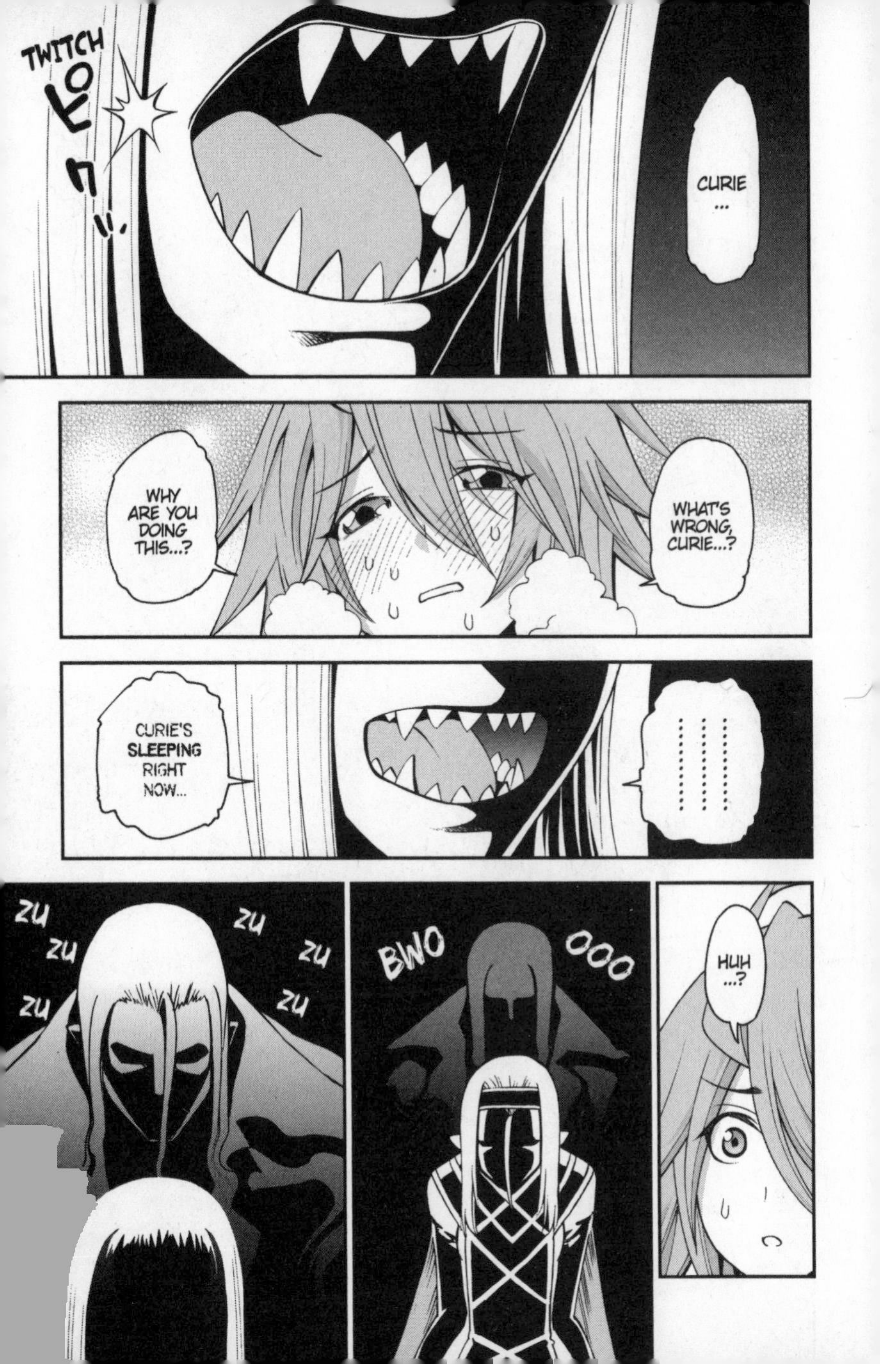
CURIE ...
TWITCH
WHAT'S WRONG, CURIE...?
WHY ARE YOU DOING THIS...?
......
CURIE'S SLEEPING RIGHT NOW...
HUH ...?
BWO OOO
ZU ZU ZU ZU ZU ZU

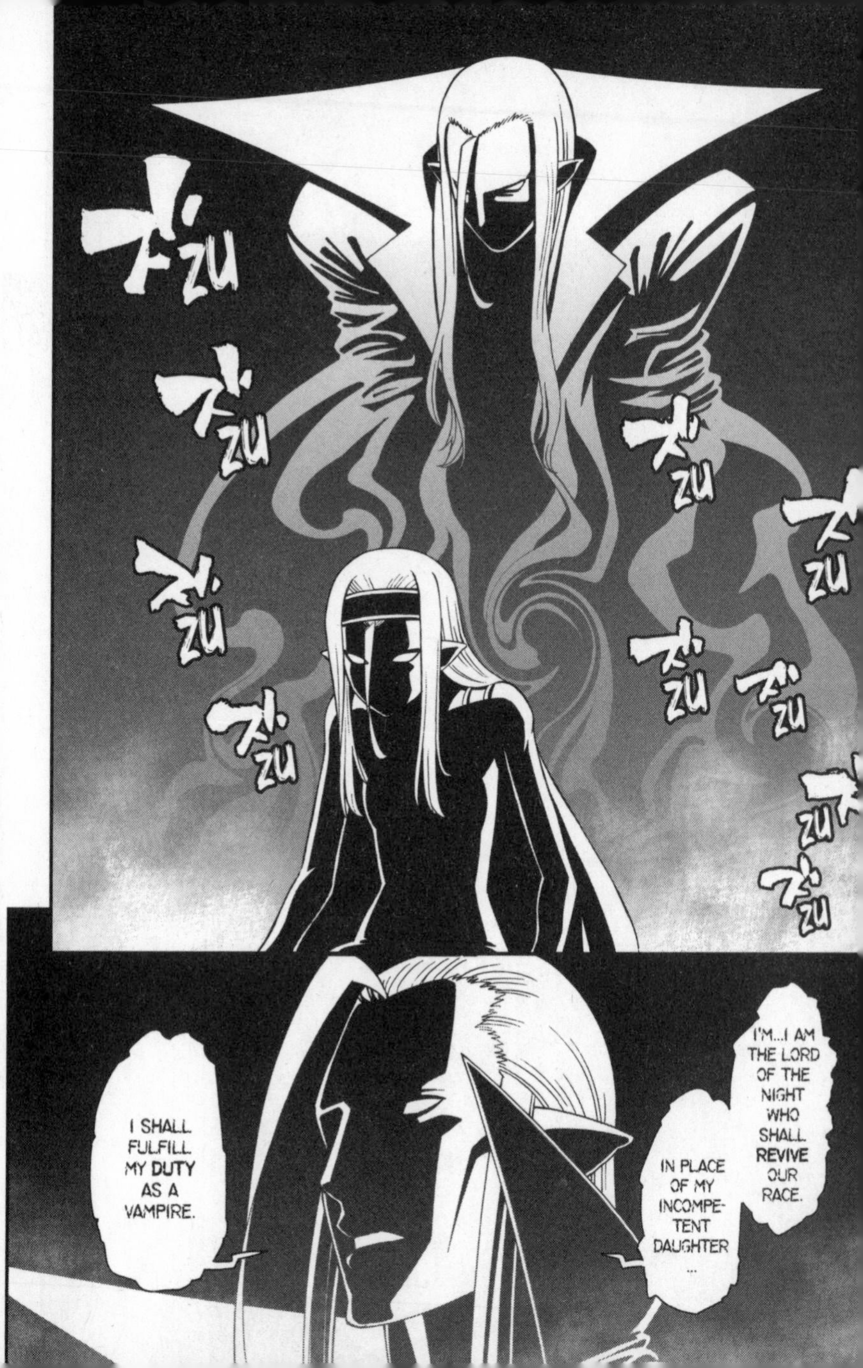
ZU
ZU
ZU
ZU
ZU
ZU
ZU
ZU
ZU
ZU
I'M...I AM THE LORD OF THE NIGHT WHO SHALL **REVIVE** OUR RACE.
IN PLACE OF MY INCOMPE- TENT DAUGHTER ...
I SHALL FULFILL MY **DUTY** AS A VAMPIRE.

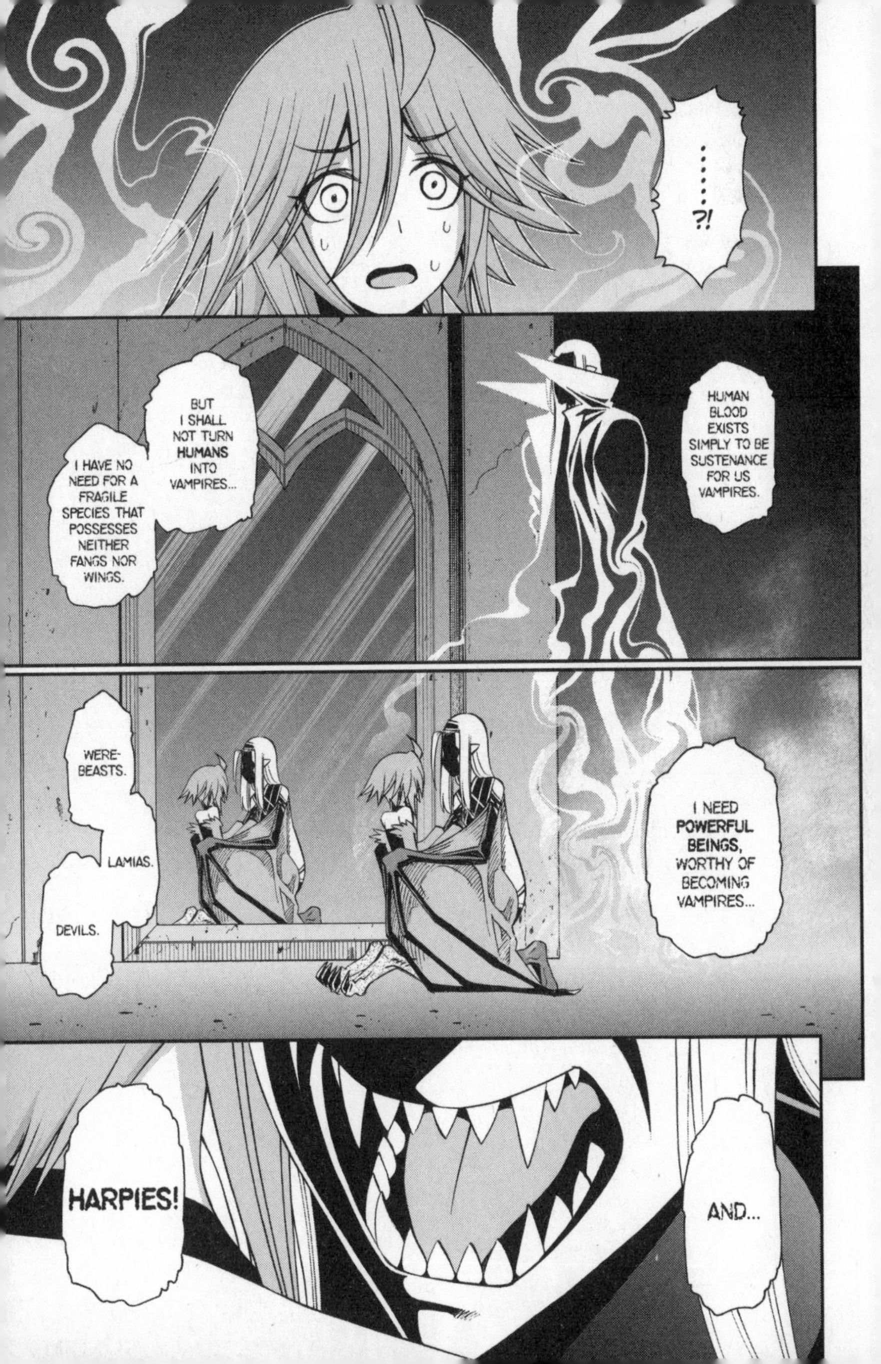
......?!
HUMAN BLOOD EXISTS SIMPLY TO BE SUSTENANCE FOR US VAMPIRES.
BUT I SHALL NOT TURN HUMANS INTO VAMPIRES...
I HAVE NO NEED FOR A FRAGILE SPECIES THAT POSSESSES NEITHER FANGS NOR WINGS.
I NEED POWERFUL BEINGS, WORTHY OF BECOMING VAMPIRES...
WERE-BEASTS.
LAMIAS.
DEVILS.
AND...
HARPIES!

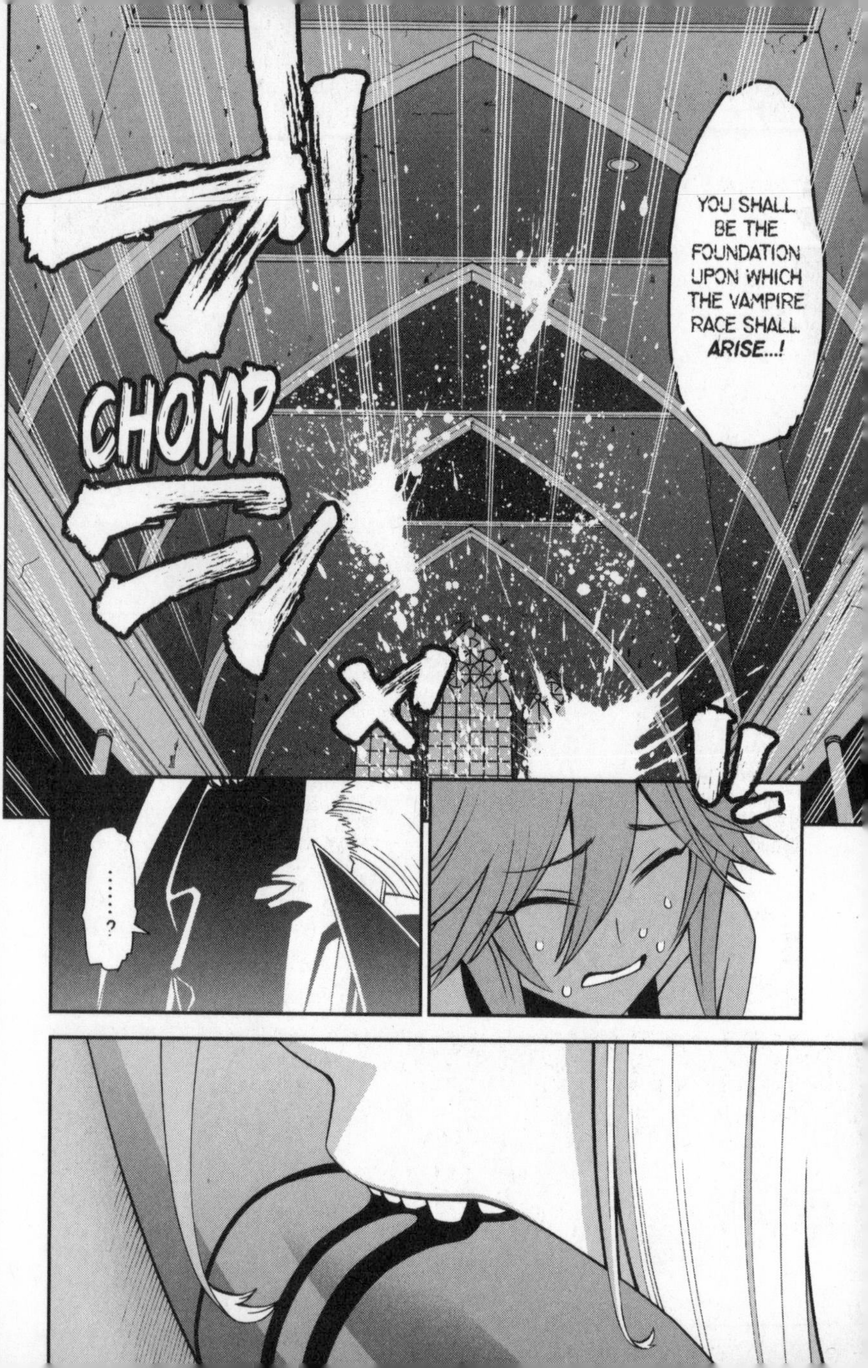
YOU SHALL BE THE FOUNDATION UPON WHICH THE VAMPIRE RACE SHALL **ARISE**...!
CHOMP
......?

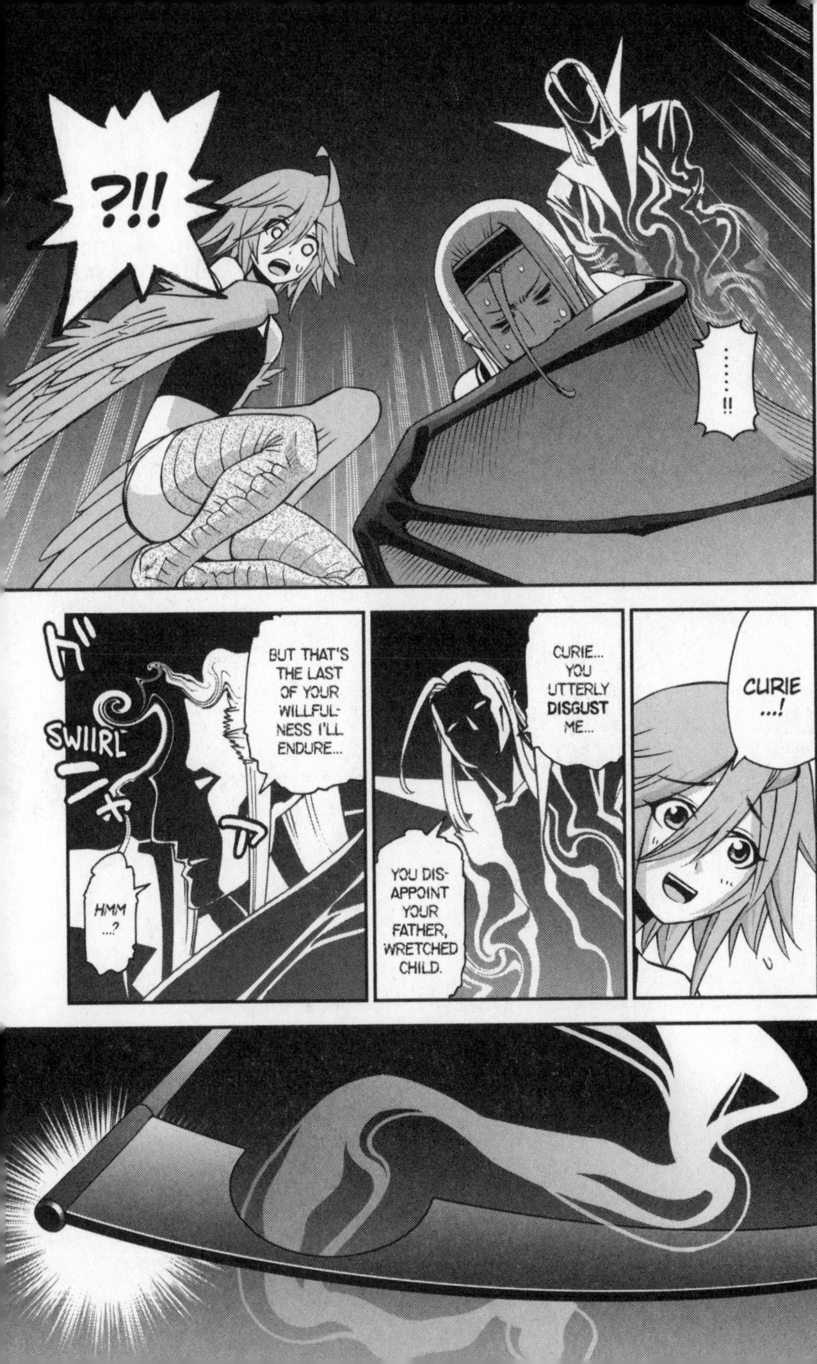
......!!
?!!
CURIE ...!
CURIE... YOU UTTERLY DISGUST ME...
YOU DIS-APPOINT YOUR FATHER, WRETCHED CHILD.
BUT THAT'S THE LAST OF YOUR WILLFUL-NESS I'LL ENDURE...
SWIIRL
HMM ...?

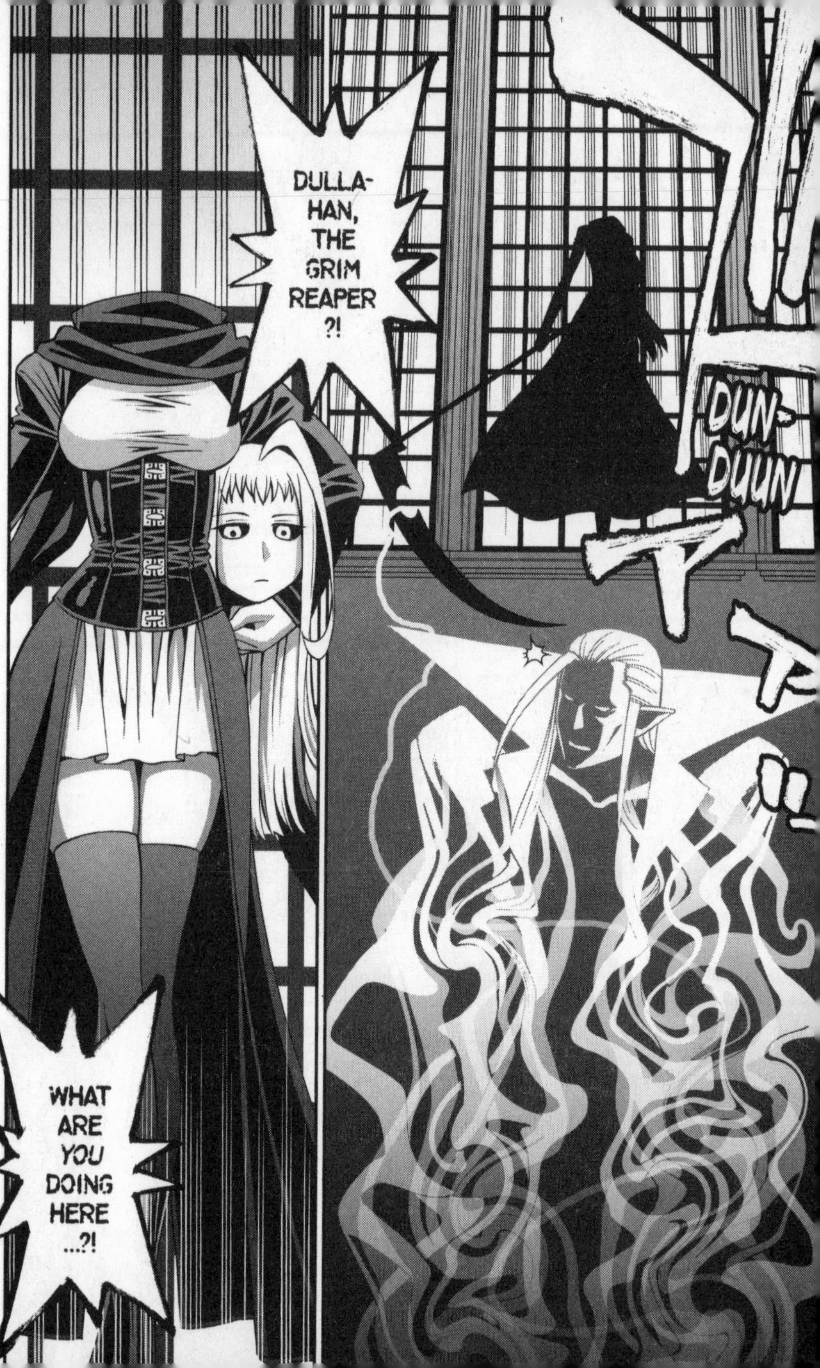
DUN-DUUN
DULLA-HAN, THE GRIM REAPER ?!
WHAT ARE YOU DOING HERE ...?!

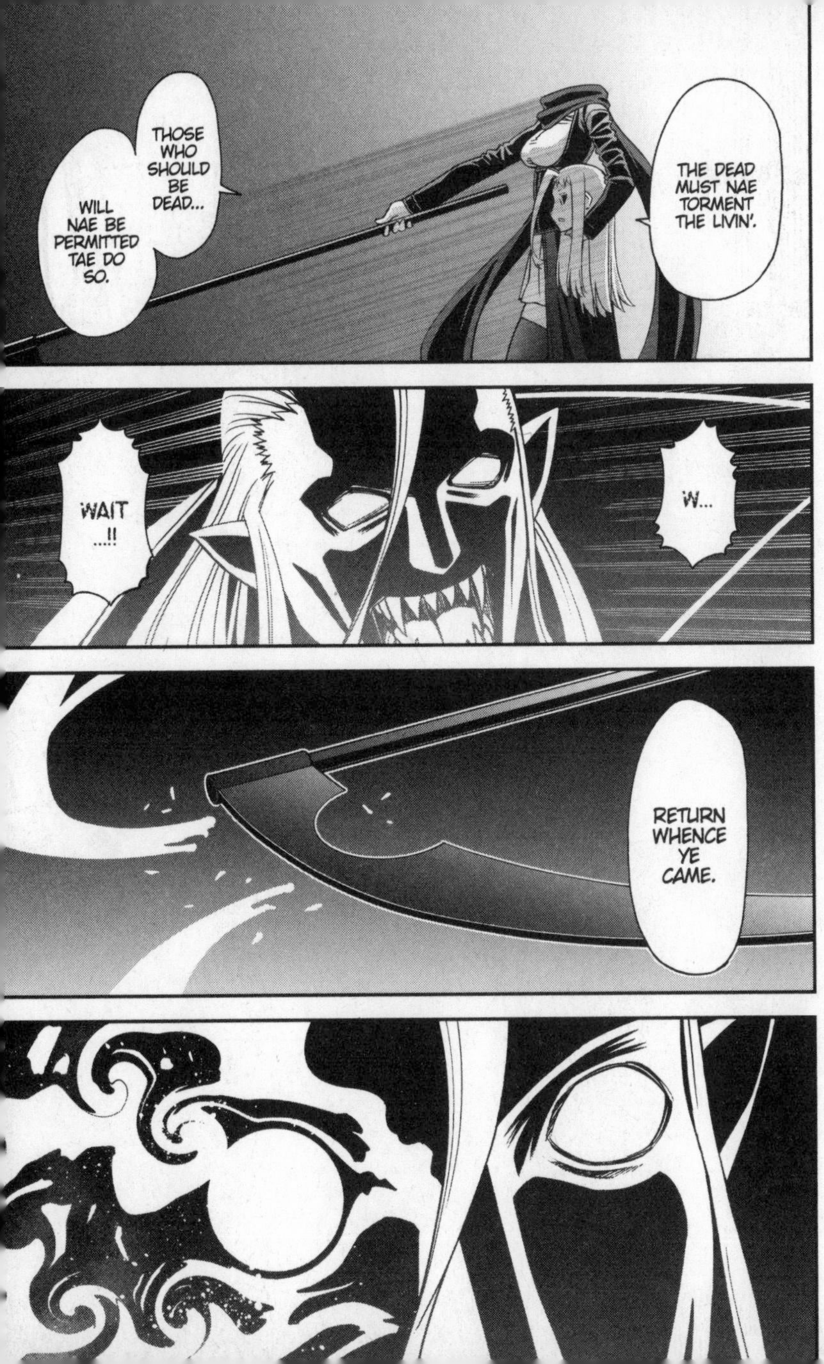
THE DEAD MUST NAE TORMENT THE LIVIN'.
THOSE WHO SHOULD BE DEAD...
WILL NAE BE PERMITTED TAE DO SO.
W...
WAIT ...!!
RETURN WHENCE YE CAME.

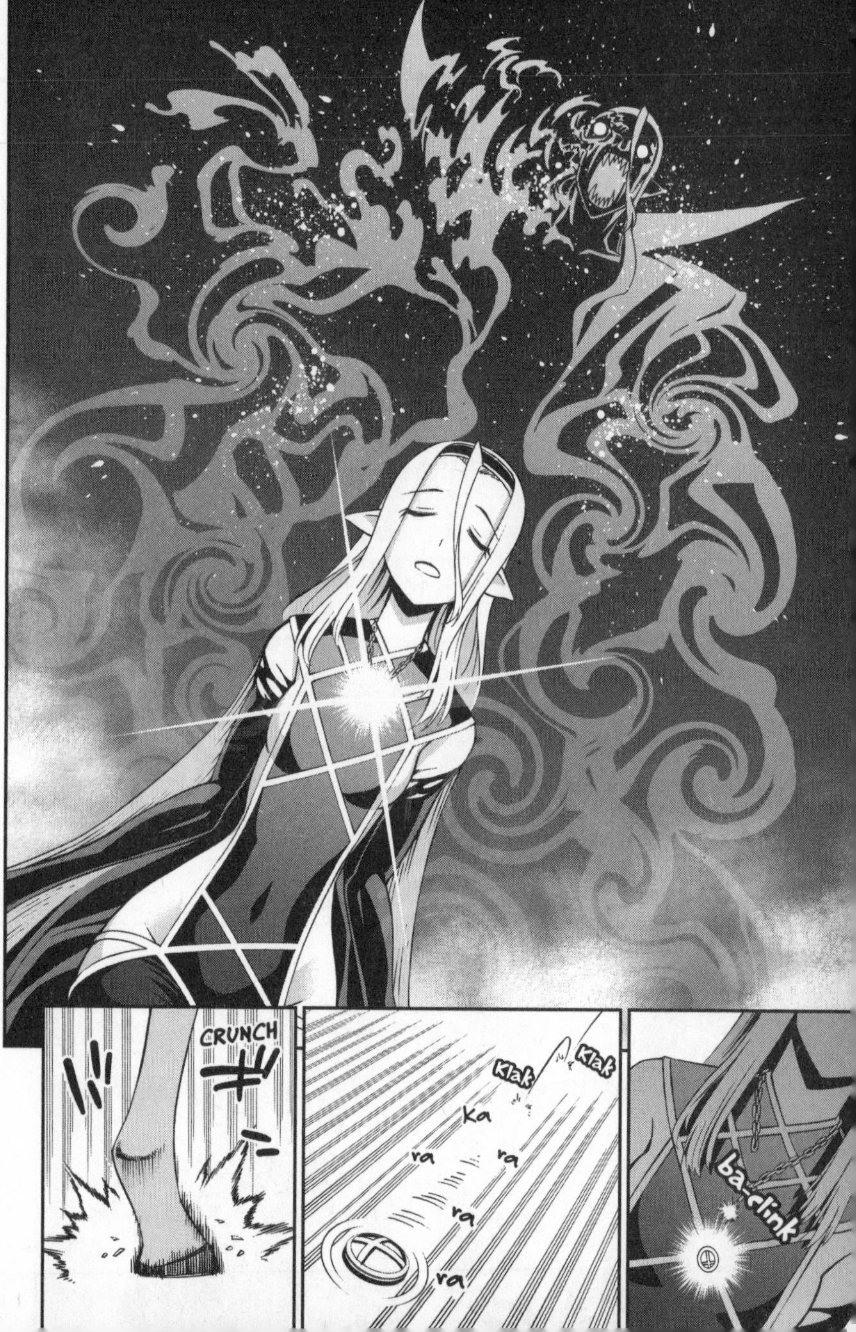
ba-clink
Klak
Klak
Ka
ra
ra
ra
ra
CRUNCH

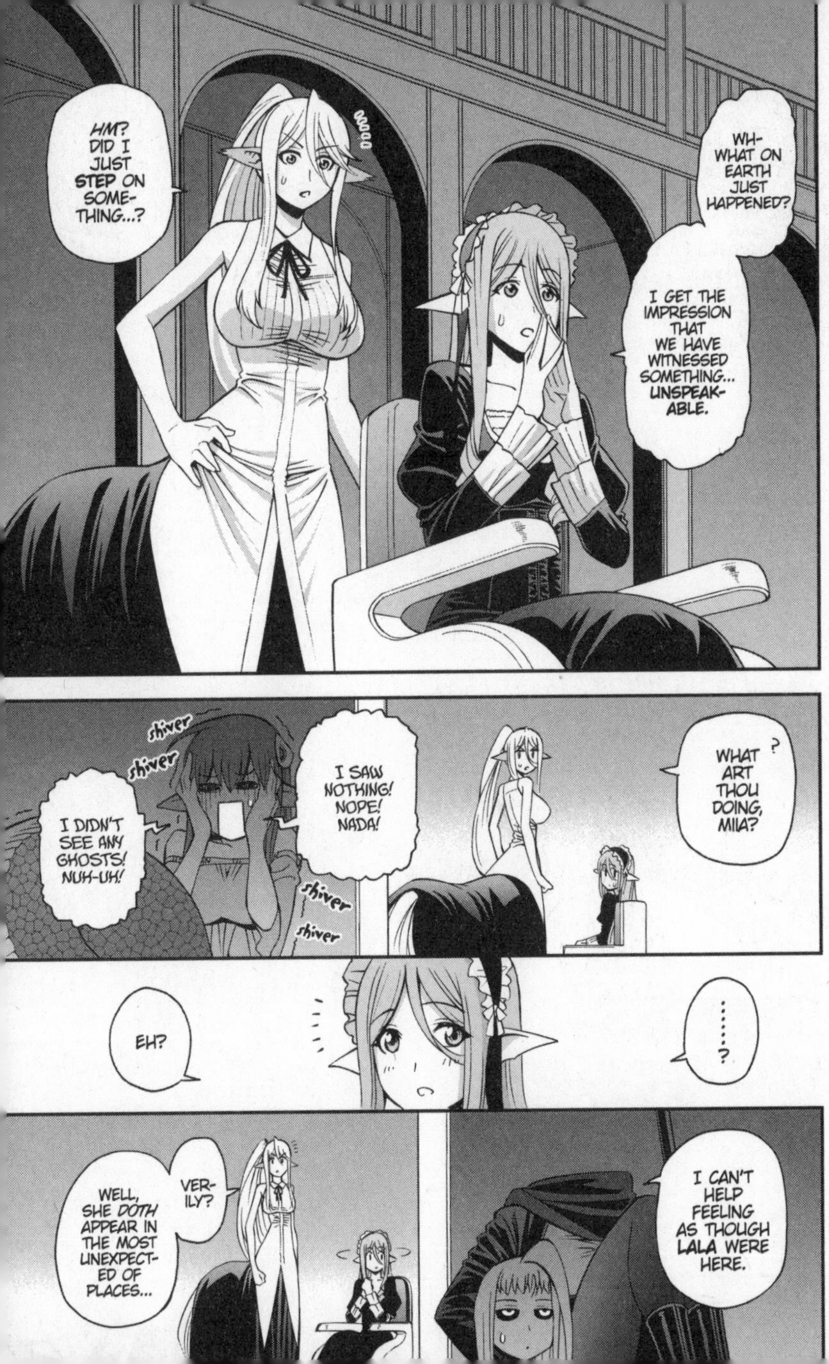
WH- WHAT ON EARTH JUST HAPPENED?
I GET THE IMPRESSION THAT WE HAVE WITNESSED SOMETHING... UNSPEAKABLE.
HM? DID I JUST STEP ON SOME-THING...?
WHAT ART THOU DOING, MIIA?
?
I SAW NOTHING! NOPE! NADA!
I DIDN'T SEE ANY GHOSTS! NUH-UH!
shiver shiver
shiver shiver
......?
EH?
I CAN'T HELP FEELING AS THOUGH LALA WERE HERE.
VER-ILY?
WELL, SHE DOTH APPEAR IN THE MOST UNEXPECT-ED OF PLACES...

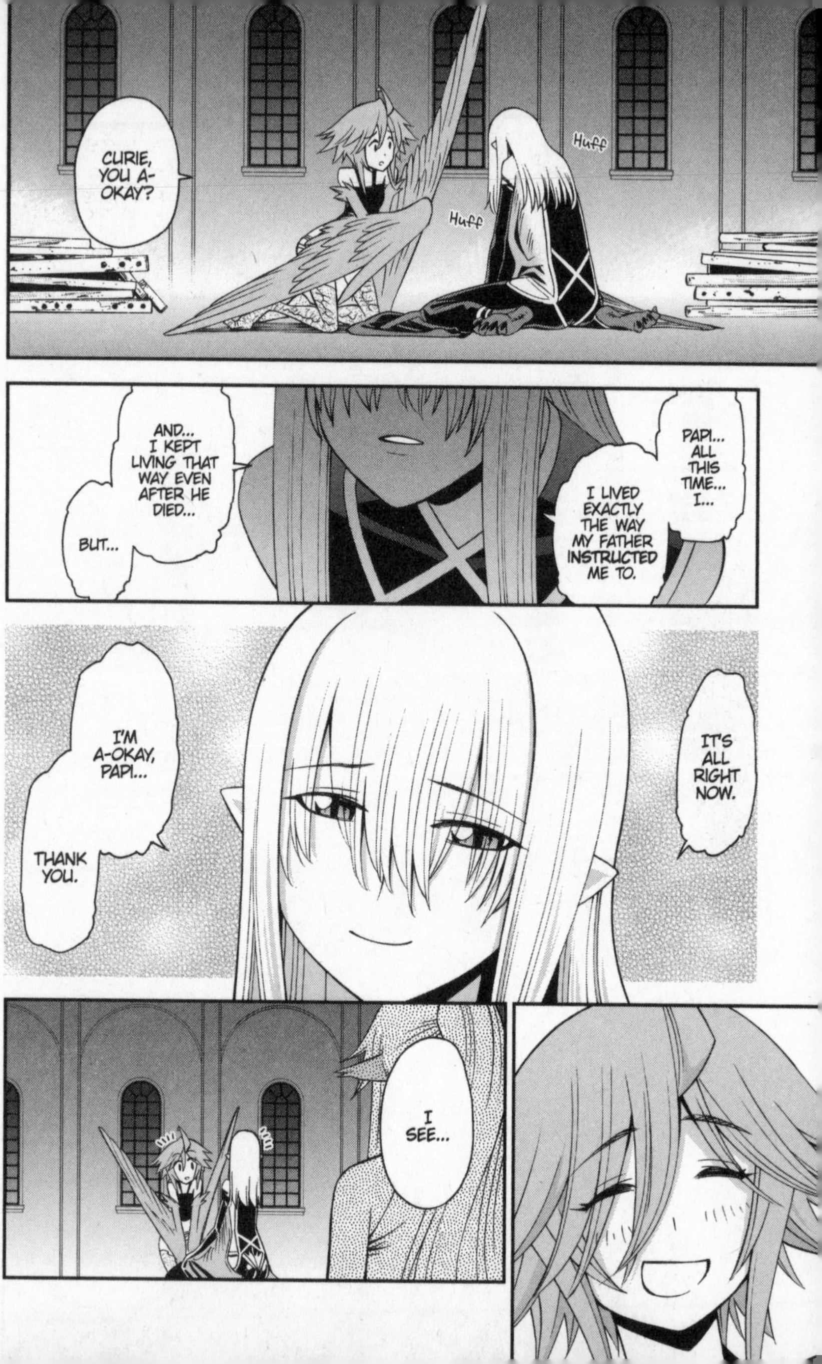
Huff
Huff
CURIE, YOU A-OKAY?
PAPI... ALL THIS TIME... I...
I LIVED EXACTLY THE WAY MY FATHER INSTRUCTED ME TO.
AND... I KEPT LIVING THAT WAY EVEN AFTER HE DIED...
BUT...
IT'S ALL RIGHT NOW.
I'M A-OKAY, PAPI...
THANK YOU.
I SEE...

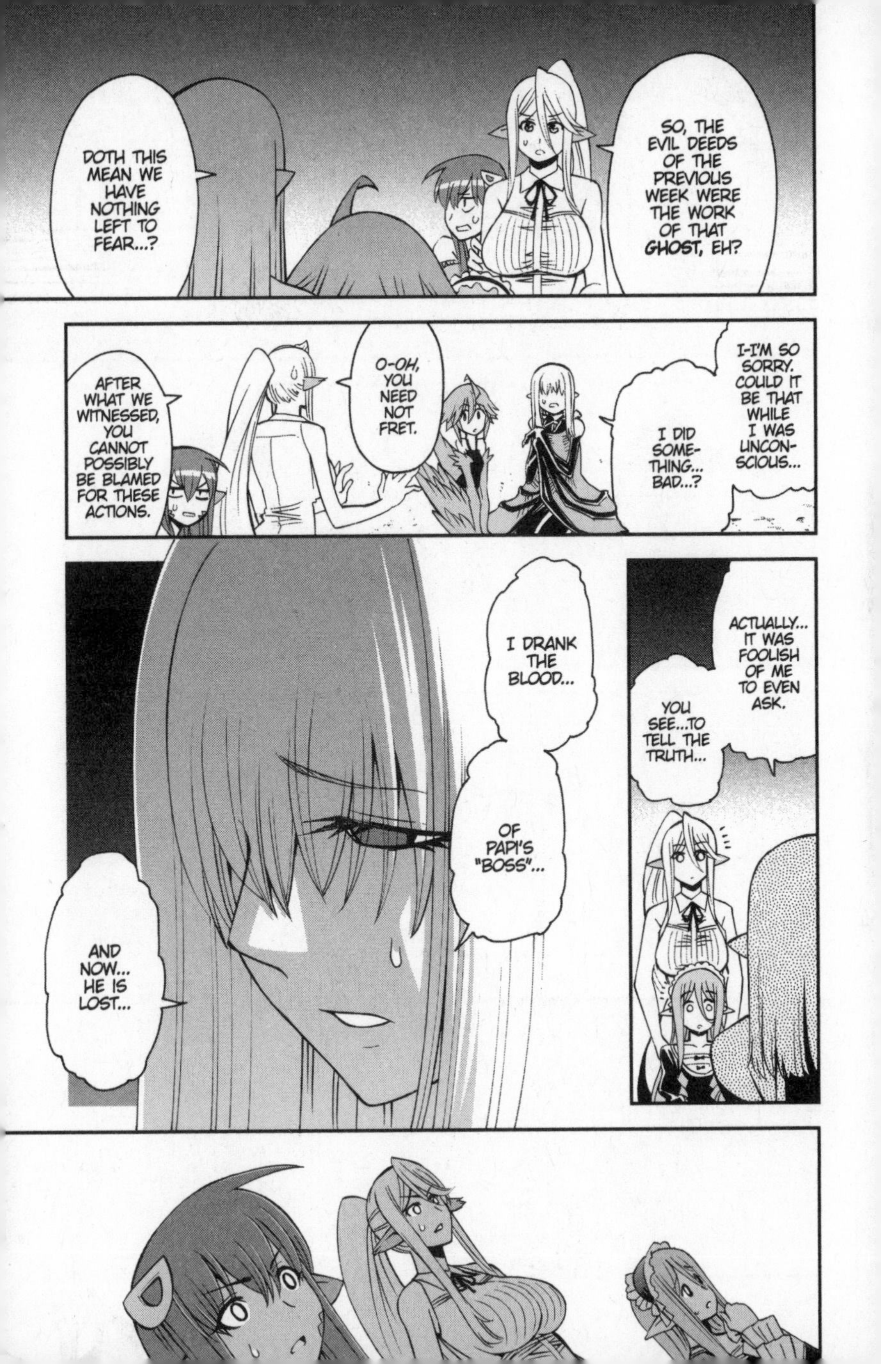
SO, THE EVIL DEEDS OF THE PREVIOUS WEEK WERE THE WORK OF THAT GHOST, EH?
DOTH THIS MEAN WE HAVE NOTHING LEFT TO FEAR...?
I-I'M SO SORRY. COULD IT BE THAT WHILE I WAS UNCONSCIOUS...
I DID SOMETHING... BAD...?
O-OH, YOU NEED NOT FRET.
AFTER WHAT WE WITNESSED, YOU CANNOT POSSIBLY BE BLAMED FOR THESE ACTIONS.
ACTUALLY... IT WAS FOOLISH OF ME TO EVEN ASK.
YOU SEE...TO TELL THE TRUTH...
I DRANK THE BLOOD...
OF PAPI'S "BOSS"...
AND NOW... HE IS LOST...

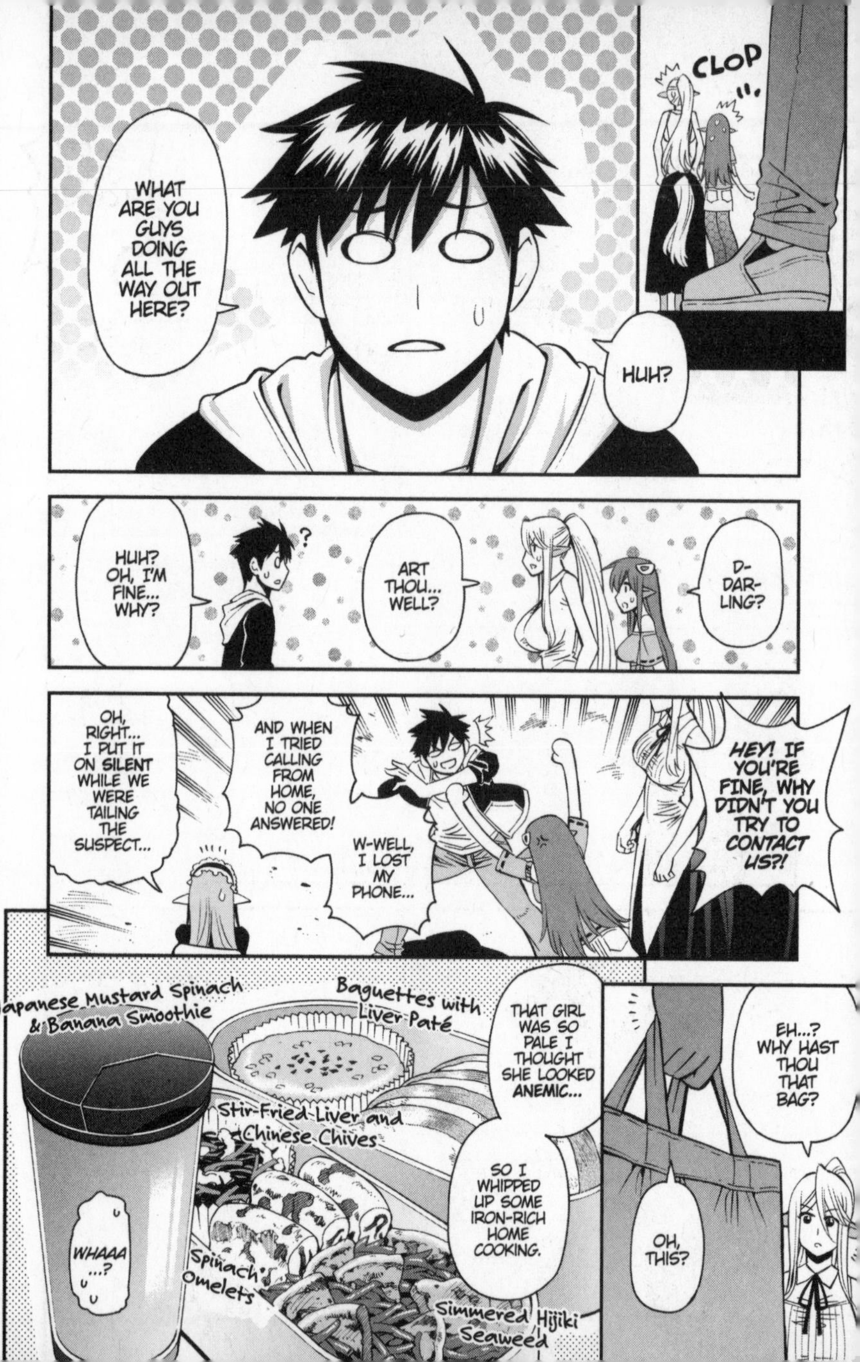
CLOP
HUH?
WHAT ARE YOU GUYS DOING ALL THE WAY OUT HERE?
D-DAR-LING?
ART THOU... WELL?
HUH? OH, I'M FINE... WHY?
HEY! IF YOU'RE FINE, WHY DIDN'T YOU TRY TO CONTACT US?!
W-WELL, I LOST MY PHONE...
AND WHEN I TRIED CALLING FROM HOME, NO ONE ANSWERED!
OH, RIGHT... I PUT IT ON SILENT WHILE WE WERE TAILING THE SUSPECT...
EH...? WHY HAST THOU THAT BAG?
OH, THIS?
THAT GIRL WAS SO PALE I THOUGHT SHE LOOKED ANEMIC...
SO I WHIPPED UP SOME IRON-RICH HOME COOKING.
Baguettes with Liver Paté
Japanese Mustard Spinach & Banana Smoothie
Stir-Fried Liver and Chinese Chives
Spinach Omelets
Simmered Hijiki Seaweed
WHAAA ...?

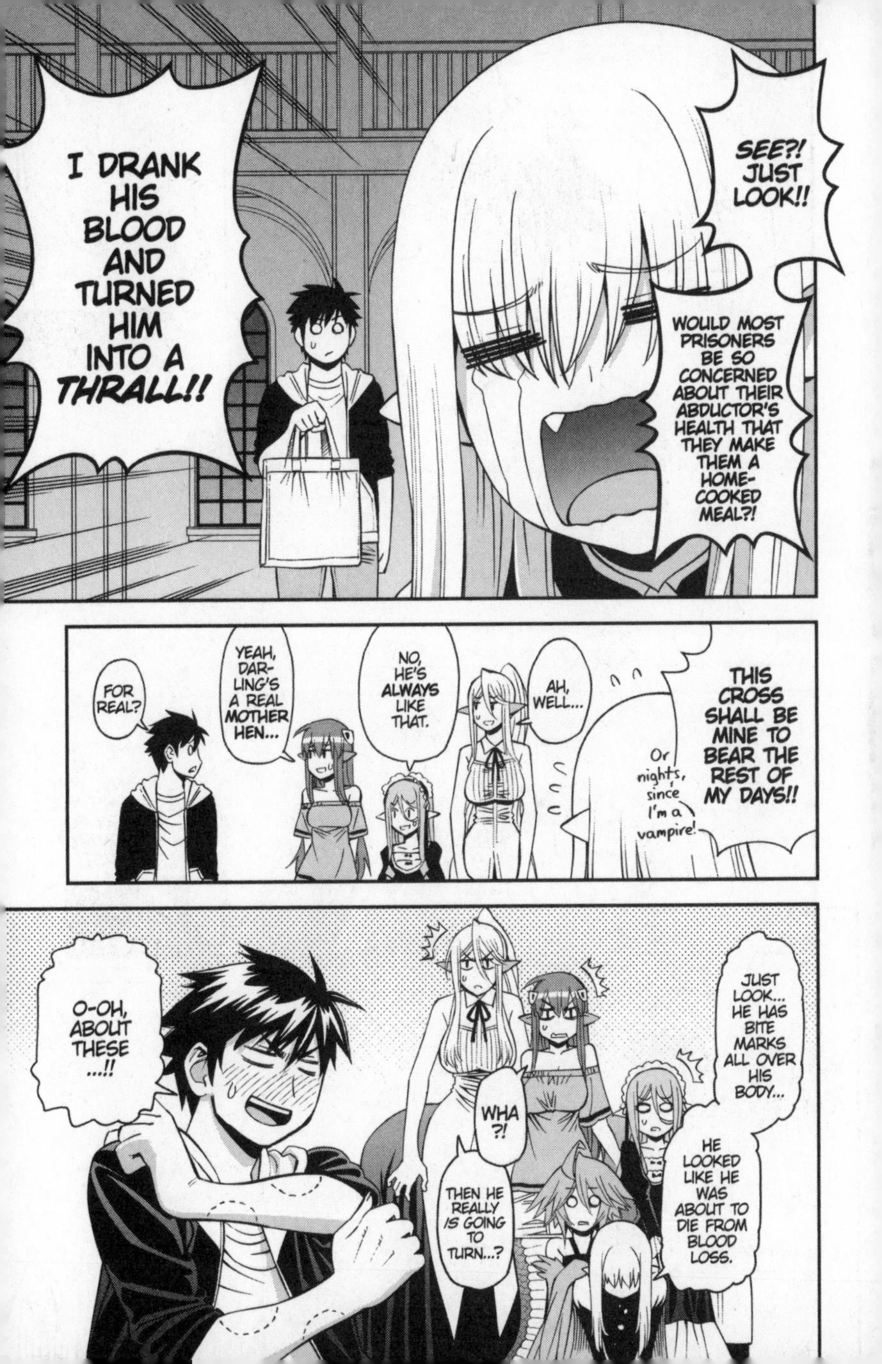
SEE?! JUST LOOK!!
WOULD MOST PRISONERS BE SO CONCERNED ABOUT THEIR ABDUCTOR'S HEALTH THAT THEY MAKE THEM A HOME-COOKED MEAL?!
I DRANK HIS BLOOD AND TURNED HIM INTO A THRALL!!
THIS CROSS SHALL BE MINE TO BEAR THE REST OF MY DAYS!!
Or nights, since I'm a vampire!
AH, WELL...
NO, HE'S ALWAYS LIKE THAT.
YEAH, DARLING'S A REAL MOTHER HEN...
FOR REAL?
JUST LOOK... HE HAS BITE MARKS ALL OVER HIS BODY...
HE LOOKED LIKE HE WAS ABOUT TO DIE FROM BLOOD LOSS.
WHA?!
THEN HE REALLY IS GOING TO TURN...?
O-OH, ABOUT THESE ...!!

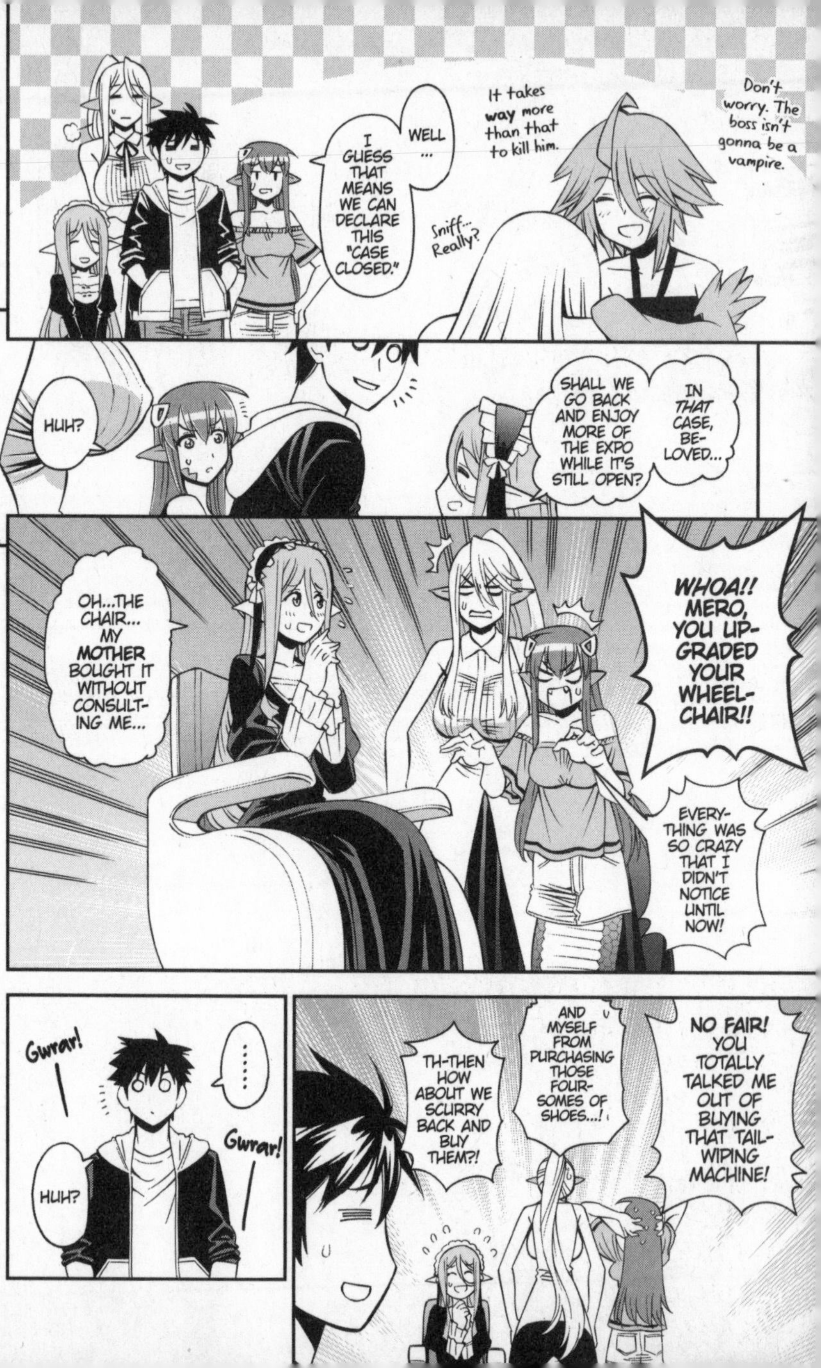
Don't worry. The boss isn't gonna be a vampire.
It takes way more than that to kill him.
Sniff... Really?
WELL...
I GUESS THAT MEANS WE CAN DECLARE THIS "CASE CLOSED."
IN THAT CASE, BE-LOVED...
SHALL WE GO BACK AND ENJOY MORE OF THE EXPO WHILE IT'S STILL OPEN?
HUH?
WHOA!! MERO, YOU UP-GRADED YOUR WHEEL-CHAIR!!
EVERY-THING WAS SO CRAZY THAT I DIDN'T NOTICE UNTIL NOW!
OH...THE CHAIR... MY MOTHER BOUGHT IT WITHOUT CONSULT-ING ME...
NO FAIR! YOU TOTALLY TALKED ME OUT OF BUYING THAT TAIL-WIPING MACHINE!
AND MYSELF FROM PURCHASING THOSE FOUR-SOMES OF SHOES...!
TH-THEN HOW ABOUT WE SCURRY BACK AND BUY THEM?!
......
Gwrar!
Gwrar!
HUH?

WHERE'S
SUU?

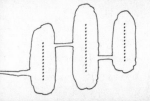

MERO?

CENTO-
REA?

MIIA?

PAPI?

?

?

WHERE
DID
EVERYONE
GO?

......
?

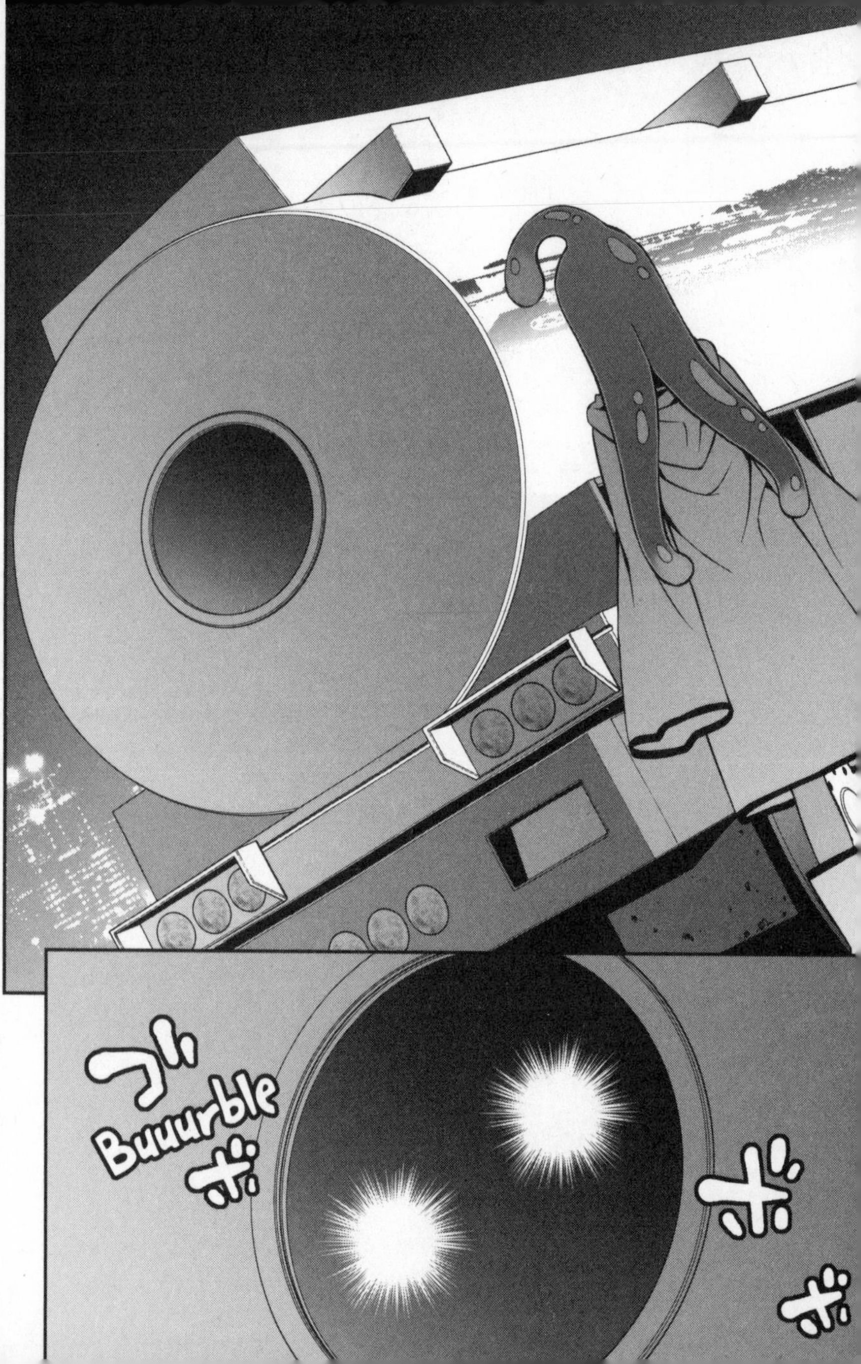
Buuurble

Monster Musume

Everyday Life with Monster Girls

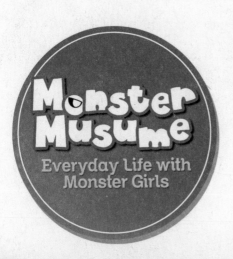

The Blood Sucking Foursome Living Together

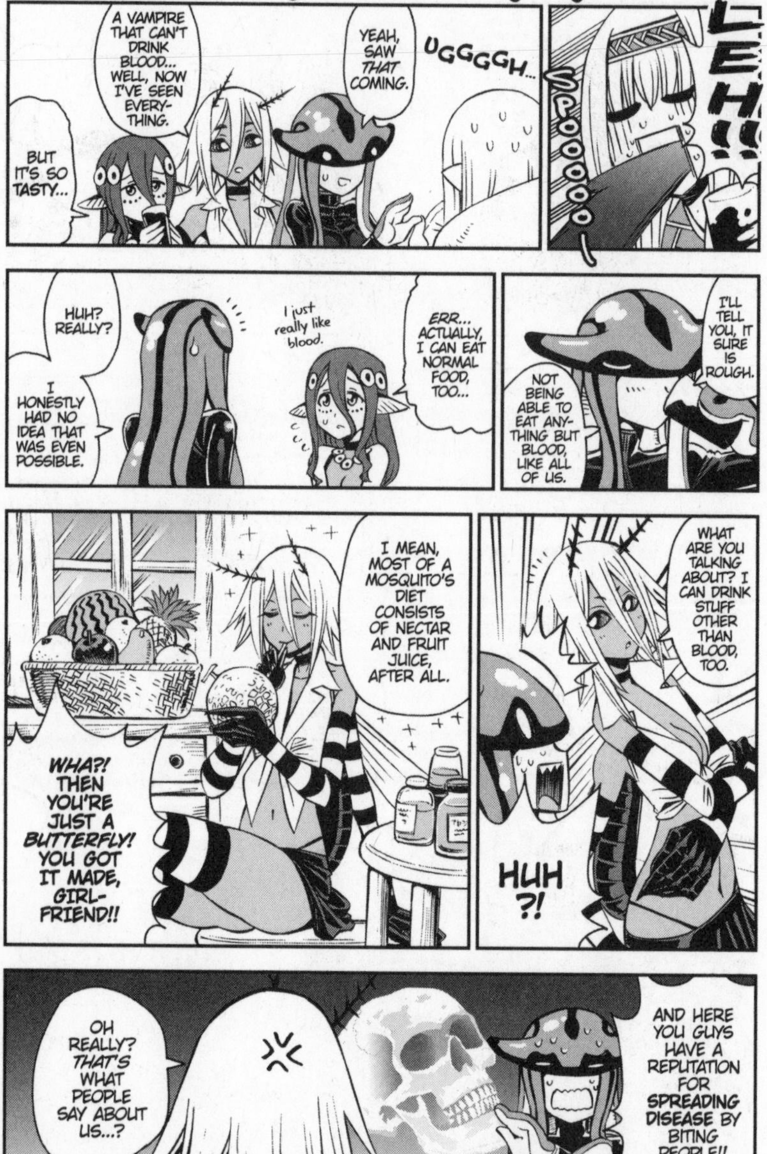
BLEH!!
SPOOOOOO
UGGGGH...
YEAH, SAW THAT COMING.
A VAMPIRE THAT CAN'T DRINK BLOOD... WELL, NOW I'VE SEEN EVERYTHING.
BUT IT'S SO TASTY...
I'LL TELL YOU, IT SURE IS ROUGH.
NOT BEING ABLE TO EAT ANYTHING BUT BLOOD, LIKE ALL OF US.
ERR... ACTUALLY, I CAN EAT NORMAL FOOD, TOO...
I just really like blood.
HUH? REALLY?
I HONESTLY HAD NO IDEA THAT WAS EVEN POSSIBLE.
WHAT ARE YOU TALKING ABOUT? I CAN DRINK STUFF OTHER THAN BLOOD, TOO.
HUH ?!
I MEAN, MOST OF A MOSQUITO'S DIET CONSISTS OF NECTAR AND FRUIT JUICE, AFTER ALL.
WHA?! THEN YOU'RE JUST A BUTTERFLY! YOU GOT IT MADE, GIRLFRIEND!!
AND HERE YOU GUYS HAVE A REPUTATION FOR SPREADING DISEASE BY BITING PEOPLE!!
OH REALLY? THAT'S WHAT PEOPLE SAY ABOUT US...?

Leeches are Annelids, Not Mollusks

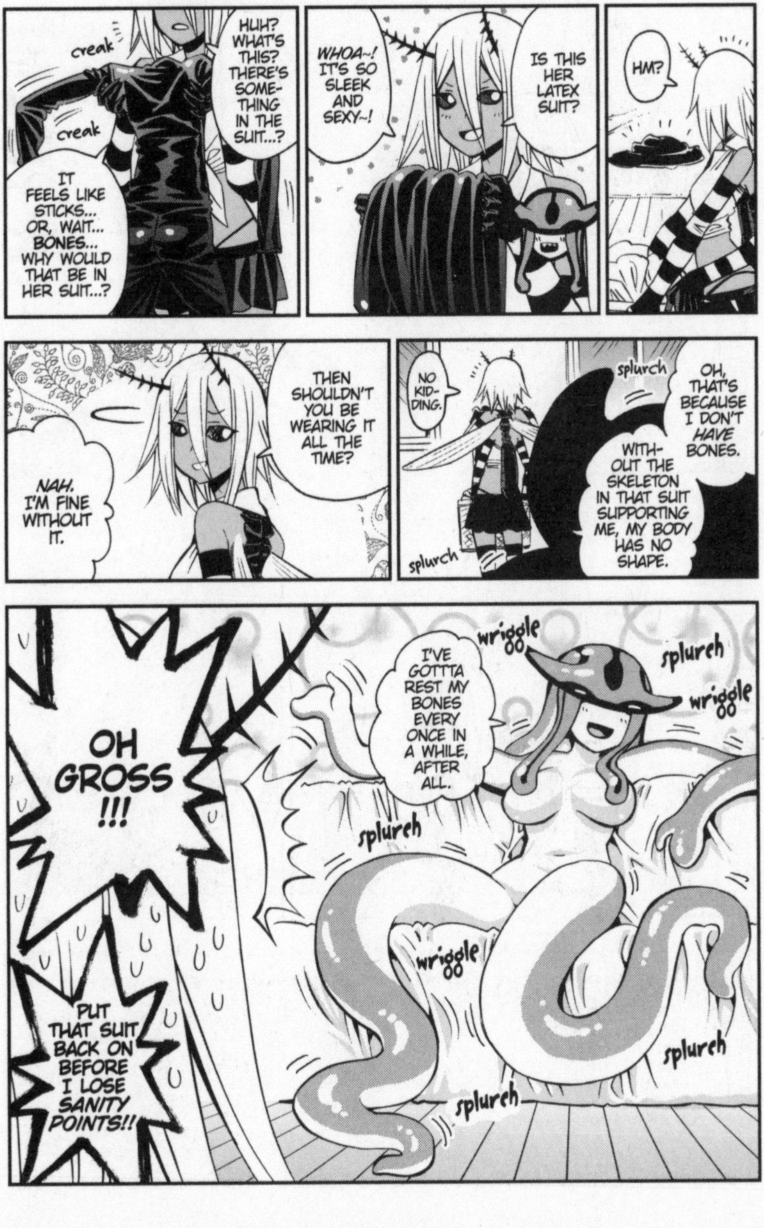
HM?
IS THIS HER LATEX SUIT?
WHOA~! IT'S SO SLEEK AND SEXY~!
HUH? WHAT'S THIS? THERE'S SOME-THING IN THE SUIT...?
creak
creak
IT FEELS LIKE STICKS... OR, WAIT... BONES... WHY WOULD THAT BE IN HER SUIT...?
OH, THAT'S BECAUSE I DON'T HAVE BONES.
splurch
NO KID-DING.
WITH-OUT THE SKELETON IN THAT SUIT SUPPORTING ME, MY BODY HAS NO SHAPE.
splurch
THEN SHOULDN'T YOU BE WEARING IT ALL THE TIME?
NAH. I'M FINE WITHOUT IT.
splurch
wriggle
wriggle
I'VE GOTTA REST MY BONES EVERY ONCE IN A WHILE, AFTER ALL.
OH GROSS!!!
splurch
wriggle
splurch
splurch
PUT THAT SUIT BACK ON BEFORE I LOSE SANITY POINTS!!

Structural Defects

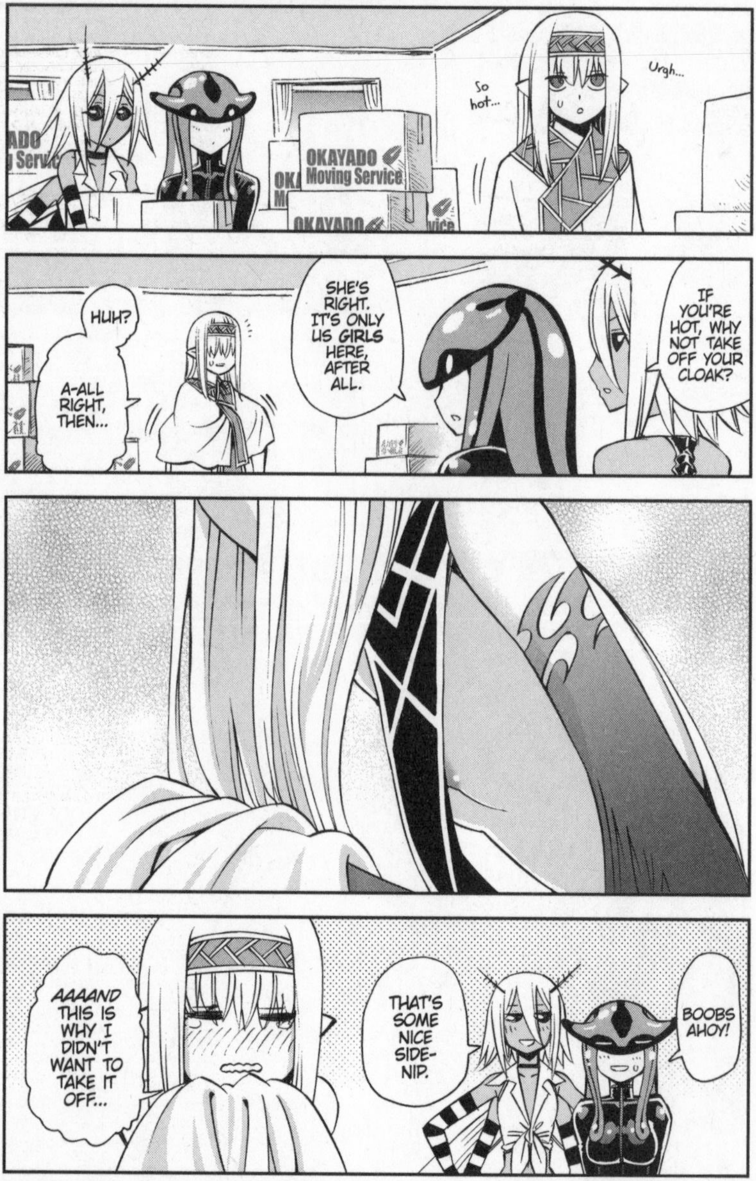
Urgh...
So hot...
OKAYADO Moving Service
IF YOU'RE HOT, WHY NOT TAKE OFF YOUR CLOAK?
SHE'S RIGHT. IT'S ONLY US GIRLS HERE, AFTER ALL.
HUH?
A-ALL RIGHT, THEN...
BOOBS AHOY!
THAT'S SOME NICE SIDE-NIP.
AAAAND THIS IS WHY I DIDN'T WANT TO TAKE IT OFF...

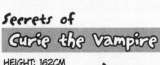

Secrets of Curie the Vampire

HEIGHT: 162CM
WEIGHT: 38KG
3 SIZES 72-52-76

A CUP

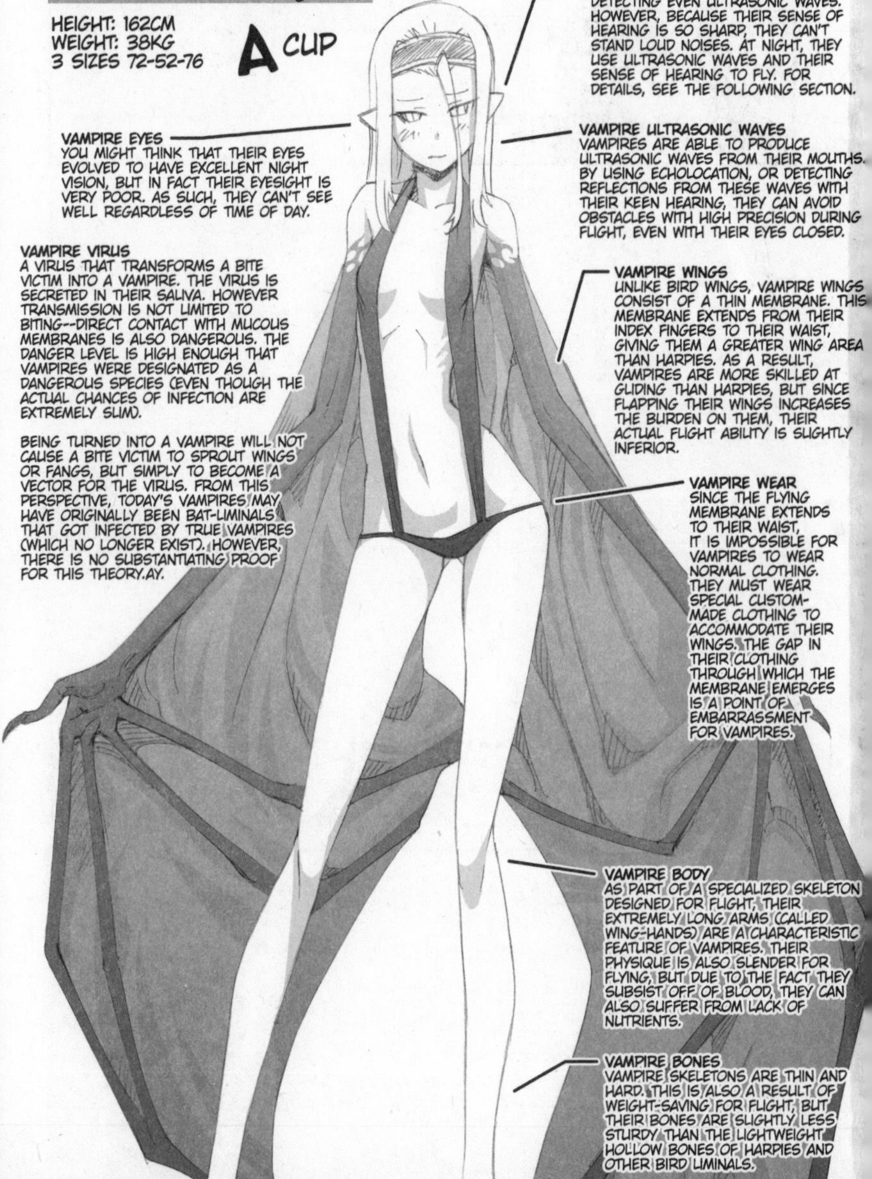
VAMPIRE EARS
VAMPIRES HAVE DEVELOPED AN EXTREMELY KEEN SENSE OF HEARING TO COMPENSATE FOR THEIR POOR EYESIGHT. THEY ARE CAPABLE OF DETECTING EVEN ULTRASONIC WAVES. HOWEVER, BECAUSE THEIR SENSE OF HEARING IS SO SHARP, THEY CAN'T STAND LOUD NOISES. AT NIGHT, THEY USE ULTRASONIC WAVES AND THEIR SENSE OF HEARING TO FLY. FOR DETAILS, SEE THE FOLLOWING SECTION.
VAMPIRE EYES
YOU MIGHT THINK THAT THEIR EYES EVOLVED TO HAVE EXCELLENT NIGHT VISION, BUT IN FACT THEIR EYESIGHT IS VERY POOR. AS SUCH, THEY CAN'T SEE WELL REGARDLESS OF TIME OF DAY.
VAMPIRE ULTRASONIC WAVES
VAMPIRES ARE ABLE TO PRODUCE ULTRASONIC WAVES FROM THEIR MOUTHS. BY USING ECHOLOCATION, OR DETECTING REFLECTIONS FROM THESE WAVES WITH THEIR KEEN HEARING, THEY CAN AVOID OBSTACLES WITH HIGH PRECISION DURING FLIGHT, EVEN WITH THEIR EYES CLOSED.
VAMPIRE VIRUS
A VIRUS THAT TRANSFORMS A BITE VICTIM INTO A VAMPIRE. THE VIRUS IS SECRETED IN THEIR SALIVA. HOWEVER TRANSMISSION IS NOT LIMITED TO BITING--DIRECT CONTACT WITH MUCOUS MEMBRANES IS ALSO DANGEROUS. THE DANGER LEVEL IS HIGH ENOUGH THAT VAMPIRES WERE DESIGNATED AS A DANGEROUS SPECIES (EVEN THOUGH THE ACTUAL CHANCES OF INFECTION ARE EXTREMELY SLIM).
BEING TURNED INTO A VAMPIRE WILL NOT CAUSE A BITE VICTIM TO SPROUT WINGS OR FANGS, BUT SIMPLY TO BECOME A VECTOR FOR THE VIRUS. FROM THIS PERSPECTIVE, TODAY'S VAMPIRES MAY HAVE ORIGINALLY BEEN BAT-LIMINALS THAT GOT INFECTED BY TRUE VAMPIRES (WHICH NO LONGER EXIST). HOWEVER, THERE IS NO SUBSTANTIATING PROOF FOR THIS THEORY.AY.
VAMPIRE WINGS
UNLIKE BIRD WINGS, VAMPIRE WINGS CONSIST OF A THIN MEMBRANE. THIS MEMBRANE EXTENDS FROM THEIR INDEX FINGERS TO THEIR WAIST, GIVING THEM A GREATER WING AREA THAN HARPIES. AS A RESULT, VAMPIRES ARE MORE SKILLED AT GLIDING THAN HARPIES, BUT SINCE FLAPPING THEIR WINGS INCREASES THE BURDEN ON THEM, THEIR ACTUAL FLIGHT ABILITY IS SLIGHTLY INFERIOR.
VAMPIRE WEAR
SINCE THE FLYING MEMBRANE EXTENDS TO THEIR WAIST, IT IS IMPOSSIBLE FOR VAMPIRES TO WEAR NORMAL CLOTHING. THEY MUST WEAR SPECIAL CUSTOM-MADE CLOTHING TO ACCOMMODATE THEIR WINGS. THE GAP IN THEIR CLOTHING THROUGH WHICH THE MEMBRANE EMERGES IS A POINT OF EMBARRASSMENT FOR VAMPIRES.
VAMPIRE BODY
AS PART OF A SPECIALIZED SKELETON DESIGNED FOR FLIGHT, THEIR EXTREMELY LONG ARMS (CALLED WING-HANDS) ARE A CHARACTERISTIC FEATURE OF VAMPIRES. THEIR PHYSIQUE IS ALSO SLENDER FOR FLYING, BUT DUE TO THE FACT THEY SUBSIST OFF OF BLOOD, THEY CAN ALSO SUFFER FROM LACK OF NUTRIENTS.
VAMPIRE BONES
VAMPIRE SKELETONS ARE THIN AND HARD. THIS IS ALSO A RESULT OF WEIGHT-SAVING FOR FLIGHT, BUT THEIR BONES ARE SLIGHTLY LESS STURDY THAN THE LIGHTWEIGHT HOLLOW BONES OF HARPIES AND OTHER BIRD LIMINALS.

SEVEN SEAS ENTERTAINMENT PRESENTS

Monster Musume

story and art by OKAYADO

VOLUME 12

TRANSLATION
Ryan Peterson

ADAPTATION
Shanti Whitesides

LETTERING AND LAYOUT
Meaghan Tucker

LOGO DESIGN
Courtney Williams

COVER DESIGN
Nicky Lim

PROOFREADER
Janet Houck

ASSISTANT EDITOR
Jenn Grunigen

PRODUCTION ASSISTANT
CK Russell

PRODUCTION MANAGER
Lissa Pattillo

EDITOR-IN-CHIEF
Adam Arnold

PUBLISHER
Jason DeAngelis

ISBN: 978-1-626925-17-5

Printed in Canada

First Printing: August 2017

10 9 8 7 6 5 4 3 2 1

FOLLOW US ONLINE: ***www.gomanga.com***

READING DIRECTIONS

This book reads from ***right to left***, Japanese style. If this is your first time reading manga, you start reading from the top right panel on each page and take it from there. If you get lost, just follow the numbered diagram here. It may seem backwards at first, but you'll get the hang of it! Have fun!!

1
2
3
4
5
6
7
8
9

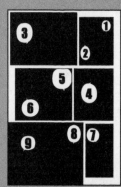